Operating Systems
Techniques

A.P.I.C. Studies in Data Processing
General Editor: C. A. R. Hoare

1. Some Commercial Autocodes. A Comparative Study
   E. L. Willey, A. d'Agapeyeff, Marion Tribe, B. J. Gibbens and
   Michelle Clarke.

2. A Primer of ALGOL 60 Programming
   E. W. Dijkstra

3. Input Language for Automatic Programming
   A. P. Yershov, G. I. Kozhukhin and U. Voloshin

4. Introduction to System Programming
   Edited by Peter Wegner

5. ALGOL 60 Implementation. The translation and use of Algol 60
      Programs on a Computer.
   B. Randell and L. J. Russell

6. Dictionary for Computer Languages
   Hans Breuer

7. The Alpha Automatic Programming System
   Edited by A. P. Yershov

8. Structured Programming
   O. -J. Dahl, E. W. Dijkstra and C. A. R. Hoare

9. Operating Systems Techniques
   Edited by C. A. R. Hoare and R. H. Perrott

A.P.I.C. Studies in Data Processing
No. 9

Operating Systems Techniques

Proceedings of a Seminar held at Queen's
University, Belfast, 1971

edited by

C. A. R. HOARE
R. H. PERROTT

*Department of Computer Science
Queen's University,
Belfast, Northern Ireland*

1972

ACADEMIC PRESS · LONDON AND NEW YORK

ACADEMIC PRESS INC. (LONDON) LTD.
24/28 Oval Road,
London NW1

United States Edition published by
ACADEMIC PRESS INC.
111 Fifth Avenue
New York, New York 10003

Library of Congress Catalog Card Number: 72–84347
ISBN: 0–12–350650–6

Text set in 10/11 pt. IBM Press Roman and printed by photolithography
in Great Britain at Galliard (Printers) Ltd, Great Yarmouth

LIST OF PARTICIPANTS

A. Alderson*, Computing Laboratory, University of Newcastle-upon-Tyne, England.

D. A. Bell, A.C.T.P./National Physical Laboratory, Teddington, England.

P. Brinch Hansen*, Carnegie-Mellon University, Pittsburgh, Pennsylvania, U.S.A.

C. Brindley, I.C.L., Putney, London, England.

M. Clint, Queen's University of Belfast, Northern Ireland.

M. Falla, I.C.L., Putney, London, England.

D. P. Fenton*, Burroughs Corporation, London, England.

A. G. Fraser*, Bell Telephone Company, Murray Hill, New Jersey, U.S.A.

G. Goos*, University of Karlsruhe, Germany.

J. Hall, Queen's University of Belfast, Northern Ireland.

D. F. Hartley*, Computer Laboratory, University of Cambridge, England.

A. L. Hillman*, National Physical Laboratory, Teddington, England.

C. A. R. Hoare*, Department of Computer Science, Queen's University of Belfast, Northern Ireland.

D. J. Howarth*, Institute of Computer Science, University of London, England.

D. H. R. Huxtable, I.C.L., Putney, London England.

H. Lipps*, Data Handling Division, C.E.R.N., Geneva, Switzerland.

R. M. McKeag*, Department of Computer Science, Queen's University of Belfast, Northern Ireland.

R. McLaughlin, Queen's University of Belfast, Northern Ireland.

R. M. Needham*, Computer Laboratory, University of Cambridge, England.

G. Newell, I.C.L., Putney, London, England.

M. Patel, I.C.L., Putney, London, England.

R. H. Perrott, Queen's University of Belfast, Northern Ireland.

B. Randell*, Computing Laboratory, University of Newcastle-upon-Tyne, England.

D. Rimmer, A.C.T.P./A.E.R.E. Harwell, England.

P. Schuler, Queen's University of Belfast, Northern Ireland.

J. Sherlock, A.C.T.P./R.R.E. Malvern, England.

F. J. Smith, Queen's University of Belfast, Northern Ireland.

A. Sutcliffe, I.C.L., Putney, London, England.

P. W. Thomas, I.C.L., Putney, London, England.

N. L. Vince, I.C.L., Putney, London, England.

A. Walker, I.C.L., Putney, London, England.

J. Warne, Queen's University of Belfast, Northern Ireland.

M. T. Warwick, I.C.L., Putney, London, England.

B. A. Wichmann*, National Physical Laboratory, Teddington, England.

R. Wilson, Queen's University of Belfast, Northern Ireland.

Submitting papers *in absentia*

J. K. Broadbent*, Queen Mary College, University of London, Mile End Road, London, England.

C. Bron*, Technological University, Eindhoven, The Netherlands.

G. F. Coulouris*, Queen Mary College, University of London, Mile End Road, London, England.

E. W. Dijkstra*, Technological University, Eindhoven, The Netherlands.

H. P. Goodman*, I.C.L., Putney, London, England.

W. C. Lynch*, Case Western Reserve University/Computing Laboratory, University of Newcastle-upon-Tyne, England.

D. J. Roche*, Telecommunications Development Department, G.P.O., London, England.

J. R. Thomas*, Telecommunications Headquarters, G.P.O., London, England.

*Indicates contributor to this volume

PREFACE

This book reports the proceedings of an International Seminar on Operating Systems Techniques held at the Queen's University, Belfast between 30th August and 3rd September 1971. The Seminar was sponsored jointly by International Computers Limited and the Advanced Computer Technology Project, by whose kind permission the book is published.

The Seminar formed a part of a continuing research project supported by the same sponsors and carried out in the Department of Computer Science of the Queen's University in 1971 and 1972. The purpose of the research is to investigate, classify and evaluate the practical techniques which have been used in the implementation of successful operating systems. It is hoped to relate each technique to its objective, and to the range of circumstances in which it is applicable; and thus produce a reliable guide upon which an operating system designer can base his decisions.

The participants of the Seminar were invited on grounds of their extensive experience of the implementation and use of successful operating systems. Having assembled such a group of designers and users we were anxious not only to discuss the major principles of operating system design but also minor modifications and enhancements to their techniques, and other small but important matters that are not normally written up and submitted for publication. We believe that operating system designers of the present day can benefit greatly from the study of the methods adopted by their predecessors.

This study will also be interesting to the users of operating systems; it may help them to evaluate the techniques adopted by rival systems, to select the best options and parameter settings available to them, and where necessary to introduce variations oriented towards their own requirements. By highlighting some of the problems and dilemmas facing an operating system designer, it may help them to moderate their complaints and organise their workload to improve the flexibility and performance of an existing operating system.

The book will be of interest to students and teachers of Computer Science, because many of the problems discussed are the same as those facing designers of any large program, particularly real-time programs, which have to react sensibly to peripheral equipment and human users, and take frequent decisions of policy on partial evidence.

Many people were involved in the organisation of the Seminar and the subsequent production of this book, and to them we wish to extend our sincerest thanks. In particular the Queen's University Belfast for their help and co-operation in adverse circumstances. The actual recordings of the Seminar amounted to some 30 hours of tape and special thanks are due to Mike McKeag and Bob Wilson for their considerable help in the initial editing stages of this material. Finally thanks are due to Miss Ella Noble for the large amount of typing and office duties she so expertly executed, and to John Hall for his invaluable assistance throughout the period of the Seminar.

October, 1972   Tony Hoare
Queen's University, Belfast.   Ron Perrott

EDITORS' NOTE

The views expressed in this book represent (to the best of the editors' ability) the views of the contributors to whom they have been attributed. The sponsors of the Seminar and the organisations to which the contributors belong are in no way responsible for the accuracy of the contents, in detail or in general, nor for any consequences resulting from their publication or use.

"Our problem is that we never do the same thing again. We get a lot of experience on our first simple system, and then when it comes to doing the same thing again with a better designed hardware, with all the tools we know we need, we try and produce something which is ten times more complicated and fall into exactly the same trap. We do not stabilise on something nice and simple and say 'let's do it again, but do it very well this time'."

D. J. HOWARTH

CONTENTS

List of Participants   v

Preface   vii

Editors' Note   ix

OPERATING SYSTEM REQUIREMENTS
Some User Reactions to Operating Systems: A Selective Survey
    G. F. Coulouris and J. K. Broadbent   3

Operating Systems: their Purpose, Objectives, Functions and Scope
    C. A. R. Hoare   11

OPERATING SYSTEM PRINCIPLES
An Outline of a Course on Operating System Principles
    P. Brinch Hansen   29

On the Meaning of Names in Programming Systems
    A. G. Fraser   37

OPERATING SYSTEM STRUCTURE
Towards a Theory of Parallel Programming
    C. A. R. Hoare   61

Hierarchical Ordering of Sequential Processes
    E. W. Dijkstra   72

Some Basic Principles in Structuring Operating Systems
    G. Goos   94

Monitors (Special Discussion)   109

STORE MANAGEMENT TECHNIQUES
A Survey of Store Management Techniques
    C. A. R. Hoare and R. M. McKeag
    Part One   117
    Part Two   132

Thrashing in a Multiprogrammed Paging System
    A. Alderson, W. C. Lynch and B. Randell   152

Allocation of Virtual Store in the T.H.E. Multiprogramming System
    C. Bron   168

Job Scheduling Techniques (Discussion)   194
Process Dispatching Techniques (Discussion)   201
Resource Allocation Techniques (Discussion)   208
Input/Output Control Techniques (Discussion)   218

FILING SYSTEM TECHNIQUES
File Integrity in a Disc-based Multi-access System
  A. G. Fraser   227

Miscellaneous Topics (Discussion)   255
The User's Problem (Discussion)   264

TITAN OPERATING SYSTEM
Techniques in the Titan Supervisor
  D. F. Hartley   271

Tuning the Titan Operating System
  R. M. Needham   277

CDC OPERATING SYSTEMS
Batch Processing with 6000-Series Scope
  H. Lipps   291

BURROUGHS OPERATING SYSTEMS
Burroughs B5500 MCP and Time-sharing MCP
  D. J. Roche   307

B6700 "Working Set" Memory Allocation
  D. P. Fenton   321

MISCELLANEOUS OPERATING SYSTEMS 1
Experience with the Eldon Operating System for KDF9
  A. L. Hillman and B. A. Wichmann   337

An Operating System Designed for the Computer Utility Environment
  W. C. Lynch   341

The Structure of a Time-sharing System
  J. R. Thomas   351

MISCELLANEOUS OPERATING SYSTEMS 2
A Re-appraisal of Certain Design Features of the Atlas I Supervisory System
  D. J. Howarth   371

On Unifying a Batch System with a Multi-access System
  H. P. Goodman   378

OPERATING SYSTEM REQUIREMENTS

Speaker: C. A. R. Hoare: "Operating systems: their purpose, objectives, functions and scope."

Repliers: G. Goos, B. Randell.

In absentia: G. F. Coulouris and J. K. Broadbent: "Some user reactions to operating systems: a selective survey."

SOME USER REACTIONS TO OPERATING SYSTEMS: A SELECTIVE SURVEY

G. F. Coulouris and J. K. Broadbent

Queen Mary College,
Mile End Road,
London

INTRODUCTION

It has become clear to many of the users of third generation computer systems that the effective exploitation of those systems is at least as dependent upon the properties of their operating systems as upon those of the high-level programming languages implemented on them.

High-level languages are now standardized to a significant degree. These standards have been and remain the subject of disagreements, especially between the users of such languages and the designers of systems implementing them. Any development of standards for operating systems is liable to encounter similar disagreements unless the channels for communication between users and system designers are improved. This study is intended as a step in that direction.

The main source of information for this study is a technical survey of six industrial computer users. The survey was aimed at obtaining information from users whose computer applications make special demands on operating system facilities. The applications concerned are therefore principally in the real-time field, but include some applications environments with a smaller real-time component where a high degree of dynamic resource allocation occurs.

The study was carried out during the period June to October 1969 and its content and conclusions on specific systems relate to the systems in use and the applications handled by the users during that period.

The topics considered in the survey are discussed on p. 4, and the applications involved on p. 6. The users surveys are described on p. 7 and conclusions are given on p. 7. Fuller reports of the discussions held with users are available as part of a separate report [1].

METHOD OF INVESTIGATION

The "consumer survey" method of determining design criteria for software and hardware systems does not often appear in the literature but has been used before by an associate in connection with the development of some user-orientated extensions to an experimental machine language [2].

The approach does not correspond to a conventional "market survey" since that type of survey clearly cannot yield reliable information on such complex and ill-defined items as operating systems. Instead, a detailed understanding of the

3

requirements and environments of a limited number of selected users is obtained by intensive discussions.

In most cases, a list of topics was first submitted in the form of a questionnaire (see p. 5). Explicit replies were not requested since they were not considered likely to be useful unless accompanied by a large amount of explanatory detail. The questionnaire was submitted to stimulate interest and to ensure that the basic information requested could be made available in the discussions which followed. The differences in application environments and in approach to system design problems meant that the discussions ranged over many topics not included in the list, and answers were not always available or forthcoming to all of the questions listed. Furthermore, the discussions with the earlier users helped in formulating questions for the others.

Reports of the discussions with each user were prepared and sent to the user for confirmation. All the reports were agreed after only minor modifications. In drawing conclusions from the survey we have relied as far as possible on the agreed reports, but in the absence of specific information in some cases, we have also included assessments based on our knowledge of users' systems and applications.

TOPICS COVERED

The questionnaire used was designed to initiate a dialogue with the computer users interviewed. It therefore includes several questions designed to raise specific problems known to exist in current operating systems. Other questions suggested technical developments that might offer solutions to these problems. These questions reflect to some extent the authors' own views on trends in operating system design.

The features of operating systems selected for special consideration included:

Address mapping
Ease of system modification
Inter-process communication
Interrupt handling
Job language
Process changing
Program error detection
Store management
System integrity
System performance monitoring

The parameters selected to indicate operating system performance were:

Main store utilization
Processor time utilization

and, in the case of real-time applications, maximum transaction processing rate.

Since the design and performance of operating systems is heavily dependent on the organization of the hardware systems on which they operate, we did not consider it useful to carry out this study of operating system features in complete isolation from the hardware architectures that support them. Many of the features studied are often aided by special hardware features. For similar reasons, the study concentrated on the design and performance of basic system components. Somewhat less attention was paid to the details of the user interface, which is of great importance to the individual user, but does not normally influence strongly the ability of a system to perform effectively.

OPERATING SYSTEMS QUESTIONNAIRE

1. Please state hardware and operating systems used and indicate applications.
2. Does (do) your operating system(s) meet your current requirements? If not, please summarize the limitations.
3. In what respects is your current equipment unsuitable for future requirements, as far as these are known? Which, if any, of these potential limitations would you attribute to the operating system?
4. Do you use high level languages? Please state which.
5. If you do not use high level languages or if you considered them unsuitable for a particular application, please give brief reasons.
6. Would it be (or is it) important for all your organization's computers to be compatible?
7. Are you prepared to rewrite assembly programs if/when you change/enhance your current equipment?
8. Would it be (or is it) important for all your organization's computers to use compatible operating systems (i.e. a common job description language, but not necessarily fully implemented for machines with inadequate hardware)?
9. Is compatibility between your existing operating system(s) and future operating systems for the same machine (or its enhancement) important?
10. Would you approve of the integration of job control and programming language? If not please give reasons.
11. Are you able to make modifications to your operating system(s)? If yes, what facilities are available to do this? If no, would you like to be able to do so?
12. Please give examples of modifications made, if any.
13. Are modifications   (*a*) easy to design and code
    (*b*) easy to test
    (*c*) easy to incorporate in the system
    Please indicate specific points of difficulty.
14. Please give approximate core occupancy of your operating system(s). If this can be varied, please say so and give approximate figure for optimum performance.
15. Do you regard the figures Q14 as acceptable. If not, what would you consider acceptable?
16. Are sufficient parameters available to alter system performance?
17. In what additional respects (if any) would you like a variable performance?
18. Have system/hardware failures ever caused the operating system to corrupt user's program or data files? Please give examples. If none, do you think it is possible?
19. Do you ever have to run a machine without its operating system? If yes, please give reasons and say whether you regard this as satisfactory.
20. Is the operating system documentation adequate?

21. Is the operating system easy to use from the points of view of
    - (*a*) programmer
    - (*b*) operator

    If possible please give examples of difficulties.
22. How easy is it to incorporate standard software or applications programs into the system, and what is the method of doing this?
23. Is it possible for one program to initiate another so that they run in parallel as independent jobs with independent resources? If yes, do you use the facility? If no, would you like to have the facility? In either case please elaborate with examples.
24. What facilities do you have for writing pure procedures?
25. How are standard subroutines or blocks of other users code made available to the user?
26. If you have ever changed from using a less powerful operating system to a more powerful one on the same machine with roughly the same workload, how was the throughput affected? If it decreased which extra facilities would you regard as justifying the loss?
27. Can you issue job control commands by program? If yes, which facilities do you find particularly useful?
28. How frequent are involuntary system re-starts?

APPLICATIONS

An attribute common to the six computer users interviewed was the existence of a real-time element in their computer applications. Despite this there was a wide variation in the type of application encountered. This variation implies that any attempt to give comparative ratings for specific systems on the basis of this survey would not be valid. Detailed descriptions of the applications encountered can be found in [1].

For the purpose of the tabulated summaries in Table I, we have classified users' descriptions of their main applications under six headings; the characteristics of each are as follows:

(i) *Scientific*

Batch-processed jobs that are mainly processor-limited and require access only to relatively small sequential files.

(ii) *Commercial*

Batch-processed jobs which are mainly input-output limited and manipulate large and complex files.

(iii) *Remote entry*

Jobs of classes (i) and (ii) filed and edited by interactive methods, but compiled and run in batch mode.

(iv) *Interactive programming*

Continuous interaction with the computer in order to achieve a problem solution. Usually processor limited and making heavy demands on operating system functions. Response time dependent on system performance and processor scheduling algorithm.

(v) *Transaction-orientated*
Interactive interrogation and updating of files. Usually transfer-limited and hence not dependent on processor scheduling for response time.
(vi) *Graphics*
Similar characteristics to (iv) but with a much higher rate of interaction.

SELECTION OF USERS TO BE INTERVIEWED

Each of the users selected had at least one year's experience of using the operating system concerned in several application areas including some with a real-time element. At the time we were carrying out the survey, these requirements were sufficiently restrictive to reduce the number of available candidates to eight users. Of these, six were willing to collaborate in the study. Two of the six organizations wished to remain anonymous. We have not considered it necessary to identify any of the users for this report.

CONCLUSIONS

Table I is a summary of basic conclusions drawn from discussions with users, giving the users' gradings for each of the topics listed on p. 6. It is important to remember that these are with reference to specific applications and in a few cases represent our own extrapolations from the agreed reports.

The more general conclusions that can be drawn from the study are:

1. Most users want and are willing to pay for a system of hardware and software performance monitoring. In the words of user B, "without this facility, we don't know whether to buy more core storage or more disc drives to improve our system's throughput". A figure of 5% was mentioned by the user as an acceptable overhead for processor use incurred by such a facility. Most other users were also willing to accept such an increase in overhead.
2. Greater control over critical operating system parameters and resource allocation algorithms is required in most systems. In general, only the user can determine the best strategies for his installation and the system should be sufficiently parameterized to allow him to do so.
3. Most operating systems had acceptable overheads in terms of direct processor utilization (but not necessarily in idle processor time), but the amount of main store overhead incurred was extremely high except for machines with hardware assisted dynamic store allocation (paged or descriptor-based). In the installations surveyed this overhead alone accounts on average for about 10% of main-frame costs.
4. Real-time systems are very difficult to test in a realistic environment and check-out systems to simulate such environments are desirable. These systems probably call for hardware extensions.
5. The need for rapid interrupt handling and process changing facilities is now widely recognized but they were not available in most of the systems studied.
6. Greater operating system modularity, and a job language which reflects the modular structure of the system can both contribute to a reduction in overhead

TABLE I

Summary of results

User	A	B	C	D	E	F
Applications	Scientific, interactive programming	Scientific, commercial, graphics, interactive programming	Transaction-oriented	Transaction-oriented	Transaction-oriented	Scientific, commercial, remote entry
Hardware	Burroughs B5500	3 x IBM 360/65	IBM 360/50	3 x IBM 360/65	3 x Univac 494	Univac 1108
Operating system	MCP	OS360(MVT)	OS360(MFT)	OS360(MFT) & special real time	CONTORTS	EXEC 3
Languages used for:						
(a) Applications	Algol, Fortran	PL/1, Fortran	Assembler	PL/1 & assembler	Neliao & assembler	Fortran
(b) System software	Algol, Espol	Assembler	Assembler	Assembler	Assembly	Assembly
Operating system performance						
Core store used	18–24 Kbytes (15%)	180–350 Kbytes (15–20%)	70 Kbytes (25%)	(Not available)	122 Kbytes (20%)	(Not applicable)
Processor time used (estimated)	15–20%	10%	10%	(Not available)	?	?
Software features						
Store management	Good	Inadequate	Inadequate	?	Good	–
Program error detection	Good	Adequate	Poor	Good	Adequate	Poor
System integrity	Adequate	Adequate	Poor	Adequate	Adequate	Adequate
System performance monitoring	Poor	Poor	Poor	Poor	Poor	Poor
Job language	Adequate	Poor	Poor	Poor	Adequate	Good
Inter-process communication	Adequate	Adequate/good	Poor	Good	Adequate	–
Ease of system modification	Good	Poor	Poor	?	Poor	Adequate
Hardware features						
Address mapping	Good	Poor	Poor	Adequate	Adequate	Adequate
Process changing	Good	Poor	Poor	Poor	Good	?
Interrupt handling	Good	Poor	Poor	Poor	Good	?

costs for all classes of users. Users expect this structure to be well documented and to remain fixed during system enhancements, since their software may depend on the structure of the system.

7. Most users in the class studied expect to program major operating system modifications and sub-systems using a language that gives adequate control over machine and system functions. In most cases this was an assembly language. These gave little or no security during program testing and were inadequately monitored even during production running. Furthermore, some users were dissatisfied with the security of the object code in high level language programs. Conclusion 5 is relevant to these problems.

8. Facilities for the execution of operating system functions under program control were considered valuable by most users as an aid to system development. The integration of a command language and programming language was favoured as a method of providing such facilities, although only one user had any practical experience with such a system.

In addition to the above eight main conclusions, three further points made by users are considered worthy of note:

9. In any system there will be facilities whose use may have an adverse effect on the service offered to other users. This is particularly true of interactive programming and batch processing environments with dynamic job creation. A controlled system for the allocation of such facilities is required.

10. Privileged orders are a source of system insecurity and failure. The level of privilege in the main part of existing systems is often unnecessarily high.

11. The dynamically allocated store used in transaction-orientated applications cannot be securely addressed without a protected datum-limit pair for each area allocated. Amongst the systems studied only the Burroughs B5500 had such facilities.

FURTHER COMMENTS

The conclusions drawn apply only to the systems in current use at the time of the study. Some of the deficiencies mentioned might be removed by more recent systems, or by the use of proprietary or in-house system extensions. In general, however, the user sample studied is composed of some of the most sophisticated industrial users in the U.K.; we were not able to make contact with users of more advanced systems. Moreover, the deficiencies identified appear in many cases to be direct consequences of hardware architectural features and could not be effectively remedied without further hardware support. Operating systems on some more recent computer architectures do not suffer from all of these deficiencies; the results of this study for the Burroughs B5500 system appear to support this assertion.

Clearly, the results of our study cannot be claimed as a statistically significant measure of users' reactions to operating systems. At the lowest evaluation the results can be taken as evidence for the existence of certain unfulfilled requirements amongst a certain class of operating system users. If current requirements of the advanced users whom we chose for study are accepted as typical of future requirements amongst more pedestrian users, then the results carry greater weight.

The method of working that we have described here therefore appears to have a useful role in the total operating system design activity. In particular, it offers one alternative to the much-criticized method of "design-by-committee".

ACKNOWLEDGEMENTS

The willingness of the six organizations and their representatives to undergo our rather searching and time-consuming questionings made this study possible. We owe them our warmest thanks.

The work was carried out with the help of financial support from International Computers Limited when the authors were at the Centre for Computing and Automation, Imperial College of Science and Technology.

REFERENCES

[1] Evans, J. M., "Commercial data processing in basic language". Imperial College Computer Science Report 15, October 1969.
[2] Broadbent, J. K. and Coulouris, G. F., "A study of operating systems and their applications". Imperial College Computer Science Report 16, November 1969.

OPERATING SYSTEMS:
THEIR PURPOSE, OBJECTIVES,
FUNCTIONS AND SCOPE

C. A. R. Hoare

Department of Computer Science,
Queen's University,
Belfast

PURPOSE AND OBJECTIVES

The basic purpose of a computer operating system is to *share* the hardware which it controls among a number of users, making unpredictable demands upon its resources; and its objectives are to do so efficiently, reliably, and unobtrusively.

Amplification

The definition of a *user* is left deliberately vague; it may be a single person or a team; a single program or a suite of related programs carrying out some task. Each user is regarded at least on occasion as more or less isolated from all other users, and is not supposed to be concerned or aware of what the other users are doing at any given time. Consequently an operating system should protect each user from the accidental or deliberate effects of the actions of other users; this is accomplished by presenting to each user an apparent or virtual machine configuration (usually smaller and/or slower than the actual hardware available), which the user may regard as his own separate machine, relatively independent of the virtual machines presented to other users.

The main problems faced by an operating system arise from the *unpredictability* of the demands made by its users. If all demands were made in predictable combinations at predictable times, the whole operation of the machine could be planned in advance by a single prewritten program. Indeed, any ALGOL program using block structure (or FORTRAN program using EQUIVALENCE for a similar purpose) is "sharing" the store of a computer among different "users" (blocks or procedures) at different times. But since the pattern of sharing is completely predetermined by the program, one cannot argue that such a program is an operating system.

The *efficiency* of the sharing achieved by an operating system can be measured in terms of the density of utilization of resources. Each item of hardware (e.g. peripheral device, word in core store, channel, central processor) is allocated to a user (on his request) for only a certain percentage of the time. Each such item can be given a comparative weighting related to its capital and running cost and possibly also scarcity value; multiplying each weight by the percentage of time in use, it is possible to obtain a figure for the density of utilization of the installation as a whole. Naturally, this figure will depend on the degree of balance between the hardware configuration and the user workload; but even in the case of perfect balance and a well-designed

11

operating system, unpredictable variations in the behaviour of the users, and their demands for good service, are likely to place quite a low limit on the efficiency achievable.

The *reliability* achieved by an operating system must obviously depend on the reliability of the underlying hardware; nevertheless, a good operating system should certainly mitigate the effects of occasional hardware malfunction, for example by automatically repeating unsuccessful operations, or restoring corrupt data; and if automatic recovery is not possible, an operating system should confine the effects of error to as few users as possible, and assist each user in making good after a breakdown. To some extent, the objective of increasing the apparent reliability of the hardware also derives from the primary purpose of sharing a computer; for the effects of hardware failure on a shared machine would be many times as serious as on a single unshared computer, in that it will affect many more users; and also, on a shared computer, no single user without software assistance would have sufficient understanding or control over the installation as a whole to enable him to take steps to recover from a fault in the sort of *ad hoc* way which is often possible on a single stand-alone computer.

Another objective of an operating system is to give each user the same *predictability of service* that he would have on his own separate (slower) computer, to which he would have immediate access whenever he wished. A user should know the apparent speed and capacity of his virtual machine, and thus be able to predict how long he will have to wait after submitting his program and data before getting his results back. If he is disappointed in his expectation, it does not matter whether this is due to a hardware breakdown, or to a deficiency in the scheduling strategy of the operating system. Thus the achievement of reasonable predictability of turnround for the individual user is an important corollary of the objective of reliability; but it is difficult to achieve in view of the unpredictability of the workload presented at any given time by the other users of the system, and there is no doubt that a user must occasionally be disappointed.

There is one clear consequence of the view that the purpose of an operating system is to share a computer installation among a number of users: for the individual user, the use of the operating system is not optional but compulsory. He must therefore regard an operating system as a necessary evil, tolerated as the only means of obtaining a share of an expensive computer installation, when he would really prefer to have exclusive use of a rather cheaper one, which he presumably cannot afford. Thus as far as the user is concerned, the best operating system is one which is most *unobtrusive* – which appears least to stand between his requirements and the virtual machine which is to satisfy them. The complex control-languages and obscure output messages which are such a feature of modern software are certainly widely recognized as evils, even if it is claimed that they are necessary.

There is another consequence of the compulsory nature of the use of an operating system which should be taken to heart by its designers and implementors – the obligation upon them to achieve the very highest quality of their product. Any other item of software is at least in principle optional for the user; if the quality of a library program is unacceptably low, he can write or select a better program. In the case of an operating system, however, the individual user has no choice; he cannot replace the parts which are of substandard quality. It is to be hoped that future designers of operating systems will accept the obligation of high quality; will recognize that quality is measured by efficiency, reliability and unobtrusiveness; and will produce software which is a major improvement on current products in widespread use, which display none of these qualities in any high degree.

Alternative views

It must be recognized that the unsatisfactory nature of many current operating systems is not wholly due to lack of good will or competence on the part of designers and implementors; but rather to the fact that they started with a view different to that proposed here both of the purpose of an operating system, and of its objectives. These alternative views will now be discussed.

The Universalist view

One widely accepted view is that the term "Operating System" should cover the entire range of software support offered by a computer manufacturer. Naturally, there is no point in arguing about terminology; nevertheless, indiscriminate use of a single term to cover so wide a range of software is very unhelpful, and may have serious consequences in blurring the functions and objectives of different items of software. In this paper we choose to adopt a more precise terminology, to single out some important particular part of a manufacturer's software range.

The Compatibilist view

A second view, which certainly underlies the practice of many manufacturers' operating systems, is that the objective of an operating system is to secure "compatibility" for user programs so that they can be transferred between installations of widely differing speed, size and configuration. Naturally, it is a sensible objective of a manufacturer's commercial policy that the lower machines of a range should be identical in their hardware structure to the virtual machines which are set up by an operating system within the more powerful shared installations. Furthermore, there is an obvious role for simulators, emulators, service routines and library programs, and machine-independent languages, which will assist in the transfer of programs from one machine to another. However, it should not be the province of an operating system to enforce compatibility when this is not wanted or appropriate for the user; for compatibility is seldom achieved without a cost which surprises user and implementor alike.

The Perfectionist view

Finally, there is a widespread view that an operating system should present to each user a virtual machine which is in some way preferable to the original hardware, in the sense that it possesses more facilities or is easier to program. This view arrogates to operating system designers a number of responsibilities which are better discharged by others: for example the provision of better hardware should be the responsibility of hardware designers; useful facilities should be provided by designers of service programs and library routines; and the task of making a computer easier to program belongs to programming language designers and implementors. In the past, when presented with badly designed hardware and even worse programming languages (which cannot be changed for reasons of compatibility), there has been a great temptation for the operating system designer to attempt to remedy the situation by software. The resulting systems have inevitably grown very large and expensive,

and far from mitigating previously existing defects, they have introduced many new
ones of their own. There are few writers of major programs who would not prefer to
interface directly to the hardware rather than to an operating system.

The main reason for taking a very strict view of the proper province of an operating
system is that the use of an operating system is compulsory on a shared installation.
Any resources of core storage, backing storage, channel capacity and processor time
which are used by the operating system present a permanent and inescapable overhead on the installation and the user; whereas any compiler, library routine or
service program which is invoked by a user may be selected, adapted or even specially
written for his particular requirements. Even worse, any attempt to present a user
with a "more convenient" virtual machine than that provided by hardware must
almost inevitably be based on assumptions about the nature of his use of the machine,
which will in particular cases be unjustified. Thus the provision of additional software
support as part of an operating system nearly always leads to *loss* of flexibility in
application. A machine empty of software is always the most flexible; the addition of
even a few instructions of "compulsory" software can only reduce the range of its
application, never increase it.

Nevertheless, as in all successful design, a certain scope for compromise must be
recognized, and the following special cases can be made:

1. When the operating system itself needs a service (for example, binary-decimal
conversions) such a service can often be made available to users at no extra overhead.
2. When considerations of compatibility and convenience are very strong, and the
extra overhead quite small, a suitable concession can be made.
3. The hardware designers must be permitted to interpret instructions by software
if on certain machines in a range this is more economic than building their
interpretation into hardware.

As mentioned above it is a legitimate objective of an operating system to simulate
a virtual machine which is more *reliable* than the actual hardware of the machine,
and software services associated with this objective may legitimately be ascribed to
an operating system.

FUNCTIONS AND SCOPE

This section surveys the range of functions which an operating system is properly
called upon to perform in sharing a computer installation among many users. The
survey starts from the simple rudimentary forms of operating system suitable for
small machines and specialized applications, and progresses to the larger and more
complex systems providing a service to many users with differing needs.

Rudimentary systems

It is instructive to start a survey with an "empty" or "null" case where no
operating system is needed at all. Such cases are found in the application of computers
to laboratory automation or process control, where a small computer is wholly and
continuously dedicated to a single task. In an application such as airline seat
reservation a larger computer is generally used, and it shares its attention among a

number of separately identifiable tasks or transactions. But usually the paramount importance of reliability and predictable response times in these applications force the programmer to work out fairly precisely in advance the potential "behaviour" of the transactions, and to take advantage of this knowledge throughout the design of his sharing strategy and its implementation. To date, it has proved impossible to design a "real-time" operating system which will give real-time service on a general bureau basis. We shall therefore omit real-time applications in the remainder of this survey.

Returning to a more conventional environment, where users submit more or less disjointed *jobs* to be run on a computer, it is obvious that the simplest method of "sharing" is just by succession in time. Each user follows another, and has sole use of the machine during the period allotted to him (usually controlled by a booking system). The role of operating system software is minimal: its main function is to *reset* the machine to some known state at the beginning of each user's session; and if some suitable output device is available, it may provide the facility of *dumping* the user's job if his period expires before the job is complete; and *reinstating* it at the beginning of the next session. The facility for reinstating programs may be used to load service programs or compilers on behalf of the user. This operating regime is suitable for small machines installed in scientific laboratories.

In a commercial environment a similar method is quite suitable for a small machine. But such an installation should not be regarded as only a central processor, but also as the set of removable tapes, discs, etc., which contain essential user files; and which are usually stored centrally in or near the computer room. Thus when each user starts his session, the files relevant to his job must be set up by operators, and there is a severe risk that the incorrect data will be mounted. Thus the user may inadvertently process the wrong data; or worse still, overwrite valuable information still required by another user.

The solution to this problem is to write a *header label* at the beginning of each file, containing the name of the file and the date up to which the information must be preserved; and these are checked before the file is read or overwritten. This obviates a reliability problem arising out of the sharing of the computer, and is thus properly an operating system function.

Another function connected with reliable sharing is the error correction and recovery procedure carried out by standard read/write routines. These should perhaps be regarded as part of the "hardware", in that it is a choice of the hardware designer how to minimize the cost of reliability by a mixture of hardware and software techniques.

Batch monitors

As machines get faster, the time taken to execute a typical single job submitted by a user reduces until it is very much less than the time taken by the manual changeover between one job and the next. Indeed in a scientific workload with a high component of program testing, a significant proportion of jobs will fail in the first few seconds. The reduction of the interjob gap may be achieved by introducing a *batch monitor* to automate the transition between one job and the next, and to replace intervention by the user or operator. The main additional function of a batch monitor is to detect the end of a job either by expiry of a time limit or exhaustion of input data, the overflow of some resource constraint, or other detectable error; and to indicate to the operator the point where the output of one job should be separated from that of the next.

After virtual elimination of the inter-job gap, the main limitation to the throughput of the machine is the slow speed of the input and output devices (card readers, line printers, etc.); it is essential to minimize the time spent waiting for these devices, particularly during periods of card loading, paper change, routine maintenance and hardware breakdown. This can be achieved by off-lining of information: jobs and data are read from a slow device onto backing store as a continuous operation well in advance of processing; the information destined for printing is also written first to backing store, and later transcribed to a slower device as a continuous operation. When off-lining is carried out simultaneously with computation on the same computer, it is known as *pseudo-offlining*. The continuity of the input/output ensures that the slower devices operate at full speed for as long as they are in service and there is work for them; and when they are out of service, the computer can continue transferring information to and from the backing store until they are operational again. Thus an improvement in efficiency and reliability is simultaneously achieved.

When the information is transferred between main store and backing store, there is usually a large average overhead on each transfer; it therefore pays to perform input and output in fairly large *blocks,* each containing some ten to fifty cards or lines of information. Thus information from cards is assembled into blocks before being written to backing store, and in reading back, the blocks are disassembled into lines again before being presented to the user program. Similarly, lines destined for output on the printer are assembled into blocks before being written to backing store, and disassembled again on printing.

If the hardware of the computer permits backing store transfers simultaneous with computing, the operating system can further increase efficiency by a *buffering* scheme, which allows the user program to proceed while a block is being output, and attempts to keep one block ahead on input. This blocking, unblocking and buffering is a function of the operating system, since it improves the efficiency of a shared installation; and it should be of no concern to the individual user whether his input and output information resides for a period on backing store or not. The part of the operating system which administers the above-mentioned aspects of an operating system is known as an *input/output control system.*

When pseudo-offlining is used, and the central processor develops a fault which is repaired, it is very important to be able to continue output of the results of jobs which had been completed before the fault occurred; and to continue processing jobs which had been previously input, preferably starting again the job during which the fault occurred. Such an action is known as a *warm start*, and is one of the means by which an operating system limits the potentially more extensive effects of hardware unreliability on the efficiency and service of a shared machine.

One major disadvantage of a batch monitor is that once a long job has been initiated, any short jobs input later must wait until the long job is complete. This leads to long and unpredictable delays in the turnround of the majority of jobs, which are short. The inconvenience can be mitigated if the operating system has the power to select for execution an arbitrary job from the input queue, and thus give favour to shorter jobs even if they were input after a longer one. An even better service can be given if a long job can be interrupted and dumped to backing store to permit short jobs to pass by. This function of an operating system is known as *job scheduling*.

In a batch monitor system, programs which require operator action, for example the mounting and dismounting of tapes or discs, present particular problems, since such a program will in general have to wait completion of operator action before proceeding. This problem can be mitigated by the job scheduler, which can ensure that the proper files are mounted before selecting the job for initiation. Nevertheless, the mounting of special files inhibits "queue-jumping" by shorter jobs; and furthermore if a high proportion of jobs require such action, the efficiency of the computer installation will be severely limited.

This problem can be solved by keeping the information required by most users on a large disc store, from which it is immediately available on demand. The task of sharing a disc store among many users falls to the *filing system* which splits the disc space into areas, and allocates and deallocates them to each user on request. Thus each user of the filing system has a virtual machine with a "non-volatile" backing store, which can store information between one run and the next. In fact one of the major problems of a filing system is to guarantee absolute permanence of stored information, in face of disc hardware failure; or even worse, breakdown of the central processor during the process of updating vital information on disc. The required security seems to be achieved only by the periodic dumping of information from disc on to magnetic tapes, which can then be removed from risk by dismounting. A second requirement of a filing system is of course to ensure that no user can deliberately interfere with the information belonging to another user, either by reading or by writing. The third requirement is to provide an environment in which a library of commonly used programs and subroutines can be stored on disc, and efficiently shared by all users. Finally, a filing system may also provide a communication facility which permits one user to give to selected colleagues a controlled access to his files.

A further function which falls to an operating system is that of maintaining a *log* of significant events. The purpose of this is three-fold:

1. To assist in diagnosis and recovery from error or breakdown;
2. To provide statistical information on the workload and the performance of the operating system, so that it can be improved;
3. To provide the information for charging each user for the resources he has used. The calculation of the charge and the invoicing of users may also be regarded as an operating system function.

Multiprogramming systems

Up to this point, our survey has assumed that only one user program is being executed at a time. However, on larger machines, a denser utilization of resources may be achieved if several programs are initiated together to run simultaneously, in a mode of operation known as multiprogramming. If there is more than one central processor in the system, multiprogramming is needed to make effective use of the extra computing power. Even if there is only a single processor, it may pay for it to alternate attention between several programs, and thus avoid delays while one program is communicating with backing store or with the operator. The part of the operating system responsible for sharing a central processor or processors between several concurrent programs is known as the *dispatcher*.

When a general facility of this kind has been set up, it is convenient to allow the operating system itself to take advantage of it, and to delegate certain of its tasks (for example, pseudo-offlining) to programs which run in parallel with each other and with the user's programs. Operating system tasks differ from normal user programs in that they require to communicate with each other while they are running; and each communication may involve some form of *synchronization*. Similarly, user programs must occasionally synchronize with each other if they are competing for some limited resource. Some means of administration of synchronization must be part of the responsibility of the dispatcher.

In the absence of multiprogramming, it is assumed that the user program, once initiated, will have access to all resources of the computer installation other than those occupied by the system itself. In many cases, a proportion of these resources will not be required at all for a given job; and in other cases, the resources are required only for a proportion of the total running time of the job. One of the main advantages of multiprogramming on a large machine is that the unused resources can be allocated to another program. Thus the task of *resource allocation* belongs to the operating system. The objective of resource allocation is to give each user the resources he needs exactly when he needs them, and thus secure a general high density of utilization. In some systems, the user defines the required resources for his job, or each job step, by means of *job control* cards included in his submitted job; the interpretation of these is the task of a resource allocator. Of special interest is the management of core storage, which is usually one of the most valuable and scarcest resources in a multiprogrammed computer installation; many ingenious schemes (paging, segmentation, etc.) have been devised to postpone allocation of core storage to programs until the very moment that they first need it, and to take areas of core storage away from programs which are not currently using them and to lend them to other programs; and also to share subroutines and data among programs which may happen to be using them simultaneously.

With the advent of multiprogramming, it again becomes economically feasible to permit the user to communicate with his own program while it is running, in exactly the same way as he would if he had a machine of his own. The provision of a console on the user's virtual machine involves no new principle in the functioning of an operating system; nevertheless, the strict requirements for good response time and acceptable cost entail that many of the techniques used to carry out the major functions of an operating system must be specially designed for this new mode of operation.

CONCLUSION

This paper has put forward a theory of the purpose and objectives of an operating system, and has shown how many of the traditional functions of operating systems arise from their primary purpose of sharing a computer installation.

The paper contains no new technical proposals to solve the many problems which face implementors and users of operating systems at the present time. Nevertheless, it is hoped that the general philosophy propounded here may prove to be of some general benefit:

1. To the users of an operating system, it explains the major source of the problems, namely the provision of a predictable service in the face of a highly varied and unpredictable workload; and suggests that disciplines designed to reduce variability and unpredictability may show a valuable return in the form of improved service and reduced cost.

2. To the designer and implementor a clear statement of purpose and objectives of the system as a whole and each part of it may be an invaluable guide in taking the many thousands of decisions of principle and detail involved in any large programming system.

DISCUSSION

HOARE: It is with some diffidence that I present a paper of this sort to such a learned gathering; my intention was to make it as boring as possible. You may gather on reading this paper that one of my academic interests is philosophy, about which long papers are written which take more space explaining what they haven't said than what they have.

I wanted to get clear in my own mind what I would like if I were using or implementing an operating system, and what I would like my managers to know, so that they understood my objectives: to leave out all technical terms and isolate a language of purposes, qualities, criteria and objectives, in which a user or manager can communicate with the designer; a language consisting of vague terms, ordinary English, and many concepts with vague definitions. I think it is important even in technical discussions to attempt to define concepts in terms of their purpose, rather than by describing how they accomplish that purpose.

Many programmers when you ask them the meaning of a term take out a scrap of paper and write a program which isn't really the level of communication wanted. It should rather be — what's it there for? what can I do with it? what good is it to me? and very often the users and designers of software do not have the required abstractions to conduct discussions of this sort.

Compare my approach with that of Mr. Coulouris, who attempts to establish communication between the designer and users by means of questionnaires and visits. His customers rate various operating systems which they happen to be using, in the manner of a market survey of a rather technical nature. There are two dangers in this approach: (1) people tend to fall in love with whatever prison cell they happen to be in, so it is very difficult to get an unbiased view; (2) when you come to discuss a remedy for an unsatisfactory situation you find the user using catch words to describe what he thinks is the remedy. These catch words may have been fed to him by a salesman from a rival organization and it is very difficult to find out exactly what is wrong. The reason he has a problem is because of some original deficiency in the software he was given; and he thinks a superimposed solution will solve this.

Mr. Coulouris suggests, quite rightly, that greater contact between customers and designers is necessary, and offers this as an alternative to the much criticised method of design by committee. If I know of any alternative worse than the much criticised design by committee, it's design by the customer. The customer has very little breadth of knowledge, no knowledge of the needs of others, or the way in which his particular solutions are going to make life difficult for others. He attempts to obtain from the manufacturer, not an objective and a set of criteria by which the accomplishment of the design is to be judged, but specific technical demands. In programming language design or implementation he doesn't say "I want a technique for efficient use of magnetic tapes on this machine" he says "I want multiblocking with self indexing and automatic factor control". So you get a queue of customers who tell you what "extensions" they need. The designer must ask: "what exactly do you want that for?"; and usually there is some reason, probably peculiar to their installation. "All right", the designer says, "if you want to do that, surely you can do it this way" and indicates a brief and efficient little program; but the user says "No, I want to do it the way I did it before". Now you have contact between designer and users at far too detailed a level for the good of either of them.

In drafting this paper, I came to the view that the task of the designer of a modern manufacturer's operating system is: on a machine with unknown power and size inherent unreliability and unpredictability of effect, to write an operating system which will satisfactorily cater for the unpredictable demands of an unknown group of users. This is why operating system design is difficult and probably impossible. I suggest no solutions, just perhaps that designers should have the right to look for the easiest solution to their problems, rather than the most general and most sophisticated.

An objection to my paper is that it views the users as an indiscriminate and large class of individuals, whereas they tend to be grouped in more or less hierarchical fashion, usually into different classes. For example there is the group of users who are setting up a data processing system on magnetic tapes. A suggestion is often made that the structure of the operating system should, as far as possible, take account of this and other grouping of users. You could perhaps have a hierarchical operating system. At the top level it shares between large classes of user so that within each class there is a separate sub-operating system which is particularly adapted to its needs. A very good example of the successful use of this sort of hierarchical operating system is the in-core compiler, where by grouping the users who agree to use the same compiler and not to mix languages you can write a specialized operating system, incorporated more or less in the compiler, which will share a partition of the machine among this particular sub-group of the users. I believe the benefit of a hierarchical structure derives from the fact that cross references (e.g. references to brothers, sisters, uncles) are an order of magnitude less frequent than references up and down the chain of the hierarchy (e.g. references to fathers, sons). You can then take advantage of the virtual isolation of each group of users to achieve efficiency and other objectives of your operating system. Unfortunately, the customer does not always co-operate, and this can have a serious impact on performance and then everyone suffers. In general whenever a manufacturer's software sets up barriers in the flexibility of the use of the machine, customers are always asking to jump over these barriers.

In practice the promise of hierarchical operating systems has not been fully realized. The decision to set up an operating system as a hierarchy should be one of the technical decisions of a designer if he feels this is a good compromise solution. It's not an objective of an operating system to be hierarchical, but it is an important technique to take advantage of any known structure in the user population to achieve efficiency, reliability and unobtrusiveness.

RANDELL: I feel that the emphasis on sharing in Hoare's paper is not quite right, sharing is a remedy not a problem. My own characterization of an operating system is that it is something which allows one (or attempts to allow one) to achieve the performance which the hardware should be capable of, and to surpass the reliability which it is capable of. As the system gets bigger and more expensive, sharing is very obviously a way of dealing with the first of these.

The paper is a very good discussion of sharing and therefore those aspects of an operating system which are important in this regard. However, there are some functions (such as spooling) which are mentioned as being part of an operating system which do not fit in under sharing, rather under performance. They don't fit in under sharing; rather they fit in parallel with sharing.

Finally, it is very useful to draw a distinction between an operating system intended for a known environment and known configuration and a generic operating system. One of the biggest distinctions between operating systems can often be the extent to which an operating system is intended for a known environment rather than being a massive kit of tools of unbelievable flexibility.

HOARE: I too have considerable difficulty in justifying input/output control as part of an operating system. The existence of a stream of jobs larger than those submitted by a single person is the reason why spooling contributes to efficiency. It is a result of the interaction effects between sharing and efficiency rather than being directly attributable to sharing. You would hardly use spooling if you were not sharing the computer. Things like buffering seem to be difficult to justify as the direct result of sharing. In practice, since input/output is time shared and tends to have interactions with other users, the most convenient place to conduct its administration is in the operating system.

GOOS: I have two points on Coulouris's paper. Firstly, if we have to design systems for future use, we must remember that the skill of the users will also have changed, and hence the value of such questionnaires will not be so relevant. Secondly, if you try to get reactions from the outside world either you get no answer or you get the answer that future systems need to be 300% more powerful than the present ones, while you know that at most they need 20% more power. However, the paper indicates that it may be a good idea to start some kind of market research, but by software engineers.

I think Hoare's paper is perhaps too weak in definitions — the people you are talking to know how an integrated system behaves. Also it does not point out clearly how the system should preserve hardware properties. Either the hardware is given (if you are designing a second or a third system for the same hardware), or the software and hardware should be designed together and in this case you should only speak of the system rather than of hardware properties. I have found that designers first design a system and then define a user rather than starting with a clear definition of the user.

Logical clarity is part of what you call efficiency, or sometimes it may be seen as part of reliability or unobtrusiveness. But in all cases it has a value of its own and should not be confused with other objectives.

HOARE: I have found that the logical clarity and ease of use of machine hardware to be greater than that of the virtual machine presented by most software systems. If you can give to your virtual machine a logical clarity equivalent to that of an empty machine, then you have achieved quite a high target. Of course, your hardware must be free of gross awkwardness I have once tried to ameliorate an oversight in the hardware by means of software. It was a disaster.

GOOS: It depends what is meant by hardware, whether you are considering conventional hardware of a second generation machine or the hardware properties as designed for use by the operating system.

HOARE: I haven't forbidden my hardware designers to write programs. The hardware man is the person to decide how much of his machine to implement in hardware and how much in a low level micro-program or program.

GOOS: Another point I should like to make is that for reasons of efficiency it might be possible to construct virtual machines which at the time of compilation allow for checks which otherwise would be made by the operating system at run time. Therefore you increase the reliability and robustness of the system.

RANDELL: You have a slightly more optimistic view than I have of the ability of logic designers and hardware designers to create a thing of beauty in absolute isolation from the people who have to use the object.

SUTCLIFFE: I agree with what has been said in praise of Mr. Coulouris's approach provided we do not impose a doctor/patient relationship on this exchange. We want to know what is wrong with the user but we do not want him coming to us and telling us what to prescribe and just where to do the surgery.

HARTLEY: I agree entirely, but how are we to protect ourselves from manufacturers of hardware or software who are going to be unscrupulous and try and persuade us that their product will do our job.

SUTCLIFFE: That's certainly true in this developing field, but doctors also can be misled by advertising.

NEWELL: When you feel unwell you do not consult six doctors and take the medicine you fancy best.

GOOS: It is an operating systems consultant who should conduct such a questionnaire, for he doesn't have any responsibility either to the users or the people who want to know the results.

RANDELL: We have been assuming the designers of the system are completely separate from the users of the system.

FRASER: The best operating systems are made by the people who have to use them. Also a survey has to be closely related with the actual use of software that one can witness, not just asking people what they think the hardware should do.

VINCE: We should have an operating system architecture which can be evolved to the user's requirements as we know about them, since in a few years' time this sort of survey will no longer be accurate.

LIPPS: I have one comment concerning the relationship between manufacturer and user. I know of at least one manufacturer who is very reluctant to present his machine to the users in terms of what either the hardware or the software will do. The manufacturer takes the attitude that "I am telling you what the system does for you, and you have to put up with that". I have tried to use one of his machines, without going through the operating system, to read cards and find out what each column contains. The longer I talked to the manufacturer, the more difficult it became to disentangle what that machine could do. I therefore support the point that the hardware should be separated from the software and that the hardware should be simple and straightforward.

HOARE: This illustrates the point between those who believe in virtual machines and those who believe in the sad necessity of sharing and hope that it is unobtrusive. The reason why it is impossible for your program to find out what actual holes were in what pieces of cardboard is because his operating system constructs a virtual machine on which what you read from the card reader is characters, not holes in a piece of cardboard. Now it may be necessary, for reasons of efficiency or other reasons that the virtual machine presented to each user by an operating system does make this abstraction, but what that manufacturer has said is "I know better than you what you want; you want characters, not holes in cardboard" and has written an operating system which is obtrusive, which stands between you and the machine that you want your program to control.

RANDELL: It strikes me as standing in exactly the same way that printed circuit boards stand between me and the transistors. The manufacturer may well have decided that by specializing on certain services he has found a market which is satisfactory to his shareholders. Hence some people are no longer appropriate customers for him. It is as if the machine is absolutely perfect for you, except that the way the round-off works isn't quite what you want; and you ask "Will you please tell us where the wires are, etc.". Wouldn't you feel this is a slightly less reasonable request to make of him?

It's not obvious to me that the level of secrecy should be at the level of hardware. It may well be that on top of the hardware one puts some program and a manufacturer may well have very good reasons for refusing to allow you to delve into that program.

HOARE: As long as he *has* good reasons. Manufacturers are sometimes fooled by their software writers into thinking that the construction of the virtual machines is an end in itself, quite independent of the commercial objectives of the company or indeed the interests of the customer.

GOOS: My own view is that every level of abstraction which is implemented by an operating system is a new level of hardware and the user is completely on top of the whole scheme. He is unaware of what is implemented by hardware or software.

VINCE: I think the lowest level of abstraction of software that is seen on certain manufacturers' machines has in fact proved difficult for certain people, not because it presents a higher level of hardware in its place but because certain aspects of system organization were included in the software. It's not so much the fact that we can't get a particular punched hole rather than a character that is important. The unfortunate point is that this lowest level piece of software is already dictating the strategy that one can use in designing any software which sits above that level of abstraction.

LIPPS: It is an oversimplification to expect that a certain user should use a machine such that the hardware and software form one unit. I think one of the requirements as seen from the user's angle is that he should be able to dig into a system as far as he likes. It is a mistake for a manufacturer not to allow this. It may be satisfactory for the majority of his customers and may be perfect from a general point of view of economics, but he should not take such a hard line. He should provide documentation from which the user who wants to can go into any necessary detail.

BRINCH HANSEN: We should try to accept the validity of the papers within their own stated objectives and try to reach agreement on the principles of operating systems. For example Randell pointed out that the main objective was not sharing, but the efficient use of equipment. If you're the manager of a computer installation the efficient use of the system matters more than anything else. But the resource requirements of most programs cannot efficiently use the machine continuously, which leads to the immediate need for sharing. I don't see any great difference between Randell's and Hoare's views. With operating systems we are trying to pursue the consequences of a seemingly simple economic necessity, namely that of sharing, and the design of virtual machines with nice features is a sort of compensation to the poor user who has to suffer from this economic necessity.

FRASER: When I have thought of sharing in terms of a computer system I always thought of it as a constructive help rather than an obstacle. The reason why people share a bed is not just shortage of beds. As time goes on, and more data and tasks become committed to machines, people will want to lie in the same bed even if there's a spare one available because they will want to share, they will want to use the same programs.

SUTCLIFFE: There are two types of sharing; non-contentious, like the sharing of the atmosphere in this room; and contentious sharing.

BRINCH HANSEN: Sharing has two aspects, the competition for resources and the possibility of happy co-operation by the exchange of resulting programs. As software designers, the blessings of sharing need not worry us too much, we ought to be more concerned with the problematic aspect of sharing.

NEWELL: The point I found most interesting in Hoare's paper was the aspect of the predictability and reliability of the virtual machine. You implied that most users would rather run their Fortran programs on a mini-computer of power n, than go on a big fancy system and share with everybody else, where the turnround time might vary by a factor of 10 or more. How much do we make the virtual machine predictable in that sense? and also how can the reliability of the virtual machine be very different from the reliability of the actual hardware? Another point concerned resources: how do you schedule so as to encourage users to use the resources to best advantage? How do you encourage users to double buffer, assuming you think it's a good thing? The programmer uses more core store than if he didn't double buffer, so you are going to penalize the man who double buffers. How do you schedule the resources in order to encourage such a tendency?

HOARE: This may be a pragmatic argument for putting double buffering as a part of an operating system when, in principle, it ought to be part of the user program. As far as predictability is concerned, most programmers are programming in high level languages nowadays. I have done a lot of work on predictability of performance on high level languages. That is the place where I would first tackle the problem, it being more serious there. Unfortunately present day fashions are for languages in which compilers generate arbitrarily unpredictable programs, and I haven't been able to make much headway on this investigation.

NEWELL: What do you mean by arbitrarily unpredictable?

HOARE: Most people prefer to use a compiler which makes the performance of their programs unpredictable to them. Nobody likes to take responsibility for his designs and so he buys software which apparently takes this responsibility away from him.

NEWELL: I haven't known of anybody going round manufacturers with a bench mark and saying I'll buy the machine which will give the worst results when I run the bench marks.

HOARE: On the other hand people don't buy machines that run the best bench mark, and they use compilers that certainly don't produce the best bench mark. An optimizing PL1 compiler has probably about two orders of magnitude of unpredictability. If you accidentally invoke an automatic type conversion you'll get at least a factor of 10 expansion in your code and in run time. If you happen to obey the rules for switching on the optimizer you may well gain a factor of 10 or more in the other direction. The rules are so complicated no user could possibly predict.

NEWELL: That's one aspect of predictability. However, if I run a given program to-day and it takes exactly 20 minutes and I run it to-morrow It would like it to take the same time and not ten times longer. But this has a corollary, that if to-morrow the operating system finishes it in two minutes, it has to delay artificially for eighteen minutes, in order to be predictable.

HOARE: In this case the operating system would be very well advised to say, "I might break down in the next eighteen minutes, therefore let's get this job out at once, to be on the safe side".

NEWELL: But you wouldn't tell the user until the end of twenty minutes!

OPERATING SYSTEM PRINCIPLES

Speakers: P. Brinch Hansen: "An outline of a course on operating system principles."

A. G. Fraser: "On the meaning of names in programming systems."

Replier: G. Goos.

AN OUTLINE OF A COURSE ON OPERATING SYSTEM PRINCIPLES

P. Brinch Hansen

Carnegie-Mellon University,
Pittsburgh, Pennsylvania, U.S.A.

COMPUTER SCIENCE AND OPERATING SYSTEMS

In November 1970 I began writing a textbook on operating system principles at Carnegie-Mellon University. This is a description of its structure and how far it has progressed.

The goal is to give students of computer science and professional programmers a general understanding of operating systems. The only background required is an understanding of the basic structure of computers and programming languages and some practical experience in writing and testing non-trivial programs. In a few cases a knowledge of elementary calculus and probability theory is also needed. The components of the course are well-known to a small group of designers, but most operating systems reveal an inadequate understanding of them.

The first and most obvious problem is to delimit the subject and consider its place in computer science education. I define an *operating system* as a set of manual and automatic procedures which enable a group of users to share a computer system efficiently. The keyword in this definition is *sharing*: it means competition for the use of physical resources but also cooperation among users exchanging programs and data on the same computer system. All shared computer systems must *schedule* user computations in some order, *protect* them against each other, and give them means of *long-term storage* of programs and data. They must also perform *accounting* of the cost of computing and *measure* the actual performance of the system.

In early computer systems, operators carried out most of these functions, but during the last fifteen years the programs that we call operating systems have gradually taken over these aspects of sharing.

Although most components of present computer systems are sequential in nature, they can work simultaneously to some extent. This influences the design of operating systems so much that the subject can best be described as the *management of shared multiprogramming systems*.

Operating systems are large programs developed and used by a changing group of people. They are often modified considerably during their life-time. Operating systems must necessarily impose certain restrictions on all users. But this should not lead us to regard them as being radically different from other programs. They are just examples of large programs based on fundamental principles of computer science. The proper aim of education is to identify these fundamentals.

The student should realize that principles and methods of resource sharing have a general utility that goes beyond operating systems. Any large programming effort

29

will be heavily influenced by the presence of several levels of storage, by the possibility of executing smaller tasks independently, and by the need for sharing a common set of data among such tasks. We find it convenient to distinguish between operating systems and user computations because the former can *enforce* certain rules of behaviour on the latter. It is important, however, to realize that each level of programming solves some aspect of resource allocation.

I argue therefore that the study of operating systems leads to the recognition of general principles which should be taught as part of a core of computer science. Assuming that the student has an elementary background in *programming languages, data structures* and *computer organization*, the course concentrates on the following areas of computer science: *concurrent computations, resource sharing* and *program construction*.

Let us look at the course in some detail. It consists of eight parts which are summarized in the Appendix. The following is a more informal presentation of its basic attitude.

TECHNOLOGICAL BACKGROUND

The necessity of controlling access to shared computer systems automatically is made clear by simple arguments about the poor utilization of equipment in an *open shop* operated by the users themselves, one at a time. As a first step in this direction, I describe the classical *batch processing system* which carries out computations on a main computer while a smaller computer prepares and prints magnetic tapes. The strict sequential nature of the processors and their backing storage in this early scheme made it necessary to prevent human interaction with computations and schedule them in their order of arrival inside a batch.

These restrictions on scheduling disappear to some extent with the introduction of multiprogramming techniques and large backing stores with random access. This is illustrated by two simple operating systems: the first one is a *spooling system* which handles a continuous stream of input, computation and output on a multiprogrammed computer with drum storage; the other is an *interactive system* in which main storage is shared cyclically among several computations requested from remote terminals.

Through a chain of simple arguments the student gradually learns to appreciate the influence of *technological constraints* on the service offered by operating systems.

THE SIMILARITY OF OPERATING SYSTEMS

The main theme of the course is the similarity of problems faced by all operating systems. To mention one example: all shared computer systems must handle concurrent activities at some level. Even if a system only schedules one computation at a time, users can still make their requests simultaneously. This problem can, of course, be solved by the users themselves (forming a waiting line) and by the operators (writing down requests on paper). But the observation is important, since our goal is to handle the problems of sharing automatically.

It is also instructive to compare a batch processing and a spooling system. Both achieve high efficiency by means of concurrent activities: in a batch processing system independent processors work together; in a spooling system a single processor switches among independent programs. Both systems use backing storage (tape and drum) as a buffer to compensate for speed variations between the producers and consumers of data.

As another example, consider real-time systems for process control or conversational interaction. In these systems, concurrent processes must be able to exchange data in order to cooperate on common tasks. But again, this problem exists in all shared computer systems: in a spooling system user computations exchange data with concurrent input/output processes; and in a batch processing system we have another set of concurrent processes which exchange data by means of tapes mounted by operators.

So I find that all operating systems face a common set of problems. To recognize these we must reject the established classification of operating systems into batch processing, time sharing, and real time systems which stresses the dissimilarities of various forms of technology and user service. This does not mean that the problems of adjusting an operating system to the constraints of a certain environment are irrelevant. But the students will solve them much better when they have grasped the underlying common principles.

You will also look in vain for chapters on input/output and filing systems. For a particular operating system considerations about how these problems are handled are highly relevant; but again I have concentrated on the more elementary problems involved in these complicated tasks, namely, process synchronization, storage management and resource protection.

SEQUENTIAL AND CONCURRENT COMPUTATIONS

After this introduction, the nature of computations is described. A *computation* is a set of operations applied to a set of data in order to solve a problem. The operations must be carried out in a certain order to ensure that the results of some of them can be used by others. In a *sequential process* operations are carried out strictly one at a time. But most of our computational problems only require a partial ordering of operations in time: some operations must be carried out before others, but many of them can be carried out concurrently.

The main obstacles to the utilization of concurrency in computer systems are economy and human imagination. Sequential processes can be carried out cheaply by repeated use of simple equipment; concurrent computations require duplicated equipment and time-consuming synchronization of operations. Human beings find it extremely difficult to comprehend the combined effect of a large number of activities which evolve simultaneously with independent rates. In contrast, our understanding of a sequential process is independent of its actual speed of execution. All that matters is that operations are carried out one at a time with finite speed, and that certain relations hold between the data before and after each operation.

So sequential processes closely mirror our thinking habits, but a computer system is utilized better when its various parts operate concurrently. As a compromise, we try to partition our problems into a moderate number of sequential activities which can be programmed separately and then combined for concurrent execution. These processes are *loosely connected* in the sense that they can proceed simultaneously with arbitrary rates except for short intervals when they exchange data.

After a brief review of methods of structuring data and sequential programs, I consider the synchronizing requirements of *concurrent processes.* It is shown that the results of concurrent processes which share data cannot be predicted unless some operations exclude each other in time. Operations which have this property are called *critical regions.* Mutual exclusion can be controlled by a data structure, called a *semaphore,* consisting of a boolean, defining whether any process is inside its critical region, and a queue, containing the set of processes waiting to enter their regions.

A critical region is one example of a timing constraint or *synchronization* imposed on concurrent processes. Synchronization is also needed when some processes produce data which are consumed by other processes. The simplest *input/output relationship* is the exchange of *timing signals* between processes. The constraint here is that signals cannot be received faster than they are sent. This relationship can be represented by an integer semaphore accessed by *signal* and *wait* operations only.

Realistic *communication* between processes requires the exchange of data structures. This problem can be solved by synchronizing primitives operating on semaphores and data structures which are accessible to all the processes involved. It is tempting to conclude that critical regions, common data, and wait and signal operations are the proper concepts to include in a programming language. Experience shows that the slightest mistake in the use of these tools can result in erroneous programs which are practically impossible to correct because their behaviour is influenced by external factors in a time-dependent, irreproducible manner.

A more adequate solution is to include *message buffers* as primitive data structures in the programming language and make them accessible only through well-defined *send* and *receive* operations. The crucial point of this language feature is that storage containing shared data (messages) is accessible to at most one process at a time. It has been proved that when a set of smaller systems with time-independent behaviour are connected by means of messages buffers only, the resulting system can also be made time-independent in behaviour.

The most general form of process interaction is one in which a process must be delayed until another process has ensured that certain relationships hold between the components of a shared data structure. This form of synchronization can be expressed directly by means of *conditional critical regions.*

The conceptual simplicity of simple and conditional critical regions is achieved by ignoring the sequence in which waiting processes enter these regions. This abstraction is unrealistic for heavily used resources. In such cases, the operating system must be able to identify competing processes and control the scheduling of resources among them. This can be done by means of a *monitor* — a set of shared procedures which can delay and activate individual processes and perform operations on shared data.

Finally, I consider the problems of *deadlocks* and their prevention by hierarchical ordering of process interactions.

RESOURCE MANAGEMENT

Most of the previous concepts are now widely used. Far more controversial are the problems of how abstract computations are represented and managed on physical systems with limited resources. At first sight, problems caused by the physical constraints of computers seem to be of secondary importance to the computational problems we are trying to solve. But in practice most programming efforts are dominated by technological problems and will continue to be so. It will always be economically attractive to share resources among competing computations, use several levels of storage, and accept occasional hardware malfunction.

It seems unrealistic to look for a unifying view of how different kinds of technology are used efficiently. The student should realize that these issues can only be understood in economic terms. What we can hope to do is to describe the circumstances under which certain techniques will work well.

The implementation of the process concept is considered in two chapters on *processor multiplexing* and *storage organization*. The first of these describes the representation of processes and scheduling queues at the lowest level of programming and the implementation of synchronizing primitives. Hardware registers, clocks and interrupts are treated as technological tools which in many cases can be replaced by more appropriate concepts at higher levels of programming. The second of these chapters discusses the compromises between associative and location-dependent addressing, and the dynamic allocation of fixed and variable-length data structures in storage with one or more levels.

Following this, I discuss the influence of various *scheduling algorithms*: first-come first-served, shortest job next, highest response ration next, round robin, and so on, on the behaviour of the system in terms of average response times to user requests.

A CASE STUDY

At the end of the course, the conceptual framework is used to describe an existing operating system in depth using a consistent terminology.

I have selected the RC 4000 multiprogramming system [1] as a case study, because it is the only one I know in detail, and is a small, consistent design which illustrates essential ideas of concurrent processes, message communication, scheduling and resource protection.

THE CHOICE OF A DESCRIPTION LANGUAGE

So far nearly all operating systems have been written partly or completely in machine language. This makes them unnecessarily difficult to understand, test and modify. I believe it is desirable and possible to write efficient operating systems almost entirely in a *high-level language*. This language must permit *hierarchal structuring* of data and program, extensive *error checking* at compile time, and production of *efficient machine code*.

To support this belief, I have used the programming language *Pascal* [2] throughout the text to define operating system concepts concisely by algorithms. Pascal combines the clarity needed for teaching with the efficiency required for design. It is easily understood by programmers familiar with Algol 60 or Fortran, but is a far more natural tool than these for the description of operating systems because of the presence of data structures of type record, class and pointer.

At the moment, Pascal is designed for sequential programming only, but I extend it with a suitable notation for multiprogramming and resource sharing. I have illustrated the description of operating systems in Pascal elsewhere [3, 4].

STATUS OF THE COURSE

I conceived the plan for the course in March 1970 and started to work on it in November 1970. Now, in November 1971, drafts have been written of parts 1–4, and 6 (see the Appendix). Most of the work on parts 5, and 7–8 remains to be done. It is unlikely that the structure of the course will change significantly, although the details certainly will.

ACKNOWLEDGEMENTS

Without the encouragement of Alan Perlis this work would not have been undertaken. I am indebted to Nico Habermann, Anita Jones and Bill Wulf who read and criticized all or part of the manuscript. I learned much from discussions with Tony Hoare. It should also be mentioned that without the foundation laid by Edsger Dijkstra [5] we would still be unable to separate principles from their applications in operating systems. The idea of looking upon the management of shared computer systems as a general data processing problem was inspired by a similar attitude of Peter Naur towards program translation [6].

REFERENCES

[1]   Brinch Hansen, P., "The nucleus of a multiprogramming system". *Comm. ACM* **13**, 4 (April 1970), 238–250.
[2]   Wirth, N., "The programming language Pascal". *Acta Informatica* **1**, 1 (1971), 35–63.
[3]   Brinch Hansen, P., "Short-term scheduling in multiprogramming systems". The 3rd ACM Symposium on Operating System Principles, Stanford University, Oct. 1971.
[4]   Brinch Hansen, P., "A comparison of two synchronizing concepts". November 1971. (To appear in *Acta Informatica.*)
[5]   Dijkstra, E. W., "Cooperating sequential processes". Technological University, Eindhoven, 1965.
[6]   Naur, P., "Program translation viewed as a general data processing problem". *Comm. ACM* **9**, 3 (March 1966), 176–179.

APPENDIX: THE CONTENTS OF THE COURSE

1. An overview of operating systems

The purpose of an operating system. Technological background: manual scheduling, non-interactive scheduling with sequential and random access backing storage, interactive scheduling. The similarity of operating systems. Special versus general purpose systems.

2. Sequential processes

Abstraction and structure. Data and operations. Sequential and concurrent computations. Methods of structuring data and sequential programs. Hierarchal program construction. Programming levels viewed as virtual machines. Our understanding and verification of programs.

3. Concurrent processes

Time-dependent programming errors in concurrent computations. Definition of functional behaviour in terms of input/output histories. The construction of functional systems from smaller functional components. Concurrent systems with inherent time-dependent behaviour: priority scheduling and shared processes.

Disjoint and interacting processes. Mutual exclusion of operations on shared data. Simple and conditional critical regions. Process communication by semaphores and message buffers. Explicit control of process scheduling by monitors.

The deadlock problem. Prevention of deadlocks by hierarchal ordering of process interactions.

4. Processor multiplexing

Short-term and medium-term scheduling. A computer system with identical processors connected to a single store. Peripheral versus central processors. Process descriptions, states and queues. Processor execution cycle. Scheduling of critical regions by means of a storage arbiter. Implementation of the scheduling primitives wait, signal, initiate and terminate process. Influence of critical regions on preemption. Processor multiplexing with static and dynamic priorities. Implementation details: hardware registers, clock, interrupts. Timing constraints.

5. Storage organization

Properties of abstract and physical storage. Methods of address mapping: searching, key transformation and base registers.

Single-level storage: fixed partitioning, dynamic allocation of fixed and variable-length data structures. Compacting and fragmentation.

Hierarchal storage: swapping, demand paging and extended storage. Locality principle. Prevention of thrashing. Placement and replacement strategies. Hardware support.

Influence of input/output, process communication, and scheduling on storage allocation.

6. Scheduling algorithms

Objectives of scheduling policies. Queueing models of user requests and computations. Performance measures. A conservation law for a class of priority scheduling algorithms.

Non-preemptive scheduling: fixed priorities, first-come first-served, shortest job next, and highest response ratio next.

Preemptive scheduling: round robin with swapping. Methods of reducing transfers between storage levels. Scheduling with performance feedback.

7. Resource protection

The concept of a process environment of shared objects. Requirements of naming and protection. Existing protection mechanisms: privileged execution state, storage protection, file systems with private and public data, user password identification, protection levels and process hierarchies.

8. A case study

A detailed analysis of the structure, size and performance of the RC 4000 multiprogramming system.

ON THE MEANING OF NAMES IN PROGRAMMING SYSTEMS

A. G. Fraser

Bell Telephone Laboratories, Inc.,
Murray Hill, New Jersey, U.S.A.

INTRODUCTION

At the present time operating system design and language design appear as totally unrelated disciplines. This paper seeks to demonstrate that the distinction is not entirely necessary. In Part 1 we discuss the problems of file identification and programming language design. A single concept, that of *context,* underlies both problem areas.

Part 2 looks at context manipulations in more detail. For this purpose it has been necessary to find a notation in which the subject can be discussed in isolation and with precision.

PART 1: ON THE IDENTIFICATION OF DATA

Review of terminology

Any study that attempts to discuss linguistic concepts must involve the use of a notation in which each concept is separately identified. That notation, a programming language, could be placed alongside the many such languages already in existence. It would be misleading, however, if it were thereby implied that it is suitable as a tool for the preparation of computer programs. In this paper we draw upon the notations of Algol 60 [9] and CPL [6], and introduce new notations to match the linguistic concepts which we seek to expose. In the discussion we shall draw heavily on a terminology that is due to C. Strachey [5, 7].

We use *names* to identify items of data. Each item occupies a storage *location.* The content of this location is known as the item's Right-Hand Value, or *R-value,* whereas the identity of the location is the item's Left-Hand Value, or *L-value.* We assume a one-to-one correspondence between locations and L-values. At any instant every location contains one R-value which may be replaced or updated as time passes. The relationship between names and L-values may also vary and in different contexts the name/L-value associations are not necessarily the same. In one particular context we assume that each name has just one L-value although several names may share one L-value.

The discussion will assume the presence of a store that is subdivided into an indefinite number of distinct locations. No assumption is made about its physical structure. We shall use a function NEW to obtain the L-value of a location which, as far as is detectable by program, is unused and has never been obtained by a previous call on NEW. The single argument of NEW designates the type of R-value which the storage location will be expected to retain. Thus NEW [*integer*] yields the L-value of a cell capable of holding an integer.

In addition to values of type *real* and *integer* we shall find it convenient to store R-values of type *function,* or more accurately *function closure.* We take the view that a function definition, such as

$$let\ f(x) = 2x + p$$

stores a function closure in location f and it is the R-value of f that is used when we evaluate

$$f(z)$$

It is important to note that the R-value of f can be used in contexts where p is not defined; thus the function closure for f contains more than just an occurrence of the name p. (We shall discuss this again on p. 46.)

The *extent* of a location is the continuous period of time over which that location is *known* to exist. We presume that new locations can be *created* and existing ones *destroyed* and that these actions take place some time before and sometime after the period identified by the extent of the location. A location is known to exist only if there is some name which gives access to its L-value.

We shall use the term *Name Substitution* to refer to the act of replacing a name with its L-value. The process will be discussed as if it always took place at run-time although in practice we frequently use an implementation technique that minimizes this run-time activity. A discussion of name substitution at compile time appears on pp. 46 ff. of this paper.

Discussion of name substitution

Name substitution is performed with respect to a particular context and we assume that, in any specific context, there is no ambiguity about the L-value which corresponds to a particular name. In an Algol 60 program we form a separate context for each program block, and the context for an inner block is determined from the context of the immediately containing block together with any declarations appearing at the head of the inner block. Furthermore, the language design is such that a compiler can decide which names appear in the context of any block simply by inspection of the program text. There is no way in which the membership of a context can be computed at run-time. Commands such as

$$if\ \ \ .\ .\ .\ .\ then\ real\ x$$

are not permitted.

For a file system dynamic declarations are normal. We may expect to add new file names and remove others in the course of a computation. We may not, by inspection, relate a particular file to any particular body of program text. An historical file system exists to provide continuity between one task and the next. Two tasks may concurrently share a single file and tasks run at different times may use files as a means of providing continuity.

If an object created by task T_1 is to be used by T_2, then there must be a name, N, that has the same meaning to both T_1 and T_2. In what context does the substitution of the name N take place? The local contexts associated with the program blocks of

T_1 and T_2 cannot be used; we need another context which persists in time longer than both T_1 and T_2. Let this context be C_N.

Within the body of T_1 we can expect to find a declaration such as *real* N but unlike the usual Algol 60 declaration, the name N must be added to the context C_N and not merely to the local context of T_1.

Named contexts

When a new job enters the operating system it will name the context in which it is to run. But that name must itself appear in some context. It therefore seems that for each job there must be a *master context* in which we can expect to find the names of other contexts and from which the job will choose its environment. In some systems it may be convenient to arrange that there is just one master context which applies equally to all jobs, but there is no reason why this must be so. It would be quite practical to select the master context on the basis of the type of channel through which a job is submitted.

It is convenient to fit context names into the regular mechanism for handling named objects. This we can do if we allow a data element of type *context*. The R-value of such an object can be thought of as a list of name/L-value pairs.

There is some similarity between an object of type context and the more conventional file directory; both may be used for name substitution although it is customary to store more than just names and L-values in a file directory. In cases where a name in one context yields the L-value of another context we can find some similarity with the hierarchial structure of some filing systems. But there is no assumption here that the relationship between one context and another should be strictly hierarchial.

The concept of an unnamed *current context* persists in all Algol-like languages. It is this context which is used when performing name substitution. For the purposes of this discussion we shall assume that the name CC identifies the current context. The function of an Algol block heading is to define a new context which applies only to that block. On entry the new context becomes the current context and this is initialized to the value of the current context for the outer block. The Algol *begin* is equivalent to a declaration

$$let\ context\ CC = CC$$

where the CC on the right identifies the current context of the outer block and the CC on the left identifies a fresh copy of that context.

A single declaration of the form *real* x updates the current context

$$CC := CC \parallel (x, NEW[real])$$

the effect of which is to add a new name/L-value pair to the current context; the name being x and the L-value being obtained by the function called NEW [*real*].

The context CC is a list of Name/L-value pairs and the assignment

$$CC := CC \parallel (x, NEW[real])$$

adds one more term to the right-hand end of this list. In order to discover the L-value for x we scan CC from right to left and in so doing we ensure that we refer to the most recent definition of x.

The CPL declaration

$$let \quad x \simeq y$$

specifies that the name x is to refer to the same location as that identified by y. The equivalent form of this is

$$CC : = CC\|(x,y)$$

where the second operand of the pair (x,y) is assumed to be evaluated in L-mode. (Notation which makes this assumption unnecessary will be introduced on p. 46.)

Manipulations upon contexts

The expression

$$CC\|(x, NEW[real])$$

has a value which is of type *context*. The operator $\|$ takes two operands, both of type *context* and produces a result that is a new context. In the case where CC does not already contain the name x it is clear that the result is a context which contains all the name/L-value pairs found in CC together with one further name/L-value pair for x. But what is the value of

$$(x, NEW[integer])\|(x, NEW[real])$$

To disallow an expression of this form would mean that Algol-like context manipulations would be less straightforward to describe.

If expressions of the above form are permitted we will find it convenient to arrange that the resulting context is such that repeated references to the name x all yield the same L-value. For the time being we adopt the convention that the right-most definition takes precedence, and we shall discuss the subject later (p. 44). This being the case, the only way of telling whether the resulting context contains the name x once or twice is to dismantle it or use an operator that breaks it apart.

One command for dismantling a context might be

$$DELETE (C, x)$$

which removes the name x from the context C and we shall assume that it is the current interpretation of the name x that is removed. Now suppose that

$$C = (x,L_1) \| (x,L_2)$$

where L_1 and L_2 are distinct L-values. There are two possible results of applying DELETE:

(*a*) The resulting value of C has no x in it, or
(*b*) The result value of C contains (x,L_1) only.

Notice that, if we choose (*a*), we can release space taken by L_1 when we evaluate

$$C : = (x,L_1) \| (x,L_2)$$

The two possible interpretations correspond closely to the DELETE and RECOVER commands of the Cambridge University file system [1]. DELETE removes all trace of a file whereas RECOVER backs up to an old version of a recently updated file.

Space acquisition

The CPL declaration

$$let \quad x = 0$$

has three distinct effects:

(*a*) To request a new and hitherto unused storage location;
(*b*) To associate the name x with this new location, and
(*c*) To initialize the location to the value zero.

The effect described in (*a*) has been referred to already in this paper by calling on the function NEW. The value of

$$NEW \ [real]$$

is the L-value of a new and previously unused location that is capable of holding a real number.

Another function that will be found useful is

$$COPY \ [type, exp]$$

which obtains a new location capable of holding values of the specified type. The location is initialized to the value of exp. Thus, the declaration

$$let \ real \ x = 3$$

can be written as

$$CC : = CC\|(x, COPY \ [real,3])$$

We have included the type specification in the argument for NEW because it seems that it is more correctly associated with the storage location than its name. By specifying type *real* we impose a restriction upon the set of values and representations that a location might legitimately contain.

When a file is created we may expect to set some privacy restrictions that determine who can use it and in what way it can be used. We may limit general use of a file to reading only and yet allow the "owner" to delete it. It seems that there might be some similarity between the imposition of these controls and the restraints defined when we specify data type. On the assumption that it is more appropriate to protect the information than to protect its name we suggest that privacy control data should appear with type specification in the argument list for the function NEW.

Garbage collection

Both NEW and COPY assume an inexhaustible supply of unused storage locations; an assumption that is not always realistic. We need to find some way of re-using storage space when its useful life has expired.

The command

$$DELETE \ (C,x)$$

removes the name x from the context C; it does not necessarily release the location identified by the L-value of x. If we allow data sharing we cannot assume that the removal of one name implies that the location itself is no longer needed.

Perhaps the most satisfactory system is one which never allows a user to reach a situation in which he has a name/L-value pair in some potentially available context when the location to which it refers has been removed as garbage.

A direct and expensive way of implementing this principle is to use a LISP-type garbage collector [8]. If we are to be more economical than this then we must know something about the way in which the system is to be used and the restrictions which the language imposes upon the user. Indeed the need to reuse space and the need to be able to restart a system safely after an error are two of the most forceful reasons for restricting user behaviour.

In the Cambridge University system, for example, a user can copy the L-value of a file by writing a command that is equivalent to the declaration

$$let\ S \simeq FILE\text{-}NAME\ in\ CONTEXT$$

but ther is no way of making a copy of the copy; he cannot write the equivalent of

$$let\ T \simeq S$$

A consequence of this is that the system can keep a record of the number of copies that are made of each file L-value. File deletion only takes place when the original and only copy of an L-value is removed from a file directory; an attempt to remove an original while copies still exist is treated as an error.

One of the actions that must take place after a system failure is garbage collection. One cannot be sure that the free store list is correctly formed after a system crash. In order to be able to perform the restart process with maximum speed the Cambridge University system is designed so that new file directories can only be created by certain members of the administration; the normal system user cannot create additional directories. By this means the number of file directories is kept to a minimum and so too are the lengths of the chains that must be followed by the Lisp-type garbage collector.

Economic space management strategies are made possible in many programming languages by restricting user behaviour. For example, Algol 60 provides no direct way of creating or copying a context other than that provided by the block structure. Contexts are derived one from another in a strictly hierarchial fashion that is evident at compile time. Furthermore we know that contexts can be abandoned in the reverse order to that in which they are initialized. Stack-type garbage collection is based upon just this fact.

PART 2: ON THE MANIPULATION OF CONTEXTS

The absence of a rigorously defined notation in which distinct concepts are distinguished separately is one major obstacle to any discussion of system design. A notation in which contexts appear explicitly would be helpful when discussing the design of file systems and other name handling mechanisms. The object of the remaining part of this paper is to present such a notation and its associated algebra. Most of the examples will be drawn from issues of language design, not because the approach is unsuited to file system design but because the former discipline is more generally understood.

Contextual abstraction

The context manipulations already described are a special case of a form of abstraction that has general relevance to programming theory. To discuss this we introduce the operator, μ, as follows.

The expression

$$\mu[A_1, A_2, \ldots, A_n][V_1, V_2, \ldots, V_n](E)$$

can be evaluated by substituting the value V_i for the name A_i wherever the latter occurs in the expression E. Thus

$$\mu[x,y][g,h](2x + 4y) = 2g + 4h$$

The μ operator is closely related to Church's λ operator [2, 3] since the expression

$$\mu[A_1, A_2, \ldots, A_n][V_1, V_2, \ldots, V_n](E)$$

has the same value as

$$\lambda[A_1, A_2, \ldots, A_n](E)[V_1, V_2, \ldots, V_n]$$

The sole purpose of introducing μ is to allow a new form of abstraction.

We are accustomed to making certain abstractions on the basis of λ-expressions and we call these *functions*. If the function is defined as

$$let \quad f = \lambda[x,y](2x+4y)$$

Then the value of

$$f[g,h]$$

is obtained by substituting the R-value of f to give

$$\lambda[x,y](2x+4y)[g,h]$$

which can then be simplified to

$$(2g+4h)$$

Now consider the expression

$$\mu[x,y][g,h]$$

and the declaration

$$let \quad C = \mu[x,y][g,h]$$

I shall call this μ-expression a *context*. To make use of the context C we must supply the remaining operand, an expression. The *context call*

$$C(2x+4y)$$

is evaluated by substituting the R-value of C to give

$$\mu[x,y][g,h](2x+4y)$$

which can then be simplified to

$$(2g+4h)$$

A context specifies the values which are to be substituted for some of the names that appear in the operand of a context call. Indeed, if the values are L-values reference, we find that the contexts described by μ-expressions correspond to the idea of a context as proposed earlier in this paper.

It is convenient for our present purposes to adopt the convention that all values listed in the second operand of a μ-expression are L-values. For example

$$let \quad g = 0; \quad let \, h = 0; \quad let \, k = 0$$

$$let \, C_1 = \mu[x,y] \, [g,h]$$

$$let \, C_2 = \mu[x,z] \, [h,k]$$

The data item which is named h in the current context can be referred to as $C_1(y)$ and $C_2(x)$; all three share the same location.

Context valued expressions

Consider the context valued expression

$$\mu[x,y] \, [g,h] \, \| \mu[u,v] \, [j,k]$$

This can be simplified to yield a single μ-expression by concatenating the name-lists and value-lists separately. If

$$C_1 = \mu[x,y] \, [g,h]$$

$$C_2 = \mu[u,v] \, [j,k]$$

then $C_1 \| C_2$ simplifies to

$$\mu[x,y,u,v] \, [g,h,j,k]$$

Note that the names in the value-lists [g,h] and [j,k] will have been substituted from the current context at the time that C_1 and C_2 were defined; there is no question of a name-clash between the value-list of C_2 and the name-list of C_1. In the case of the expression

$$\mu[\text{Namelist}_1] \, [\text{Valuelist}_1] \, \| \mu[\text{Namelist}_2] \, [\text{Valuelist}_2]$$

names in both value-lists are substituted from the current context before the $\|$ operator is applied.

There are three possible equivalent forms for

$$\mu[x] \, [y] \, \| \mu[x] \, [z]$$

one is $\mu[x,x] \, [y,z]$ and the others are $\mu[x] \, [z]$ and $\mu[x] \, [y]$. If the first of these is accepted as a possible interpretation then the rule for evaluating

$$\mu[x,x] \, [y,z] \, (x)$$

must be chosen. By definition, this expression is equivalent to

$$\lambda[x,x] \, (x) \, [y,z]$$

which is an abbreviation for

$$\lambda x(\lambda x(x)z)y$$

and reduces to z. Therefore, for consistency we shall require that the name list is scanned from the right; the value of $\mu[x,x]\,[y,z](x)$ is z. On this basis $\mu[x]\,[z]$ is the alternative interpretation.

Now consider the expression

$$C_1(C_2(x))$$

where C_1 and C_2 are context valued expressions. This can be reduced to an expression of the form

$$C(x)$$

Although we may concatenate the name lists of C_1 and C_2 to form the name list of C, we must recognize that the value list of C_2 is to be computed within the context C_1.

Thus, if C_1 is $\mu[\text{Namelist}_1]\,[\text{Valuelist}_1]$
and if C_2 is $\mu[\text{Namelist}_2]\,[\text{Valuelist}_2]$

then

$$C = \mu[\text{Namelist}_1, \text{Namelist}_2]\,[\text{Valuelist}_1, C_1(\text{Valuelist}_2)]$$

For example:

$$\mu[x,y]\,[p,q]\,(\mu[z]\,[y]\,(x := y+z))$$

simplifies to

$$\mu[x,y,z]\,[p,q,\mu[x,y]\,[p,q]\,(y)]\,(x := y+z)$$

which reduces to

$$\mu[x,y,z]\,[p,q,q]\,(x := y+z)$$

and then to

$$p := q+q$$

Formal evaluation rules

In order to introduce the concept of contextual abstraction into a programming language we must develop a calculus in which combinations of context and function do not lead to ambiguous results. That ambiguity is a possibility can be seen from the following example.

$$\lambda[C](\lambda[x](Cx)[t])[\mu[x]\,[s]]$$

The ambiguity arises when a context, $\mu[x]\,[s]$, has the potential to interfere with a bound variable, x, of a function, $\lambda[x](Cx)$. In this case the expression would appear to reduce either to

$$\lambda[C](Ct)[\mu[x]\,[s]]$$

which reduces to t, or to

$$\lambda[x](\mu[x]\,[s]\,(x))[t]$$

which reduces to s.

By distinguishing between the bound and free variables of an expression, Church was able to devise a calculus in which conflicting results could not be obtained by permuting the sequence in which simplification rules are applied to an expression. The theorems of Church and Rosser [3] prove this point. When attempting to define a calculus with similar properties but including both functional and contextual abstraction we find it necessary to introduce a new notion, that of *binding power*. In the context application CE, where both C and E may denote elaborate expressions it may be that a free occurrence of some variable x in E is bound in CE. If that is the case we say that C has *binding power* for x.

In order to avoid ambiguity, we could legislate against any substitution of C in place of k in kE when C has binding power for a name x that is free in E and is bound in some expression containing kE. Alternatively we could rule that an occurrence of x in E is bound in kE if k can be replaced by an expression C which has binding power for x. This second alternative is more difficult to implement than the first but corresponds more closely to practice. In order to facilitate implementation we can use a distinctive syntax for expressions such as kE and rule that such expressions contain no free variables. File references are usually syntactically distinctive for this reason.

Evaluation of context-bound expressions

The context value

$$\mu[A_1, \ldots, A_n] [V_1, \ldots, V_n]$$

specifies that the values V_i are to be substituted in place of the names A_i. Hitherto (p. 43) it has been convenient to assume that V_i were always L-values but this assumption was not strictly necessary.

Given the expression

$$\mu[A_1, \ldots, A_n] [E_1, \ldots, E_n]$$

in which E_i are expressions, we may specify the mode of evaluation by which E_i gives us a value V_i. One way of doing this would be to prefix each E_i as follows.

ref E_i specifies that V_i is the L-value of E_i

val E_i specifies that V_i is the R-value of E_i

lit E_i specifies that V_i is literally the expression E_i

For example, if t = 6, A(0) = 10 and A(6) = 16 then

$\mu[x,y] [ref\, t, val\, t](x := 0; x := 2*y)$ sets t = 12

$\mu[x,y] [ref\, t, ref\, t](x := 0; x := 2*y)$ sets t = 0

$\mu[x,y] [ref\, t, lit\, A(t)](x := 0; x := 2*)$ sets t = 20

Note that we are concerned here with the mode of parameter evaluation and not the context from which the names appearing in a parameter value are substituted. Thus the effect of

$$\mu[t,y] [ref\, x, lit\, A(t)](t := 0; t := 2*y)$$

is to set 32 in x.

The mode of parameter evaluation directly affects program compilation strategy. For example, consider the context bound expression

$$\mu[x] \, [val \, E] \, (y : = x; z : = x)$$

If the value of E is known at compile time to be 8, say, then we can simplify this to

$$\mu[x] \, [lit \, 8] \, (y : = x; z : = x)$$

which we can safely reduce to

$$y : = 8; z : = 8$$

However, if E is more complex we might rewrite the program in the following way

$$p : = E; \mu[x] \, [lit \, p] \, (y : = x; z : = x)$$

where p is some working space location not otherwise involved in the calculation. With the context expressed in this way we can simplify at compile time to yield

$$p : = E; y : = p; z : = p$$

The same technique can be used to deal with parameters called by reference. For example,

$$\mu[x] \, [ref \, E] \, (y : = x; z : = x)$$

can be reduced at compile time if the L-value of E is known then. If this L-value is $\mathcal{L}$ then the program can be rewritten as

$$\mu[x] \, [lit \, \mathcal{L}] \, (y : = x; z : = x)$$

and thence as

$$y : = \mathcal{L}; z : = \mathcal{L}$$

More commonly the evaluation of E will have a side-effect as in

$$\mu[x] \, [ref \, NEW[real]] \, (x : = y; z : = x)$$

(The function NEW changes the state of the free store.) In this case we can rewrite the program but to do so we need the two operators rv and lv which appear in the language BCPL [4]. The L-value of rv x is the R-value held in x, and the R-value of lv x is the L-value of x. The rewritten program is

$$p : = lv \, NEW[real]; \mu[x] \, [lit \, rv \, p] \, (x : = y; z : = x)$$

which reduces to

$$p : = lv \, NEW[real]; rv \, p : = y; z : = lv \, p$$

Compilation strategy can profitably be discussed in this way. If we describe a source program in terms of λ and μ-expressions we may seek to rewrite it so that the text can be simplified by use of the evaluation rules referred to previously. In particular, if we can arrange that a context parameter is evaluated as a literal then we can perform the substitution completely at compile time.

We can use a context bound expression to represent the body of a function or procedure closure. Consider the function definition

$$let\ f = \lambda[x](x+p)$$

When this definition is made we make a name/L-value association that can be described by

$$\mu[f]\ [NEW[\textit{function}]]$$

and the location obtained by NEW[*function*] is initialized as a function closure.

Suppose that the free variable, p, is to be called by value. The function closure must contain an expression in which the name p is tied to its R-value at the time of function definition. This situation can be described by writing the function definition in the following form

$$let\ f = \mu[p]\ [\textit{val}\ p](\lambda[x](x+p))$$

If the context in which this declaration is made is C, the closure for f becomes

$$C(\mu[p]\ [\textit{val}\ p](\lambda[x](x+p)))$$

and, if the R-value of p in C is R_p, then the function closure is

$$\mu[p]\ [R_p](\lambda[x](x+p))$$

The function f is called by writing

$$f[\textit{val}\ z]$$

which expands by substituting for f, to become

$$\mu[p]\ [R_p](\lambda[x](x+p))[\textit{val}\ z]$$

and then reduces to

$$\lambda[x](x+R_p)[\textit{val}\ z]$$

thence to

$$\textit{val}\ z + R_p$$

Execution of complete programs

We define a *completely specified* program to be one that has no free variable name. Such a program might be *evaluated* using any of the rules referred to in previous sections of this paper, but even programs that are incomplete can often be partially evaluated. The extent to which evaluation is possible will follow from the role played by the free variables within a program; by imposing certain restraints on the use of free variables we are frequently able to perform much useful evaluation. For example, it is quite practical to compile just part of a program and later bring the various parts together in a loader. Even at load time file names and peripheral names may remain free so they can be bound in the course of program execution. Evaluation therefore proceeds in several stages, starting with compilation and ending with execution. Note that the boundaries between the successive stages of evaluation are not clearly defined but are partially determined by the extent to which program specification is complete at each stage.

The timing of certain binding operations, particularly the time of evaluating context bounds expressions, can determine the successful outcome of program execution. Within the confines of one program the evaluation sequence might be determined by rules such as those discussed previously (pages 43, 44 and 45) but when several programs employ a shared context additional rules are required. Before permitting any execution that involves reference to, or update of, a storage location we must consider whether other programs also refer to that location and, if so, what the proper sequence of updates and references should be.

The allowed sequence of updates and references is often determined by means of an *interlock* mechanism. For example, the Cambridge University file system prevents one program from updating a file while another is referencing it. The interlock mechanism consists of two parts. First a status value is associated with each file and, second, an algorithm is provided by which file accesses are authorized and file status values changed. Commonly, all file accesses are governed by a single algorithm but economy would seem to be the main justification for this. In principle the algorithm used to govern access to a particular file could be a property of that file; the algorithm should probably appear as an argument of the function NEW.

In the first section we introduced the function NEW to represent the mechanism for storage allocation and we suggested that data type be an argument of that function. Later on in this paper (p. 41) we suggested that privacy controls also appear in the argument of NEW and now we have added the lockout algorithm to the list. By implication we have embroidered the notion of a storage location and hence have suggested that the acts of reference and update become more complex. Unfortunately we have as yet no unifying concept of storage and assignment that can satisfactorily handle privacy, lockout, type and the update operation.

In the definition of NEW we avoided the possibility that storage space could be in limited supply. Where that is the case execution of a program may have to be suspended when it calls upon NEW. Once a storage location has been acquired by means of NEW that location can be considered as *allocated* to the program that called for it and the allocation persists for as long as the program has access to the location's L-value.

Storage is only one of the resources that an operating system may need to allocate. In fact, anything that is in limited supply may require to be supervised by the operating system. Our notion of a *resource* then is defined in terms of the supervisory function and is not particularly associated with a type of object. Storage space, peripherals and files might each be regarded by the operating system as having limited availability and may therefore justify supervision by the operating system. With a resource comes the notion of allocating it to a particular program (or perhaps to be shared by a particular set of programs). Conveniently we can arrange to correlate allocation with the act of binding the identity of the resource into some context of the program to which it is allocated. Indeed we might more accurately think of allocation in terms of the bindings made in certain contexts, even when those contexts are files rather than parts of executable programs. Appropriately we should recognize that each resource has a unique identity and we should introduce functions, such as NEW, that yield the identity of an allocated resource. For as long as that identity is accessible from a particular context the associated resource should be considered allocated to that context. Only when there is no means by which a context can be employed by executable program can that context be collected as garbage, and only when there is no context bearing the identity of a resource can that resource be considered unallocated.

For the purposes of the present discussion we can represent the symmetry between resources by allowing each to have a unique L-value and denoting each type of resource by a unique symbol. We then extend the definition of NEW so that the function call

$$NEW[t]$$

yields the L-value of a resource of type t.

In any practical operating system we must make provision for programs that have extravagant behaviour. For example, we must deal reasonably with a program whose execution would appear to have no natural termination. If, for any reason, we chose to abandon execution of a program then we may wish to recover certain, or all, of the resources allocated to it. For this reason at least, we may place certain restrictions upon the way in which the L-values of a certain type can be used. The problem is essentially the garbage collection problem whose solution (as noted on p. 41) can be influenced by imposing suitable linguistic constraints upon the user.

One technique for handling resource allocation and subsequent deallocation is to embed each executable program, P_i, in a special context, C_i, that is initially empty. The identity of C_i is unknown to P_i (and to any other user program). A request for a resource of type T to be identified as N within P_i is interpreted by the operating system as

$$C_i : = C_i \| \mu[N] [NEW[T]]$$

and a command to relinquish N would be interpreted as

$$Delete (C_i, N)$$

Since P_i cannot operate directly upon C_i, the operating system can assume that all resources of type T allocated to P_i are to be found in C_i. Thus, to abandon execution of P_i and recover resources of type T the operating system can confine itself to C_i.

The above example illustrates two styles of control. On the one hand the mere absence of any reference to the identity of C_i from a context within P_i makes it impossible for P_i to interfere with C_i. The use of NEW invokes a second, more elaborate, control mechanism whereby the operating system determines which, if any, resource of type T to allocate to P_i.

Our definition of resource is entirely in terms of the level of control which an operating system wishes to employ. That control can be split into two distinct parts.

(a) Allocation
NEW[T] chooses from one of a set of objects of type T to yield the identity of one that is unallocated. This function implies bookkeeping by which allocated and unallocated objects are distinguishable.

(b) Authorization
NEW[T] determines for the set of objects identified by T, whether the program has adequate authority to make a requisition, and whether such a requisition is timely.

REFERENCES

[1] Barron, D. W. *et al.,* "File handling at Cambridge University". *AFIPS Conf. Proc.* **30** (SJCC 1967) 163.

[2] Curry, H. B. and Feys, R., *Combinatory Logic,* Vol. 1. North Holland Publishing Co. (1958).

[3] Church, A., "The calculi of lambda-conversion", *Annals of Mathematical Studies,* **6**. Princeton University Press (1941).

[4] Richards, M., *The BCPL Reference Manual.* M.I.T. Project MAC Memorandum M-352 (1967).

[5] Strachey, C., "Fundamental concepts in programming languages". NATO Summer School, Copenhagen 1967. Proceedings to be published.

[6] Barron, D. W. *et al.,* "The main features of CPL". *Comput. J.* **6**, 2 (July 1963), 134–143.

[7] Strachey, C., "Towards a formal semantics", in *Formal Language Description Languages for Computer Programming.* Ed. T. B. Steel (1966).

[8] McCarthy, J., LISP 1.5 *Programmers Manual.* M.I.T. Press (1962).

[9] Backus, J. W. *et al.,* Revised report on the algorithmic language Algol 60. *Comput. J.* **5**, 4 (January 1963), 349–368.

DISCUSSION

BRINCH HANSEN: If you examine operating systems you find that they are large programs, in the sense defined by Peter Naur [6]; they are developed and used by a changing group of people, and are often modified considerably during their life-time. This is what causes the complexity of their design. In contrast to most other large programs such as compilers, operating systems by necessity impose a set of absolute restrictions on all users in order to make sharing tolerable. Programmers who have a choice between compilers will soon discover which one is most efficient and reliable. They are not forced to use a piece of software if they find it inefficient and unreliable. The enforced use of operating systems has led us to consider them uncorrectly as being radically different from other programs.

In a course on operating systems the student should realise that principles and methods of resource sharing have a general usefulness which goes beyond operating systems, indeed beyond computers themselves. The mathematical techniques of resource sharing, the techniques of structure and design, for any utility system. We need to distinguish between operating systems and user computations, because operating systems enforce certain rules of behaviour on user programs; but each level of programming, be it at the system or user level, will solve some aspect of resource allocation. For example, if in the design of a compiler you partition it into several passes which are carried out strictly sequentially, this is an attempt to schedule the use of a semi-sequential backing store in a reasonable manner. You may also consider a large data processing program for a factory, where daily loops of processing keep track of production; weekly loops perform pay-roll computations; monthly loops, and yearly fiscal loops perform other duties. The scheduling and protection considerations which go into the design of such a system are far more complicated than the short-term scheduling decisions that are made by operating systems.

So one can claim that not only are the principles of computer science found in the operating systems of a general utility, but very often they occur on a much more complicated scale in user applications. Taking that view, the study of operating systems leads to the recognition of general principles which should be taught as part of a computer science course. The Appendix of my paper gives a rough idea of the kind of course this would lead to. It is slightly different from the course you would give if you took an engineering approach to operating systems. For example, you will not find the topic of filing systems mentioned, except very briefly. From an educational point of view I think a filing system is a commercial data processing problem of fairly large magnitude, involving principles of storage allocation, synchronization and protection. My attitude is to start with these simpler topics and then, at a later stage in the education of the student, hope that he will be able to combine them by sound methods of program construction.

GOOS: It is my experience in teaching that the definition of what an operating system is requires that the student already has a working knowledge of a particular operating system. Also it is better to start with the concept of a virtual machine, and to point out that an operating system is a set of programs which implements a certain virtual machine, just as every high level language is designed with a certain machine in mind.

In practice, when designing operating systems, we consider the objectives and properties of the virtual machine and what hardware properties it should have. First we consider the ideal hardware and then design our operating system as reliably and efficiently as possible bearing in mind that it is impossible to satisfy every users' requirements.

What I miss in your course is a discussion of a set of particular algorithms which seem to be unique for operating systems, especially basic I/O handling; there is nothing mentioned about optimizing that part of the system or about the hardware required. The student should learn from this course what good hardware should do. This also applies to error correction; he should learn how to protect himself against malfunctions of the hardware and his own programs.

Lastly, considering the interface with the outside world and how the operating system should handle it, it is not sufficient just to enumerate a set of basic instructions, which should be executed by the virtual machine as a command language It is no use having desirable properties in your virtual machine if you are unable to express them in a consistent and concise way in a command language.

It is a good idea to base a course on operating systems on the assumption that the structural aspects of operating systems are the same as for most other programs, but the interface with the outside world, hardware and user, should be more clearly defined, and it should be pointed out that there are topics in operating systems which are unique.

BRINCH HANSEN: I do not think it is very fruitful to replace the stress on sharing with the stress on the design of a virtual machine. Any program that I can think of implements a virtual machine, e.g. an Algol compiler implements a virtual machine capable of executing instructions in the Algol language.

If you want to single out anything which characterizes the subject of operating systems you must examine them at the application level. The keyword "sharing" is the best one I can find. If I want to appeal to the student's intuitive understanding, when he has no background, I can point out that it is a management problem of running the system. For example, if a restaurant has more customers than chairs, and some of the customers are more prominent than others (they pay best!) then your problem is to manage this restaurant in such a way that you use the limited resources the best you can.

About the existence of algorithms which are unique to operating systems; I take your point that operating systems are so close to hardware that the properties of good hardware and the handling of things like I/O cannot entirely be ignored. It is my intention to tell the student that I/O handling is to be considered as a problem which involves synchronization by interrupts, semaphores or the like. It involves the use of a good scheduling policy, if you are thinking of a drum, for example. It also involves principles of store allocation; you must give your programs the ability to address data after it has been input, but I admit this might be at too abstract a level for the student.

I feel that everything in Randell's recent paper[1] about reliability of operating systems is equally applicable to the reliability of almost any program. I would not like to identify a set of techniques for systematic debugging, proof techniques, protection, etc., and say these are peculiar to operating systems. Although they have been discovered in connection with operating systems, I hope they are equally applicable at the user level. A user should also be able to partition his problem into a set of independent tasks which he can protect against each other.

The problem of the interface with the outside world is very important. I would present it at a later stage, after teaching the design of large programs and analyzing the requirements of particular operating systems. Again I refuse to believe that interface problems are peculiar to operating systems. I do not really see operating systems as being anything else but a very troublesome application. Hopefully, in the long run we will not hold conferences on operating systems any more than we now hold conferences on pay-roll systems.

GOOS: If you consider the problem of program construction you have the interface problem with the outside world, and for that reason I would consider it an integral part of the course.

I have chosen the term "virtual machine" rather than "sharing" as a keynote because one can easily explain what its possible properties may be. But if you start by saying I would like to share something, then I ask you "sharing what, and where is the borderline?"

BRINCH HANSEN: What one should share, I really do not know, nor do I care, because most of the problem in sharing does not really seem to be caused by what you share but by the fact that you have competition. You must somehow solve logical problems of synchronization, mutual exclusion and protection, and you must choose a certain policy of sharing which seems to be much more of a political rather than a logical decision.

HOARE: There are two questions concerning the merits of the course that arise in my mind. Firstly, is it right to teach a course on operating systems when you are not really interested in operating systems at all, and are therefore trying to use this as an excuse for teaching good programming methods? I feel that in a University

[1] Randell, B., "Operating Systems: The Problems of Performance and Reliability". IFIP Congress, Ljubljana, Yugoslavia 1971; pp. I-100–I-109.

education the illusion of studying a subject for its own sake is one that should be preserved. I feel that students will respond better if they are told that they are going to become experts in operating systems, and any general knowledge that happens to rub off on them about programming principles, techniques and strategies is, of course, an excellent thing.

Secondly, is the criterion of sharing a reasonable way to approach the subject; or is the rather more fashionable virtual machine approach the right method?

NEEDHAM: On the second point, I am sure that sharing is the right way to approach the subject. If you start with the virtual machine concept you are liable to generate confusion. You are talking about something with so much abstraction, whereas operating systems are very concrete and practical things.

With operating systems there are two aspects; what the system ought to do and how it ought to do it. My experience has been that a course on operating systems goes down better if one puts emphasis on what the thing ought to do; then you can see why complicated methods of synchronization and communication are actually necessary. If you emphasize the sordid practical things, then the student is likely to think you are proposing a lot of mechanisms for doing something which can be done in a much more simple way.

FENTON: An operating system designer has some target which he has agreed with the user. One is aiming to produce some kind of virtual machine, so if you regard your system structure as a nested series of virtual machines, sharing is something you have got to do as a technique at each level to interface the given machine with the one you have actually got to produce. So I think that both definitions are valid from a practical point of view.

SUTCLIFFE: With an unshared machine the virtual machine approach is valid. If you have a uniprogramming machine there is no sharing in multiprogramming sense, so that the sharing approach is not so appropriate. The point about any program, even a pay-roll program, is that the virtual machine approach is not adequate because there is a very real difference between the sort of virtual machine produced by an operating system and a user program.

BRINCH HANSEN: I feel that a uniprogramming batch processing machine is very much a shared machine. It is the one which is shared in the most intolerable fashion, namely one at a time; sharing is not necessarily simultaneous, it can be sequential.

VINCE: The principles of sharing and virtual machines are equally valid, and there is no difference between the operating system's virtual machine and the user's. One could take the approach that the operating system is just a part of everybody's application and that for each user there is only one virtual machine. Operating systems form a composite application, and all that one requires to do this is to have a segmented virtual store within the virtual machine giving levels of protection. The sharing can then be implemented at various levels of abstraction according to the degree of authority which the virtual processor of this machine has got at that particular time. My main objection is that differentiation is being made between virtual machines in user application and operating system software.

GOOS: I do not think this objection is correct. We all have different forms of virtual machine in mind, and it may take more than one virtual machine to describe one operating system. If you start to design a system you have got to state objectives and to define a virtual machine, or more than one, by a program. Sharing is the tool by which we realize and implement this.

FRASER: The paper is concerned with a crucial area in operating systems, though not specifically restricted to operating systems, and that is the manipulation of names. We use names in programming languages and in operating systems to refer to certain files and jobs. You can't have a language or talk about any piece of a computing system without using these names. There are a variety of methods for handling names. I do not mean decoding and discerning them, or recognizing their syntactic structure; I mean managing their scopes and the extents and values with which they are associated. What I have tried to do is bring these management techniques together, and study them separately from the function for which they are being managed. In an operating system the management technique and the syntax for job names, file names, document names, and names of variables in programming languages are different. Is this great diversity justified?

In Algol we have techniques for talking about the scope of a name. You can have an Algol block with a *begin* and a declaration *real* x, say (ignoring other complicated functions for the moment). The declarations are not statements of the language, when the block is invoked the declarations are brought into force. It is not possible, for example, to have a statement which reads: — *if* I = 0 *then real* x. It is not necessary that this construction be included in Algol; it requires that when you arrived at a specific x you must determine (at run time) which x you really are referring to. This is a dynamic change of context for x and would require a much more complicated run time administration than does an Algol program. However, this happens with files. I consider that the function "*real* x" is very close to the function of creating a file.

The name is a mechanism which allows you to refer to a value, and in the case of a file the value may be a large structure, and you may have to form it incrementally. If you want to construct a system such that the same management technique is used for file names as for names in the program, you have to solve another problem which occurs when you have two programs. Suppose the first program produces an object called y, and the other wants to refer to that same object by the name y. If both are used within one common block body, then you arrange that y has a scope associated with a block which surrounds both. With operating systems they may be separated, not just graphically, but also in time. So there must be some way the two names can be connected. What we do is invent a user directory, or master file directory, which is really just a context, a list of names created some time in the past. It is like a record of declarations which are still extant, and when you come to obey a program you specify either at the start, or in some other way, which context the name is to be evaluated in.

So now I am requiring that we specify the context of a name by giving another specification, which must be a name itself. Hence we have the same problem applied recursively. This leads to the conclusion that there must be at least one unnamed object, which I call the master file directory, which is a context that you refer to by implication.

In Algol you may have a nested block structure with references to z, in two distinct blocks. What it really means is that one particular z is to be evaluated in a slightly different context to the other. The Algol program does not have to give a name to the context, it is an unnamed quantity, the "current" context. This is like the logic in some time sharing systems in which your personal name will be used as the name of a contect. That context is then looked up in the master context, and you are, in fact, operating in the context specified by your own name. In the case of Algol there is an unnamed context for each block, and is constant throughout the block (excluding inner blocks). There is also a context which applies to the outer block.

In a file system for a time sharing system you have to allow for the possibility of two people creating files with the same name at the same time. This is allowed for by having named contexts, and allowing different people to work under different named contexts, known as user file directories. What is shared in the context is a set of pairs, consisting of a name plus a value. So when you consider building a file system, or perhaps a translator for Algol 60, it's advisable to consider objects of type *context,* and how they are going to be stored at run time or filing time.

In an operating system, because you have conditional commands, and you have commands which create or delete files, the operations have to be done at run time. Therefore it is necessary to have the object of type context available at run time, which is somewhat different from earlier programming languages. Most programming languages do not require you to have the context available at run time, whereas an operating system certainly does.

If you are going to study the consequences of having an object type *context* in a programming system then you had better try and find some way of making it consistent with all the objects which you have already got in the programming system. We do not really have very many concepts yet which are well organized in programming systems; but one which we have taken over from mathematics is functional abstraction. I use Church's λ-calculus, since it provides a fairly precise means of talking about functions. I consider a notation for describing context, and then try to find axioms that are necessary in order to provide an unambiguous system, so that the equivalent of the Church–Rosser theorem would be true, i.e. any given program has one unique answer. I soon discovered the following; basically a λ-expression consists of a λ followed by a name-list, an expression and a value-list. The axioms which Church describes associate a value with each name, and using these the expression can be simplified.

Consider another expression which has the same terms and has exactly the same value. The name-list appears first, followed by the value-list, then the expression; I have changed only the order of the terms. I investigate the way in which Church's axioms will handle this. But I have not been able to find a set of axioms such that context handling can co-exist with λ-calculus: such that any one program has only one answer, and satisfies the following objectives. (1) You can apply the reduction rules in any order and get the equivalent answer; (2) You can implement all the different roles that we normally associate with context in operating systems and programming systems, i.e. it allows you to have functions which compute context; (3) It allows you to have references appearing in programs, and in programs transferred and operated under a context which they weren't originally written under which is what we do in operating systems.

My conclusion is that I started off with the thesis that you could perhaps find one management technique to handle all names in a programming system, and found that this is very difficult because there is no simple set of rules which allows you to do so. It may be that for practical reasons we had better have different management systems for different sorts of names.

GOOS: We have for a long time been describing algorithms simply by programs. Only for the last few years have we realized that it is not the programs but the activities which result from a program being executed that we are interested in. It is very difficult to explain to a beginner what a procedure does. The dynamic basis of computing has been studied for only a few years. Fraser's paper explains the question of data structures, which is a dynamic problem and should not be considered statically only, as is usual in programming languages.

It seems to be a mistake in Algol 60 that the word scope is used for two different things; one the lifetime of an object and the other the identification of it.

This paper should contain the definition of a name. There are two different possibilities; firstly, a name is an internal object, a pointer to something which may or may not be identified externally; and secondly, a name is an identifier which we can associate with some internal object pointer.

FRASER: A name is something which has no structure or no significance except that you can decide whether two of them are the same.

GOOS: Yes, but this applies to both pointers and identifiers.

OPERATING SYSTEM STRUCTURE

Speakers: C. A. R. Hoare: "Towards a theory of parallel programming."

G. Goos: "Some basic principles in structuring operating systems."

Repliers: A. G. Fraser, P. Brinch Hansen.

In absentia: E. W. Dijkstra: "Hierarchical ordering of sequential processes."

TOWARDS A THEORY OF PARALLEL PROGRAMMING

C. A. R. Hoare

Department of Computer Science,
Queen's University,
Belfast

OBJECTIVES

The objectives in the construction of a theory of parallel programming as a basis for a high-level programming language feature are:

1. Security from error. In many of the applications of parallel programming the cost of programming error is very high, often inhibiting the use of computers in environments for which they would otherwise be highly suitable. Parallel programs are particularly prone to time-dependent errors, which either cannot be detected by program testing nor by run-time checks. It is therefore very important that a high-level language designed for this purpose should provide complete security against time-dependent errors by means of a *compile-time* check.

2. Efficiency. The spread of real-time computer applications is severely limited by computing costs; and in particular by the cost of main store. If a feature to assist in parallel programming is to be added to a language used for this purpose, it must not entail any noticeable extra run-time overhead in space or speed, neither on programs which use the feature heavily, nor on programs which do not; efficient implementation should be possible on a variety of hardware designs, both simple and complex; and there should be no need for bulky or slow compilers.

3. Conceptual simplicity. A good high-level language feature should provide a simple conceptual framework within which the programmer can formulate his problems and proceed in an orderly fashion to their solution. In particular, it should give guidance on how to structure a program in a perspicuous fashion, and verify that each component of the structure contributes reliably to a clearly defined overall goal.

4. Breadth of application. The purposes for which parallel programming have been found useful are:

   (a) To take advantage of genuine multi-processing hardware.
   (b) To achieve overlap of lengthy input or output operations with computing.
   (c) Operating system implementation.
   (d) Real-time applications.
   (e) Simulation studies.
   (f) Combinatorial or Heuristic Programming.

61

Ideally, a language feature for parallel programming suitable for inclusion in a general-purpose programming language should cater adequately for all these highly disparate purposes.

The design of high-level programming languages which simultaneously satisfy these four objectives is one of the major challenges to the invention, imagination and intellect of Computer Scientists of the present day. The solutions proposed in this paper cannot claim to be final, but it is believed that they form a sound basis for further advance.

PARALLEL PROCESSES

The concept of two or more processes occurring simultaneously in the real world is a familiar one; however, it has proved exceptionally difficult to apply the concept to programs acting in parallel in a computer. The usual definition of the effect of parallel actions is in terms of "an arbitrary interleaving of units of action from each program". This presents three difficulties:

1. That of defining a "unit of action".
2. That of implementing the interleaving on genuinely parallel hardware.
3. That of designing programs to control the fantastic number of combinations involved in arbitrary interleaving.

Our approach to the solution of these problems is based on the observation that in the real world simultaneous processes generally occur in different parts of physical space (it is difficult to give any explanation of what it would mean for two processes to be occurring in the same place). Thus our normal concept of simultaneity is closely bound up with that of spatial separation. The concept of spatial separation has an analogue in computer programs that are operating on entirely disjoint sets of variables, and interacting with their environment through entirely disjoint sets of peripheral equipment. Obvious examples are programs being run on separate computers, or on the same computer under the control of a conventional multiprogramming system.

In such cases, where there is no possibility of communication or interaction between the programs, the question whether a given action of one program preceded, followed, or was simultaneous with a given action of the other program is wholly without significance. On a "Newtonian" view, the question must have a definite answer, even if we can neither know nor care what it is. For practical purposes, it is equally acceptable to take an "Einsteinian" view that there is *no* relative ordering between events occurring in disjoint programs being executed in parallel; and that *each* action of one program is simultaneous with *all* the actions of the other programs.

We introduce the notation

$$\{Q_1//Q_2// \ldots //Q_n\}$$

to indicate that the program statements $Q_1, Q_2, \ldots, Q_n$ are disjoint processes to be executed in parallel. It is expected that the compiler will check the disjointness of the processes by ensuring that no variable subject to change in any of the Q_i is referred to at all in any Q_j for $i \neq j$. Thus it can be guaranteed by a compile-time check that no time-dependent errors could ever occur at run time. It is assumed that the high-level language in use has the decent property that it is possible to tell by inspection which variables and array names appear to the left of an assignment which might be executed in any given statement of a program.

The desired effect of the parallel statement described above is to initiate execution of each of the Q_i in parallel; and when they are *all* terminated, execution of the parallel statement is also complete. Each Q_i may contain any of the normal program features — assignments, conditionals, iterations, blocks, declarations, subroutine calls — of the base language; but if recursion or dynamic storage allocation is used, this will involve replacing the simple stack by a "cactus" stack. It would be wise to ban the use of jumps out of a parallel statement, since these would be not only difficult to define and to use correctly, but can also cause considerable implementation problems. In a language designed for parallel programming there is an even stronger case for the abolition of jumps than in more conventional high-level languages.

Some languages (e.g. PL/I) give the programmer the ability to specify and even to change the priorities of the parallel processes. For most applications this appears to be an unnecessary complexity, whose effective use will depend on many detailed machine and implementation oriented considerations. In practice it has been found that the general-purpose scheduling method of giving control to the process which has used least computer time in the recent past achieves acceptably high efficiency in most circumstances. The programmer can therefore safely be encouraged to "abstract from" the relative speeds and priorities of his processes, and allow the implementor of his programming language to decide on his behalf.

The way in which parallel programs can be proved to achieve some desired objective is simple. Suppose each Q_i is designed to ensure that R_i is true when it finishes, on the assumption that P_i is true before it starts. Then on completion of

$$\{Q_1//Q_2// \ldots //Q_n\}$$

all the R_i will be true, provided that all the P_i were true beforehand. Thus each Q_i makes its contribution to the common goal. But one caution is necessary: none of the P_i or R_i may mention any variable which is subject to change in any of the Q_j for $j \neq i$. A formal statement of this and following program proving principles will be found in the Appendix.

The facility for specifying parallelism of disjoint programs appears to be adequate for use of genuine multiprocessing hardware, and for the overlap of input and output operations with computing. But of course the more interesting problems require some form of interaction between the parallel programs; and this will be the topic of the following sections.

Example: input/output overlap.

A simple program inputs an array, processes it, and outputs it. In order to achieve overlap of input, output and processing, it adopts a simple buffering scheme.

```
input (lastone);
{process (lastone)//input (thisone)};
while some remain do
begin {input (nextone)//process (thisone)//output (lastone)}
      lastone := thisone; thisone := nextone)
end;
{process (thisone)//output (lastone)};
output (thisone).
```

RESOURCE CONSTRAINTS

One of the reasons why parallel programs need to interact with each other is because they need to share some limited resource. For example, several parallel programs may need to communicate with a single operator through a single console; or to present a series of lines for output on a single line printer. In such cases it is usually important that no other process be permitted to access the resource while a given process is using it; for example, one process must be permitted to complete its conversation with the operator without interruption from other processes; and an "arbitrary interleaving" of lines from files output by different parallel processes would be wholly unacceptable.

We may thus envisage the action of each parallel process as follows: for part of the time it operates freely in parallel with all the other processes, but occasionally it enters a so-called *critical region* C; and while it is executing C, it must have exclusive use of some resource r. On completion of C, the resource is freed, and may be allocated to any other process (or the same one again) which wishes to enter a critical region with respect to the same resource. Thus the effect of a critical region is to re-establish the necessary degree of serialism into the parallel execution, so that only one of the processes may enter its critical region at any time. Thus critical regions from different processes are executed strictly serially, in an arbitrarily interleaved order.

This reintroduction of "arbitrary interleaving" does not suffer from the disadvantages mentioned on p. 62 since:

1. The unit of action (= critical region) is defined by the programmer.
2. The necessary synchronization will be relatively infrequent, so that software-assisted implementation is acceptable.
3. The user has no desire or need to control the "interleaving" involved in the use of common resources, since these make no difference whatsoever to the results of his program.

If a parallel statement is to include critical regions with respect to a resource constraint, I suggest the following notation

$$\{resource \; r; Q_1//Q_2// \ldots //Q_n\}$$

where r is the name of the non-local quantity (e.g. lineprinter, console, etc.) which constitutes the resource.

Then inside the processes $Q_1, Q_2, \ldots, Q_n$, a critical region C is signalled by the notation

$$with \; r \; do \; C$$

The compiler is expected to check that no resource is used or referred to outside its critical regions.

The run-time implementation of this feature will depend on the nature of the basic synchronization facility provided by the hardware of the computer. If we assume that a Boolean semaphore mechanism is "built-in", the implementation is trivial. A resource declaration causes a Boolean Semaphore to be created; each critical region in the object code is preceded by seizing this semaphore (the P-operation), and followed by releasing it (the V-operation).

This method of dealing with resource constraints encourages the programmer to ignore the question of which of several outstanding requests for a resource should be granted. In general, the density of utilization of a resource should be sufficiently low that the chance of two requests arriving during the critical period of a third process should be relatively infrequent; for if the resource is a serious bottleneck, it is hardly worth setting up parallelism at all. Thus the relatively simple strategy of granting the resource to the one that has waited longest would seem to be perfectly adequate. Where it is not adequate, the facilities described on p. 66 can be used to program a more subtle strategy.

Another problem which arises from resource constraints is that of the deadly embrace. Fortunately, a simple compile-time check can guarantee against this danger, if the programmer is willing to observe a simple discipline; when one critical region is nested inside another, the resource involved in the outer region should always have been declared as such *before* that declared in the inner region. This will mean that sometimes resources are acquired rather *before* they are actually needed, just as the nested nature of critical regions may mean that resources are kept longer than needed. Even when this occurs, it may be preferable to the alternatives, which include run-time checks and the generalized banker's algorithm.

The proof of programs which share resources will be virtually identical to that of non-sharing processes. However, the non-local variables which constitute the resource must be regarded for proof purposes as though they were local to each of their regions; since their initial values must be regarded as arbitrary, and their final values are "lost" to the program on exit from the critical region. This shows that from an abstract point of view, the seizure of a common resource could have been replaced simply by a local declaration of the variable required; and the only reason for introducing the constraint is because limitations of hardware availability make it unwise or impossible to provide enough "local" quantities to enable two processes to enter their critical regions together.

COOPERATING PROCESSES

In order for processes to cooperate on a common task, it is necessary that they communicate or interact through some common item of data. Within each process, any updating of this item must be regarded as a critical region, not interruptable by similar updatings in other processes. However, on exit from a critical region, this data item *retains* its value, which can then be examined and updated by other processes. Thus with the understanding of the retention of the value of the "resource", it appears that no new language feature is required to permit the construction of programs involving cooperating processes.

In order to see how such a facility might be used, it is helpful to draw an analogy. The resource r may be a potentially large structure (building) which starts off in some null condition (empty site), and which is built up to some desired state by performance of a number of operations of different types; $C_1, C_2, \ldots C_m$ (laying a brick, fitting a window). It does not matter much in what order these operations are performed, so their execution may be delegated to a set of parallel processes (builders), each of which will on occasion invoke one of the permissible operations. Since an operation will update the common resource r, it must be invoked as a critical region. When each process detects that it has fulfilled its task, it terminates. When the tasks of all processes are complete, the structure r will also be complete.

In many cases it will not be permissible to perform the updating operations on r in a wholly random order; for example, the windows cannot be inserted in a building until the frames are installed. In general, a process must be allowed to test the state of r before entering a critical region, to see whether the corresponding operation is permissible or not; and if not, to wait until other processes have brought r into a state in which the operation can be carried out. Let B be a Boolean expression which tests the permissibility of an operation carried out by a critical region C. Then I suggest the notation:

$$\textit{with } r \textit{ when } B \textit{ do } C$$

to specify that C is not to be carried out until B is true.

Some care must be exercised in the implementation of this new feature. The first action (as before) is to seize the semaphore associated with r. Then the condition B is tested. If it is *false*, the given process will hang itself up on a queue of processes waiting for r, and must then *release* the semaphore. If B is *true*, the critical region C is executed normally; and on completion the queue of waiting processes (if any) will be inspected, in the order of longest wait.

Then the waiting condition B for each waiting process is re-evaluated. If it is still *false*, the process remains on the queue. If *true*, it executes its critical region C, and then repeats the scan of the queue. Thus it is guaranteed that B will be true on entry to a critical region prefixed by *when* B; it is also guaranteed at all times (outside critical regions) that no process is waiting when its B is *true*; for B can only *become* true as a result of some critical operation by another process, and it is retested after each such operation. The programmer must be encouraged to ensure that this retesting is not too time-consuming.

In order to verify the correctness of a system of cooperating processes, it is necessary to define what is meant by a permissible operation on the resource r. This may usually be accomplished by giving some propositional formula I, specifying some property of r, which must remain true at all times (outside critical regions); such a proposition is known as an *invariant* for the resource. Obviously I must not mention any variable subject to change in any of the parallel processes. Now the condition for harmonious cooperation of the processes is that each process after updating the resource in a critical region must leave the resource in a state which satisfies I; and in return the process may assume that I is true before each entry to one of its own critical regions. Also, each process may assume that its condition B for entry of a critical region will be true before execution of the critical region starts. If all processes of a parallel program cooperate harmoniously, and if I is true before entering the program, then it is known that on completion of the program I will still be true.

Example: Bounded Buffer.

A process Q_1 produces a stream of values which are consumed by a parallel process Q_2. Since the production and consumption of values proceeds at a variable but roughly equal pace, it is profitable to interpose a buffer between the two processes;

but since storage is limited the buffer can only contain N values. Our program takes the form (using PASCAL notations):

B: *record* inpointer, outpointer, count : Integer;
         buffer:*array* 0 . . N-1 *of* T *end*;
{*resource* B; $Q_1//Q_2$}

We maintain the following variables:

count: the number of values in the buffer.
inpointer: if count $<$ N, this is first empty place in the buffer; otherwise it equals outpointer.
outpointer: if count $>$ 0 this is the place where the next consumed value will be taken from; otherwise it equals inpointer.

The initial values of these variables are all zero.
The critical region inside the producer is as follows:

    with B *when* count $<$ N *do*
        begin buffer [inpointer] := next value;
              inpointer:=(inpointer + 1) *mod* N;
              count:= count + 1
    end

The critical region inside the consumer is

    with B *when* count $>$ 0 *do*
        begin this value:=buffer [outpointer] ;
              outpointer:= (outpointer + 1) *mod* N;
              count:= count $-$ 1
    end

Example: Spaghetti Eaters

Five Benthamite philosophers spend their lives between eating and thinking. To provide them sustenance, a wealthy benefactor has given each of them his own place at a round table, and in the middle is a large and continually replenished bowl of spaghetti, from which they can help themselves when they are seated. The spaghetti is so long and tangled that it requires *two* forks to be conveyed to the mouth; but unfortunately the wealthy benefactor has provided only five forks in all, one between each philosopher's place. The only forks that a philosopher can pick up are those on his immediate right and his immediate left.

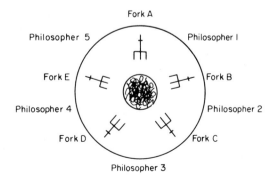

It can be seen that no two neighbours can be eating at a time. The problem is to write a program for each philosopher which will ensure that he contributes at all times to the greatest good of the greatest number.

When a philosopher is hungry, he must go to his own place and pick up two forks. Supposing each philosopher adopts the practice of picking up his left fork first. Then there is a grave danger that all philosophers will get hungry simultaneously, and all pick up their left forks; then they would slowly but inexorably starve to death. If the philosophers all put their left forks down on finding the right fork unobtainable, there is still a danger that they will continue to starve while repeatedly picking up and putting down their left forks in perfect unison.

One solution to this vicious circle is to arrange that one of the philosophers always picks up his *right* fork first. Then either he or the philosopher on his left must always have the opportunity of eating. This is basically the solution suggested earlier, of establishing a linear sequence of resources, and ensuring that all claims of more than one resource observe the standard sequence. The period of eating for each philosopher may be regarded as critical a region with respect to his right fork, nested immediately within the critical region for his left fork, for example:

> *with* fork A *do with* fork B *do* eat spaghetti;

but for the last philosopher the nesting is reversed:

> *with* fork A *do with* fork E *do* eat spaghetti.

This solution is a great improvement, and certainly prevents universal starvation; but it still does not ensure optimum utilization of resources, since it is possible for three adjacent philosophers to remain holding one fork each while one of their colleagues is eating; and one would hope that a slightly more intelligent strategy could be devised in such a case to enable the middle one to eat.

The correct solution requires the use of synchronization facilities to guarantee that each philosopher either picks up *no* forks or he picks up *both* his forks. Picking up a single fork must be avoided. Thus we introduce an array:

> *integer array* possforks [0 : 4];

> possforks [i] takes values 0, 1 or 2 (with initial value 2),

and indicates the number of forks available to philosopher i. This array itself is a resource, which can be inspected or updated by any philosopher. Each philosopher on feeling hungry first waits until two forks are available to him, and then reduces the number of forks available to his immediate neighbours, seizes the forks, and eats. On completion, he increases the number of forks available to his neighbours. Thus three successive critical regions are required in philosopher i:

> *with* possforks *when* possforks [i] = 2 *do*
>   *begin* possforks [(i−1)*mod* 5]:= possforks [(i−1)*mod* 5]−1;
>   possforks [(i+1)*mod* 5]:= possforks [(i+1)*mod* 5]−1
>   *end*;
> *with* fork A *do with* fork B *do* eat spaghetti;
> *with* possforks *do*
>   *begin* possforks [(i−1)*mod* 5]:= possforks [(i−1)*mod* 5]+1;
>   possforks [(i+1)*mod* 5]:= possforks [(i+1)*mod* 5]+1
>   *end*.

ADDITIONAL POINTS

It is hoped that the basic concepts and facilities introduced in the previous sections will be found adequate for most purposes. However, it seems that a few additional simple notations and features may increase their convenience and range of application.

Array remapping

This paper proposes that the introduction of parallelism is meaningful only when no process refers to variables changed by another process (excluding critical regions). However, a compile time check on the observance of this discipline is sometimes too restrictive, since it would prevent two processes operating in parallel on different elements of the same array. A proposal to mitigate this problem is to permit the programmer to declare a local *remapping* of an array, within a block; this splits the array down into disjoint parts, each with its own name; and these separate names can now be updated in separate processes. A notation for expressing the remapping might be:

$$\textit{begin map } a \; [1\!:\!12], b, c \; [o\!:\!i] \; \textit{on } X; \ldots \; \textit{end,}$$

which declares a as a local name for an array consisting of the first 12 elements of X, b as the thirteenth element, and the next $i + 1$ elements are renamed c. C itself should not be referred to within the block.

Example: Quicksort.

Using this facility it is possible, if sufficient parallel hardware is available, to sort an array of size N in time proportional to N.

```
procedure Quicksort (A, m, n);
    begin integer i, j;
        partition (A, i, j, m, n);
        begin map B[m:j] X[j+1: i–1], C [i:n] on A;
            {Quicksort (B, m, j)//Quicksort (C, i, n)}
        end
    end Quicksort
```

Resource arrays

The facility for remapping storage gives a simple method by which parallel processes can operate simultaneously on different parts of a data structure. However, it can be used only when it is known in advance which parts are going to be used by each process. Sometimes, the choice of which element or elements of an array are to be seized for a particular critical region can only be made on entry to that region; this means that each element of the array must be regarded as a *separate* resource, which can be allocated and deallocated independently of its neighbours. Such an array may be declared

$$\textit{resource array } R,$$

and the critical regions may take the form:

$$\textit{with } r = R\,[i] \; \textit{do } Q,$$

where r is used within Q as a local name for R[i]; and R itself must not be mentioned in Q.

One obvious application of resource arrays is in the real time maintenance of a table of information; and if a random access file is regarded as a form of sparse array, this gives the facility of the PL/I EXCLUSIVE attribute. Another application is in dealing with a set of homogeneous resources, such as disc handlers, where the programmer does not care *which* handler(s) he is allocated in a particular critical region. As an example of the use of the feature, we suppose that the number of handlers required in each critical region is different, and that as before we wish to avoid the possibility that more than one process should have a partially fulfilled request.

To achieve this, we use a resource "request", which is allocated to a process during the time that its request is being fulfilled. There is also a *set* resource "free" which contains the numbers of all free handlers; "mine" is a local *set* variable, containing the numbers of the handlers allocated to me. A critical region requiring two handlers would be surrounded by small critical regions which carry out the administration, thus:

with request *do* {*with* free *when* size (free) ≥ 2 *do*
           {mine:=first two of (free); free:= free & $\neg$ mine}}
with a = handler [first (mine)] *do* {*with* b = handler [second (mine)] *do*
          use a and b};
with free *do* free := free v mine;

ACKNOWLEDGEMENTS

It will be obvious to all how much this paper owes to the thought and writings of Professor E. W. Dijkstra, to whom I owe the concepts of the critical region, the semaphore, the deadly embrace and the simple method of its avoidance; and the examples of the bounded buffer and the spaghetti eaters. Less obvious but equally invaluable has been his constant encouragement in the search for a concept to "replace" the semaphore in a high-level programming language, and my ambition of meeting his high standards of rigour and programming style.

I am also deeply indebted to many friends and colleagues who have kindly followed me in many a wild goose chase, and in particular to Maurice Clint, whose advice and experience have been especially valuable.

APPENDIX

Formal definition

It has been suggested that a specification of proof procedures for proving correctness of programs would be a useful method of defining languages with a certain desired degree of indeterminacy. This appendix applies the formal language definition technique to parallel programming.

Let V_i be the set of variables subject to change in Q_i. Then it is assured.

1. no variable of $V_i - \{r\}$ occurs free I or in P_j, Q_j, or R_j for $j \neq i$
2. r is not free in P, R, P_i, Q_i, R_i, except in a critical region with respect to r.

Then letting r *inv* I state that I is the invariant for r, we can formulate the following two rules:

$$r \; inv \; I$$

$$\frac{B \; \& \; I \; \& \; P \; \{C\} \; R \; \& \; I}{P \; \{with \; r \; when \; B \; do \; C\} \; R} \quad \text{criticality}$$

$$\frac{r \; inv \; I \; t \; P_1\{Q_1\}R_1, P_2\{Q_2\} \; R_2, \ldots, P_n\{Q_n\}R_n}{I \; \& \; P_1 \; \& \; P_2 \; \& \ldots \& \; P_n \; \{resource \; r; Q_1//Q_2// \ldots //Q_n\}I \; \& \; R_1 \; \& \; R_2 \; \& \ldots R_n}$$

$$\text{simultaneity}$$

These two rules cover all cases if we adopt the conventions:

1. "*when true*" can be omitted.
2. If there are no critical regions with respect to r, "*resource r*" can be omitted; and I may then be taken as *true*.

HIERARCHICAL ORDERING OF SEQUENTIAL PROCESSES

E. W. Dijkstra

Technological University,
Eindhoven,
The Netherlands

The processing unit of a working computer performs in a short period of time a sequence of millions of instructions and as far as the processing unit is concerned this sequence is extremely monotonous: it just performs instructions one after the other. And if we dare to interpret the output, if we dare to regard the whole happening as "meaningful", we do so because we have mentally grouped sequences of instructions in such a way that we can distinguish a structure in the whole happening. Similar considerations apply to the store: high speed stores contain typically millions of bits stored in a monotonous sequence of consecutively numbered but otherwise equivalent storage locations. And again, if we dare to attach a meaning to such a vast amount of bits, we can only do so by grouping them in such a way that we can distinguish some sort of structure in the vast amount of information. In both cases the structure is *our* invention and *not* an inherent property of the equipment: with respect to the structure mentioned the equipment itself is absolutely neutral. It might even be argued that this "neutrality" is vital for its flexibility. On the other hand, it then follows that it is the programmer's obligation to structure "what is happening where" in a useful way. It is with this obligation that we shall concern ourselves. And it is in view of this obligation that we intend to start with a rather machine-bound, historical introduction: this gives us the unordered environment in which we have to create order, to invent structure adequate for our purposes.

In the very old days, machines were strictly sequential, they were controlled by what was called "a program" but could be called very adequately "a sequential program". Characteristic for such machines is that when the same program is executed twice — with the same input data, if any — both times the same sequence of actions will be evoked. In particular: transport of information to or from peripherals was performed as a program-controlled activity of the central processor.

With the advent of higher electronic speeds the discrepancy in speed between the central processor on the one hand and the peripheral devices on the other became more pronounced. As a result there came for instance a strong economic pressure to arrange matters in such a way that two or more peripherals could be running simultaneously.

In the old arrangement one could write a program reading information from a paper tape, say at a maximum speed of 50 char/sec. In that case the progress through that piece of program would be synchronized with the actual movement of the paper tape through the reader. Similarly one could write a program punching a paper tape, say at a maximum speed of 30 char/sec. To have *both* peripherals running

72

simultaneously and also closely to their maximum speed would require a tricky piece of program specifically designed for this mixture of activities. This was clearly too unattractive and other technical solutions have been found. Channels were invented; a channel is a piece of hardware dedicated to the task of regulating the information traffic between the store and the peripheral to which it is attached, and doing this synchronized to the natural speed of the peripheral device, thus doing away with the implicit mutual synchronization of the peripheral devices that would be caused if both were controlled by the same sequential program execution.

The introduction of channels created two problems, a microscopic and a macroscopic one. The microscopic problem has to do with access to the store. In the old arrangement only the central processor required access to the store and when the central processor required access to the store it could get it. In the new arrangement, with the channels added — channels that can be regarded as "special purpose processors" — a number of processors can be competing with each other as regards access to the store because such accesses from different processors very often exclude each other in time (for technical or logical reasons). This microscopic problem has been solved by the invention of the "switch", granting the competing processors access to the store according to some priority rule. Usually the channels have a lower traffic density and a higher priority than the central processor: the processor works at full speed until a channel requests access to the store, an arrangement which is called "cycle stealing". We draw attention to the fact that the unit of information in which this interleaving takes place — usually "a word" — is somewhat arbitrary; in a few moments we shall encounter a similar arbitrariness.

The macroscopic problem has to do with the coordination of central processor activity and channel activity. The central processor issues a command to a channel and from that moment onwards, two activities are going on simultaneously and — macroscopically speaking — independent of each other: the central processor goes on computing and the channel transports information. How does the central processor discover, when the execution of the channel command has been completed? The answer to this has been the "interrupted". Upon completion of a channel command the channel sets an interrupt flip-flop; at the earliest convenient moment (but never sooner than after completion of the current instruction) the central processor interrupts the execution of the current program (in such a neat way that the interrupted computation can be resumed at a later moment as if nothing had happened) and starts executing an interrupt program instead, under control of which all now appropriate actions will be taken. From the point of view of the central processor it interleaves the various program executions, the unit of interleaving being — similarly arbitrarily — "the instruction".

The above scheme can be recognized in all larger, modern computers that I have studied. It has been embellished in many directions but we don't need to consider those embellishments now. We go immediately to the next questions: given a piece of equipment constructed along the lines just sketched, what are the problems when we try to use it and in what direction should we look for their solution?

What are the problems? Well the main point is that from the point of view of program control such a piece of equipment must be regarded as a non-deterministic machine. Measured in a grain of time appropriate for the description of the activity of the central processing unit — clockpulse or instruction execution time — the time taken by a peripheral transport must be regarded as undefined. If completion of such a peripheral is signalled to the central processor by means of an interrupt, this means that we must regard the moment when the interrupt will take place (or more precisely: the point of progress where the computation will be interrupted) as unpredictable. The problem is that in spite of this indeterminacy of the basic hardware, we must make a more or less deterministic automaton out of this equipment: from the outside world the machine will be confronted with a well-defined computational task and it has to produce a well-defined result in a microscopically unpredictable way!

Let me give a simple example to explain what I mean by "a more or less deterministic automaton". Suppose that offering a program to the machine consists of loading a pack of cards into a card reader (and pushing some button on the reader in order to signal that it has been loaded). Suppose now that we have a machine with two readers and that we want to load it with two programs, A and B, and that we can do this by loading both card readers and pressing both buttons. We assume that the two card readers are not mutually synchronized, i.e. we regard both speeds as unpredictable. To what extent will the total configuration be a deterministic automaton? It will be fully deterministic in the sense that eventually it will produce both output A and output B. If these outputs are to be produced by the same printer, they will be produced in some order and the system may be such that the order in which the respective outputs appear on the printer *does* depend on the relative speeds of the two readers. As far as the operator is concerned, who has to take the output from the printer and to dispatch it to the customers, the installation is non-deterministic; what *he* has to do depends on the unpredictable speed ratio of the two readers, which may cause output A to precede or to follow output B. For both cases the operator has his instructions such that in both cases all output is dispatched to the proper customer. The "computation centre" — i.e. installation and operator together — are deterministic. We can regard the operator's activity as an outer layer, "wrapping up the installation", shielding from the outside world a level of interior indeterminacy.

Now, even if the operator is aware of not having a fully deterministic machine, we should recognize that he has only to deal with two cases — output A before output B or the other way round — while the number of possible sequences of occurrences at cycle time level is quite fantastic. In other words, by far the major part of the "shielding of indeterminacy" is done by the installation itself. We call the resulting installation "more or less deterministic" because as the case may be, a few degrees of limited freedom — here one Boolean degree of freedom — may be left unpredictable.

We have called the operator's activity "an outer layer", shielding a level of indeterminacy, and of course we did so on purpose. At the other end we may distinguish an inner layer, viz. in the channel signalling (via an interrupt signal) that the next card has been read: it tells the central processor that the next card image is available in core, regardless which storage cycles have been stolen to get it there. The terms "inner layer" and "outer layer" have been chosen in order to suggest that in the total organization we shall be able to distinguish many layers in between. But an important remark is immediately appropriate: I assume that with the card read command an area in core has been designated to receive this card image: the remark that the interrupt signalled the completed transfer of the card image irrespective of which cycles had been stolen to transport its constituents is only true, provided that no other access to the designated core area took place in the period of time ranging from the moment the command was given up to the moment that the completion was signalled! Obvious but vital.

It draws our attention to an element of structure that must be displayed by the remaining programs if we wish to make the total organization insensitive to the exact identity of the cycles stolen by the channel. And from the above it is clear that this insensitivity must be one of our dearest goals. And on next levels (of software) we shall have to invent similar elements of structure, making the total organization insensitive (or "as insensitive as possible") to the exact moment when interrupts are honoured. Again it is clear that this must be one of our dearest goals. And on a next level we must make our organization insensitive (or "as insensitive as possible") to the exact number of cards put into the readers for program A and B, and so on. . . . This "layered insensitivity" is, in two words, our grand plan.

I have used the term "layer" on purpose, because it has seemed to provide an attractive terminology in terms of which to talk about operating systems and their total task. We can regard an operating system as the basic software that "rebuilds" a given piece of hardware into a (hopefully) more attractive machine. An operating system can then be regarded as a sequence of layers, built on top of each other and each of them implementing a given "improvement". Before going on, let me digress for a moment and try to explain why I consider such an approach of ordered layers a fruitful one.

There is an alternative approach, which I would like to call the approach via unordered modules. There one makes a long list of all the functions of the operating system to be performed, for each function a module is programmed and finally all these modules are glued together in the fervent hope that they will cooperate correctly and will not interfere disastrously with each other's activity. It is such an approach which has given rise to the assumed law of nature, that complexity grows as the square of the number of program components, i.e. of the number of "functions".

In the layered approach we start at the bottom side with a given hardware machine A_0, we add our bottom layer of software rebuilding A_0 into the slightly more attractive machine A_1, for which the next layer of software is programmed rebuilding it into the still more attractive machine A_2 etc. As the machines in the sequence $A_0, A_1, A_2, \ldots$ get more and more attractive, adding a further layer gets easier and easier. This is in sharp contrast to the approach via unordered modules, where adding new functions seems to get progressively worse!

1. So much in favour of a layered approach in general. When one wishes to design an operating system, however, one is immediately faced with the burning question, which "improvement" is the most suitable candidate to be implemented in the bottom layer.

For the purpose of this discussion I will choose a very modest bottom layer. I do so for two reasons. Firstly, it is a choice with which for historical reasons I myself am most familiar. Secondly, as a bottom layer it is very modest and neutral, so neutral in fact that it provides us with a mental platform from where we can discuss various alternatives for the structure of what is going to be built on top of it. As a bottom layer it seems close to the choice of minimal commitment. The fact that this bottom layer is chosen as a starting point for our discussion is by no means to be interpreted as the suggestion that this is the best possible choice: on the contrary, one of the later purposes of this discussion is the consideration of alternatives.

With the hardware taking care of the cycle stealing we felt that the software's first responsibility was to take care of the interrupts, or, to put it a little more strongly, to do away with the interrupt, to abstract from its existence. (Besides all rational arguments this decision was also inspired by fear based on the earlier experience that, due to the irreproducibility of the interrupt moments, a program bug could present itself misleadingly like an incidental machine malfunctioning.) What does it mean "to do away with the interrupt"? Well, without the interrupt the central processor continues the execution of the current sequential process while it is the function of the interrupt to make the central processor available for the continuation of another sequential process. We would not need interrupt signals if each sequential process had its own dedicated processor. And here the function of the bottom layer emerged: to create a virtual machine, able to execute a number of sequential programs in parallel as if each sequential program had its own private processor. The bottom layer has to abstract of the existence of the interrupt or, what amounts to the same thing, it has to abstract from the identity of the single hardware processor. If this abstraction is carried out rigorously it implies that everything built on top of this bottom layer will be equally applicable to a multi-processor installation, provided that all processors are logically equivalent (i.e. have the same access to main memory etc.). The remaining part of the operating system and user programs together then emerges as a set of harmoniously cooperating sequential processes.

The fact that these sequential processes out of the family have to cooperate harmoniously implies that they must have the means of doing so; in particular, they must be able to communicate with each other and they must be able to synchronize their activities with respect to each other. For reasons which, in retrospect, are not very convincing, we have separated these two obligations. The argument was that we wished to keep the bottom layer as modest as possible, giving it only the duty of processor allocation; in particular it would leave the "neutral, monotonous memory" as it stood; it would not rebuild that part of the machine, and immediately above the bottom layer the processes could communicate with each other via the still available, commonly accessible memory.

The mutual synchronization, however, is a point of concern. Closely related to this is the question: given the bottom layer, what will be known about the speed ratios with which the different sequential processes progress? Again we have made the most modest assumption we could think of, viz. that they would proceed with speed ratios, unknown but for the fact that the speed ratios would differ from zero; i.e. each process (when logically allowed to proceed, see below) is guaranteed to proceed with some unknown, but finite speed. In actual fact we can say more about the way in which the bottom layer grants processor time to the various candidates: it does it "fairly" in the sense that in the long run a number of identical processes will proceed at the same macroscopic speed. But we don't tell, how "long" this run is and the said fairness has hardly a logical function.

This assumption about the relative speeds is a very "thin" one, but as such it has great advantages. From the point of view of the bottom layer, we remark that it is easy to implement: to prevent a running program from monopolizing the processor an interrupting clock is all that is necessary. From the point of view of the structure built on top of it is also extremely attractive: the absence of any knowledge about speed ratios forces the designer to code all synchronization measures explicitly. When he has done so he has made a system that is very robust in more than one sense.

Firstly he has made a system that will continue to operate correctly when an actual change in speed ratios is caused, and this may happen in a variety of ways. The actual strategy for processor allocation as implemented by the bottom layer, may be changed. In a multiprocessor installation the number of active processors may change. A peripheral may temporarily work with speed zero, e.g. when it requires operator attention. In our case the original line printer was actually replaced by a faster model. But under all those changes the system will continue to operate correctly (although perhaps not optimally, but that is quite another matter).

Secondly — and we shall return to this in greater detail — the system is robust thanks to the relative simplicity of the arguments that can convince us of its proper operation. Nothing being guaranteed about speed ratios means that in our understanding of the structure built on top of the bottom layer we have to rely on discrete reasoning and there will be no place for analog arguments, for other purposes than overall justification of chosen strategies. I trust that the strength of this remark will become apparent as we proceed.

2. Let us now focus our attention upon the synchronization. Here a key problem is the so-called "mutual exclusion problem". Given a number of cyclic processes of the form

```
cycle begin entry;
            critical section;
            exit;
            remainder of cycle
      end
```

program "entry" and "exit" in such a way that at any moment at most one of the processes is engaged in its critical section. The solution must satisfy the following requirements:

(*a*) The solution must be symmetrical between the processes; as a result we are not allowed to introduce a static priority.

(*b*) Nothing may be assumed about the ratio of the finite speeds of the processes; we may not even assume their speeds to be constant in time.

(*c*) If any of the processes is stopped somewhere in "remainder of cycle", this is not allowed to lead to potential blocking of any of the others.

(*d*) If more than one process is about to enter its critical section, it must be impossible to devise for them such finite speeds, that the decision to determine which of them will enter its critical section first is postponed until eternity. In other words, constructions in which "After you" — "After you" — blocking, although improbable, is still possible, are not to be regarded as valid solutions.

I called the mutual exclusion problem "a key problem". We have met something similar in the situation of programs A and B producing their output in one of the two possible orders via the same printer: obviously those two printing processes have to exclude each other mutually in time. But this is a mutual exclusion on a rather macroscopic scale and in all probability it is not acceptable that the decision to grant the printer to either one of the two activities will be taken on decount of the requirement of mutual exclusion alone: in all probability considerations of efficiency or of smoothness of service require a more sophisticated printer granting strategy. The explanation why mutual exclusion must be regarded as a key problem must be found at the microscopic end of the scale. The switch granting access to store on word basis provides a built in mutual exclusion, but only on a small, fixed and rather arbitrary scale. The same applies to the single processor installation which can honour interrupts in between single instructions: this is a rather arbitrary grain of activity. The problem arises when more complicated operations on common data have to take place. Suppose that we want to count the number of times something has happened in a family of parallel processes. Each time such an occurrence has taken place, the program could try to count it via

$$\text{``}n := n+1\text{''}$$

If in actual fact such a statement is coded by three instructions

$$\text{``}\begin{aligned} &R := n; \\ &R := R+1; \\ &n := R \end{aligned}\text{''}$$

then one of the increases may get lost when two such sequences are executed, interleaved on single instruction basis. The desire to compound such (and more complicated) operators on common variables is equivalent to the desire to have more explicit control over the degree of interleaving than provided by the neutral, standard hardware. This more explicit control is provided by a solution to the mutual exclusion problem.

We still have to solve it. Our solution depends critically on the communication facilities available between the individual processes and the common store. We can assume that the only mutual exclusion provided by the hardware is to exclude a write instruction or a read instruction, writing or reading a single word. Under that assumption the problem has been solved for two processes by T. J. Dekker in the early sixties. It has been solved by me for N processes in 1965 (CACM 8 (1965), 9, p. 569). The solution for two processes was complicated, the solution for N processes was terribly complicated. (The program pieces for "enter" and "exit" are quite small, but they are by far the most difficult pieces of program I ever made. The solution is only of historical interest.)

It has been suggested that the problem could be solved when the individual processes had at their disposal an indivisible "add to store" which would leave the value thus created in one of the private process registers as well, so that this value is available for inspection if so desired. Indicating this indivisible operation with braces the suggested form of the parallel programs was:

$$\textit{cycle begin while } \{x := x+1\} \neq 1 \textit{ do } \{x := x-1\};$$
$$\qquad\qquad \text{critical section;}$$
$$\qquad\qquad \{x := x-1\};$$
$$\qquad\qquad \text{remainder of cycle}$$
$$\qquad \textit{end}$$

Where the "add to store" operation is performed on the common variable "x" which is initialized with the value zero before the parallel programs are started.

As far as a single process is concerned the cumulative Δx as affected by this process since its start is $=0$ or $=1$; in particular, when a process is in its critical section, its cumulative $\Delta x = 1$. As a result we conclude that at any moment when N processes are in their critical section simultaneously, $x \geqslant N$ will hold.

A necessary and sufficient condition for entering a critical section is that *this* process effectuates for x the transition from 0 to 1. As long as one process is engaged in its critical section ($N = 1$), $x \geqslant 1$ will hold. This excludes the possibility of the transition from 0 to 1 taking place and therefore no other process can enter its critical section. We conclude that mutual exclusion is indeed guaranteed. Yet the solution must be rejected: it is not difficult to see that even with two processes (after at least one successful execution of a critical section) "After you" — "After you" — blocking may occur (with the value of x oscillating between 1 and 2).

A correct solution exists when we assume the existence of an indivisible operation "swap" which causes a common variable (x) and a private variable (loc) to exchange their values. With initially $x = 0$ the structure of the parallel programs is:

```
begin integer loc; loc: = 1;
        cycle begin repeat swap (x, loc) until loc = 0;
                    critical section;
                    swap (x, loc);
                    remainder of cycle
              end
end
```

The invariant relation is that of the N+1 variables (i.e. the N loc's and the single x) always exactly one will be $=0$, the others being $=1$. A process is in its critical section if and only if its own loc $=0$, as a result at most one process can be engaged in its critical section. When none of the processes is in its critical section, $x = 0$ and "After you" — "After you" — blocking is impossible. So this is a correct solution.

In a multiprogramming environment, however, the correct solutions referred to or shown have a great drawback: the program section called "enter" contains a loop in which the process will cycle when it cannot enter its critical section. This so-called "busy form of waiting" is expensive in terms of processing power, because in a multiprogramming environment (with more parallel processes than processing units) there is a fair chance that there will be a more productive way of spending processing power than giving it to a process that, to all intents and purposes, could go to sleep for the time being.

If we want to do away with the busy form of waiting we need some sort of synchronizing primitives by means of which we can indicate those program points where — depending on the circumstances — a process may be put to sleep. Similarly we must be able to indicate that potential sleepers may have to be woken up. What form of primitives?

Suppose that process 1 is in its critical section and that process 2 will be the next one to enter it. Now there are two possible cases.

(*a*) process 1 will have done "exit" before process 2 has tried to "enter"; in that case no sleeping occurs

(*b*) process 2 tries to "enter" before process 1 has done "exit"; in that case process 2 has to go to sleep temporarily until it is woken up as a side-effect of the "exit" done by process 1.

When both occurrences have taken place, i.e. when process 2 has successfully entered its critical section it is no longer material whether we had case (*a*) or case (*b*). In that sense we are looking for primitives (for "enter" and "exit") that are commutative. What are the simplest commutative operations on common variables that we can think of? The simplest operation is inversion of a common Boolean, but that is too simple for our purpose: then we have only one operation at our disposal and lack the possibility of distinguishing between "enter" and "exit". The next simplest commutative operations are addition to (and subtraction from) a common integer. Furthermore we observe that "enter" and "exit" have to compensate each other: if only the first process passes its critical section the common state before its "enter" equals the common state after its "exit" as far as the mutual exclusion is concerned. The simplest set of operations we can think of are increasing and decreasing a common variable by 1 and we introduce the special synchronizing primitives

$$P(s) : s : = s-1$$

and

$$V(s) : s : = s+1$$

special in the sense that they are "indivisible" operations: if a number of P- and V-operations on the same common variable are performed "simultaneously" the net effect of them is as if the increases and decreases are done "in some order".

Now we are very close to a solution: we have still to decide how we wish to characterize that a process may go to sleep. We can do this by making the P- and V-operations operate not on just a common variable, but on a special purpose integer variable, a so-called *semaphore,* whose value is by definition non-negative, i.e. $s \geqslant 0$.

With that restriction, the V-operation can always be performed: unsynchronized execution of the P-operation, however, could violate it.

We therefore postulate that whenever a process initiates a P-operation on a semaphore whose current value equals zero, the process in question will go to sleep until (another) process has performed a V-operation on that very same semaphore. A little bit more precise: if a semaphore value equals zero, one or more processes may be blocked by it, eager to perform a P-operation on it. If a V-operation is performed on a semaphore blocking a number of processes, one of them is woken up, i.e. will perform its now admissible P-operation and proceed. The choice of this latter process is such that no process will be blocked indefinitely long. A way to implement this is to decide that no two processes will initiate the blocking P-operation simultaneously and that they will be treated on the basis "first come, first served" (but it need not be done that way, see below).

With the aid of these two primitives the mutual exclusion problem is solved very easily. We introduce a semaphore "mutex" say, with the initial value

$$mutex = 1,$$

after which the parallel processes controlled by the program

```
cycle begin P(mutex);
           critical section;
           V(mutex);
           remainder of cycle
       end
```

are started.

Before proceeding with the discussion I would like to insert a remark. In languages specifically designed for process control I have met two other primitives, called "wait" and "cause", operating on an "event variable", which is a (possibly empty) queue of waiting processes. Whenever a process executes a "wait" it attaches itself to the queue until the next "cause" for the same event, which empties the queue and signals to all processes in the queue that they should proceed. Experience has shown that such primitives are very hard to use. The reason for this is quite simple: a "wait" in one process and a "cause" in another are non-commutative operations, their net effect depends on the order in which they take place and at the level where we need the synchronizing primitives we must assume that we have not yet effective control over this ordering. The limited usefulness of such "wait" and "cause" primitives could have been deduced a priori.

3. As a next interlude I am going to prove the correctness of our solution. One may ask "Why bother about such a proof, for the solution is obviously correct". Well, in due time we shall have to prove the correctness of the implementation of more sophisticated rules of synchronization and the proof structure of this simple case may then act as a source of inspiration.

With each process "j" we introduce a state variable "C_j", characterizing the progress of the process.

$$C_j = 0 \quad \text{process}_j \text{ is in the "remainder of cycle"}$$
$$C_j = 1 \quad \text{process}_j \text{ is in its "critical section"}.$$

While process$_j$ performs (i.e. "completes") the operation P(mutex)$_j$ the translation $C_j=0 \to C_j=1$ takes place, when it performs the operation V(mutex)$_j$ the transition $C_j=1 \to C_j=0$ takes place. (Note that the C_j are *not* variables occurring in the program, they are more like functions defined on the current value of the order counters.) In terms of the C_j the number of processes engaged in its critical section equals

$$\sum_{j=1}^{N} C_j$$

In order to prove that this number will be at most =1, we follow the life history of the quantity

$$K = \text{mutex} + \sum_{j=1}^{N} C_j$$

The quantity K will remain constant as long as its constituents are constant: the only operations changing its constituents are the 2N mutually exclusive primitive actions P(mutex)$_i$ and V(mutex)$_i$ (for $1 \leqslant i \leqslant N$).

We have as a result of

$$P(\text{mutex})_i: \Delta K = \Delta\text{mutex} + \Delta\left(\sum_{j=1}^{N} C_j\right)$$
$$= \Delta\text{mutex} + \Delta C_i$$
$$= -1 + 1 = 0$$

and similarly, as a result of

$$V(mutex)_i : \Delta K = \Delta mutex + \Delta C_i$$
$$= +1 - 1 = 0$$

As these 2N operations are the only ones affecting K's constituents, we conclude that K is constant, in particular, that it is constantly equal to its initial value,

$$K = 1 + \sum_{j=1}^{N} 0 = 1$$

As a result

$$\sum_{j=1}^{N} C_j = 1 - mutex.$$

Because mutex is a semaphore, we have

$$0 \leqslant mutex,$$

and from the last two relations we conclude

$$\sum_{j=1}^{N} C_j \leqslant 1.$$

Because this sum is the sum of non-negative terms we know

$$0 \leqslant \sum_{j=1}^{N} C_j;$$

Combining this with

$$mutex = 1 - \sum_{j=1}^{N} C_j$$

We conclude

$$mutex \leqslant 1.$$

i.e. mutex is a so-called "binary semaphore", only taking on the values 0 and 1.

Finally we observe that no process will be kept out of its critical section without justification: if all processes are outside their critical sections, all C_j's are =0 and therefore mutex is =1, thereby allowing the first process that wants to enter its critical section to do so.

For later reference we summarize the structure of this proof. A central role is played by an invariant relation among common variables (here only the semaphore) and "progress variables" (here the C_j's). Its invariance is proved by observing the net effect of the (mutually exclusive) operators operating on its constituents, without any further assumptions about their mutual synchronization, about which we can then make assertions on account of the established invariance. In the sequel we shall see that this pattern of proof is very generally applicable.

4. Before proceeding with more complicated examples of synchronization we must make a little detour and make a connection with earlier observations. When a process is engaged in its critical section, a great number of other processes may go to sleep. When the first one leaves its critical section, it is undefined which of the sleepers is woken up, the only requirement being that no single process is kept sleeping indefinitely long. (This latter assumption we have to make when, later, we wish to prove assertions about the finite progress of individual processes.) In this sense our "family of sequential processes" is still a mechanism of an undeterministic nature, but the degree of undeterminacy is a mild one compared with the original hardware, in which an interrupt could occur between any pair of instructions: the only indeterminacy left is the relative order of much larger units of action, viz. the critical sections. In this respect the bottom layer of our operating system achieves a step towards our goal of "layered insensitivity".

It is in this connection that I should like to make another remark of quantitative nature. The choice of the process to be woken up is left undefined because it is assumed that it does not matter, i.e. we assume the system load to be such that the total period of time that any of the processes will be engaged in its critical section will be a negligible fraction of real time, in other words, nearly always mutex = 1 will hold. It is for that reason that such a neutral policy for waking up a sleeper is permissible. This is no longer true for our macroscopic concerns regarding so-called "resource allocation". In the case of a number of programs producing their output via the same printer, these printing actions have to exclude each other mutually in time, but it is no longer true that the total time spent in printing will be a negligible fraction of real time! On the contrary: in a well-balanced system the printer will be used with a duty cycle close to 100 per cent! In order to achieve this – and to satisfy other, perhaps conflicting design requirements – such a neutral policy which is adequate for granting entrance into critical sections will certainly be inadequate for granting a scarce resource like a printer. For the implementation of a less neutral granting policy we shall use the critical sections, entrance to which is granted on a neutral basis. (For an example of a more elaborate synchronization implemented with the aid of critical sections we refer to the Problem of the Dining Philosophers to be treated later.) This is the counterpart of the "layered insensitivity": going upwards in levels we gain more and more control over the microscopic indeterminacy, but simultaneously macroscopic strategic concerns begin to enter the picture: it seems vital that the bottom layer with its microscopic concerns does not bother itself with such macroscopic considerations. This observation seems to apply to all well-designed systems: I would call it a principle if I had a better formulation for it.

5. We now turn to a slightly more complicated example, viz. a bunch of producers and a bunch of consumers, coupled to each other via an unbounded buffer. In this example all producers are regarded as equivalent to each other and all consumers are regarded as equivalent to each other. Under these assumptions – which are not very realistic – the semaphores provide us with a ready-made solution.

In the commonly accessible universe we have

(*a*) a buffer, initialized empty

(*b*) a semaphore "mutex", initialized =1; this semaphore caters for the mutual exclusion of operations changing buffer contents

(*c*) a semaphore "numqueuepor"; this gives (a lower bound of) the number of portions queueing in the buffer.

Then a producer may have the form

> *cycle begin* produce next portion;
> > P(mutex);
> > add portion produced to buffer;
> > V (numqueuepor);
> > V(mutex)
>
> *end*

with consumers of the following structure

> *cycle begin* P(numqueuepor);
> > P(mutex);
> > take portion from buffer;
> > V(mutex);
> > consume portion taken
>
> *end*

Note 1: The order of the V-operations in the producer is immaterial, the order of the P-operations in the consumer is absolutely essential.

Note 2: The assumption is that the operations "produce next portion" and "consume portion taken" are the slow, time-consuming operations — possible in synchronism with other equipment — for which parallelism is of interest, while the actions "add portion produced to buffer" and "take portion from buffer" are very fast "clerical" operations.

In the above program the semaphore "numqueuepor" is a so-called "general semaphore", i.e. a semaphore whose possible values are not restricted to 0 and 1. We shall now give an alternative program, using only binary semaphores.

In the commonly accessible universe we have

(*a*) a buffer and an integer "n", counting the number of portions in the buffer. The buffer is initialized empty (incl. n:=0)

(*b*) a semaphore "mutex" initialized =1; this semaphore caters for the mutual exclusion of the operations changing the buffer contents, the value of "n" and the inspection of "n".

(*c*) a semaphore "consal", initialized =0; if this semaphore is =1, a next consumption is allowed.

Then a producer may have the form

> *cycle begin* produce next portion;
> > P(mutex);
> > add portion to buffer (incl. n:=n+1);
> > *if* n=1 *do* V(consal);
> > V(mutex)
>
> *end*

with consumers of the following structure

> *cycle begin* P(consal);
>   P(mutex);
>   take portion from the buffer (incl. n:=n−1);
>   *if* n > o *do* V(consal);
>   V(mutex);
>   consume portion taken
>   *end*

Although it is not too hard to convince ourselves "by inspection" − whatever that may mean − that the above bunch of programs work properly, it is illuminating to give a somewhat more formal treatment of their cooperation. (I am now used to calling such a more formal treatment of their cooperation "a correctness proof", although I did not formalize the requirements that such a piece of reasoning should satisfy in order to be a "valid proof".)

The proof consists of two steps. The first step uses our earlier result, viz. that the P(mutex) and V(mutex) establish mutual exclusion of the critical sections. (Inside these critical sections we find no P-operations, as a result they cannot give rise to deadlock situations.) This observation allows us to regard the critical sections as indivisible operations and to confine our attention to the state of the system at the discrete moments with mutex = 1 (i.e. no one engaged in its critical section).

In the second step we define three mutually exclusive states for the whole system and shall show that whenever the system is started in one of these states, it will remain within these states. For the purpose of state description we introduce a function defined on the progress of the consumers, viz.

K = the number of consumers that have performed "P(consal)" but have
    not yet entered the following critical section.

Now we can introduce our three states

> S1 : n=0 *and* K=0 *and* consal=0
> S2 : n>0 *and* K=0 *and* consal=1
> S3 : n>0 *and* K=1 *and* consal=0

Three operations; (viz. P(consal) and the two critical sections) operate on the constituents of these Boolean expressions; for each state we investigate all three.

> S1 : (initial state)
> P(consal) : impossible (on account of consal=0)
> critical producer section : transition to S2
> critical consumer section : impossible (on account of K=0)
>
> S2 :
> P(consal) : transition to S3
> critical producer section : transition to S2
> critical consumer section : impossible (on account of K=0)
>
> S3 :
> P(consal) : impossible (on account of consal=0)
> critical producer section : transition to S3
> critical consumer section : transition to S1 or S2

This concludes the second step, showing the invariance of

$$S1 \; or \; S2 \; or \; S3$$

(from which we conclude $N \geqslant 0$ and consal$\leqslant 1$).

A few remarks, however, are in order, for we have cheated slightly. Let us repair our cheating first and then give our further comments. In our second step we have investigated the *isolated* effect of either P(consal) or the critical producer section or the critical consumer section. For the critical sections this is all right for they exclude each other mutually in time; the operation P(consal), however, can take place *during* a critical section, and we did not pay any attention to such coincidence. We can save the situation by observing that in the case of coincidence the net effect is equal to the execution of the critical section immediately followed by P(consal). This is really a messy patching up of a piece of reasoning that was intended to be clean. Now our further comments.

1. The proof shows why the mutual exclusion problem is worthy, of the name "a key problem". Thanks to the mutual exclusion of critical sections we only need to consider the net effect of each single, isolated section. If these sections were not critical i.e. could take place in arbitrary interleaving, we would have to consider the net effect of one section, the net effect of two sections together, of three sections together, of four etc.! With N cooperating processes the number of cases to be investigated would grow like 2^N (i.e. the powerset!). This is one of the strongest examples showing how the amount of intellectual effort needed for a correctness proof may depend critically on structural aspects of the program, here the aspect of mutual exclusion. It is this observation that is meant to justify the inclusion of the above proof in this text.

2. The proof is complicated considerably by the fact that P(consal) is an operation sequentially separate from the following critical section: this caused the messy patching up of our piece of reasoning, it called for the introduction of the function "K". If the conditional entrance of critical sections is going to be a standard feature of the system, a more direct way of expressing this would be essential. A minimal departure of the current formation would be the introduction of the parallel P-operation, allowing us to combine the two P-operations of the consumer into

$$P(consal, \; mutex)$$

3. For the sake of completeness we mention that in the T.H.E. multiprogramming system, where we used general semaphores to control synchronization along information streams, each information stream had at any moment in time at most one consumer attached to it. As a result a general semaphore could block at most one process and when a V-operation was performed on it there was never the problem which process should be woken up. The absence of the possibility that more than one process is blocked by a general semaphore is not surprising: it is the semaphore "consal" that may be equal to zero for a long period of time; as a result it is not to be expected that it is irrelevant which of the processes will be woken up when a V-operation is performed on it. In the design phase of the T.H.E. multiprogramming system the parallel P-operation has been considered but finally it has not been implemented because we felt that it contained the built-in solution to an irrealistic problem. But it would have simplified proof procedures.

6. We now turn to the problem of the Five Dining Philosophers. The life of a philosopher consists of an alternation of thinking and eating:

> *cycle begin* think;
> 　　　　eat
> *end*

Five philosophers, numbered from 0 through 4 are living in a house where the table is laid for them, each philosopher having his own place at the table:

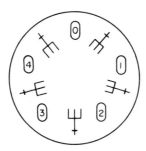

Their only problem — besides those of philosophy — is that the dish served is a very difficult kind of spaghetti, that has to be eaten with two forks. There are two forks next to each plate, so that presents no difficulty: as a consequence, however, no two neighbours may be eating simultaneously.

A very naive solution associates with each fork a binary semaphore with the initial value =1 (indicating that the fork is free) and, naming in each philosopher these semaphores in a local terminology, we could think the following solution for the philosopher's life adequate

> *cycle begin* think;
> 　　　　P(left-hand fork); P(right-hand fork);
> 　　　　eat;
> 　　　　V(left-hand fork); V(right-hand fork)
> *end*

But this solution — although it guarantees that no two neighbours are eating simultaneously — must be rejected because it contains the danger of the deadly embrace. When all five philosophers get hungry simultaneously, each will grab his left-hand fork and from that moment onwards the group is stuck. This could be overcome by the introduction of the parallel P-operation, combining the two P-operations into the single

P(left-hand fork, right-hand fork)

For the time being we assume the parallel P-operation denied to us — later we shall reject the solution using it on other grounds — and we shall show how (using only single P-operations and binary semaphores) we can derive our solution in a reasonably controlled manner.

In order to be able to give a formal description of our restriction, we associate with each philosopher a state variable, "C" say, where

$C[i]$ = 0 means: philosopher i is thinking
$C[i]$ = 2 means: philosopher i is eating.

In accordance with their first act, all C's will be initialized =0. In terms of the C's we can state that it is disallowed

$$\exists_i (C[i] = 2 \text{ } and \text{ } C[(i+1) \text{ } mod \text{ } 5] = 2), \tag{1}$$

in words: no philosopher may be eating while his left hand neighbour is eating as well. From this formula it *follows* that for a C the transition from 2 to 0 can never cause violation of the restriction (1), while the transition from 0 to 2 can. *Therefore* we introduce for the last transition an intermediate state

$C[i]$ = 1 means: philosopher i is hungry

Now each philosopher will go cyclically through the states 0, 1, 2, 0. . . . The next question to ask is: when has the (dangerous) transition from 1 to 2 to take place for philosopher K? Well, three conditions have to be satisfied

(1) $C[K]$ = 1, i.e. he himself must be hungry
(2) $C[(K+1) \text{ } mod \text{ } 5] \neq 2$, because otherwise
       $C[K]$:=2 would cause violation of (1) for i=K
(3) $C[(K-1) \text{ } mod \text{ } 5] \neq 2$, because otherwise
       $C[K]$:=2 would cause violation of (1) for i=(K−1) *mod* 5.

As a result we have to see to it that the state

$$\exists_K (C[(K-1) \text{ } mod \text{ } 5] \neq 2 \text{ } and \text{ } C[K] = 1 \text{ } and \text{ } C[(K+1) \text{ } mod \text{ } 5] \neq 2) \tag{2}$$

is unstable: whenever it occurs, it has to be resolved by assigning $C[K]$:=2 and sending philosopher K to the table.

In a similar analysis we ask: which transitions in the life of philosopher w can cause the unstable situation and for which values of K?

(1) when $C[w]$:= 1 is executed, instability may be created for K = w
(2) when $C[w]$:= 0 − i.e. when $C[w]$ loses the value 2 − instability may be
       created for K = (w+1) *mod* 5 and for K = (w−1) *mod* 5.

In words: when philosopher w gets hungry, the test whether he himself should be sent to the table is appropriate, when he leaves the table the test should be done for both his neighbours.

In the universe we assume declared

(1) the *semaphore* mutex, initially = 1
(2) the *integer array* C[0:4], with initially all element = 0
(3) the *semaphore array* prisem [0:4] with initially all elements = 0
(4) *procedure* test (*integer value* K);
       if $C[(K-1) \text{ } mod \text{ } 5] \neq 2 \text{ } and \text{ } C[K] = 1 \text{ } and \text{ } C[(K+1) \text{ } mod \text{ } 5] \neq 2 \text{ } do$
       begin $C[K]$:= 2; V(prisem [K]) *end*;

(This procedure, which resolves instability for K when present, will only be called from within a critical section.)

In this universe the life of philosopher w can now be coded

```
cycle begin think;
            P(mutex);
                C[w] := 1; test (w);
            V(mutex);
            P(prisem [w]); eat
            P(mutex);
                C[w] := 0; test [(w+1) mod 5]; test [(w−1) mod 5];
            V(mutex)
     end
```

And this concludes the solution I was aiming at. I have shown it, together with the way in which it was derived, for the following reasons.

(1) The arrangement with the private semaphore for each process and the common semaphore for mutual exclusion in order to allow for unambiguous inspection and modification of common state variables is typical for the way in which in the T.H.E. multiprogramming system all synchronization restrictions have been implemented that were more complicated than straightforward mutual exclusion or synchronization along an information stream (the latter synchronization has been implemented directly with the aid of a general semaphore).

(2) The solution (including the need for the introduction of the intermediate state called "hungry") has been derived by means of a formal analysis of the synchronization restriction. It is exemplar for the way in which the flows of mutual obligations for waking up have been derived in the design phase of the T.H.E. multi-programming system. It is this analysis that I have called "A constructive approach to the problem of program correctness".

With respect to this particular solution I would like to make some further remarks.

Firstly the solution as presented is free from the danger of deadlock, as it should be. Yet it is highly improbable that a solution like this can be accepted because it contains the possibility of a particular philosopher being starved to death by a conspiration of his two neighbours. This can be overcome by more sophisticated rules (introducing besides the state "hungry" also the state "very hungry"); this requires a more complicated analysis but by and large it follows the same pattern as the derivation shown. This was another reason not to introduce the parallel P-operation: for the solution with the parallel P-operation we did not see an automatic way of avoiding the danger of individual starvation.

Secondly we could have made a more crude solution: the procedure "test" has a parameter indicating for which philosopher the test has to be done; also in the critical sections we call the procedure "test" precisely for those philosophers for whom there is a chance that they should be woken up and for no others. This is very refined: we could have made a test procedure without parameter that would simply test for any K if there was an unstability to be removed. But the problem could have been posed for 9 or 25 philosophers and the larger the number of philosophers, the more prohibitive the overhead of the crude solution would get.

Thirdly, I have stated that we "derived our solution in a reasonably controlled manner": although the formal analysis has been carried out almost mechanically, I would not like to suggest that it should be done automatically, because in real life, whether we like it or not, the situation can be more complicated.

We consider two classes of processes, class A and class B, sharing the same resource from a large pool. (The situation occurred in the T.H.E. multiprogramming system with the total pool of pages in the system.) Suppose now that processes from class A ask and return items from this pool at high frequency, while those from class B do so at low frequency only. In that case it is highly unattractive to pose upon the highly frequent item releases of class A the (possibly) considerable overhead involved in the analysis of whether it is necessary to wake up one or more blocked processes. This high-frequency overhead was avoided by delegating the waking-up obligation to (some) processes of class B and by guaranteeing that at least one of these processes would be active when the boundary of the resource restriction was in danger of being approached. In other words, in order to reduce system overhead we removed the highly frequent inspection whether processes had to be woken up at the price of increasing the "reaction time" there where an ultra short "response" was not required. The taking of such decisions seems a basic responsibility of the system designer and I don't see how they could be taken automatically.

The above concludes my discussion of the chosen bottom layer. In the final part of this paper I would like to discuss briefly an alternative solution.

7. The chosen bottom layer implements a family of sequential processes plus a few synchronizing primitives, the remaining part of the system, to be composed on top of it, will exist of a set of harmoniously cooperating sequential processes. The interface is characterized by a number of features

(*a*) the bottom layer treats all sequential processes on the same footing
(*b*) the sequential processes communicate with each other via commonly accessible variables
(*c*) critical sections ensure the unambiguous interpretation and modification of these common variables.

One or two objections can be raised to this organization; they centre around the observation that each sequential process can be in one of two mutually exclusive radically different states: either the process is inside its critical section or it is not. Inside its critical section it is allowed to access the common variables, outside it is not. In actual fact this difference does not only pertain to accessibility of information, it has also a bearing on processor allocation as implemented in the bottom layer. Given a process without hurry it is permissible to take the processor away from it for longer periods of time, but it is unattractive to do so in the middle of a critical section: if a process is stopped within a critical section it blocks for the other processes the mechanism needed for their cooperation and the remaining processes are bound to come to a grinding halt. In the T.H.E. multiprogramming system this has been overcome by giving processes two colours – red or white – by making each process red while it is in a critical section and by never granting the processor to a white process if a red one is logically allowed to proceed.

Furthermore there is the aspect of reproducibility. To an individual user, offering a strictly sequential program to the system, we should like to present a strictly deterministic automation. In the system a number of sequential processes are dedicated to the processing of user programs, they act as slots into which a user program can be inserted; whenever the user program refers to a shared resource the translator effectively inserts — via a subroutine call — the critical section required for this cooperation. As a result, what happens in this slot is perfectly reproducible as long as the sequential process remains outside critical sections. But if we wish to charge our user and also insist that the charge be reproducible, we can only charge him for the activity of the slot outside critical sections! What happens inside the critical sections is situation dependent system overhead: it does not really "belong" to the activity of the process in which the critical section occurs.

Finally, we know how to interpret the evolution of a sequential process as a path through "its" state space as is spanned by "its" variables. But for this interpretation to be valid, it is necessary that all variables "belong" uniquely to one sequential process.

It is this collection of observations that was an incentive to redo some of our thinking about sequential processes and to reorder the total activity taking place in the system. Instead of N sequential processes cooperating in critical sections via common variables, we take out the critical sections and combine them into a N+1st process, called "a secretary"; the remaining N processes are called "directors". Instead of N equivalent processes, we now have N directors served by a common secretary. (We have used the metaphor of directors and a common secretary because in the director—secretary relation in real-life organization it's also unclear who is the master and who is the slave!)

What used to be critical sections in the N processes are in the director's "calls upon the secretary".

The relation between a set of directors and their common secretary shows great resemblance to the relation between a set of mutually independent programs and a common library. What is regarded as a single, unanalysed action on the level of a director, is a finite sequential process on the level of the secretary, similar to the relation between main program and subroutines.

But there is also a difference. In the case of a common library of re-entrant procedures, the library does not need to have a private state space: whenever a library procedure is called its local state space can be embedded (for the duration of the call) in the (extendable) state space of the calling program.

A secretary, however, has her own private state space, comprising all "common variables". One of the main reasons to introduce the concept of "a secretary" is that now we have identified a process to which the "common variables" belong: they belong to the common secretary.

To stress the specific nature of a secretary, I call her "a semi-sequential process". A fully sequential process consists of a number of actions to be performed one after the other in an order determined by the evolution of this process. A secretary is a bunch of actions — "operators in her state space" — to be performed one after the other, but in an undefined order, i.e. depending on the calls of her directors.

A secretary presents itself primarily as a bunch of non-reentrant routines with a common state space. But as far as the activity of the main program is concerned there is a difference between the routine of a secretary and a normal subroutine. During a normal subroutine call we can regard the main program "asleep", while the return from the subroutine "wakes" the main program again. When a director calls a secretary — for instance when a philosopher wishes to notify the secretary that now he is hungry — the secretary may decide to keep him asleep, a decision that implies that she should wake him up in one of her later activities. As a result the identity of the calling program cannot remain anonymous as in the case of the normal subroutine. The secretary must have variables of the type "process identity" whenever she is called the identity of the calling process is handed over in an implicit input parameters, when she signals a release — analogous to the return of the normal subroutine — she will supply the identity of the process to be woken up.

In real time a director can be in three possible states with respect to his secretaries.

(*a*) "active", i.e. his progress is allowed
(*b*) "calling", i.e. he has tried to initiate a call on a secretary, but the call could not be honoured, e.g. because the secretary was busy with another call.
(*c*) "sleeping", i.e. a call has been honoured but the secretary's activity in which he will be released has not ended.

The state "calling" has hardly any logical significance: it would not occur if the director was stopped just before the call that could not be honoured.

With respect to her directors a secretary can be

(*a*) "busy", i.e. engaged in one of her (finite) algorithms
(*b*) "idle", i.e. ready to honour a next call from one of her directors.

Note that a secretary may be simultaneously busy with respect to her directors and calling or sleeping with respect to one of her subsecretaries.

In two respects, the above scheme asks for embellishments. Firstly, a secretary may be in such a state that certain calls on her service are inconvenient. With each call we can associate a masking bit, stating whether with respect to that call she is "responding" or "deaf". A secretary managing an unbounded buffer could be deaf for the consumer's call when her buffer is empty. Here we have another reason why a director may be in the state "calling": besides being busy the secretary could be deaf for the call concerned. For the reasons stated I have my doubts as to whether this embellishment is very useful, but I mention it because it seems more useful than similar embellishments that have been suggested, e.g. making a secretary responding to an enumerated list of directors. The secretary has to see to it that certain constraints will not be violated, i.e. she may be in such a state that she can not allow certain of her possible *actions* to take place. This has nothing to do with the identity of the director calling for such an action.

A more vital embellishment is parameter passing: in general a director will like to send a message to his secretary when calling her — a producing director will wish to hand over the portion to be buffered; in general a director will require an answer back from his secretary when she has released his call — a consuming director will wish to receive the portion to be unbuffered.

Note that this message passing system is much more modest than various mail box systems that have been suggested in which processes can send messages (and proceed!) to other processes. In such systems elaborate message queues can be built up. Such systems suffer from two possible drawbacks. Firstly, implementation reasons are apt to impose upper limits to lengths of message queues: "message queue full" may be another reason to delay a process and to show the absence of the danger of deadly embraces may prove to be very difficult. Secondly, and that seems worse, with the queueing messages we have reintroduced state information that cannot be associated with an individual process.

From an aesthetic point of view the relation director-secretary is very pleasing because it allows secretaries to act as directors with respect to subsecretaries. This places our processes in a hierarchy which avoids deadly embraces as far as mutual exclusion is concerned in exactly the same way in which mutual exclusion semaphores would need to be ordered in the case of nested critical sections. Whether, however, actual systems can be built up with a meaningful hierarchy of secretaries of reasonable depth — say larger than two — remains to be seen. That is why I called this point of view "aesthetically pleasing".

Finally: I can only view a well-structured system as a hierarchy of layers and in the design process the interface between these layers has to be designed and decided upon each time. I am not so much bothered by designer's willingness and ability to propose such interfaces, I am seriously bothered by the lack of commonly accepted yardsticks along which to compare and evaluate such proposals. My "playing" with a bottom layer should therefore not be regarded as a definite proposal for yet another interface, it was meant to illustrate a way of thinking.

Acknowledgement is due to my former students J. Bomhoff and W. H. J. Feyen and to Professor C. A. R. Hoare from the Queen's University of Belfast.

REFERENCES

Koestler, A., *The act of creation.* Macmillan, New York, 1970.
Simon, H. A., *The sciences of the artificial.* MIT Press, Cambridge, 1969.

SOME BASIC PRINCIPLES IN STRUCTURING OPERATING SYSTEMS

Gerhard Goos

Institut Für Informatik,
Universität Karlsruhe,
Germany

INTRODUCTION

The design of a general purpose operating system consists of four major steps:

(i) deciding which tasks should be carried out by the system and which should be left to the user, e.g. the extent to which data management is considered to be part of the system;

(ii) deciding the types of algorithms which should be used in the system, e.g. the interrelationship between the notion of a job and a process, also the use of the paging hardware;

(iii) establishing the structuring principles of the planned system;

(iv) the detailed elaboration of the algorithms used in the system.

Step (ii) is the responsibility of the design group and should be greatly diminished in future. Presently its necessity stems from our inability to define precisely the scope of the operating system and the needs of our users. Another contribution is our lack of understanding of the implications of certain algorithms in a given hardware and user environment.

Steps (iii) and (iv) constitute the design process itself and are interrelated in content and time. Establishing the structuring principles may be compared to the guidelines for building a house. The latter is based on assumptions of the needs and habits of the future occupants; at the same time it regulates the behaviour of these occupants but the actual properties of the occupants are still unaffected. In the same way principles for structuring operating systems should allow us an overview of the system, to define communication lines or — more generally — interfaces between different parts of the system. They should allow for the division of the system into different modules, and for proving completeness and consistency of the system definition. The resulting structure should serve as a base for splitting the design and implementation into subtasks to be solved by different groups of people. The existence of clear principles for establishing interfaces and the structure of the system as a whole greatly simplifies the communication in a design or implementation group and makes people aware of the global effects of their particular decisions.

Principles for structuring operating systems therefore should be judged according to the following criteria:

— Can it be applied to the first design phase?

— Does it guarantee the completeness, correctness and reliability of the system?

  – Does it provide a base for getting and maintaining an overview on the system?
  – Does it ease the communication inside of the design or implementation group? (e.g. by reducing the amount of information to be distributed).
  – Is it "natural" to think in terms of this principle? (Ease of application, reduction of error.)

While the first questions can be discussed in technical terms, the last question is psychological in nature. Answers to it may depend on the particular people concerned.

This paper resulted from the design of a general purpose system for a Telefunken TR440 multiprocessor configuration. The computer has a paging hardware mechanism with separate page tables for each job. Each page table defines a virtual memory; however, this memory may contain holes and consists of two (possibly overlapping) address spaces which correspond to two addressing modes differing in base address and address limits. The result of a supervisor call in "normal" addressing mode is to switch to the second of these addressing modes called "private" mode. Only a supervisor call in the private mode enters the "supervisor" mode in which addressing is absolute. Thus, the hardware design is based on the assumption that every job has its private operating system executed in private mode. This brings us to our first principle.

NESTING

In designing a large ALGOL-program each outer block defines a new environment for the execution of inner blocks. This environment is established by declarations of variables and procedures and the execution of statements before entering the inner block. It provides data structures, values and new basic operations expressed by procedures – for the inner block.

This interpretation is extended beyond ALGOL-programs by regarding the hardware as the environment of an operating system which itself defines the environment for one or more run-time systems for ALGOL-programs; the run-time system being the environment of the ALGOL-program. By refining the steps we get a sequence of transformations which, starting with the hardware as machine M_0, we can define an ALGOL-program as some other virtual machine M_n. Therefore structuring into layers as described by Dijkstra [2] – [4] turns out to be a slight generalization of the well known principle of nesting.

It should be noted, however, that every system designed using this principle distinguishes in each layer L_i between those (system-) variables and procedures which are visible to the following layers L_{i+k} and those entities which serve merely as technical tools in establishing the desired level of abstraction. Access to the latter should be denied to all processes which do not belong to that layer, e.g. no user job should have direct access to the tables controlling any type of dynamic resource allocation. Within the framework of programming languages this consideration demands a restriction of the scope of certain entities such that they cannot be accessed from inner blocks (in the sense of ALGOL). But neither ALGOL 60 nor any of its successors contains such a feature.[1]

[1] Overwriting of a declaration by a new one should be considered as a dirty trick in this context.

Suppose that we have to construct a system containing two completely different file access methods α and β which are independent. Every process P using a file can select one of these access methods. It is then appropriate to implement α and β in the same layer L_i leaving it to process P to dynamically select that part of the layer which actually should be used. This approach may be compared to a compiling process which dynamically selects certain library subroutines while others are not considered. This example shows that structuring into layers is twofold:

(i) dynamically: In that sense that we can trace a linear sequence of transformations from the top level of abstraction described as a virtual machine M_n back to the basic level M_0. There may exist different machines M_n and different sequences of transformations. It is this interpretation with which we started this section although our arguments did not explicitly mention the dynamic aspect.

(ii) statically: every layer L_i defines a set of "capabilities" $C_i = \{C_{i_1}, \ldots, C_{i,k_i}\}$. Every capability $C_{i+1,k}$ defined by L_{i+1} depends on a set $\{C_{i,j_1}, \ldots, C_{i,j_m}\}$ $m \leqslant k_i$, but possibly $m < k_i$.

The connection between these two pictures is given by the fact that every machine M_{i+1} comprises a subset of C_i not necessarily the full set. M_{i+1} defines a subset C'_{i+1} of C_{i+1} but possibly $C'_{i+1} \neq C_{i+1}$. We therefore get a tree of machines rooted in M_0 and this idea forms the basis for defining recursively (private) operating systems within the more general ones. We have a lattice of capabilities, where $C_{i,j} \prec C_{i+1,k}$ if the definition of $C_{i+1,k}$ depends on the existence of $C_{i,j}$. Moreover for every machine M_{i+1} and every capability $C_{i,j}$ we have the relation "M_{i+1} possesses $C_{i,j}$" or does not possess it.

Obviously in practice there remains the question which subsets of C_i allow a consistent definition of a M_{i+1} (there may be inconsistent capabilities which must not occur in the same machine), and how can we actually prevent M_{i+1} using capabilities it does not possess. Answers to the first question have to be based on an analysis of the meaning of the existing capabilities. The second question requires some form of protection mechanism. Every mechanism useful in guaranteeing file security is applicable. In our system we have found it sufficient and efficient to provide a pattern x for every capability C_i and a key y for every machine M_{i+1} such that $x \wedge y = x$ represents the relation of possession.

PROCESSES

Let us assume for the moment that the program modules are reentrant; hence the question of when and how to share code is irrelevant. Execution of one or more program modules require the existence of an associated data space and of an environment providing certain real or abstract resources, e.g. the use of certain files or I/O-devices, the capability of issuing certain supervisor calls or privileged instructions. This environment is represented by a virtual machine M_i and provisions must be made expressing the capabilities which must be possessed by that abstract machine. Although the existence of a certain data space may itself be seen as a capability provided by M_i. It differs from others since we are interested not only in its existence but also in its internal structure and contents.

Thus, we define a process to be the sequential execution of a piece of program in a given data space on a certain (virtual) machine. There may be more than one process on a given machine M_i; but any other process having the same data space as a given process is part of some larger process which also contains the given one.

Conversely, it follows from this definition that every section of a sequential process must be considered as a sequential process in its own right. This point of view is useful in the design stage where we consider the system as a collection of sequential processes which — depending on their tasks — have to be synchronized, e.g. using Dijkstra's P- and V-operation. As soon as we study the details of the implementation of the synchronization primitives or of any kind of resource allocation it appears that our collection of processes contains some maximal elements which can be identified by the rest of the system; every other sequential process of our original collection being a subprocess of one of these maximal processes. It is important to notice that in structuring operating systems we need both aspects: the sequential nature of a process is needed as a basis for assigning a pseudo-processor (simulated by the existing CPU's) to each process; for running them asynchronously and for synchronizing them; the possibility of identifying a process is needed as a basis to administer the processes. This administration comprises the following aspects:

(i) Scheduling (depending amongst other things on synchronization conditions)
(ii) Identification of the process as a possible issuer or recipient of messages and events in interprocess-communication
(iii) Identification of the process as the "owner" of certain resources
(iv) Accounting.

In fact, the possibility of identifying a process may be regarded as independent from its sequential nature. At least for the purpose of accounting it would be much easier to identify a user job as the owner of all the resources used by its constituent sequential processes. On the other hand, every request for a resource by a job is represented by an action taken by one and only one sequential process. The use of that resource in parallel by any other process must be organized by proper techniques for sharing resources whether the other process belongs to the same job or not. It is this type of reasoning which forces system designers to unify the concepts of a sequential process and an identifiable process into one.

INTERPROCESS-COMMUNICATION

There are four logically different ways in which two processes P1, P2 may communicate with each other in a system structured in different layers:

(a) P1 and P2 communicate by means of P- and V-operations (mutual exclusion). This type of communication required P1, P2 residing in the same layer.
(b) P1 communicates to P2 that it has reached a certain stage in fulfilling its tasks; P2 may wait for that event. Basically this type of communication requires the existance of private semaphores and its implementation contains critical sections in which P1 and P2 access certain state variables. It then follows from (a) that P1 and P2 belong to the same layer. Note that there may be more than one process P1 which may cause the event on which P2 waits ("disjunctive waiting").

(*c*) P1 delegates a part of its task to P2 and waits until P2 has finished the subtask. To distinguish this case from a normal subroutine call we assume that there is more than one process which can call P2 and that P2 contains at least one critical section in which all calls of P2 must synchronize themselves. It follows that P2 must belong to the same layer or to a lower layer[1]: otherwise P1 cannot know anything about the existence of P2.

(*d*) P1 can interrupt P2, i.e. it can force P2 to execute a jump to a label specified by P1. This is the only way in which unexpected events can be communicated from a lower level to a higher level and in which a faulty process can be forced to pay attention to its environment. Furthermore, the speed by which interrupts may be served in contrast to the usual communication methods permits treatment of certain real-time conditions which otherwise cannot be dealt with.

Except in real-time systems, interrupts should be used only to communicate unusual hardware or software conditions, i.e. in error-handling (except if the hardware handles interrupts as an unexpected procedure call with automatic saving of the former process state, cf. the Burroughs B6700 system [1]).

I/O-interrupts should be interpreted as the reactivation of a process which was deactivated at the time of a formerly issued I/O-start. Although this interpretation is very formal it has been shown to be very useful in the design stage (clearly the implementation deviates for reasons of efficiency). Obviously it assumes that the V-operation is implicit in the reactivation of the interrupt-handler. Its removal from the blocked queue is regarded as part of the basic machine M_0 which therefore does not include hardware alone.

There is a similarity between cases (*b*) and (*c*): in case (*b*) P1 "calls" P2 to proceed but in contrast to (*c*) P2 is not requested to send a reaction back to P1. However, in practice most communications P1 → P2 require the existence of the converse communication line P2 → P1 also. It is therefore useful to unify (*b*) and (*c*) by installing a central message-switching system as described by Brinch Hansen [6]. A communication P1 → P2 or a call from P1 to P2 is then described as a "message" from P1 to P2 to which an "answer" from P2 to P1 must be sent later on (the wake up of P1 in case (*c*), the communication from P2 to P1 in case (*b*)). The maintenance of the message-queues which must now exist is done by a process of type (*c*) (from the point of view of the issuer of a message: by a "supervisor call").

From the theoretical point of view it would be sufficient to think of this message-handler as the only process of type (*c*). Theoretically we need the process on each layer and the transfer of a message from P1 to P2 and the corresponding answer from P2 to P1 acts as follows (P2 is assumed to belong to a layer other than P1):

P1   sends the message to the message-handler M1 on its own layer
M1   sends the message to the message-handler M2 on the P2 layer and waits for the answer (or another message)
M2   enters the message into the queue of P2 and waits for the answer (or another message) after having activated P2
P2   sends the answer to M2, reactivating M2
M2   sends the answer to M1, reactivating M1
M1   enters the message into the queue of P1 and activates P1.

[1] Dijkstra calls P2 a "secretary" (cf. [4]).

Of course, this is a theoretical description of what happens. In practice there should be only one message-handler having access to the queues of all other processes.

Actually, our system allows for semaphores and mutual exclusion only. Every other communication is established by the message-handler, by introducing processes of type (*c*) and in exceptional cases interrupts.

Mutual exclusion can only occur for processes belonging to the same layer and every mutex-semaphore can be attributed to shared data, the use of which is either opened or blocked by the semaphore. Consequently all data either belongs to the private data space of a process or is shared among processes of the same layer. The use of data outside the layer to which they belong is only allowed if they are transferred as actual parameters of a call. This subdivision of the system data causes trouble especially in data management, where people liked to intermix data from different layers in one table for reasons of efficiency and security (in the case of warmstarts).

Our message-handler deviates from the one described by Brinch Hansen in that every inspection of an entry in a message-queue automatically implies the deletion of that entry from the queue. The method has been found particularly useful for two reasons:

(i) it allows the construction of a deadlock-finding process for identifying those processes which break the rules of the synchronization game. This process is needed if user processes are allowed to communicate with each other.
(ii) it has been found much easier to think in terms of messages and answers instead of private semaphores and inspection states.

Although it is possible to handle mutual exclusion by messages there was never any doubt in which places messages and in which places mutex-semaphores should be used. This shows that the distribution between the two features is quite natural although they are not logically independent.

Today's experience still shows two deficiencies in the communication system. Firstly there are cases in which messages are sent to a process in a lower layer merely in order to receive an answer in case unusual conditions arise, e.g. the system runs short of disc space. Although this is theoretically correct it has been found to be unnatural. Secondly there are cases in which messages or answers should be received by more than one process, e.g. for performance measurement or accounting. We tried to solve this problem by providing "listener" processes which receive all the messages or answers for a specified internal structure. As a general principle this was later abandoned mainly for reasons of efficiency and logical clarity. It seems to be preferable to have as a third synchronization primitive, "events" as well as mutex-semaphores, messages and answers. Events should be used instead of messages or answers if there is more than one process which is interested in it. Events should be classified to be either irreversible, e.g. completion of a process, or reversible, e.g. the removal of a page from core.

CONCLUSIONS

The principle of structuring a system into layers has been found very successful in obtaining a structural description of the system as a whole. This structure can be determined before clarification of which algorithms should be used to solve the actual problems. Every layer is considered to be a set of algorithms with its data, to be specified in the later design stages. Those processes which form the layer dynamically are selected from the set partly at system generation time, partly at run-time. Provisions can be made to dynamically enlarge the system at every layer except in the basic ones in which basic I/O, process scheduling and dynamic core allocation are established. The use of a message switching system allows the definition of interfaces between layers and processors, independently from the decision of which processes should be implemented by subroutines and which by independently running processes. The latter decision can be delayed until the actual algorithms which should be used are designed. This greatly simplifies the communication in the design group and allows for distributing the design tasks among many people. It is possible to maintain an overview of the system without knowing all the particular constructions used in different parts of the system. It is therefore guaranteed by the structure that the leaders of the design group can investigate the implications of their particular decisions in the context of the system as a whole.

ACKNOWLEDGEMENTS

I have to thank the members of the system group at the Technische Universität München, and in particular Mr. J. Jürgens and Dr. K. Lagally for many fruitful discussions.

REFERENCES

[1]   Burroughs Corp., B6700 Master Control Program, Information manual, Burroughs Corp., Form 5000086, 1970.
[2]   Dijkstra, E. W., "The structure of the T.H.E. multiprogramming system". *Comm. ACM* 11 (1968), 341–346.
[3]   Dijkstra, E. W., "Complexity controlled by hierarchical ordering of function and variability", Report on a conference on software engineering, Garmisch, Oct. 1968.
[4]   Dijkstra, E. W., "Hierarchical ordering of sequential processes". Proceedings of an International Seminar on Operating Systems Principles, Belfast 1971.
[5]   Goos, G., "Communication in process structures". Lecture notes, International Summer School, Marktoberdorf 1970.
[6]   Hansen, P. B., "The nucleus of a multiprogramming system". *Comm. ACM* 13 (1970), 238–241, 250.

DISCUSSION

HOARE: My paper presents a proposal for incorporation of parallel programming in a high level language.

Many language designers accept that the introduction of parallel programming into a language should not entail heavy overheads on programs which do not use the feature; Algol 68 and PL1 were designed on this principle. I've chosen a slightly more stringent condition; they should not involve heavy overheads even on programs which *do* use the feature. Secondly, I maintain that the property of being able to look at a piece of program and tell which variables it changes and uses is a decent property. I wouldn't be prepared to insert extensions or make language proposals for a language which did not aim at this objective.

My design uses scope rules to do two things (1) to enforce certain forms of security by means of compile time checks and (2) to clarify the structure of programs, in particular, the relationships between program and data.

Simula 67[1] uses scope rules for similar purposes in a pseudo-parallel environment but my paper applies them to the problems of critical regions, the access of common data, and communication and co-operation between parallel processes.

One can't achieve all these objectives in a single design, and the one that I sacrificed is breadth of application. Considering the list given in the paper, I would like to say which ones I have reasonably well achieved. This design can be used quite well to take advantage of genuine multiprocessing hardware and to achieve overlap of input/output with computing. It can be used for real time applications where an application is designed as a specific real time program, which needs to branch into parallel actions and synchronize. It is not good for simulation studies because pseudo-parallel programming as implemented in Simula 67 is more suitable for that purpose. It is not useful for combinatorial or heuristic programming in the manner suggested by Floyd[2] (non-deterministic algorithms), because it's much more efficient. The suggested use of parallelism for combinatorial back-tracking programs suffers from the defect that every time the program goes parallel, it makes a copy of the entire machine state; hence each parallel process updates the different machine state. This solves the problem of conflict of data access at a quite unrealistic expense.

Finally, as a result of discussions with Brinch Hansen and Dijkstra, I feel that this proposal is not suitable for operating system implementation. I mention the problem of low-level scheduling or process dispatching and make the entirely unjustified assumption that a rather simple low-level scheduling strategy for allocation of processor time is useful in many circumstances. In operating systems, and certain parts of a real time system where very specialized high-speed response is required, this general purpose implementation technique will not be satisfactory. In fact I have made the same sort of oversimplification when dealing with resource constraint; my proposed method encourages the programmer to ignore the question of which of several outstanding requests for a resource should be granted. Now in general, the density of utilization of a resource should be sufficiently low that the chance of two requests arriving during the critical period of a third process will be relatively infrequent. If it does occur, the relatively simple strategy of granting a resource to the one that has waited longest (first come first served) would seem to be perfectly adequate. In a real time application you would tend to buy enough hardware to ensure that your response times to a given request for use of that hardware will be acceptable. In other words, the answer to resource conflicts can very often be to buy more hardware; and this seems to be, in many cases, a very reasonable answer.

Operating systems have the rather different objective of density of utilization of

[1] Dahl, O.-J., Myhrhaug, B. and Nygaard, K., "The Simula 67 common base language." Norwegian Computer Centre Report, Oslo.
[2] Floyd, R. W., "Non-deterministic algorithms". *J. ACM* **14**, 3 (Oct. 1967), 636–644.

resources. Their objective is, virtually speaking, to overload the resources; to provide more work for them to do than they can reasonably be asked to do. Thus the bottleneck case, where there is genuine conflict for a resource to be used by two programs, is the normal rather than the exceptional condition. Now decisions about which one is to get the resource is the crux of the matter, certainly to the operating system designer. A year ago I would have said this was a very serious criticism indeed of a language proposal that it encouraged the programmer to ignore certain essential problems. I now believe that a language should be usable at a high level of abstraction, and at high levels of abstraction it is an excellent thing to encourage the programmer to ignore certain types of problem, in particular scheduling problems. He should be concerned only with the logical structure of his program; the co-operation and the synchronization of his processes; and he needs the conceptual apparatus to ignore the really tedious details of scheduling; of deciding between two waiting processes which of them should get the resource. However, at a lower level of abstraction a means must be provided to express these decisions, the conditional critical region is a sufficient tool for expressing scheduling decisions of this sort also, but it may be for this purpose inferior to other methods.

One criticism due to Dijkstra, is that when designing algorithms and techniques for sharing a single resource among a number of different processes, the program for doing this should belong to the resource (which is a single object) and this program should regard the customers as separate nameable objects which can be looked at and dealt with by the scheduling process. It does seem slightly inappropriate to ask the individual processes, who are not really supposed to know of each other's identity, to perform their own scheduling by a form of ritual gesturing.

This is illustrated by the example of the spaghetti eaters. Here we have expressed quite a complicated scheduling decision by surrounding a genuine critical region with respect to a resource (the resource conflict for forks) by a pair of small critical regions with respect to certain common administrative variables. Now this seems to be conceptually incorrect. Firstly, the close relationship between the allocate and the release critical regions is not very clearly expressed. Even more important, it is not clear, when all these three critical regions are written in a row, that the middle one is the only one that is important at this level of abstraction and the two small regions which guard the entry and exit to the critical region, are relevant only at a different level of abstraction. It is essential for the correct working of the guarded critical region that the guardians operate in a grain of time which is an order of magnitude smaller than the original grain of time in which the major critical region, the eating of the spaghetti, occurs. If you find that you are spending more time protecting your resources than using them, this would be practically and conceptually wrong. Whatever the level of abstraction, the guardians, which sit at the beginning and end of every critical region, only work because they occur in a grain of time which is smaller than the grain of time in which the central part of the critical region works.

The solution is that the guardian critical regions which do the complex scheduling around a major critical region should be textually separated from the critical regions with respect to a resource. These should be brought out in what Dijkstra calls a "secretary" and I call a "monitor", and it is intimately associated with the resource in question. This is important because the scheduling decision cannot always be expressed by means of a single Boolean expression without side effects. You sometimes need the power of a general procedural program with storage in order to make scheduling decisions.[1] So it seems reasonable to take all these protecting critical regions out, and put them together and call it a secretary or monitor.

There is one additional feature of the critical region philosophy; and that is, the actual use of the resource inside a critical region is protected by a *compile time* check. This prevents you from using the resource outside the critical region, and thereby protects against certain forms of interference. It is possible to maintain this aspect of my proposal to give security, and at the same time permit scheduling decisions to be taken by a secretary, so that you apparently get a combination of the advantages of both. But this would be wasteful. A successful secretary has the property that it always tries to move the machine away from the boundaries imposed by resource constraints. It will begin to detect that there is a high demand for a certain resource, and will attempt to steer its customers away from the resource boundary it seems most likely to bump into. As a result it will also, almost inevitably, have the good property of preventing that boundary from ever being passed. If you look at the example of the dining philosophers you will see that it is logically impossible for two philosophers ever to use the same fork. This is guaranteed by the run time check which is imposed by the secretary, and therefore the compile time check, which also involves run time action, is unnecessary and redundant. This is a nasty fact of life which makes it difficult to nicely reconcile the benefits of the Dijkstra secretary with the benefits of the critical region and the conditional critical region.

RANDELL: It's very difficult to disguise the fact that processes do have identities, and that process identity is a concept that has to be dealt with explicitly. The idea that mutual exclusion is recursive is very important and this can be implemented either by the notion of a secretary or, even by the notion of P and V. I prefer the notion of a secretary. The idea of a secretary preventing boundaries ever being hit at all depends to a large extent on the secretary's foreknowledge of the director's future behaviour. In many cases this can at best be statistical, but to assume that her work is only to make sure that deadlock could never occur is a considerable over-simplification of the problem.

GOOS: Your method implies that there are no global procedures which are shared by different processes.

HOARE: Yes, there are no procedures with global variables.

GOOS: That is a very severe restriction in practice.

HOARE: A process which calls a global procedure effectively updates any variable updated by that procedure. If that procedure itself updates global variables then these global variables are indirectly updated by the process. If the procedure is shared between two processes, and updates global variables, then obviously there is a potential interference between these two processes which is ruled out by my insistence that processes be non-interfering, except inside critical regions. Obviously if the global procedure does not alter variables global to itself, it can be shared. If one wishes to use a procedure which updates globals, the procedure call must be a critical region, and then we have conceptually something rather different from a pure procedure. We have a procedure, each of whose calls as it were updates itself, and this is logically rather a different entity to the sort of procedure that can be more easily shared. So to some extent you are really describing a secretary.

[1] A proposal which makes this possible is made in Brinch Hansen, P., "Structured multiprogramming (Invited paper, *Comm. ACM*, 1972.)

GOOS: Suppose you have a file consisting of thousands of records and this file is a resource, and more than one process wants to access it. Synchronization should take place at the record level to decide whether a certain record can be accessed. It's practically impossible to use normal synchronization techniques to regulate this, as it would involve the creation of thousands of private semaphores, and the number will vary. It is better to have a model in which more than one process accesses the same resource, and to have some refined means for guaranteeing that they do not access it at exactly the same moment.

HOARE: I did make the proposal towards the end of my paper that any variable, even a component variable, could be protected by being called a resource. The intention is that this variable should be protected in the same way as a simple variable, by means of attaching a semaphore to it. Now I don't understand why (perhaps because I haven't implemented it) you can't afford to have a lot of semaphores. There are ways of implementing semaphores in which you can afford to have an arbitrary number of them in the computer.

GOOS: If the number approaches some thousands it may be difficult to handle them and it creates a problem somewhere else in the resource allocation.

FRASER: There now seems to be two different styles of producing not only an operating system but anything which has to handle asynchronous events. One seems to involve multiple invocations of the same procedure and then the use of critical regions within that procedure in order to provide some sort of serialization. The other style has to do with the maintenance of queues of messages and a single invocation of a procedure which processes a queue and, presumably, this procedure can see the whole queue while it's going on. The same applies to file systems which either process a queue of file access requests or invoke the file management procedure every time a file access request is made, depending on how your operating system is organized. If we consider the technique of applying interlocks on files so that no two people can simultaneously update one file, we find that the interlocks should be applied serially in time. It is, of course, possible to provide this facility in both forms of implementation, but it is easier to optimize when handled by a single sequential process.

If you are going to have a system which handles asynchronous processes, and if these processes are going to go into wait status, then it is important that they should be in a tidy state while they wait. The cross section of the information which records their state should be kept small. Such is usually the case with the queueing system but not with the critical region system.

Turning now to the question of the hierarchical structuring of programs which is raised in both Goos's and Dijkstra's papers: I have noticed that those people who can write programs which work and are robust in a changing environment are those people who can express themselves and their ideas in an organized fashion on paper. However, what Dijkstra preaches is not only that we should cultivate the ability to express ourselves on paper in an orderly form. What he really requires us to do is to organize our thoughts. A program is an assembly of abstract notions dreamed up for the purpose of solving a particular task, and much of the programming activity is a matter of self-organization. The significance of Dijkstra's writing is that he is trying to bring into existence a study of form.

So far I've talked as if the operating system was going to be written by one person. If you are going to manage a group of people then the constraints become even more complicated. However, when we talk about the advantages, for example, of using the scope rules to determine who may and who may not operate upon an item of data it seems like a management operation, either with respect to one's own activities or a group. The privacy mechanism which we have in the file system at Cambridge is not hierarchically based; the list of permissions which are stored in the system are not a hierarchy but a network of interconnections. In any organization the only person who sees a hierarchy is the managing director who likes to think in terms of single lines of authority. In practice there is a lot of interplay between components of any one organization, and although the technique of using scope to control or determine the possibility of access is an important idea, I don't think that all protection should be handled by this technique.

The thing I like about the conditional critical region is that it is a control structure which is compact and may help to reduce the amount of undisciplined control transfers in a program.

BRINCH HANSEN: We now have a multiplicity of proposals for synchronization, such as P and V on semaphores, conditional critical sections, message passing and the monitor concept. These proposals can be judged on the basis of whether they permit you explicit control over complicated scheduling decisions, in which case I prefer the monitor concept. They can also be judged by the extent to which they simplify your understanding or the formulation of correctness in programs, and I would like to judge the proposals in that light.

Starting with semaphores and using Pascal[1] for illustration: you can assign an initial value, c, to a semaphore; it is then assumed that the only operations performed on the semaphore will be P and V. If you stick to these rules the primitives P and V ensure that $i \geqslant 0$, remains true. Dijkstra uses this to prove the correctness of the implementation of critical sections by a pair of P and V operations and to prove the correctness of the producer and consumer problem. Some time ago I proposed a structured notation for critical sections in which you could declare a variable x as being an arbitrary Pascal variable of type T, shared. This means that it should only be accessed inside a critical section associated with that data structure x. You must now imagine that the compiler will allocate a variable x of type T and associate an anonymous semaphore S with that variable. The construction for critical sections now looks as follows:

$$var \ x: shared \ T$$

$$critical \ x \ do \ S(x)$$

where S(x) is a statement operating on x.

It is an axiom about this construction that only one process can refer to x at a time. At compile time you can check that the variable x is only referred to within statements of this type.

Now consider private semaphores declared explicitly

$$var \ x : semaphore$$

Habermann proposed that associated with each private semaphore there are three integers: W, the number of times you have successfully completed P or wait operations, and S, the number of times you have successfully completed V or *signal*

[1] Wirth, N., "The programming language Pascal". *Acta Informatica,* 1 (1971), 35–61.

operations. There is also an initial value C. The invariant relation maintained by the P and V operations is then

$$W (V) \leqslant S (V) + C(V)$$

i.e. the number of signals W(V) consumed cannot exceed the number of signals S(V) produced plus the number of signals C(V) initially available. This definition of semaphore properties greatly simplifies the proof of correctness which Dijkstra has in his paper.

One problem on which I have been considering using the above tools is that of readers and writers. It involves to classes of parallel processes sharing a single resource under the following constraints. More than one reader can share the resource but writers demand exclusive access to it. Furthermore, you have the priority rule that as soon as a writer wishes to write he should be permitted to do so as soon as possible, but pre-emption of readers is not permitted. I found a very nice program for doing this and wrote down an informal correctness proof which turned out to require fifteen pages explanation, which I thought was due to the intricate scheduling rules. However, using the conditional critical sections proposed by Hoare I found I could write down a solution requiring only half the statements and variables. The solution was so evident that a proof was felt to be unnecessary, this I guess is characteristic of all good programs, they are self-evident. The complexity of the previous proof was due to the use of semaphores.[1]

A very frequent requirement is that a process wishes to use a resource under certain conditions. So, using critical regions and semaphores, you enter a critical section and look at the shared variables to see whether you can use that resource. If a certain condition, B, is fulfilled then indeed you can reserve the resource, and perform a signal or V operation on a semaphore S. Otherwise you indicate your request for that resource and leave the critical section and wait outside on semaphore S. This is a construction which anyone who has used semaphores will find himself using time and time again. If you use Habermann's definition you can state the proof of correctness in terms of the number of times you have successfully completed signal and wait operations, but the difficulties of expressing this proof are twofold. First of all, in order to wait for the resource I have to leave the critical region, otherwise another process can't get into the critical region to release the resource and signal that I can continue. Inside my critical section I make certain assertions about the state of affairs. Some assertions are based on variables which belong to that critical section; they hold unconditionally, because I'm the only one inside that critical region. Other assertions are based on the relationship between the number of signal operations performed on the semaphore and the number of wait operations completed. It may be that while I'm making these assertions another process is in the middle of a wait operation, so I do not know precisely when these assertions hold. Dijkstra refers to this in his paper I would call it the split critical region problem; you are forced to leave the critical region to wait for a condition which strictly speaking is part of your critical region.

The other problem is that since you will be woken up by another process which is releasing the resource, in order to make sure that you are indeed only proceeding when condition B is true, you will have to examine all possible critical sections to

[1] Brinch Hansen, P., "A comparison of two synchronizing concepts", *Acta Informatica*, 1 (1972), 190–199.

ensure that they only signal the semaphore S when you have expressed the desire to do so, and condition B holds. But if you use Hoare's construction

with V *when* B *do* S[1]

you can directly see that statement S is executed only when condition B holds. I don't have to inspect to other critical sections and see that I only proceed under condition B. Furthermore, other processes which release this resource do not have to be aware of the fact that there are some processes which might want it provided condition B holds. You don't have the responsibility for waking up other processes; this is also implicit in the construction.

The reason this construction hasn't been invented before is Dijkstra's well motivated statement that busy waiting should be avoided like the plague. Nobody can deny that Hoare's construction will sometimes have the effect that you tentatively enter the critical section and find that condition B doesn't hold. Then you leave it until another process successfully completes a critical section, after which you wake up the former process and let it evaluate condition B again. It is hoped that this amount of re-valuation can be held within reasonable limits so that one can benefit from the conceptual simplification of conditional critical sections without too much loss of efficiency.

GOOS: Structuring an operating system is like building a house. First, you construct a skeleton which to some extent regulates the behaviour of the future occupants of the house; but this does not dictate how many rooms are in the house and the size of these rooms. The principles of a structured system are not intended to be algorithms, but rather principles with which to construct the system, and to regulate communication lines between the different parts of the system.

Consider the principle of nesting a block in Algol. An interesting application occurs if you use a certain block to establish procedures and certain data structures, which are used in some of the inner blocks of that program. This leads to the structuring of programming systems into layers, with interfaces between these layers, e.g. each block constitutes a layer. None of the known programming languages allows you to quote variables and structures, which are the sub-layers of the inner block from the layers above.

The structuring of an operating system leads to a linear sequence of machines. Each one constitutes a virtual machine which has certain properties overriding certain hardware properties; and the next machine is built on the basis of the previous one. The sequence appears as semi-ordered, in which we have on one layer several different machines implemented, using the properties which are provided by the underlying layers. Some of the inflexibilities and deficiencies of a virtual machine can be remedied by introducing principles which govern the use of the different capabilities introduced by each programming layer. For instance, this can be achieved if you have a means of protecting against the use of certain system functions, by providing a set of alternatives, such that everyone can use one of them, but not all of them.

The programming layers of an operating system, give rise to at least one set of co-operating processes. This means that we can split the processes into at least two sets which do not communicate; such splittings are layered in the system. The term

---

[1] I have suggested an additional facility for waiting at the end of a critical region:

with V *do* S *await* B.

"process" is used with two different meanings. Firstly, as a sequential process; and if we have another sequential process containing the first one then it's perfectly all right, it's just an extension. Secondly, as some unit which is specially scheduled, i.e. it the owner of certain resources. These different meanings create confusion; especially when implementing processes in the form of a subroutine called by some other process. It's satisfactory if the process takes over all the resources, perhaps adding some data. However, when we consider scheduling it causes difficulties, because usually the called process takes over the priorities of the calling process. This may cause some high priority job to be stopped, waiting on a low priority job, which is calling some system process.

If you have a two-processor machine, it very often happens that you have two different processes running on the processors and calling the same process. You must therefore install some means of synchronization between the two processes, between the calls of the process. In doing so, it is as if you had made one separate process of the whole thing, scheduled in itself. How can one process ask another process to perform certain functions and how can two different processes communicate with one another? We decided to use the normal semaphore techniques only for mutual exclusion purposes. We avoided the use of private semaphores by using messages in most parts of the design, as proposed by Brinch Hansen. This gave us a means for calling one process by another process.

The splitting of the system into layers enables you to use semaphore techniques in that layer only; since you have no possibility of synchronizing two processes in different layers. The use of a message switching system enables you to communicate between the different layers of the system. It was a mistake that we did not use events as a means of communication. The process which causes the event does not have any knowledge of the other processes which may be interested in that event. A reason for introducing events can be seen from the following example: if you want to have a monitoring process to look after the system and extract information from it, then allow the process to receive every message and answer which is switched between processes. It has therefore a complete picture of the dynamic interrelations between the different parts of the system. However, message switching doesn't allow you to send a message to the normal receiver as well as to the special process which monitors the system. On the other hand, if you construct the system with the help of event variables it is possible to have two different receivers. I am not yet convinced whether messages or events are the best means of communication. I feel, however, there should be some restriction placed on the programmer when deciding.

The result of the application of these principles enables us to split the design into sub-tasks so that people can work on their own, providing the means of communication is established.

VINCE: In your event scheme, when an event is caused and a number of processes are waiting, do you inform the highest priority waiting process or the process which has been chronologically waiting longest?

GOOS: We inform all processes because they may have all started independently.

HARTLEY: I think the basic co-ordinating mechanism should include all the possibilities and that the system designers should use whichever one they need at a particular time.

VINCE: Supposing you're using events from lower level software which communicate a termination interrupt, you don't want to go and wake up every process.

HARTLEY: This is just an example that disproves the rule, just because we're not being wide enough or explicit enough.

RANDELL: Every time we take a decision we are putting some of the past behind us and cutting off the possible future decisions we can take. Part of the process of design involves taking these sort of decisions, realising what was lost and hopefully what was gained.

NEEDHAM: You mentioned the question of a language difficulty. Possibly a little restriction of the scope of certain entities, so that they can't be accessed from inner blocks, and so forth, would be helpful. One has the appearance of a difficulty if one uses a language which doesn't have a facility like that; but can it really be important? It will only be important if you are relying on the scope drills of your language and the fact that your programs will all be compiled by an authorized compiler for that language, to give you the kind of protection which ought to be done by the hardware anyway.

GOOS: Sometimes we have to get the protection by hardware. In a normal programming language you can get the kind of protection you want by separately compiling different parts of the program.

MONITORS

Due to the widespread interest expressed in the monitor concept a special session of the Seminar was arranged. An account of that session now follows.

HOARE: The monitor or secretary concept, like all important programming ideas, is something which people have been using all the time but have only just realized it. A monitor is a high-level language construction which has two properties which are not possessed by most monitors as actually implemented in machine code. Firstly, like all good programming ideas it can be called in at several levels: monitors can call other monitors declared in outer blocks. Secondly, the use of the high-level language feature enables you to associate with each monitor the particular variables and tables which are relevant for that monitor in controlling the relative progress of the processes under its care. The protection, which prevents processes from corrupting this information and prevents monitors from gaining access to information which has no relevance, is established by Algol-like scope rules. Also, it appears that by use of semaphores and references it is possible to implement a monitor in a reasonably efficient fashion. Brinch Hansen will present a simple example of the use of a monitor in order to program a semaphore. This is purely an academic exercise so don't be put off by its simplicity.

BRINCH HANSEN: Suppose you have a set of processes and a monitor — a dormant process consisting of non-reentrant procedures which can be called by the processes. Now there will be parameter passing between the processes and the monitor, with different formats depending on the procedures called. You can imagine the calls as a queue of messages being served one at a time. The monitor will receive a message and try to carry out the request as defined by the procedure and its input parameters. If the request can immediately be granted the monitor will return parameters in the same message record and allow the calling process to continue. However, if the request cannot be granted, the monitor will prevent the calling process from continuing, and enter a reference to this transaction in a queue local to itself. This enables the monitor, at a later time when it is called by another process, to inspect the queue and decide which interaction should be completed now. From the point of view of a process a monitor call will look like a procedure call. The calling process will be delayed until the monitor consults its request. The monitor then has a set of scheduling queues which are completely local to it, and therefore protected against user processes the latter can only access the shared variables maintained by the monitor through a set of well defined operations as the monitor procedures.

As an example, imagine you have a monitor consisting of two actions called *enter* and *leave* critical section as follows:

monitor enter, leave	1
var R: enter *ref*; Q: *queue of* enter *ref*; free : Boolean;	2
when enter (P) *do*	3
if free *then* {free := false ; continue (P)}	4
else put (P) in (Q) ;	5
when leave (P) *do*	6
{*if not* empty (Q) *then* {select (R) from (Q); continue (R)}	7
else free := true ;	8
continue (P)}	9

My example is highly unrealistic because there are no parameters, and parameters are what makes this concept interesting. Local to the monitor I have declared the shared variables it is in charge of. A variable R which is a pointer or reference to one of the transactions invoked by calling the *enter* procedure. Since I want to be able to delay processes and schedule them according to my own rules I postulate a data structure Q. The elements of this data structure are references to calls of type *enter*. Also I have a Boolean free which describes whether the critical section is open or closed.

So now I have inside the monitor a declaration of what to do when various interactions are caused. You can imagine the monitor as a dormant process which is waiting on a hidden message queue, the moment you invoke an interaction it will recognize the type of the interaction (*enter* or *leave*) and switch to the relevant statement [3 or 6]. So when someone is trying to enter a critical section the following happens; if the section is free then change *free* to false and allow the process which invoked this transaction, identified by variable P, to continue [4]. Associated with each call to the monitor is a reference to a particular transaction (defining a set of parameters, and the identity of the process that called that interaction). This reference is assigned to the variable P on either entry to the monitor [3, 6]. If, however, the critical section is closed I put the reference P to that interaction in the queue Q and terminate the monitor action. As soon as you terminate a monitor action it will return to the point where it is waiting for the next interaction to occur.

Suppose we have now reached the stage where a process leaves its critical section. If the queue of references is not empty then select any process from that queue, according to your own rules, and assign the reference to the transaction you have selected to the variable R [7] ; and enable the corresponding process to continue. If nobody is waiting to enter a critical section we now define that it's an open critical section [8] and finally we allow the process which left the critical section to continue also [9].

So what you have inside a monitor is a set of actions associated with shared variables. Suppose you have to prove that if you enclose a critical section with "enter" and "leave" calls this achieves mutual exclusion. You'll find that the proof depends essentially on the fact that the shared variables are accessed only by the enter and leave actions. The monitor ensures that shared variables are *only* accessed through well defined operations. Apart from that, since you are trying to perform explicit scheduling, you normally need variables of type *process reference*. I did not point this out in my example, since I was able to hide the process identity as part of interaction references. Should you want to be able to recognize processes and favour some of them more than others, you must introduce variables of type *process reference* and a standard procedure which says "Please give me the identity of the process which invoked this particular interaction".

RANDELL: Surely a process calling a monitor gives it one message and then has to stop; the fact that you can shuffle these references doesn't destroy the one-to-one relationship between processes and messages, so that the monitor can think in terms only of the messages.

BRINCH HANSEN: It can be argued that you always have somewhere in a monitor a data structure which describes the resources and the capability of a process. What you want is a direct means of identifying a process whenever it invokes something. But there are cases in which you want to concentrate on the type of the interaction rather than the specific process which is doing it, and for that the abstraction of an interaction reference is the proper one.

HOARE: I have a technical solution which would make it possible for processes to pass their identity as part of the message without realizing it. A monitor needs to associate with each process certain facts about the process which in the process itself ought not to or doesn't want to know. Therefore when you declare a monitor you declare the shape of the messages that you're prepared to receive and hand back. At the same time you could declare that some of these messages are implicit. When a process is created, values are assigned to these hidden variables which will be effectively part of every message that is passed to the monitor, and the monitor can store results in this variable too. The reason for this is to implement process queues and tables, which are mappings from processes on to certain facts like priorities, time so far, etc., which are needed and which would be difficult to implement unless you could use part of the process work space to hold these items.

RANDELL: That's made the case for process reference, but what about message reference?

BRINCH HANSEN: If you go down to the level where you have to worry about the identity of processes then things get very detailed indeed, so I'm preserving an intermediate abstraction called a transaction for two reasons. One is that there are cases in which the scheduling rules depend only on the kind of transaction you're doing and not on the identity of individual processes. Secondly, since you need to have the concept of being able to return parameters at a different time from that at which the monitor is originally called, you need the concept of storing the identity of where these parameters should be transferred back to as part of the working space of the process which falters.

RANDELL: And you still have the one-to-one correspondence.

BRINCH HANSEN: Yes. One point which worries me about the monitor concept is that it isn't altogether clear that this is the equivalent of the

with C *do* S construction.

It's a horrible mess if you want to be in control of scheduling rules. I can't really seriously defend the monitor concept, as Dijkstra does, as a better way of structuring the simple cases in which you can live with Hoare's construction

with C *when* B *do* S.

RANDELL: It ought to be best to program the monitor, and afterwards you don't let people look inside it and they're protected from whatever is there.

GOOS: Can I implement this by subroutines or does the monitor have to be a separate process present in the process dispatching table?

HOARE: It doesn't have to be in the process dispatching table. It could take over the identity of the process that called it.

BRINCH HANSEN: That gets confusing when you have a situation where you have nested monitor calls. I think it's more natural to say that each monitor has a private semaphore associated with itself rather than saying it somehow takes over the identity of the calling process. When you first call it, it pretends to be you; but a little later it says "Ah, you're not worth talking to", and then puts you in a queue and pretends to be someone else. Later when someone else calls to release a resource, is the monitor, part of the person who calls or the one whom it is reactivating?

HOARE: A monitor has an inherently higher priority, and perhaps for this reason should be regarded as a process separate from the processes which call it.

HARTLEY: Can you describe it as a separate process but it's one level up? There are different levels of processes.

HOARE: Yes.

VINCE: My idea of the dormant process was something that was invoked for emergency action. What I'm concerned about is the overhead of entering a monitor, in order to claim the semaphore or go through a critical section. In operating systems the critical sections are something like ten machine code instructions long because you are just updating a central system table and we can't afford enormous overheads for this.

HOARE: We do not use monitors to implement semaphores: we use semaphores to implement monitors. This was wholly an educational example.

RANDELL: You could use a monitor to create a semaphore but it would be a much smaller monitor, at least conceptually. But inside the smaller monitor you'd realize you'd need a critical section and therefore you need some semaphore concept on it. Eventually you're going to get down to an electronic switch; conceptually there is complete division all the way down to the hardware level.

HOARE: Yes. If you really cared which of the processes waiting for a semaphore actually got it, you'd have to write it like that.

VINCE: There is still one question to do with the length of the critical section. By what criteria do we choose to interact with the schedulers? A critical section might be so long that if interrupted in the middle, say, by a low priority process we might be holding up a high priority process: perhaps we should have told one of the schedulers about this, so that the low priority process could be continued in spite of the fact that there are other high processes which can still go.

GOOS: It's my experience that you must interchange the priorities and later on re-set them, otherwise you waste too much time.

HOARE: One of the attractions of the monitor is that priorities do not have to be passed, and that when properly used the simple technique of giving the monitor higher priority than all those processes which it controls will always be adequate; because the proper use of a monitor involves the fact that you are only spending a very small proportion of your time at the higher level inside the monitor. If you don't obey this principle, you are then going to need another monitor to schedule the entries of the monitor.

BRINCH HANSEN: The difficulty with a classical "monolithic" monitor is not the fact that while you are performing an operation of type A you cannot perform another operation of type A, but that if you implement them by a single critical section which inhibits further monitor calls then the fact that you are executing an operation A on one data set prevents all other operations on completely unrelated data sets. That is why I think the ability to have several monitors, each in charge of a single set of shared data, is quite important.

STORE MANAGEMENT
TECHNIQUES

Speakers: R. M. McKeag and C. A. R. Hoare: "A survey of store management techniques."
A. Alderson, W. C. Lynch and B. Randell: "Thrashing in a multi-programmed paging system."

Replier: N. Vince.

In absentia: C. Bron: "Allocation of virtual store in the T.H.E. multiprogramming system."

A SURVEY OF STORE MANAGEMENT TECHNIQUES
PART ONE

C. A. R. Hoare and R. M. McKeag

Department of Computer Science,
Queen's University,
Belfast

1. INTRODUCTION

Before embarking on the survey it is desirable to give an indication of what will be taken to be the functions and objectives of store management.

1.1. Store

The word "store" stands for the sets of stored information that can be more or less directly or randomly addressed by a running program. Excluded from this concept is the storage of material which is made available to a running program by input instructions, or which is altered by means of output instructions.

1.2. Functions

The functions of a store management system are the scheduling and allocation of storage to various purposes at various times on various physical devices. The physical devices which come under the control of a store management system will include *main storage*, that is, core store or some other immediate access store, and also, sometimes, *backing storage*, on drums, discs, or sometimes even on magnetic tape. However, backing storage is included in a store management system only insofar as it temporarily holds information which when accessed by a running program is normally resident in main or immediate access storage.

1.3. Objectives

The objectives of store management are to obtain high efficiency of resource utilization and a satisfactory performance in the overall aims of the computer installation. It is not therefore surprising that the technique to be chosen for store management should be closely dependent on the exact nature of the workload of the installation and on the particular characteristics of the hardware available.

2. THE EMPTY MACHINE

In order to clarify an understanding of store management, the survey starts with the null case in which there is no store management at all — the empty machine. Storage in main store is allocated wholly and permanently to a single user program; and if backing store is available information is transferred only by explicit transfer instructions from that program.

Figure 1 shows how main store can be represented

Figure 1. The empty machine.

pictorially in the case of the empty machine; the lowest address is zero and indicates the top of the available store, and the highest address is typically (say) 8191 referring to the bottom of the store. The word length is assumed to be sufficient to hold a typical addressed instruction; on the smallest computers such as this one it will be from twelve to eighteen bits, but on the larger computers it is more likely to be between twenty-four and thirty-six bits.

It is obvious that no special hardware is needed to implement the technique; a straightforward homogeneous addressing space for the main store is all that is required.

The advantages of this scheme are, firstly, that it provides maximum possible flexibility. It is a truism to say that any application that can be programmed with the aid of sophisticated store management software can also be programmed on the empty machine — since this software itself must ultimately be programmed on the empty machine. However, once a proportion of the storage capacity of the machine is occupied by administrative software, the range of applications to which the machine can successfully be applied must in principle be reduced — although it is to be hoped that there will be compensating advantages.

A second advantage is maximum simplicity. The programmer has direct access to the hardware addressing system of the computer; there is no need for him to study an elaborate software interface; and in the event of error a dump of the store will be directly comprehensible to him. Few software systems can offer the user as simple an interface as that presented by the addressing structure of core storage — although again it is to be hoped that the software will make the machine in other ways easier to use.

A third and obvious advantage in minimum cost, both in implementation and use. There is of course no administrative overhead. The reason for mentioning these obvious points is that they set the ultimate standards against which any software store management technique must be judged, even though these standards can in principle never be reached and may even be surprisingly difficult to approach.

The main immediate disadvantages of the empty machine follow from the fact that if it costs you nothing it gives you nothing in return. The empty machine is particularly inappropriate to an installation that is expected to run a multiplicity of more or less separate jobs at various times since it provides no job sequencing method and cannot make an efficient transition between one job and the next. Furthermore, if several jobs individually require only a small proportion of machine resources (i.e. storage, processor time and peripherals), the empty machine provides no method whereby the several jobs may share these resources by being simultaneously run (multiprogrammed) in the same store.

These disadvantages tend to confine the application of the empty machine approach to small computers with usage dedicated to a single project, for example, on-line monitoring or control of an industrial process. Since the computer is small and wholly and permanently devoted to its single function, there is no purpose to be served in introducing software techniques to schedule and allocate storage between various functions at various times. This, the simplest of techniques, has been used satisfactorily on such machines as the IBM 1130 and the Elliott 905.

3. SINGLE USER, PLUS RESIDENT

The next store management technique is one which attempts to tackle the problem of automatic job sequencing between separate jobs of a batch. This is accomplished by a software routine which resides permanently in main storage, shown in figure 2 at the bottom end. Such a routine is variously known as a monitor, a supervisor, or an executive; however, the more neutral term "resident" is used here, to indicate that it resides permanently in store. The greater part of the store is allocated as user space to the current program. The resident is normally entered on the completion of each program; it clears down the store and then loads the next program for running; it also re-initializes peripheral equipment.

Apart from the primary function of ensuring a smooth transition between programs, many resident software routines are designed to perform useful functions even during program execution, for example, the monitoring of machine and program errors, administration and monitoring of peripheral transfer instructions, and the establishment of operator communication and control. However tempting it may be to add further useful functions (for example, standard mathematical functions, sin and cos, etc.) to a resident routine, this temptation should be resisted. There is little useful purpose in giving resident status to an item of software that could equally well be included by the programmer in his own user area; to do so would be to reduce the area available to users who do not want the included function and thereby to reduce flexibility rather than increase it. The inclusion of a given function can be justified only by the fact that it is required by the job sequencing routine itself, as well as by the vast majority of jobs which are run under its control.

The special hardware required by this system is merely a fixed protected area at one end of the store, commonly the bottom end. While instructions are being executed within this area, any location of store may be altered; but an instruction obeyed from the user space may change (or jump to) only a location which is also in user space; thus the only way in which control can be passed to the protected area is through its

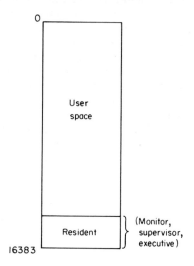

Figure 2. Single user, plus resident.

first instruction. The reason for this protection is to ensure that when a user's program contains an error it cannot corrupt the resident and thereby make it impossible to secure smooth transition to the next job.

The advantages of the single user plus resident approach are that it achieves the efficiency of automatic job sequencing while retaining most of the simplicity and low cost of the empty machine.

Like the empty machine, this technique makes no attempt to secure resource sharing by multiprogramming. It also fails to alleviate one of the major inconveniences of batch processing – the poor turnround. Turnround is defined as the interval of time between the submission of a job to a batch processing installation and the availability of the results of that job. The reason for the poor turnround is that once a long job has been loaded into the machine, any small jobs which are submitted later must wait until that job is completed, even if a later job is much shorter and can be completed in only a minute fraction of the time that it spends waiting.

In spite of its disadvantages, this store management technique has for many years been widely used on small and medium machines [1]. It is used particularly for scientific batch processing, an area in which the absence of resource sharing is not a serious drawback since most jobs use all of the available processor time. An early example of the use of this technique was in the FORTRAN monitor system for the IBM 7090; and it is still probably the most suitable choice for machines of similar hardware characteristics, for example, the cheaper scientific configurations of Elliott 4130 or ICL 1900.

4. MULTIPLE USER, FIXED PARTITIONS

The third store management technique is designed to permit resource sharing by allowing multiple users to be accommodated together in main storage; they are separated by partitions which are fixed at least for the duration of a job. Figure 3 shows the store split into three partitions, for three separate user programs, with a small area of unused storage between two of them, and a protected area for the resident as before. The method of operation is to allow one of the user programs to be executed until it is held up by an input or output instruction and then to transfer control to another program that is not held up. In this way the resources of central processor, main storage, and peripheral equipment can be shared among several programs running in apparent simultaneity.

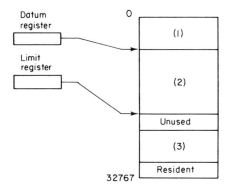

Figure 3. Multiple user, fixed partitions.

While a given program is being executed all storage locations outside the area allocated to it must be protected from it. This may be accomplished by a pair of hardware registers, shown in the figure as the *datum register* and the *limit register*. Each address generated during execution by, say, program number 2 is compared against these two registers, if it is found to be outside them control is automatically transferred to the resident which will terminate the offending program. When control passes from program 2 to one of the other programs, the resident must adjust the contents of these registers accordingly. These registers are one of the possible special hardware designs capable of ensuring variable upper and lower protection limits. In addition, it is desirable to include in hardware or software some mechanism for the relocation of programs so that each program may be written as though it were positioned at the first location in store. Thus the programmer does not have to be concerned about which partition his program will be executed in.

An advantage of the multiple user approach is obviously that it permits resource sharing. An additional advantage may be obtained if each partition is used to run a whole batch of jobs; and small jobs are allocated to one partition while larger jobs are allocated to another. In this way many small jobs may be executed during the running of a single long job, thereby achieving significantly improved turnround.

One of the disadvantages of this scheme is obviously its increased complexity; the job sequencing and general administration of multiple partitions are considerably more complex than the same tasks for a single user. In addition, each user is confined to only a part of the available main storage and must fit into an area between fixed partitions. This means that there will in general be unused space within each partition, whereas larger programs which could be run under the single user scheme now cannot be run at all.

The multiple fixed partition technique is applicable primarily on medium to large computers which have sufficient main storage, peripherals, and processor speed to make resource sharing worthwhile [2]. It is particularly suited to commercial data processing and to tasks which make heavy use of peripheral transfers and relatively light use of main store. The inflexibility of the partitions can best be tolerated in an environment in which the workload can be planned in advance to fit within partitions; or in which the users are willing to place their jobs into rigid categories in accordance with the amount of time and space used.

5. MULTIPLE USER, VARIABLE PARTITIONS

This store management technique is an extension of the last one to permit more flexible and efficient use of the main store. Again there is a protected area for the resident, and the rest of the store is partitioned into several areas with a job running in each, the jobs being multiprogrammed as before. The difference is that the resident can adjust the size of the partition to suit the job to be run in it; it may also adjust the number of partitions.

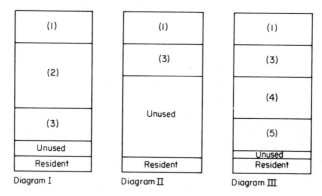

Figure 4. Multiple user, variable partitions.

Figure 4 shows, in the first diagram, two small jobs and one large job being multiprogrammed; there is, generally, a portion of unused storage as the partition sizes are tailored to the needs of the programs. Whenever a program is deleted, as in the case of program 2 in the second diagram, the remaining programs are moved up in the store thus making all the unused space contiguous. The resident may then assign storage to a further job; in the third diagram two small jobs replace the former long one.

As with the fixed partition technique the special hardware required includes some form of variable protection limits; some form of hardware program relocation is also required since dynamic relocation by software is not generally feasible.

An advantage of this scheme is its increased flexibility: the resident adjusts the partitioning of the main store to accord with the workload, perhaps having many small areas or a few large ones. Unlike the fixed partition approach, very large jobs may be run by having just one partition. In general, however, several programs will be in the store simultaneously, thus permitting a satisfactory degree of resource sharing.

The main disadvantage is the time spent in moving programs around the store as other programs are completed. In addition, the resident has to ensure, before moving a program, that no input or output operation is taking place into or out of that program's area; waiting for the termination of such an operation adds to the delay in re-arranging the partitions. The increased flexibility of the variable partition approach has to be paid for by a corresponding increase in complexity in the store management algorithm.

The characteristics of the multiple user, variable partition technique make it suitable suitable for batch processing on medium to large computers with sufficient resources to make sharing worthwhile [3] ; it is, for example, suitable for university batch processing environments with many small jobs and a few large ones. The overheads due to the movement of programs would, however, make the scheme unsuitable where jobs are only in core for a relatively short time such as in a multi-access environment. The technique has been used in the basic multiprogramming system of the ICL 1900 series.

6. ONION SKIN ALGORITHM

All the techniques described so far have operated exclusively in main storage, and have assumed that any use made of backing storage is accomplished by explicit input and output or overlay instructions. The remaining techniques under survey attempt to make automatic use of backing store in order to achieve fast turnround and high efficiency of main store utilization, without the inflexibility of having to keep all the programs currently being executed permanently in main store.

The first such technique is known as the Onion Skin Algorithm, for reasons that will become obvious shortly. The best way to consider this algorithm is as a development of the multiple partition approach, but with all the partitions superimposed upon each other rather than occupying disjoint storage regions. The obvious paradox is resolved by ensuring that all information belonging to the program that is currently in control will be in main store, and information belonging to programs not in control will be saved on backing store and will be copied back to main store when the time comes to run the corresponding program. The Onion Skin Algorithm is designed to ensure that the amount of information to be written away and copied back will be kept to a reasonable minimum: when space in main store has to be made for a program shorter than the current program, the tail end of the longer program is kept in main store while the shorter program runs.

Figure 5 depicts the store at a time when there are four programs, numbered 1 to 4, in various stages of execution. The amount of store used by each program is shown by the corresponding column on the right: the white section of the column indicates the part of the program currently in main store, and the shaded section indicates the part currently held on backing store. The shortest program, number 4, is currently in control and therefore wholly in core store. An upper limit register is set to protect the area of storage that it is not intended to use. The next shortest

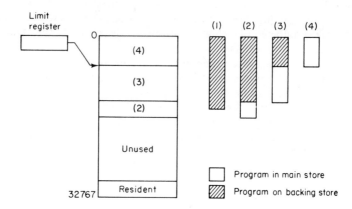

Figure 5. Onion skin.

program, number 3, has its first half written away to backing store to make room for the currently running program, as shown at the top of the corresponding column. However, the second half of program 3 still remains in main store waiting for its turn of execution. Similarly, program 2 is partially held on backing store and partially in main store. Program 1, however, has been wholly written to backing store to make room for program 2. Thus the main store is likened to an onion, whose inner heart is constituted by the running program, and whose outer skins are formed by the leftover remains of currently dormant programs. Note that the area beyond that used by the largest program remains permanently unused.

The Onion Skin Algorithm itself is shown in the Appendix. The maximum number, N, of programs under consideration at one time would typically be, say, four; the procedure to run program i is shown: the first part is concerned with saving the information which currently occupies the upper portion of main store, the second part restores the first portion of program i for execution.

The only special hardware required by this algorithm is an upper protection register which can be set by the resident.

One advantage of the method is that it provides fast turnround for short programs. It is particularly efficient if the shorter programs also require less running time than the large programs, which is quite commonly the case. It also permits the running of programs which require up to the whole available user space — although it loses its main efficiency if it has to deal with too many programs of this size.

The disadvantages of the Onion Skin Algorithm are threefold. Firstly, it does not permit effective resource sharing on a multiprogramming basis; each change of program requires access to a backing store, so that it is not feasible to change programs whenever a program is held up by a peripheral device. It is, however, perfectly feasible to change over when a program is waiting for a response from a human user, communicating for example by means of a multi-access typewriter. Secondly, there is no overlap of dump or restore operations; each change of program requires that the processor be wholly occupied in the transfer of information to and from the backing store. Since no user program is wholly in store during this period, it is not possible to overlap the transfers with useful work. Thirdly, there is some waste of space in cases where there is no program present which uses the whole of available store.

The application of the Onion Skin Algorithm is best suited to medium sized machines with a highly variable workload that cannot be planned or categorized in advance. Typical of such a workload is the one that is generated by a multi-access operation; and this algorithm was first devised and is successfully used in the Project MAC Compatible Time Sharing System at M.I.T. on a somewhat modified IBM 7094 [4]. The selection of this algorithm was originally considered as a simple and temporary expedient; subsequent experience has shown it to be just as effective for its purpose as other far more elaborate systems which were supposed to supersede it.

7. MINIMUM OVERLAY

The next algorithm, the minimum overlay, is a slight modification of the Onion Skin Algorithm and can be used on machines which provide the possibility of both lower and upper protection. This permits a relaxation of the rule that each program's area starts at the beginning of store, and enables the program as a whole to be located in any convenient consecutive area. This area is selected in such a way as to minimize (or even eliminate) the amount of main store that is allocated simultaneously to several programs, and thereby minimize the amount of material to be dumped and restored on program change. Hence the name of the algorithm – minimum overlay.

Figure 6 shows a picture of the store during execution of the same four programs as before. Program 1 was the first to be initiated, and was located at the beginning of store. When program 2 was loaded it went into the end of the store so as to minimize the amount of overlay in the middle; however, a small region at the end of the first user's area had to be dumped. On loading program 3 it was impossible to avoid dumping a large part of one of the two programs already present; however, the algorithm ensured that the area that was already used twice was not overlaid yet again. A similar consideration caused program 4 to be placed at the beginning of store, and, as it happens, this program is able to co-exist wholly in main store with program 3.

The administration of this scheme requires that the main store be split into small regions of uniform size, which may be called *page frames,* and which constitute the standard unit of allocation and release. The unit of program held in such a frame is called a *page,* and a typical size for a page would be 1024 words. To implement this technique two tables must be set up: the overlay count table, which contains for each page frame in main store the number of programs that are currently using that frame, and the owner table, which contains for each page frame the number of the program which currently occupies that frame in the main store. The first of the two minimum overlay algorithms in the Appendix shows the procedure required to initiate a run of program i; all the page frames which this program requires in store are scanned; if the current owner is already program i, nothing needs to be done. Otherwise, the information is dumped onto the backing store region of its current owner, and program i's information is input.

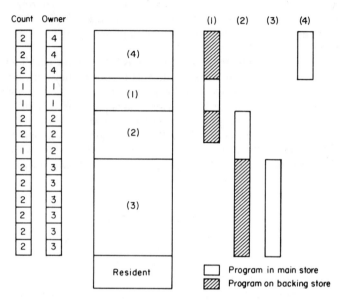

Figure 6. Minimum overlay.

The main objective of the minimum overlay technique is to find an appropriate location in store for a new program entering execution. This is achieved by the second of the two algorithms in the Appendix. The concept of a *weight* attached to each program has been introduced here: for important software routines (for example a filing system, a loader, or a compiler) it is important that they should have the best possible chance of residing in main storage together with programs submitted by users. To discourage these programs from being overlaid, they are given a high weight W, and a page frame occupied by such a program will be treated for overlay calculations as if it were equivalent to W distinct unweighted programs.

The effect of this algorithm is to compute the result of locating program i in any of its possible positions. It adds up for each possible position the sum of the overlay counts for all page frames that would be overlaid yet again by the incoming program, and it chooses that position which minimizes the sum. It then increments each affected overlay count by W units.

The special hardware required by the minimum overlay technique is the same as that required by the multiple user, fixed partition technique, namely upper and lower protection in units of at most a page, which can be varied by the resident; and relocation of programs by hardware or software. The advantages of this scheme are firstly, that it will permit a certain amount of resource sharing when there is sufficient main storage. However, programs that make use of peripherals should in general be loaded prior to the normal user programs, and should be given a high weight, to ensure that they will remain in store permanently, except when a very long program is loaded.

Secondly, the technique would permit one program to be executed while another is being brought in, provided that the two programs do not overlay each other; this achieves overlap of dump/restore with useful computing.

The disadvantages of the technique are shared by all the methods described before. The first disadvantage is that each program must be wholly in main store while it is being run; this is serious in those cases when a program only in fact uses a small proportion of its stored information before being thrown out of main store again. Unless special care is taken, this could be particularly common in cases when a user is communicating with a program on-line. Secondly, no two programs are permitted to share identical stored material. This may be desirable when the programs use the same subroutines, for example standard mathematical functions, binary/decimal conversion, etc. Thus there is the possibility that the algorithm may laboriously copy these subroutines onto backing store in order to make room to copy these identical subroutines into main store again as part of the incoming program.

The application of this technique is the same in principle as that of the Onion Skin Algorithm – medium-sized machines and a varied scientific workload. It was devised originally by Edgar Irons and implemented on a CDC 1604 at the Institute for Defense Analysis at Princeton as part of a successful fast turnround system which ran for a number of years [5]. An outstanding feature of this system was that the size of the resident, including disc input/output routine, was kept to a thousand words, and the entire remainder of the core (with the exception of 500 words) was available as user space.

8. DELAYED SWAP

This approach to store management overcomes one of the disadvantages that has hampered all the previously described techniques, namely that programs could not be run without being wholly in main store. In this technique all of the available store is again divided into page frames, but the pages of each program are not brought into core until they are actually required. Thus, in the example in figure 7, program 4 has only needed to use its first page so far, while program 3 has used most of the pages in its allocated space.

In order to implement this technique, an owner table, as used in the previous technique, is required with an entry for each page frame in main store (excluding the area occupied by the resident) to indicate the number of the program currently using that frame. When a program is to be run, the resident assigns it an area containing the required number of pages, sets a special hardware register, which may be termed the "current program register", to the number of the program, and the program starts execution with just its first page in main store. At each address generated by the program, the hardware checks the contents of the current program register against the corresponding entry in the owner table; if the numbers match then the required page is in main store and the instruction is obeyed; if they do not match then an interrupt occurs, the resident reads down the required page of the program into the frame in main store, the entry in the owner table is re-set by the resident and the instruction in the program is obeyed.

Before the new page is brought into main store the resident must decide the fate of the page currently occupying the area; three cases may be distinguished. Firstly, no program may have been using the frame in which case the new page may be read down immediately. Secondly, a page of some other program may have been occupying the area and, if if has been changed during its sojourn in core, it must be swapped onto backing store before the area can be re-used. Thirdly, a page of another program may be occupying the area but may have remained unchanged while being in main store, in which case it may be over-written without first being dumped as a copy already

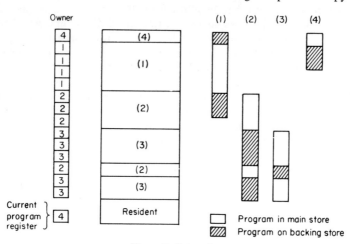

Figure 7. Delayed swap.

exists on backing store. To distinguish between the second and third cases a "write bit" must be associated with each page frame of main store: this is cleared by the resident whenever it loads a page of program into main store, then, whenever a location in the page is altered, the bit is set by hardware; when the page is to be overwritten the resident examines the write bit to decide whether or not the page must first be dumped. If the hardware does not provide these write bits then the third case must be assimilated to the second.

The special hardware required to implement this technique must include some means, such as that described above, to lock out individual pages from access by the current program; a write bit for each main store page frame is an advantage. Some form of program relocation is also required, either by hardware or by software.

The main advantage of this scheme is that the amount of traffic from backing store to main store is usually considerably reduced. This Method is used in conjunction with some other technique of store allocation; the most suitable technique is the minimum overlay algorithm, which gives a fair chance that a main store page frame being used by one program will not be needed by another. It is, however, of particular value in cases where a program does not use all of its available main storage area while being executed in core; this is most often the case with multiple-access programs which, in most systems, are frequently dumped onto backing store while awaiting some human response, thus considerably boosting the traffic between the stores. It is also useful when there is a significant program-testing component in the workload, since programs which fail early during their execution will only ever have allocated to them a small proportion of the storage they thought they were going to use.

The main disadvantage of the technique is that a particular page frame may happen to be heavily used by two or more programs, while other frames happen to remain unused. Thus the pages occupying this frame will be constantly swapped in and out of main store, even though there would have been space in main store for several of these pages to be accommodated simultaneously. The solution to this problem was suggested by Irons: all that is necessary is to adjust the frequency of program change (i.e. the time-slice) to ensure that time spent on swapping is kept to an acceptable minimum, say 10%. Further disadvantages are, of course, the increased complexity and reduced speed of the hardware which has to check the page's presence with each store access, and also the increased complexity of the resident.

The technique is a somewhat generalized form of that used in the Titan operating system at Cambridge University [6] where it has been found that extremely economical use is made of the core store. However, in the Titan, the space saved is used solely for buffers and supervisor overlays; it is not re-usable by a second user program. It might also be found suitable on computers like the IBM 360 series, which appear to have the requisite hardware protection facilities.

9. CONCLUSION

It has been shown that, for each of the techniques that have been examined, there is some machine or application for which it is the most suitable approach to store management, and for which its simplicity, relative to more sophisticated schemes, is an advantage that outweighs its limitations.

This paper omits the more complicated and flexible techniques, such as segmentation and paging, in which a program need not occupy one contigous area of physical store. We believe that it is important that those who advocate such systems should be aware that highly satisfactory results are obtainable in a wide variety of circumstances by very much simpler and less expensive techniques.

APPENDIX

Programs are given here for two of the techniques described in the paper; firstly, the Onion Skin Algorithm is listed, and then two programs are given for the Minimum Overlay technique: the first procedure shows how to initiate a run of the program belonging to user i, while the second shows how the location for the program i is chosen.

1. Onion Skin Algorithm

DATA:

let N be the maximum number of programs at one time.

upper [i] : for $0 \leqslant i \leqslant N-1$, gives number of words of store required by program i; set to zero when there is no program i.

lower [i] : for $0 \leqslant i \leqslant N-1$, gives lowest address of program i that is actually in main store; set to upper [i] when program is wholly on backing store.

32768xi: the first address of the backing store space allocated to program i.

PROGRAM: to run user i

for j :=0 *step* 1 *until* N−1 *do*
    if lower [j] < lower [i] *then*
        begin m:=min(lower [i] , upper [j]);
          output(lower [j] , m−1) to:(32768xj + lower[j]);
          lower[j] := m
        end clearance of space;

    input(0, lower [i] −1) from:(32768xi);
    lower [i] :=0;
    set limit register to upper[i] .

2. Minimum overlay

2(*a*). DATA:

let P be the number of words in a page.
lower [i] : for $0 \leqslant i \leqslant N-1$, gives the lowest address allocated to program i;
upper [i] : for $0 \leqslant i \leqslant N-1$, gives the highest address allocated to program i.

PROGRAM: to run user i

for j :=lower [i] *step* P *until* upper [i] *do*
    if owner[j÷P] ≠ i *then*
        begin output(j,j+P−1) to:(32768xowner[j÷P] + j − lower[owner[j÷P]]);
          input(j,j+P−1) from:(32768xi + j − lower[i]);
    end;

set datum register to lower [i] ,
    and limit register to upper [i] .

2(*b*). DATA:

let S be the size of store in pages.
let L be the length of the program in pages.
overlay count [p] : for $0 \leqslant p \leqslant S-1$, gives the number of programs sharing page frame p. let W be the "weight" of the program, i.

PROGRAM: to locate program i.

    sum:=0;
    for p:= 0 *step* 1 *until* L−1 *do* sum:=sum+overlay count [p] ;
    pos:=L−1; min:=sum;
    for j:=L *step* 1 *until* S−1 *do*
      begin sum:=sum−overlay count [j−L] + overlay count [j] ;
        if sum<min *then*
          begin pos:=j; min:=sum *end*
    end;

    lower [i] := (pos−L+1)xP; upper [i] := posxP+P−1;
    for j:= pos−L+1 *step* 1 *until* pos *do*
    overlay count [j] := overlay count [j] + W.

REFERENCES

[1] Lynch, W. C., "Description of a high capacity, fast turnaround computing center", *Comm. ACM* 9, 2 (February 1966), 117–123. [A successful operating system, using the single user plus resident approach to store management, is described.]

[2] IBM Corp., "IBM System/360 Operating System. Concepts and Facilities". IBM form C28-6535-5 (July 1969). [Section 5 describes the methods of core allocation that may be used in OS/360. These are the single user plus resident technique, the fixed partition technique and the variable partition technique to which may be added a program swapping strategy.]

[3] Knight, D. C., "An algorithm for scheduling storage on a non-paged computer". *Computer Journal,* 11, 1 (May 1968), 17–21. [The method described is the multiple user, variable partition technique extended to make use of program swapping.]

[4] Corbató, F. J., Daggett, M. M. and Daley, R. C., "An experimental time-sharing system". *Proc. AFIPS, SJCC,* 21 (1962), 335, Spartan Books, Baltimore. [A description of the Project MAC compatible time-sharing system for which the Onion Skin Algorithm was devised.]

[5] Irons, E. T., "A rapid turnaround multi-programming system". *Comm. ACM,* 8, 3 (March 1965), 152–157. [The minimum overlay technique is explained in the context of the operating system for which it was designed.]

[6] Hartley, D. F., Landy, B. and Needham, R. M., "The structure of a multi-programming supervisor". *Computer Journal,* 11, 3 (November 1968), 247–255. [Includes a description of the store management technique used in the Titan operating system at Cambridge University – it is the basis of the delayed swap method and is superimposed on a multiple user, variable partition scheme. The design of the algorithm is affected by some unusual hardware features.]

A SURVEY OF STORE MANAGEMENT TECHNIQUES
PART TWO

1. INTRODUCTION

The final section of the first part of this paper described the Delayed Swap technique of store management, which attempted to economize on main storage in a multi-programming environment by permitting a program to run even when only a part of its code and data were present in main store, the remainder being held on backing store until required. When the running program first refers to an absent page, the reference is trapped, and the program is suspended until the required page is brought into its proper position in main store.

One serious disadvantage of this technique is that when a page is brought into store, it must go into a fixed position in order that it may be correctly addressed by the running program. But it may happen that this particular position is also being used intensively by some other concurrent program. One of the two programs will then have to be suspended for relatively long periods, since otherwise their competition for a particular page frame in store would cause intensive *thrashing*, i.e. continuous movement of pages between main and backing store, preventing both programs from making satisfactory progress.

A second problem, for which none of the previously described methods gave a satisfactory solution, is that of sharing common code (or data) among several concurrent programs which happen to wish to access it at the same time. It is certainly more economical to avoid making two copies of such material, either in main store or on backing store; and much preferable to permit several programs to share the same copy.

A final disadvantage of all previously described techniques is that they do not readily cater for programs that are too large to fit wholly into the main store of the computer. For such programs, the programmer must himself organize transfers of data and code between main store and backing store. Apart from the inconvenience to the programmer, the programmer's own use of backing store may seriously interfere with that of the store management system, since it will use the channel capacity at unpredictable times, and pages involved in a transfer must be locked down in main store for the duration of the transfer; and then they run the risk immediately afterwards of being copied *again* to backing store by the automatic system. Furthermore, the programmer has no clear guidance for planning whether to squash his program into the smallest amount of main storage at the expense of frequent backing store transfers, or whether to use rather more store and rather less transfers. Indeed, such a decision should depend on the behaviour of other programs with which a given program is running, and the programmer in general has no way of knowing this; thus only the automatic store management system can make sensible decisions in these circumstances.

2. PAGING

A solution to the first problem is to permit any incoming page to be held anywhere in main store where an unused space (known as a *page frame*) can be found (Kilburn *et al.* [9]). If this solution is adopted, the pages of a program will come to be scattered throughout the store of the computer, in positions that cannot possibly be known to the individual program. Consequently, the addresses used by the program (known as *virtual* addresses) must all be automatically translated to actual addresses before they are used to reference the store, in a manner rather more complicated than the mere addition of a single datum register. Effectively, this is accomplished by holding a table containing many datum registers, one for each page used by the program. If a page is currently in main store the corresponding table entry contains its main store address, and if the page is currently on backing store, the entry contains the backing store address; evidently it must also contain a tag to distinguish between the two cases. Thus, figure 1 shows the structure of storage for a particular user.

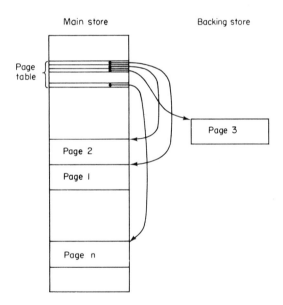

Figure 1. Storage structure for paging

2.1 Address mapping

When a program is running, a hardware register points to the start of its page table. Figure 2 shows how each address used by the program is split into two parts: the more significant part indicates the number of the page, and the less significant part gives the position of the word within the page (this assumes, realistically, that the size of the page is an exact power of two). The page number is used to index the page table to obtain the appropriate entry (known as a *page descriptor*) which contains a tag and a datum field; the tag indicates whether the required page is in main store and, if it is, the datum points to the page frame. Finally, the word number is concatenated with the page frame number to access the required main store location. This address mapping is carried out on "paged" computers by the hardware as an indivisible part of every access to store by a user program. Should an address mapping fail because the tag is set "absent" then an interrupt known as a *page fault* results so that the resident's store management routine can read the required page from backing store, before permitting the access to proceed.

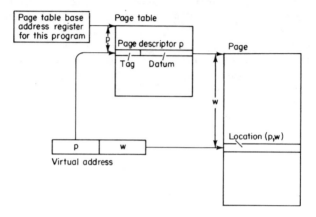

Figure 2. Address mapping for paging.

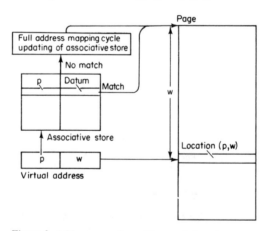

Figure 3. Address mapping with associative store.

It can be seen that this mechanism results in two store accesses for each reference: one to the page descriptor and the other to the required location. To combat this it is usual to have a few (say 8 or 16) fast *associative registers* containing copies of the page descriptors most recently referenced. Each associative register consists of two fields: the first (the associative field) containing the number of a page in main store, and the second containing the address of its associated page frame. Whenever an address is generated it is split into page number and word number, and the page number is compared, simultaneously, with the associative fields of all registers. Most references will be to pages that have been recently referenced and so generally a match will be found and the address of the page frame obtained. If no match is found it is necessary to look up the page table to obtain the page descriptor which is loaded into the associative store after unloading some other descriptor: this is usually done on a first in, first out basis.

When the processor is handed over to another program the associative store must be cleared since the new program will refer to a different set of pages using the same numbers. On a genuinely multiprocessing computer, there should probably be a separate set of associative registers for each processor, since to share a single larger set is likely to cause hardware delays owing to increased size, physical distance from the individual processor, and extra complexity of distinguishing ownership of an individual register.

2.2 Sharing of pages

The main characteristic of paging (as compared with the previously described techniques) is that each program may make use of a number of non-contiguous regions of main storage. This flexibility is often used to enable two or more programs to share one copy of, say, a library routine, as depicted in figure 4.

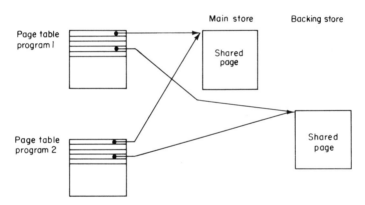

Figure 4. Sharing of pages

The main problem arising from sharing is that when a page is transferred from main store to backing store *all* pointers to the shared page must be updated. Also, whenever a page is brought into main store, each pointer to that page must be updated either when the transfer takes place or when the pointer is next used. Several techniques can be used.

1. The most straightforward technique is to scan all the page tables whenever a shared page is moved. This has the disadvantage of being time-consuming, and is especially wasteful if it is not known whether the page in question is being shared or not. This disadvantage can be mitigated to some extent by chaining together all the descriptors for each shared page – the technique used in the B5500 MCP [5] – thus when a page is moved it is a simple matter to find and update all the other relevant descriptors in turn.

2. Another technique is to keep a separate page table for shared pages. This table, rather than the program's own page table is consulted for all addresses in some fixed range. The disadvantage of this technique is that it forces a fixed and somewhat limited pattern of sharing upon the system, although in a great many environments this is a perfectly acceptable restriction. After all, it is only certain very commonly used library routines that are likely to be in multiple use for any appreciable fraction of time.

3. Yet another technique is to associate one "master" descriptor with each page; any other descriptor for the page has a tag indicating that its datum field is to be interpreted as being the address of the master descriptor. Although such master descriptors must of course be located whenever a program first refers to a shared page, there is the advantage that only the one master descriptor need be updated whenever the page is moved.

4. Another technique is to lock pages in main store while they are being shared. Associated with each page descriptor is a *lock* count which is initially zero, and which is incremented by each program using the page, and which is decremented by each program no longer needing the page. Pages with a count of two or more are never removed from main store. This solves the problem of moving a shared page *out* of core, but not of moving it *in*.

When program or data is to be shared among several programs, it is essential to prevent any of the programs from changing it by accident (or otherwise). The usual method of achieving this is to insert an *access control* bit in the page descriptor, which causes the hardware to inhibit unauthorized alteration of the page to which it points. In an environment in which a shared routine may be a commercial asset, a second bit (obey only) is sometimes provided to ensure that a user program can only execute a routine, and cannot read it as data. This prevents him from making an unauthorized copy. The obey only bit can also be used to protect the user's own code from a crude form of programming error.

2.3 Increased address space

A further advantage of paging is that the writer of a large program need not concern himself with the administrative details of organizing his program as a set of overlays; instead he assigns disjoint addresses to each item of program and data, even if this involves using more addresses than exist in the main store of the computer. Of course, a large program should be planned in such a way that the amount of main store needed at any given time does not exceed the available capacity; otherwise the program, even when executed alone on the computer, will give rise to an unacceptable amount of thrashing. The only cost of this increased addressing space is one extra word for each extra page required.

A programmer can sometimes take advantage of an increased addressing space, even if he seldom or never in fact uses the whole of it. For example, a compiler can allocate quite large areas of store for each of the tables it needs, and so avoid the risk of failure due to table overflow. A high proportion of pages allocated to such a table will in practice be seldom used; but since a page which is never used will never be allocated a place in main store or backing store, the cost is confined to provision of a single extra word in the page table. Sparse addressing can also be used to allocate to each subprogram a very large space of its own, and thereby to bypass some of the expensive link editing, which is a common feature of modern software.

However, if sparse addressing is used systematically, even the cost of the page tables will be unacceptable. A solution to this is to split the addressing space into large *segments*, each containing a number of pages under control of its own page table. A programmer who requires an area of unknown length will always start it at the beginning of a segment. Then the length of the page table for that segment need only contain entries for pages which have actually been used. Of course, a table is now required to hold the addresses and lengths of all the page tables belonging to a program; and this is known as the *segment table*. A register is allocated to hold the address of the current program's segment table.

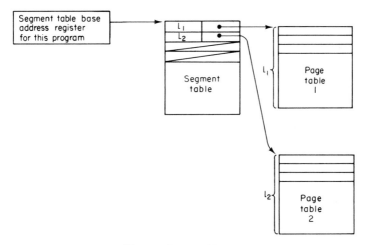

Figure 5. Sparse addressing.

Now the address mapping involves splitting each virtual address into three parts: the segment number is used as an index to the segment table to obtain the *segment descriptor* which points to the page table, if any; this is indexed by the page number to obtain the page descriptor which points to the page frame if there is one, and causes an interrupt to a segment expanding routine if there is not. Each reference thus entails three store accesses and it is important that the mapping be speeded by the use of associative registers or some other technique. Figure 6 shows how the mapping is conducted.

An alternative, or additional, scheme for bypassing the full address mapping cycle is to have several hardware *segment registers* which are explicitly loaded with copies of the descriptors of those segments currently being used; each virtual address then specifies the segment register in place of the segment number; this approach, used on the GE645 computer (Daley and Dennis [6]) enables addresses to be compacted into fewer bits if the number of segment registers is less than the number of segments a program may use, at the expense of causing stored addresses to change their interpretation when the segment registers are reloaded.

The introduction of segmentation of this form involves a considerable increase of complexity, owing to the need to administer page tables of dynamically varying

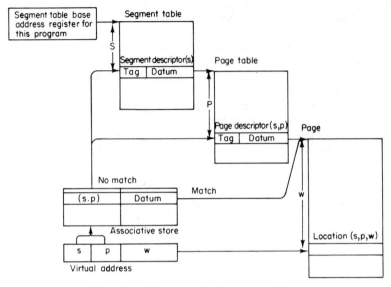

Figure 6. Address mapping for segmentation.

length; and it is doubtful whether in many cases the programmer can take effective advantage of it, since in the last resort, an increase in the size of one segment must be compensated by a reduced size in another. Furthermore, each segment will have up to an entire page unused at the end of each segment. Even an average of half a page unused at the end of each segment is rather expensive if the page size is large and many segments are used. There are cheaper and more effective ways of by-passing the link editor.

2.4 Tree addressing

In paging systems described above, the page descriptors and the page tables are wholly hidden from the user's program, which operates simply on a large linear address space. An interesting variation is to use only a small page table (perhaps only two entries, held in special registers), and to permit the programmer to create, manipulate, and store any additional page descriptors that he may require. Since one or more page descriptors may be stored in a page pointed to by a single descriptor elsewhere, the programmer may build up storage as a sort of tree, which can be pruned or sprout new branches at any point. Such a structure may be useful in setting up "cactus stacks" for the implementation of coroutines or parallel processes in the presence of recursion to an arbitrary depth. It also neatly solves the problem of variable length page tables, by making them the responsibility of the programmer.

The disadvantages of the scheme are:

1. The possibility of taking copies of descriptors involves the full complexity of sharing even within a single program.
2. In a deeply nested tree, every reference to an ultimate component must be made by following the entire chain of descriptors. It is not permitted to store a computed address, since the page may be moved in between accesses.

3. It is essential that no program corrupts any page descriptor. This is usually assured by use of a high-level language, but unfortunately no widely known high-level language permits the programmer to take full advantage of the tree-shaped addressing structure.

This technique is used in the Burroughs B5500 MCP [5], and in the T.H.E. Multiprogramming System (Dijkstra [8]).

3. ASSOCIATED ALGORITHMS

This section describes the algorithms that are involved in the administration of a paging system.

3.1 Page replacement algorithms

The original motivation for introducing the store mapping scheme of paging was to permit freedom in the physical positioning of a page coming in from the drum, so that it is no longer necessary to overwrite a predetermined page, which may happen to be required in store by another program very shortly afterwards. But this freedom brings in its train the responsibility for deciding which page to throw out of main store and overwrite. The algorithm which chooses such a page is known as the *page replacement* algorithm. It is normal practice to choose the next page for overwriting (the so-called *victim*) in advance, so that if it requires recording on backing store, this may often be completed before the space is needed, and the average delay in servicing a page fault is reduced from two transfer times to one.

The "ideal" policy for page replacement is to replace the page that will remain unreferenced for the longest period of time; in practice this is of course not known, so that an approximation must be made: thus the strategy is usually to select some page that, it is expected, will not be referenced for some appreciable time, the choice being guided by knowledge of the current and past behaviour of the programs being run. In order to gain information about past usage of a page, a *use* bit is introduced into the page descriptor. This bit is set by hardware whenever any word of a page is referenced by a program, and is examined and reset at regular intervals by software. Thus it is possible to maintain a reasonable estimate of the interval since a page was last used. In addition, it is usual to associate a *write* bit with each page descriptor, which is set by hardware whenever a program changes the content of any word of the page, and is initialized to zero by software when the page is brought from backing to main store. If it is still zero when the time comes to replace the page, it is possible to avoid a transfer, since the copy of the page already on backing store is still valid. If a "write" bit is not available, the "obey" or "read only" bit may be used for the purpose at the expense of some otherwise unnecessary page faults.

Many different strategies have been proposed for page replacement; some of the more important of them are described below.

3.1.1 *Loop detection*

The designers of the Atlas paging system attempted to select pages for replacement on the assumption that most programs exhibit a tendency to loop (Baylis *et al.* [4]).

Thus they compare the length of time since a page was last used with the length of time that it was previously inactive, and determine whether the loop to which the page belongs appears to be no longer in use; if all pages in main store still seem to be required, the page that will be the last to be referenced, assuming the recent pattern of use to be continued, is overlaid.

To implement this technique the "use" bit associated with each page in main store is periodically read and cleared to see whether that page is still in use; for each such page a count, t, is kept to denote the time since it was last referenced; also a value, T, denotes that page's previous duration of inactivity. When a page is to be replaced, any of those for which $t>T$ can be assumed to be no longer required and thus eligible for removal. Failing that, the page with the maximum value of $T-t$ is selected (excluding those pages currently in use, for which $t=0$), since that is the one that is likely to remain unreferenced for longest. Should all pages currently be in use, with $t = 0$, then there is no suitable candidate for removal although one might choose the page with the maximum value of T.

The cost of the algorithm could be high in a computer having many main store page frames since the values of t have to be updated periodically and there is quite a lot of work involved in selecting a page for replacement.

Such a technique could well be satisfactory when used with long programs which might be expected to obey many loops but it seems unnecessarily complicated for the many programs that do not exhibit such behaviour.

3.1.2 *Least recently used*

This is another technique that attempts to forecast the future behaviour of a program from its past performance. The assumption here is that the longer a page has remained unreferenced the more likely it is that it will not be required again in the near future and may therefore be removed.

As with the last technique, the "use" bit associated with each page in main store is periodically sampled and used to maintain a count, t, of the time that has elapsed since the page was last referenced. When a page is to be replaced the one with the largest value of t is selected.

Almost as expensive as the Loop Detection algorithm, this technique would appear to be applicable to a more general workload. Consequently it is a popular strategy and has been used in the T.H.E. system, amongst others.

3.1.3 *First in first out*

One of the simplest strategies proposed for page replacement is the First In, First Out (FIFO) technique, by which the page which has resided in main store for the longest time is always selected as a victim. This technique may be justified by reasoning that a page that was brought in a long time ago is more likely to be out of current use than one that has been brought in recently. But a further justification is the extreme simplicity of implementation. All that is required is a single pointer which points to the victim. When this victim has been replaced, the pointer is merely stepped on to point to the next page frame, starting again at the beginning of main store whenever it reaches the end. Such a technique has been found to be quite successful on the B5500 [5] .

3.1.4 *The second chance algorithm*

This algorithm is an effective combination of the simplicity of FIFO with much of the predictive power of the Least Recently Used. In this case the same cyclic pointer is used as in FIFO; but instead of always throwing out the next page, the "use" bit is inspected. If it has been set by hardware it is merely reset and the pointer stepped on. But if it is still unset, this means that the page has remained unused since the pointer last visited it; it is therefore selected immediately as the next victim.

If the available hardware does not support a "use" bit then the descriptor's tag may be used instead: on being passed by the pointer the page is tagged "absent" but is permitted to remain in main store; on being passed subsequently the page is removed unless it has been referenced meanwhile in which case a page fault would have occurred and the tag would have been reset to "present".

This technique has the advantage of being cheap to implement. Furthermore, being a reasonably good approximation to the Least Recently Used algorithm, it keeps in store those pages currently in use and disposes of those no longer in use.

3.2 Latency reduction

Each time a page is displaced, there is a strong likelihood that it will eventually require to be brought back again into main store, and this cannot be achieved without cost. The more obvious component of the cost is the central processor time taken to administer the page fault and change programs; but this can usually be kept to only a small proportion of the time taken to transfer a page; and if so, can never be significant. Far more significant is the hidden cost of the *latency,* i.e. the period which a program must wait until the required page is brought into store. During this period the program is unprofitably occupying resources, including main store. In fact, if a program spends more than a small proportion of its time waiting for pages, its actual occupancy of main store (space occupied multiplied by time occupied) will actually be longer than if the whole program were held fully in main store during execution; and thus the use of paging will be actually counterproductive. The extreme situation is reached when pages are actually removed from a program while it is waiting for another page coming in; and when this begins to happen, the system inevitably locks down into a thrashing episode.

It has been suggested that high latencies can be tolerated provided that the degree of multiprogramming is increased to ensure that the central processor is always occupied. In practice, this suggestion is strongly deleterious; high latencies are a symptom of bottleneck in core storage; to load another program intensifies the bottleneck, increases the latencies, and thereby actually *increases* main store occupancy. In fact, the only way of avoiding lockdown in thrashing episode is to *reduce* the number of programs competing for main store; techniques for achieving this are described in the next section, on load shedding.

Naturally, the forced reduction in multiprogramming level is an undesirable admission of failure of the paging system, and should be invoked only infrequently. To ensure this, it is necessary to ensure that the latency delay suffered by each program is kept to a minimum, especially during periods of peak load, when queue-lengths are high, and delays would normally grow unless strong measures are taken to prevent their growth.

3.2.1 *Preselection of victims*

The simplest way of reducing latency times is to select the next victim in advance of its page frame being required, so that if it needs to be written away to backing store this can hopefully be accomplished before the frame is needed, thereby reducing the latency to the one transfer required to read in the new page.

3.2.2 *Drum scheduling algorithms*

The delay involved in using a drum is due partly to the latency time, during which the drum rotates until the start of the required page is under the reading heads, and partly to the actual transfer time. This latency may be reduced if the hardware permits a transfer to begin at several points on the track, and then continue the transfer at the beginning of the page until the revolution is completed. Alternatively, the starts of each track may be "staggered" round the drum, so that at any time a certain proportion of all the pages is approaching the reading heads. Then, when a page has to be written to drum, a free drum page can be selected among those which are currently nearest the reading heads. This technique is used in the T.H.E. multiprogramming system (Dijkstra [8]). Unfortunately, delays due to writing are not in general so critical as delays for reading, since the victim is usually chosen in advance, and in any case, quite frequently does not have to be written back at all.

If each page occupies a complete track, the transfer time will be a whole revolution, and the average latency only half a revolution. A more effective way to tackle the overall delay is to reduce the transfer time. This can be done by increasing the number of read/write heads on the drum which can operate simultaneously, thereby multiplying the transfer rate, and presenting the computer with an apparently increased track size. Now instead of allocating a whole track to each page, many pages will be accommodated on each track, and so the transfer time will be reduced to insignificance in comparison with latency delay. The technique of writing out a page to the most suitable page frame will become even more effective, but there will no longer be anything appreciable to be gained by starting a page transfer in the middle.

But none of these methods can reduce the revolution latency on reading, which will on average be half a revolution. Even worse, if a second program demands a page before the first one has completed the transfer, its expected delay will be even longer; and as more programs join the queue, the problem will get worse still. But as we have seen, it is exactly under these conditions that a paging system must avoid any reduction in efficiency. Thus it seems worth while to introduce a fairly complex technique, which will ensure (up to a certain limit) that latency for each program remains reasonably constant, even when the queue is long. This technique involves reordering the queue so that the demand for the page which is nearest the reading heads always gets serviced first. It is used in the Michigan Terminal System. This means that expected latency for each program remains roughly constant, in spite of the increased queue length.

On a moving head disc, latency delays are very much more serious, and the wisdom of automatic paging methods is open to question. However, on such a device, the importance of optimum scheduling is even greater.

3.2.3 *Prepaging*

So far it has been assumed that a page is not brought into main store until it is actually referenced: this is termed *demand paging,* and necessarily involves an element of unprofitable delay. From time to time proposals are made for the use of *prepaging,* in which a page is brought into main store in advance so that it is present when first required. By reducing or eliminating page waits, not only are resources used more fully, but also the degree of multiprogramming necessary to maintain high CPU utilization can perhaps be reduced, thus further lessening the pressure on the system resources.

In order to ensure that no page faults (or at most very few) occur, it is necessary that the forecast for a page requirement be made sufficiently in advance to enable the transfer to be completed before the page is referenced, but not so long before that the page occupies main store idly for a significant period before it is used. Since the store management routines do not have sufficient knowledge of the future behaviour of the programs, these forecasts must be made by the programs, either explicitly by the programmers or else by the compilers. Backing store devices (especially those with moving heads) have very long mean latency and transfer times when compared with a computer's instruction time, and in practice programmers and compilers are quite incapable of predicting the behaviour of a program over such large intervals. Even worse, the transfer times are subject to high variability, depending for example, on the rotational position on drum, the position of the heads on the disc, and the current lengths of the queues. Furthermore, the rate at which a program will be executed in a multiprogramming environment is unknown at the time the program is written and compiled. Thus even with perfect fore-knowledge of his program's logical behaviour, the programmer can never know how far in advance he should prepage. Thus it seems that prepaging is not only difficult to use but may be actually prejudicial in its effect. The best solution is to use a demand paging system, and to take steps to prevent an excessive rate of page faults, so that it is unlikely that the time that a program has to spend waiting for pages will be more than a small fraction of its overall time in the computer.

3.2.4 *Blocking*

In the operation of a computer, it is sometimes recognized that a currently running program is to be suspended for a relatively lengthy period; for example on initiating an interaction with a human user, or on completing a time slice imposed by a job scheduler, or even on a decision to reduce the multiprogramming level. When such a program is resumed, it would be more efficient to bring into core all the pages which it was using when suspended, since with appropriate drum scheduling it may be possible to do this with relatively short delay, compared with the sum of the delays of bringing the pages in one at a time in the order that the program first references them. This method is used on the EMAP system.

3.2.5 *Chaining*

An ingenious method of permitting the programmer to help the operating system reduce paging delays has been suggested by Michael Melliar-Smith. A programmer naturally splits his use of store into a number of consecutive regions, each of which is occupied by a single subroutine, table, or array. Quite often the pattern of access to each of these regions is such that whenever any one word of a region is accessed, the whole of the rest of the region will be required shortly afterwards. Now if the region extends over several consecutive pages, any page fault for any of the pages will be very shortly followed by page faults for all the other pages. If the programmer were to inform the paging system which pages should be grouped into regions, all these page faults could be predicted, and all the transfers could take place on the occasion of the first fault, with consequent reduction in total delay. This form of prepaging seems more likely to be used effectively by the programmer than one involving explicit transfer instructions; and is especially desirable if the pages are small.

This technique may easily be implemented by associating with each entry in the page table a "chain" bit: this is set if the page lies wholly within a logical region but is clear if the page includes a region boundary. A fault for a page with a set chain bit results in not only that page being read into main store but also the adjacent pages of the region. When a fault occurs for a page with a clear chain bit, it is not known which of the two regions is required so just the one page is brought in.

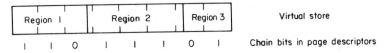

Figure 7. Chaining of pages.

3.3 Load control

As described above, however well designed a paging system may be, there is a limit to the extent to which it can share main store among concurrent programs which make heavy demands upon it. When this limit is passed, the efficiency of the system in economizing main store disappears, and unless steps are taken, there will be an almost permanent degradation of performance, symptomized by excessive thrashing. Even if a paging system spends most of its time in a lightly loaded condition, there must inevitably be occasions on which random coincidence of peak demand drive it beyond the limit; indeed if such occasions are too infrequent, this means that the paging system is not playing its full potential role. Therefore these occasions must be detected, and the load must be lightened by removing a program from the multiprogramming mix. If there is only one program in the mix this program must also be removed; it has evidently attempted to make inappropriate use of more store than actually exists.

Several techniques have been suggested for detecting overload.

3.3.1 *Operator intervention*

A simple solution, used in the ATLAS and T.H.E. systems, is to rely on the operator noticing excessive drum activity, and providing him the facility for aborting or suspending a program, preferably the one which is responsible for the situation. This method appears to be adequate on a batch processing computer, in which the loading is relatively constant and where any peaks are likely to be a result of programming error or malice; but in multiple access a situation, some more automatic load control is desirable. Such a technique must also detect underload, so that a suspended or a new program may be loaded again.

3.3.2 *Virtual/real ratio*

A simple method of controlling the pressure on the main store is to keep a count of the number of virtual pages used by all the programs in the mix. This count may then be compared with the number of real pages of main store available. High and low threshold values of the ratio are used to detect extremes of load, and in the case of over-loading, some of the load is shed and the virtual page count reduced.

The disadvantage of this approach is its assumption that, for a given page fault rate, a program requires in main store a reasonably constant fraction of its total number of virtual pages. While this assumption may be satisfactory in a large computer running many programs, it may well be optimistic for a small mix showing a large variation.

A variant of this technique is used in the Michigan Terminal System on the IBM 360/67 (Arden [2]): programs using more than 12 pages are restricted in number by the imposition of the constraint that if the total number of pages used by such programs exceeds 40, then any further large programs will be suspended.

3.3.3 *Working set*

A number of techniques are based upon the following theory: in order to run without thrashing, each program in the mix must, at any given moment, maintain in main store a *working set* of those pages it is currently using. Thus the store management strategy must in some way identify these working sets and restrict the page replacement algorithm to selecting pages that do not belong to any working set; if there is no such page then recourse must be made to the load shedding algorithm. The way in which these techniques differ is in their attempts to identify the working sets.

This type of technique could be used in Loop Detection when the replacement algorithm finds that all the pages in main store are currently in use. Likewise the Least Recently Used algorithm could impose a lower limit on the length of time that a page has remained unreferenced and invoke load shedding rather than removing a page that has not reached the limit.

Similarly with FIFO and the Second Chance algorithm, the cycle time of the pointer provides an indication of the degree of load on the main store. The time the pointer takes to complete a full cycle of the store is measured and compared with two threshold values. If the cycle time is less than some lower threshold then a program is suspended, or if greater than the upper threshold then a suspended program is resumed or a new job is scheduled. The underload case where the pointer is stationary or almost stationary must also be detected. Denning [7] has suggested that the interval of non-use should be measured in the timescale of the program owning the page, so that programs that are getting only a small share of a multiprogrammed central processor should not be penalized. It is doubtful whether this degree of refinement is necessary.

3.3.4 *Fault rate monitoring*

The most direct way of controlling the load is by monitoring the fault rate. Wulf [13] has used a scheme which may be summarized as follows: the dispatching algorithm maintains damped counts of the time spent servicing page faults, the processor time used, and the input/output channel time used. If the fault time count exceeds some threshold then a program is suspended; if it is less than some lower threshold then a suitable program is resumed or scheduled providing either the processor or the channel is underloaded. Using this technique Wulf virtually eliminated thrashing on a Burroughs B5500.

Techniques that monitor page fault rates appear to be both effective and cheap to use. In using the page fault rate as the control they would appear to be nearer the heart of the matter than those techniques that depend on the interval of non-use.

3.3.5 *Priority ordering*

Another technique used is to order the programs in the mix according to some priority and, when attempting to find a page frame for a program of a particular priority, to ensure that the selected victim belongs to a program of lower priority. For example, in the RCA Spectra 70/46 Time-Sharing Operating System (Oppenheimer and Weizer [11]), in the absence of free frames the lowest priority program is suspended from the mix so that its page frames are freed. This can continue until only one program remains and it has to cannibalize itself. Eventually a program will terminate and the suspended programs can be resumed.

This technique has the obvious disadvantage that those pages that are no longer required by high priority programs are not removed from main store. However, a thorough evaluation of techniques of this type and their problems is now in progress at Newcastle University (Alderson *et al.* [1]).

4. VARIABLE LENGTH PAGES

The main outstanding problem is the choice of a suitable page size. Suggestions for an appropriate size have varied from one to 8192 words. Some machines such as the GE645 have offered a choice of page lengths (64 or 1024 words) and the experimental machine MU5 offers an even wider choice. The real problems are as follows:

1. If the page size is too small, the overhead of page tables increases. Furthermore, when a program comes to need a contiguous region of store consisting of several pages (say a subroutine or an array), this will involve (in the absence of chaining) two or more latency delays; and when this region goes out of use, there will be the overhead on reclaiming each page individually.
2. If the page size is too large, a region of store required by a program may be considerably smaller than a page, or may cross two pages; thus there will be areas of store at the beginning of the page, or the end, or both, which are unused for long periods of time, but which cannot be reclaimed by the paging system owing to the

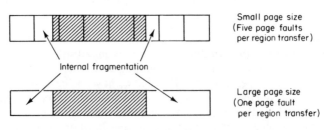

Small page size
(Five page faults
per region transfer)

Internal fragmentation

Large page size
(One page fault
per region transfer)

Shaded region denotes the logical region

Figure 8. Page size and internal fragmentation.

coarseness of its grid. This wasted space caused by the rounding up of store requirements to multiples of the page size has been termed *internal fragmentation* (Randell [12]).

Thus it appears that there are penalties both for making the page smaller than a logical region and for making it larger; and furthermore, the natural region of a program will be of widely varying lengths.

It is therefore a reasonable evasion of the problem of choosing a page size to allow it to vary in accordance with the lengths of the logical regions into which a programmer's use of the store happens to fall. This technique of matching pages with regions may be called *variable length paging* or *segmentation* (but should not be confused with the "segmentation" described earlier for the implementation of large address spaces).

This technique has been used successfully on the Burroughs B5500 [5] : each page corresponds to the main routine or to one subroutine or to a data vector. A maximum page size must be chosen and on the B5500 this is 1023 words (48 bits each).

Unfortunately, the introduction of variable length pages introduces certain additional problems in the implementation of the associated algorithms and gives rise to an entirely new problem; these are discussed in this section.

4.1 Page placement

In fixed length paging, a page may be placed in any empty page frame, but with variable length paging a gap must be found or freed that is large enough to hold the page being brought in. Typically, main store is managed using two chains: one linking together all the used pages in main store and the other linking together all the gaps. There are two main ways of finding a gap of sufficient size to hold a page, Best Fit and First Fit: in the former the smallest gap that is large enough is selected, and in the latter, the gap that is nearest to one end of store. In both cases each unused part of a gap is returned to free store; and any used segment that is freed is amalgamated with an adjacent gap (if any). Although at first sight Best Fit would seem to be the more satisfactory ploy, Knuth [10] has shown that in practice First Fit performs better, the reason being perhaps that First Fit causes the small pages to congregate at one end of the store and the large ones to go to the other, and this minimizes their mutual interference. Experiments (Batson *et al.* [3]) show that the median page size is generally smaller than the mean, so with First Fit the search of the free chain is not, on average, very time-consuming.

Should an attempt to find a suitable gap fail, a page replacement strategy must be invoked. An alternative stratagem is to *compact* all the pages in main store down to one end so as to merge all the gaps into one. On the first occasion that compaction is used it is almost certain to provide a large enough gap, but eventually this will be used up and the page replacement algorithm will have to be invoked. Therefore, unless a program has terminated or released a lot of its pages, compaction will subsequently fail; consequently its benefit is only marginal. Moreover, compaction is a costly manoeuvre, and its effectiveness is reduced if some pages are locked down, because, for example, they are engaged in input/output transfers. Furthermore, unless the system is overloaded, a good page replacement algorithm will tend to remove those pages that are no longer required and which are unprofitably occupying main store. Thus it appears not worth while to invoke compaction at all.

Although a variable length paging system does not suffer from internal fragmentation, there is bound to be wasted space in the form of gaps; this is termed *external fragmentation* (Randell [12]) and may be expected to account for something of the order of 20% of the main store (Batson *et al.* [3]). This space is usually entirely wasted, and does not contain material which is even potentially of value to a running program. There is also the (small) cost of chaining information associated with each used page in main store.

4.2 Page replacement

The remarks made earlier about replacement algorithms for fixed length pages apply equally to variable length pages, as do those on thrashing and its control. It is worthy of note that the crude FIFO algorithm gains in attraction, since the space that it liberates will necessarily be contiguous.

One extra problem does, however, arise when dealing with variable length units of store allocation: whereas a fixed length page may be locked down in main store without adversely affecting the replacement strategy, this is not so in the case of variable length paging. Burroughs' solution to this problem in the B5500 is to use First Fit from one end of store for normal pages, and the same technique from the other end for pages which are locked down, with the proviso that any normal page will be removed to permit a locked down page to reside closer to the appropriate end of store [5].

4.3 Backing store allocation

There is a further difficulty in using variable length pages on backing stores: information is usually split into fixed-length sectors, and reading and writing must begin at the beginning of a sector. Now if the sectors are large compared with a typical region, there will be significant waste of space at the end of sectors; and if the sectors are small, a significant proportion of the space will be taken by the intersector gap required by hardware. However, choice of a suitable compromise here is not too difficult.

4.4 Segmentation plus paging

One way to combat the problems peculiar to the use of variable length pages is to divide each such page into a number of fixed length pages. This technique is essentially that described in section 2.3 for implementing large address spaces. Each segment corresponds to a logical region of the program and is split into a number of fixed length pages which must be small to keep the internal fragmentation low. As with chaining, segments rather than pages are brought in at a time. The cost lies in the extra complexity of the hardware and the overheads of maintaining segment tables as well as page tables.

4.5 Conclusion

In view of these remarks, it appears that the use of small fixed-length pages with chaining is simpler and in no way inferior in performance to variable length pages, provided the necessary hardware (associative registers) is available to "glue together" the disjoint pages of a region, and provided that the administrative overhead is kept low.

5. CONCLUSION

The choice of a suitable technique for store management is one of the fundamental decisions in the design of an operating system. Many different techniques have been proposed, and many have been tried in practice, some with a conspicuous lack of success. Much effort has been expended in the comparative analysis and in the simulation of the various techniques, particularly those involving the use of fixed length pages, but unfortunately without any clear conclusion. The choice of fixed versus variable length pages; the choice of what size a fixed length page should be; the choice of replacement algorithms — in no case has any result been generally agreed.

Thus in place of selection of "best buy", we indicate the major considerations which which should be applied in the design and evaluation of a paging system.

1. The most important economy achieved by a dynamic storage allocation system is that it does not allocate storage that, for one reason or another, is never used by the program which claims it; the second most valuable economy is the delay in allocation of storage that is not required until late in the execution of the program; and the third most important economy is the storage that is required near the beginning of a program but never again. Indeed, for large numbers of short programs with run times measured in seconds, these are the only savings that are worthwhile. A paging system must be designed to make the most of these savings, which can all be achieved without page-fault (although the third economy cannot be achieved without risk of page fault). Experience (Alderson *et al.* [1]; Oppenheimer and Weizer [11]) shows that satisfactory performance can be achieved by systems making only the first two economies.

2. A paging system should be able to support efficiently a high paging rate; for other things being equal, this will ensure the maximum density of utilization of a valuable resource — the main store. Even if the average paging rate is far below the maximum supportable, the rate will undoubtedly fluctuate widely, and it is most important that the system maintains high efficiency during peak loading, for otherwise it will rapidly lock into a counter-productive overload condition.

Thus a paging system should be able to deal with a paging fault (including program change) with a minimum of central processor overhead; and some method should be adopted to keep delays from rising in a heavy load condition.

3. Having planned to support efficiently a given paging rate, some method of load-shedding must be available for dealing with those occasions when this maximum rate is exceeded. In some cases, operator intervention has proved adequate, but in other circumstances a more automatic control would be desirable.

4. It is desirable to ensure that the paging rate is not unnecessarily inflated by frequently throwing out pages which are going to have to be brought in again shortly afterwards. The FIFO technique has proved surprisingly useful in practice, but the Second Chance algorithm is probably preferable and involves very little extra complexity. The further complexity of the Least Recently Used algorithm is probably not justified.

5. Finally, whatever techniques are used, they should be simple enough to be explained to a software writer or designer of a large program, so that he knows how

best to take advantage of the system; for in the case of large and frequently used programs, better results will always be obtained with a modicum of human assistance. After all, the difference in access time between main store and backing store is something like five orders of magnitude (compare a baby crawling with a supersonic jet). It is not always wise to keep wholly hidden a difference of this magnitude.

If these five considerations have been adequately taken into account, the other decisions are probably far less critical than is generally imagined; and certainly if these considerations have been ignored, it is known from bitter experience that no amount of subsequent tinkering with details of data structure or an algorithm will rescue the situation.

ACKNOWLEDGEMENTS

This work was supported in part by a Research Contract into Operating Systems Techniques, sponsored jointly by International Computers Limited and the Advanced Computer Techniques Project. The paper has been released on the understanding that the views expressed are those of its authors, and the sponsors of the contract are in no way responsible for its accuracy, in detail or in general, nor for any consequences resulting from the dissemination or use of the information contained therein.

REFERENCES

[1] Alderson, A., Lynch, W. C. and Randell, B., "Thrashing in a multiprogrammed paging system". International Seminar on Operating System Techniques, Belfast (August 1971). [Description of an experiment to evaluate page replacement algorithms that incorporate implicit load-shedding techniques].

[2] Arden, B. W., "Multi-processing systems". On the Teaching of the Design of Large Software Systems, University of Newcastle-upon-Tyne Computing Laboratory (1970) pp. 3–19. [Includes a description of the Virtual/Real Ratio technique used for avoiding the onset of thrashing in the Michigan Terminal System].

[3] Batson, A., Ju. S.-M. and Wood, D. C., "Measurements of segment size". 2nd ACM Symposium on Operating Systems Principles, Princeton (October 1969) pp. 25–29. [Describes the behaviour of the variable length paging system used in the Burroughs B5500].

[4] Baylis, M. H. J., Fletcher, D. G. and Howarth, D. J., "Paging studies made on the ICT Atlas computer". Preprints, IFIP Congress, Edinburgh (August 1968) pp. D113–D118. [Compares the performance of the Atlas Loop Detection technique with several other page replacement algorithms].

[5] Burroughs, "A narrative description of the Burroughs B5500 Disk File Master Control Program". Burroughs Corporation, Detroit, Michigan (1966). [Describes the techniques employed in the B5500 MCP, including those for the management of variable length pages].

[6] Daley, R. C. and Dennis, J. B., "Virtual memory, processes, and sharing in Multics". *Comm. ACM*, 11, 5 (May 1968), 306–312. [Description of the storage and addressing structure of the GE645 computer used for Multics].

[7] Denning, P. J., "The Working Set Model for program behaviour". *Comm. ACM*, 11, 5 (May 1968), 323–333. [Introduces the concept of a working set and describes its use to prevent thrashing].

[8] Dijkstra, E. W., "The structure of the T.H.E. – Multiprogramming System". *Comm. ACM*, 11, 5 (May 1968), 341–346. [Includes an outline of the software paging system].

[9] Kilburn, T., Edwards, D. B. G., Lanigan, M. J. and Sumner, F. H., "One-level storage system". *I.R.E. Transactions*, EC-11, 2 (April 1962), 223–235. [This paper describes the first paging system: that used on Atlas].

[10] Knuth, D. E., *The Art of Computer Programming*, Vol. 1: "Fundamental Algorithms". Addison-Wesley (1969) pp. 435–455. [Compares several placement techniques for variable length pages].

[11] Oppenheimer, G. and Weizer, N., "Resource management for a medium scale time-sharing operating system". *Comm. ACM*, 11, 5 (May 1968), 313–322. [Includes a description of a technique with, in effect, paging in and load-shedding, but not paging out].

[12] Randell, B., "A note on storage fragmentation and program segmentation". *Comm. ACM*, 12, 7 (July 1969), 365–369, 372. [Discusses the problems of fixed versus variable length pages and internal versus external fragmentation].

[13] Wulf, W. A., "Performance monitors for multiprogramming systems". 2nd ACM Symposium on Operating System Principles, Princeton (October 1969) pp. 175–181. [Describes techniques for avoiding thrashing and for improving resource utilization, which have been used with success on the B5500].

THRASHING IN A MULTIPROGRAMMED PAGING SYSTEM

A. Alderson, W. C. Lynch and B. Randell

The University of Newcastle-upon-Tyne
Computing Laboratory

INTRODUCTION

One of the problems facing the designer of a paging system that uses multiprogramming in order to overlap processing with input/output activity is that of avoiding page thrashing [1, 2]. If too many programs are allowed to compete for a share of working storage, they will be unable to obtain sufficient storage, and will suffer from very frequent page faulting. As a result the system will achieve very low performance, coupled with an excessive amount of page transfers.

It is not usually satisfactory to choose a constant level of multiprogramming, since such a level, if low enough to avoid any chance of thrashing occurring, will not necessarily give sufficient I/O overlap. On the other hand if the multiprogramming level is allowed to vary, unless care is taken the response of the system to the onset of thrashing will be to bring pages from yet further programs down into working storage, and thus accentuate the thrashing.

Techniques for dynamically controlling the level of multiprogramming have been described by Shils [3] and Denning [2]. Both techniques involve an explicit feedback mechanism. The "Load Leveller" described by Shils takes decisions based on CPU utilization and paging rate, whereas the scheme outlined by Denning involves an attempt at obtaining an explicit estimate of the size of each job's working set. (In this usage the term "working set" is intuitively the set of pages which a job requires in order to progress without undue paging.)

The purpose of this paper is to describe some of the results obtained in an investigation of the problem of thrashing, and in particular the experiments conducted on several simple algorithms for controlling multiprogramming level by means of implicit feedback mechanisms.

THE SYSTEM MODEL

The computing system that has been simulated consists of a processor, core storage and a paging drum. Each job is modelled as an alternating sequence of intervals of processing punctuated by page faults and of waiting (for unmodelled I/O activity). In our model we regard paging activity to be concerned with the drum and input/

output to be concerned with disks. However, we do not model contention for I/O devices nor do we require that any of the jobs' pages should be regarded as I/O buffers and so be required to be present in core during I/O activity. Most paging simulators keep track of each individual page, and are either capable of actually executing programs, or are driven by address traces previously gathered from such programs. Such simulators are extremely laborious even for modelling the behaviour of just a single program. Instead our model keeps track of only the numbers of pages that each job has, and uses appropriate probability distributions to simulate the status of the pages. The amount of processing that a job will achieve before it suffers a page fault is calculated from a probability function which has as a parameter the number of pages that the job currently has in core storage. This has proved to be a most convenient level of simulation, being far less demanding in terms of code, storage and execution time than the address trace level simulations, and has enabled us to perform a large number of experiments modelling lengthy periods of system operation.

The form of the probability distribution of the time to next page fault is based on published data, most notably that gathered on the M44/44X system [4], and attempts to model two distinct aspects of the behaviour of programs running in a paging environment. The first of these concerns the relationship that has been observed to hold between page fault rate and amount of core storage that a job is allowed to use. The fault rate remains at a quite reasonable level as the number of real core pages is reduced until a critical point is passed, when the fault rate rises very rapidly. Above this point the program is capable of retaining its "working set" of pages in core storage, for perhaps quite lengthy periods of processing. However, the pages which constitute the working set can change during the execution of the program. The second aspect of program behaviour that we model is the gradual "drift" of working set membership – abrupt changes, such as occur between different phases of a job, particularly if the job has been designed using an overlay structure, can be modelled by treating the phases as constituting distinct jobs.

The observed relationship between page fault rate and available core storage has been modelled in a perhaps oversimplified fashion by taking the probability that a given instruction causes a page fault to be

$$2^{-16\frac{RCP}{DWS}}$$

where RCP is the number of pages which the job has in core, and DWS is the working set size of the job. Even more arbitrarily, in the set of experiments described in this paper, we have assumed that the gradual drift of a job's working set is steady and involves the job completely changing its working set three times during the course of its execution. The appropriate probability here is

$$\frac{3 \times DWS}{CPUTIME \times 1000}$$

where CPUTIME is the total CPU time, in milliseconds, required by the job the factor 1000 converting this to instructions.

From the combination of these two factors we obtain that the expected length of processing time that a job will achieve before page fault is given by

$$m = \frac{1-k}{k \times 1000} \text{ milliseconds}$$

where

$$k = \frac{2^{-16\frac{RCP}{DWS}} \dfrac{3 \times DWS}{+\; CPUTIME \times 1000}}{1 \qquad +\; \dfrac{3 \times DWS}{CPUTIME \times 1000}}$$

is the per instruction probability of a page fault being caused by a given instruction.

A given simulation experiment would involve one or more different classes of job. Each class of job would be represented by a job "profile" indicating the size of working set and the amount of CPU and I/O time required. The parameters for individual jobs are obtained by using the parameters of the job profile as the means of appropriate probability distributions. The parameters DWS in the above formula is sampled from the uniform distribution $U(X-\frac{1}{2}X, X+\frac{1}{2}X)$, where X is the value of the appropriate job profile parameter, and CPUTIME is sampled from the exponential distribution.

The simulator allows different drum organizations to be used. The scheme employed in the simulations described in this paper is a sector-queued organization with priority ordering of the sector queues. We simulate the drum as being able to revolve every 17.5 msec, and capable of holding 4.5 pages on each track. The drum is considered to be laid out as in the Michigan Terminal System, where each track is divided into 9 sectors each of one half page. Two adjacent tracks may then be employed to record 9 pages, so that 1 page may be read in 2/9 of a physical drum revolution (1/9 of a "logical" drum revolution) by splitting each complete page between two adjacent tracks in the appropriate manner.

A queue of requests is maintained for each of the 9 sectors and these queues are priority ordered. The maintenance of these queues is idealized in our model, in that we assume the supervisor to be capable of maintaining the queue instantaneously, so that re-ordering of a queue may take place up to the instant at which the drum read is to be performed. That is to say we ignore the time required to set up the channel programs. We make the further assumption that the system is aware of the completion of the page transfer from the instant at which the transfer is completed physically, whereas in a real system this "posting" might not occur until the end of the logical drum revolution, or some other convenient time.

WORKLOAD EXPERIMENTS

The simulation model described above has been used to conduct a series of experiments into the behaviour of a number of scheduling algorithms, which have been designed to minimize the loss of processor utilization that occurs when all jobs in core are held up waiting for either an I/O operation to be completed or a page fault to be serviced. The workload simulated in these experiments was an attempt to model a workload representative of that presented to the Michigan Terminal System at Newcastle. This model workload is composed of three distinct components.

(*a*) Small jobs requiring a working set of 5–15 pages and of the order of 1 second of CPU time and 3 seconds of I/O. These are intended to represent interactive work such as editing and listing files and perhaps APL sessions. This type of work was estimated to demand 10% of the available CPU time.

(*b*) Medium jobs requiring a working set of 15–45 pages and of the order of 20 seconds CPU time and 20 seconds of I/O. These are intended to represent the compilations and runs of simple programs, which, due to the teaching work of the establishment, represent the bulk of the jobs presented to the system. These were estimated to demand 40% of the available CPU time.

(*c*) Large jobs requiring a working set of 25–75 pages and of the order of 100 seconds of CPU time and 33 seconds of I/O. These are intended to represent the CPU bound component of the workload which accrues from the research work, which was estimated to demand 25% of the available CPU

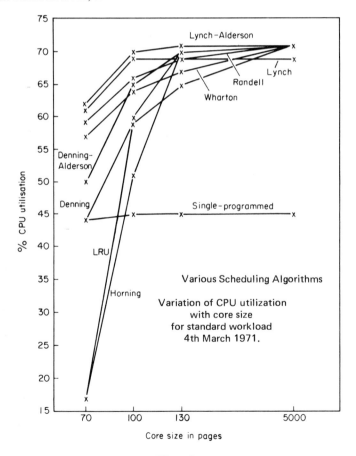

Figure 1

time. No attempt was made to model the really large jobs often required by numerical work, since these are unlikely to be run during the normal daytime MTS session at Newcastle. Overall, the load demands 75% of the available CPU time.

Figure 1 shows a graph of CPU utilization versus core size, obtained on this model workload by various algorithms, all of which contained provisions intended by their designers to prevent the occurrence of thrashing. The core size of 5000 pages may be thought of as an "infinite" core, since with the above workload no page replacements are required with this amount of core available. This core size enables us to establish the maximum CPU utilization obtainable for the load presented since there is no page wait caused by contention for core. The results labelled SINGLE-PROGRAMMED are the utilizations obtained by running the jobs serially through the system and may be used as a basis for comparison of the various algorithms. This graph illustrates the fact that given enough core even the most ill-conceived algorithms can be made to perform satisfactorily!

In figure 2, we present a graph of CPU utilization against multiprogramming level for a fixed core size of 70 pages. The value of multiprogramming level is set as an initial parameter of the system and effectively limits the length of the scheduler queue. The scheduler queue is a priority ordered queue of all the jobs in the system (jobs are detached only when they terminate), with flags set to mark whether the job is in I/O wait, page wait or requires the CPU.

A job is "CPU-ready" if it is not in wait state. In the algorithms described in this paper, when the value of multiprogramming level has been set to X, the scheduler scans only the first X positions of the queue and allocates the CPU to the first CPU-ready job that it encounters. If there is no such job the system goes into CPU-idle state until one of the jobs in wait state becomes CPU-ready once more. From the graph in figure 2 it can be seen that some algorithms have the very desirable property that their performance improves essentially monotonically with multiprogramming level. Despite this, however, some algorithms do not significantly improve upon uniprogramming. At the other end of the spectrum, some algorithms can be seen to fail dismally at avoiding thrashing and very quickly become less efficient than uniprogramming.

A further aid to insight into the behaviour of the various algorithms is the "core map", an example of which is shown in figure 3. The core map gives a pictorial representation of the way in which the core is divided amongst the jobs in the mix. Each character represents a page of core, the code being the job number modulo 10. That is, each "1" represents a page belonging to job 1 or job 11 or job 21, etc. Since the codes are laid out according to the priority order of the jobs we can easily find from the context, to which job a certain page, represented in the core map, belongs. An "*" represents a free page frame. The contents of core may be sampled at any pre-set interval. We have found sampling every simulated second to be adequate.

Such maps have been our major tool in confirming or understanding the behaviour of each scheduling algorithm, thus leading on several occasions to the development of new algorithms. We now have reason to believe that the model workload is in fact more severe than the actual workload that the 360/67 is subjected to at Newcastle. In fact in some ways this excessive severity has been useful, as the core maps have shown us how the various algorithms have reacted in a wide variety of circumstances.

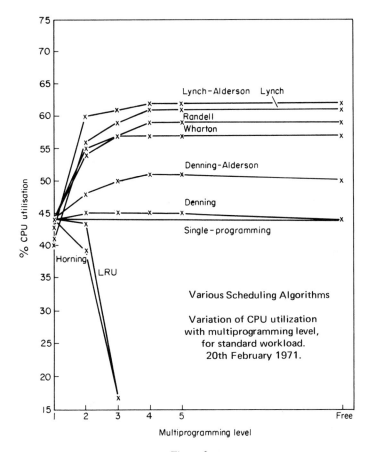

Figure 2

```
364    222222222222222233333333333344444444455555555556666666666666666777788888***
365    2222222222222233333333333334444445555555555566666666667788888888888888888
366    222222222222222233333333333333334444444445555555555666666666666677778888884
367    222222222222222333333333333333334444444455555555555556666666666677889011111
368    222222222222233333333333333344444444444455555555555666666666666677777888813*
369    222222222222233333333333334444444455555555666666666666677777788888888888888
370    222222222222222222333333333334444444444455555555556666666666677777778
371    2222222222222233333333333334444445555555555566666666666777777788888888*
372    222222222222222233333333333333334444444455555555555555555666666666666677777
373    2222222222222233333333333333555555555555555555566666666666666677788889993
374    2222222223333333333333355555555555555556666666666666666677777788888888
375    2222222222222233333333333555555555555555666666666666666777777788888888857
376    222222222222222233333333333555555555555556666666666666677777777777888888888
377    222222222222222233333333333355555555555777777788888888888888888888888888
378    2222222222222333333333377777888888888888888888888888888889900111*
379    22222222222222333333333333333377777788888888888888888888888888888888888
380    222222222222222233333333333337777888888888888888888888888888888888888889
381    222222222233333333333377777788888888888888888888888888888888888888899990
```

Figure 3. Core map with standard workload.

However, in order to simplify and shorten the present paper, we will base our discussions on graphs and core maps obtained using a much simpler workload than that described above. Furthermore, we will concern ourselves with just three of the more basic algorithms from the set whose behaviour is illustrated in figures 1 and 2. The workload consists of a single job entering the system at time O, requiring a working set of a certain size, and equal amounts of CPU and I/O time. The I/O operations require a mean time of 100 msec, to complete and therefore a computation period of mean 100 msec, between I/O operations is required to give the chosen I/O to CPU ratio. All further jobs are identical in their requirements to the first and enter the system at time 1 second. From this we observe that the lowest CPU utilization which we would expect to obtain is 50%, since this is the utilization which the first job, running by itself, would attain. This figure may be depressed due to time spent in page wait during the initial period, when the job is being loaded by demand paging, and also when a page fault occurs because of the slow drift of working set.

WHARTON'S ALGORITHM

This algorithm, which led to the development of interest in the class of implicit algorithms, was proposed by R. M. Wharton [5], a student of J. J. Horning at Toronto.

An external priority structure is imposed upon the jobs submitted to the system, this priority ordering being fixed externally of and not being modifiable by the scheduler. The scheduler allocates the CPU to the highest priority job waiting for the CPU.

On occurrence of a page fault, any free page frame is allocated, if such a page frame is available. When all of core has been allocated, the lowest priority job with pages in core, of priority less than or equal to the job causing the page fault, has a page replaced from amongst its in-core set according to some appropriate strategy. If no such job exists then the page request is denied and the requesting job cannot proceed until a higher priority job terminates its execution thus freeing pages of core.

This situation may arise because we assume that all pages are loaded on demand, there being no initial loading phase. A job which has no pages in core may then be scheduled but will page fault immediately. Such a job may then, because of its priority, find that there is no valid page replacement for it to make.

Page requests for pages to be transferred to core from the drum are serviced according to the same priority ordering as the scheduler queue priority.

The philosophy behind Wharton's algorithm is to give the top priority job the service which it would obtain if it were running by itself in the system. Further jobs are then run as a background stream utilizing any resource not required by the top priority job. By this scheme the worst utilization that will occur is that utilization obtained by running the jobs serially through the system. We acknowledge that if we were in fact producing a uniprogramming system we could introduce improvements and also that we are ignoring the interference caused by the supervisor dealing with the interrupts of the lower priority jobs. However, these should not cause very large discrepancies and so the statement is fairly accurate.

The control upon the level of multiprogramming is obtained by the allocation of core storage. If a job has no core then it cannot affect the effective multiprogramming level of the system. Since a job may only obtain more core space by replacing pages of jobs of equal or lower priority (we employ priority orders in which there is no repetition), the lowest priority job may only obtain core by utilizing free page frames. Also as the jobs of higher priority acquire more pages the lower priority jobs will be deleted from core. This is because their pages will be replaced by jobs of higher priority and since they will be unable to obtain page frames, they will be suspended until a job of higher priority terminates execution, thus freeing core.

We can observe the manner in which this occurs by studying the core map shown in figure 4. The contents of core were sampled at the end of each simulated second.

```
 1  11111111111111111111111|**********************************************************
 2  111111111111111111111111112222222222222223333333333333333333344444444444444455555555
 3  1111111111111111111111111112222222222222222222222233333333333333333333333344444444444
 4  111111111111111111111111111222222222222222222222222233333333333333333333333333344444444
 5  11111111111111111111111111112222222222222222222222222233333333333333333333333333344444444
 6  111111111111111111111111111112222222222222222222222222223333333333333333333333333344444
 7  1111111111111111111111111111122222222222222222222222222233333333333333333333333333444
 8  11111111111111111111111111111222222222222222222222222222333333333333333333333333333444
 9  1111111111111111111111111111112222222222222222222222222223333333333333333333333333344
10  111111111111111111111111111111222222222222222222222222222233333333333333333333333333344
11  1111111111111111111111111111112222222222222222222222222223333333333333333333333333344
12  1111111111111111111111111111111222222222222222222222222222333333333333333333333333333
13  11111111111111111111111111111112222222222222222222222222223333333333333333333333333333
14  11111111111111111111111111111112222222222222222222222222223333333333333333333333333333
15  11111111111111111111111111111112222222222222222222222222223333333333333333333333333333
16  11111111111111111111111111111112222222222222222222222222222333333333333333333333333333
17  11111111111111111111111111111112222222222222222222222222223333333333333333333333333333
18  11111111111111111111111111111112222222222222222222222222223333333333333333333333333333
19  11111111111111111111111111111112222222222222222222222222223333333333333333333333333333
20  11111111111111111111111111111112222222222222222222222222222333333333333333333333333333
```

Figure 4. Wharton's algorithm.

The core map shown here is the first part of that for the simulation of Wharton's algorithm when we limit the multiprogramming level to 10, and all of the jobs are identical, each requiring a 20 page working set.

We can see after time 2 seconds that the core allocations of jobs 1, 2, 3, increase at the expense of job 4 until that job is deleted from core. Thus multiprogramming has been "implicitly" reduced. After this time we see that the allocations of jobs 1, 2 increase at the expense of job 3, which is the lowest priority job with pages of core.

It is interesting to examine the number of page frames jobs 1, 2, and 3 have at the time job 4 is deleted from the mix. Job 1 has 29, job 2 has 26 and job 3 has 25. We see then that the top priority jobs accumulate pages in core for which they no longer have a requirement, and unless a job becomes the lowest priority job in core, there is no mechanism included by which these pages can be removed until the job terminates. Thus, whilst we are ensuring that contention for core will not be allowed to depress CPU utilization, we are making poor utilization of our limiting resource. A particularly bad case of the working of this algorithm is that of the top priority job being an I/O bound job which is dumping a large area. It will require many different pages during its execution but each page will be required for a very short period and will subsequently be superfluous to the progress of the job.

Let us now consider the graph of CPU utilization versus multiprogramming level (figure 5). The working set size was given the value 20(10)80 pages for a system in which 80 pages of core were available. The level of multiprogramming was varied from 1 (uniprogramming) up to 10.

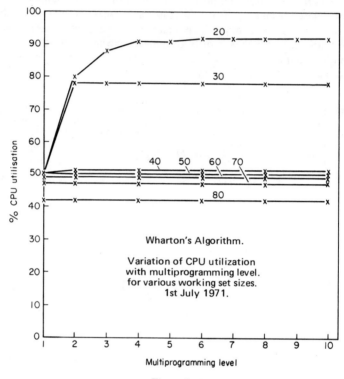

Figure 5

We see for Wharton's algorithm that as the multiprogramming level increases from 1 for a particular working set size the CPU utilization increases to some maximum value which it then maintains with only slight variations. The interpretation of this behaviour is that Wharton's algorithm implicitly sets a value of the multiprogramming level and any further jobs in the mix are ignored. When the pre-set limit of multiprogramming level is less than the level at which Wharton's algorithm is capable of working then the CPU utilization will be below the maximum attainable. As we increase the pre-set limit the CPU utilization improves to the maximum.

HORNING'S ALGORITHM

We have observed in the discussion of Wharton's algorithm that the higher priority jobs retain pages which are superfluous to their progress. This algorithm, proposed by J. J. Horning, was derived from Wharton's algorithm and attempted to include a mechanism which would free this unproductive core storage.

As before, external priority structure is imposed upon the jobs submitted to the system, this priority ordering being fixed externally of and not modifiable by the scheduler. The scheduler allocates the CPU to the highest priority job waiting for the CPU.

On occurrence of a page fault, any free page frame is allocated, if such a page frame is available. When all of core has been allocated, a job is chosen at random from amongst those which have real core pages, the probability of choosing a job being directly proportional to the number of page frames which it has, and a page is replaced from amongst this job's page frames according to some appropriate scheme.

Page requests, for pages from the drum, are serviced according to the same priority ordering as the external priority ordering. The scheduler and drum organizations of Wharton's algorithm are again employed.

The reasoning that led to the Horning algorithm was as follows. If we superimpose graphs of drum reads versus multiprogramming and CPU utilization versus multiprogramming we would expect to obtain a figure like figure 6. Obviously that level

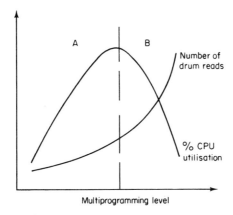

Figure 6. Superimposed graphs of CPU utilization against multiprogramming level and number of drum reads against multiprogramming level.

of multiprogramming which will give us the maximum CPU utilization is the level at which we would like to run the system. However, this level is dependent upon the load at any time. We are, therefore, interested in a mechanism which will vary the effective level of multiprogramming so that we may obtain this optimum. The form of this control will be the introduction of jobs into, or removal of jobs from core. Thus when we are in area A of the graph we would like there to be a net drift of pages from high to low priority jobs, thus increasing the multiprogramming level, and from low to high priority jobs when in area B, thus decreasing the level. This should be achieved by the random page replacement policy.

The policy is biased towards "stealing" pages from the jobs with the most pages, which are probably the highest priority jobs. When page demand is low, area A, the queues for drum service will be short, and high and low priority jobs will obtain essentially equal service. A net drift of pages from high to low priority jobs will result. When page demand is high, area B, the lower priority jobs will be blocked from obtaining drum service due to the rapid requeueing of the service requests of the higher priority jobs. The priority ordering of the drum queues will therefore bias the gain of pages to high priority jobs and so low priority jobs will eventually be deleted from core. As paging activity subsides then the service requests of the low priority jobs will become unblocked and these jobs will once more be able to gain page frames.

```
1  111111111111111111111111*************************************************************
2  1111111111122222233333333444444444444555555555566677777777777888888888999900000
3  111111111112222223333334444444444445555555555666666677777777788888889999999990000000
4  11111111111222222222222333333444444455555666666666777778888888889999999999990000000
5  111111111222222222333333344444444455555555555555666666666777777788888999999999000000
6  11111122222222233333344444455555555555666777777777777778888888889999999990000000000
7  11111111111222233333333444444445555555556666666677777777777788888888999999990000000
8  11112222222233333333333444444445555666666666666777777777788888888999999999990000000
9  1111111111111112222333344444444455555555556666666666666777777777888888899999999990
10 111111222222233333333334444444455555556666666666667777777888888899999999000000000
11 11222222223333333333333444444444555555555555666666666677777888888999999990000
12 1111111112222222333333333333444444444444455555556666666777777777888888999999000
13 1111222222223333333333444444444444455555556666666777777777788888888999999999990000
14 11111122223333333344455556666666666666666777777777788888999999999999990000
15 11111111222233333333334444444444555556666667777777777778888888999999990000000
16 111111222222233333444444444444555555555566666666777778888889999990000000000000
17 1111111112222222222223333444444444444455556666777778888888888888999999999999990000
18 1111111222222233333444444555555555555666666777777777788888888889999999000000000
19 1112222222333333333333444444444444555555555566666666777,777788888889999999999000000000
20 111111111122222222223333333333444445555555555666666666(7,/,7778888888999999999000000000
```

Figure 7. Horning's algorithm.

Let us now consider the core map, figure 7, which was obtained for Horning's algorithm with the multiprogramming level limited to 10 and all jobs identical, as for Wharton's algorithm, each requiring a 20 page working set. We observe that, in contradiction to the above reasoning, all of the jobs quickly obtain pages in core and that no job has the number of pages required for its working set. Also, the higher priority jobs obtain no greater share of core than do the lower priority jobs. For instance at time 6 seconds, job 1 has 6 pages whilst job 10, the lowest priority job, has 11 pages. We can explain the failure of this algorithm as follows.

The premise upon which this algorithm was founded is that when drum queues are short the core is not overpartitioned with the implication that the effective level of multiprogramming may be increased. A simple example is sufficient to display that this is not always true. Suppose that the top three jobs in the scheduler queue have a combined working set requirement greater than the number of pages in core, so that thrashing would ensue if avoiding action were not taken. The longest possible queue for drum service would contain just three elements which would be insufficient to block the requests of the third job. (Even if this were sufficient the request of the third job would be unblocked as soon as the higher priority jobs obtained their working set. Thus, the top priority jobs would have their working sets only for very short periods.) However, with a sector-queued drum organization, this queue length is of low probability. Thus we see that the problem is caused because lightly loaded queues act like FIFO queues with the result that the competing jobs get almost equal service from the drum. This, coupled with the random page-steal strategy causes the core to become equally divided amongst the jobs on the scheduler queue.

We see also that the other blocking mechanism, the priority scheduler, is similarly ineffective. In a thrashing situation the CPU is grossly under-utilized and so all jobs in the scheduler queue will obtain all of the CPU they demand, which is very little. Thus the other method of blocking low priority jobs from gaining core pages, not scheduling them, is undermined. We see then that once thrashing has begun this algorithm will cause further degradation. Similarly, we see that if the CPU is not fully utilized the reaction of this algorithm is to introduce further jobs to utilize it, such a policy must eventually lead to thrashing.

Let us now consider the graph of CPU utilization versus multiprogramming level, figure 8, which was obtained with the same mixes as those for Wharton's algorithm.

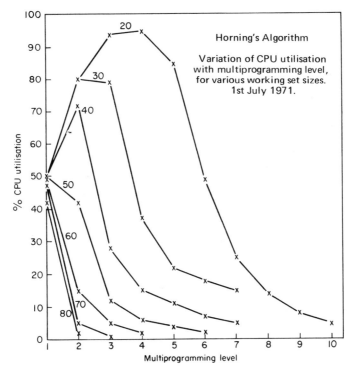

Figure 8

We see that the CPU utilization increases up to some maximum before decreasing, as multiprogramming level is increased. The maxima for those job mixes where the working set size is at least 50 pages occur at level of multiprogramming = 1. It is sufficient to multiply the working set size of the jobs by the multiprogramming level at which the maximum occurs, to explain this. We observe that the maximum occurs at the multiprogramming level for which that product is closest to the core size, that is, at the highest level at which the core is not overcommitted. A continual degradation of CPU utilization is then seen as each further job is introduced into the mix, causing greater overcommitment of core.

LYNCH'S ALGORITHM

This algorithm, proposed by W. C. Lynch, is a more successful attempt at modifying Wharton's algorithm to deal with the problem of unrequired pages being accumulated in core. The proposal is to couple a "drain" with the Wharton algorithm. The "drain" consists of writing out of core one page every second logical revolution of the drum from

    (a) the job using the CPU at that time
    (b) all jobs in I/O wait at that time

and freeing those page frames.

    The reasoning is that if a job has more page frames than it requires to contain its working set then we will gain page frames from it. If we were to steal a page which belonged to the top job's working set, then we would expect the job to page fault almost immediately and to re-acquire that page within half of a logical revolution of the drum on average. Thus, if we were to steal from that same job each time we applied the drain, we would only impair that job's performance by 25%, a loss we would hope to recoup by the improved performance of the background stream. We would also expect that the jobs most likely to be doing I/O or utilizing the CPU, would be those jobs which have at least their working set of pages in core. Thus we will, for the most part, be draining pages from the correct set of jobs.

    One does not drain pages from a job which is in page wait, because page requests are not a function of the job's "local" time (i.e. the CPU and I/O time the job demands from the system). Thus by deleting pages only from jobs which are in I/O wait or occupying the CPU, the extent to which a job may be delayed in the system is bounded. This is not so if we drain pages when a job is in page wait.

    Let us now consider the core map for Lynch's algorithm for multiprogramming level = 10 and each job having a working set of 20 pages (figure 9). We observe that the core is evenly divided amongst the top four jobs on the scheduler queue and that

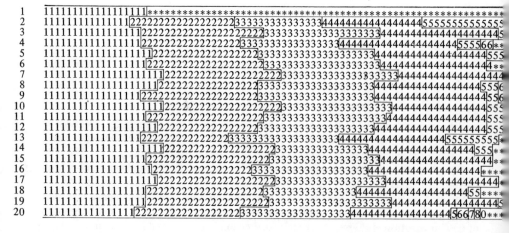

Figure 9. Lynch's algorithm.

the number of pages which each of these jobs has is in the region of their working set size of 20 pages. The situations in which a job has less than its working set correspond to I/O waits during which the job was losing pages due to the drain and was unable to regain them until it began processing once again. We see then that the "drain" is successful in ensuring that jobs do not claim more space than their working sets demand.

Now let us consider the graph of CPU utilization versus multiprogramming level (figure 10); we have omitted the results for working sets of 60 and 70 pages since they are very similar to those for 50 and 80 pages and only confuse the graph.

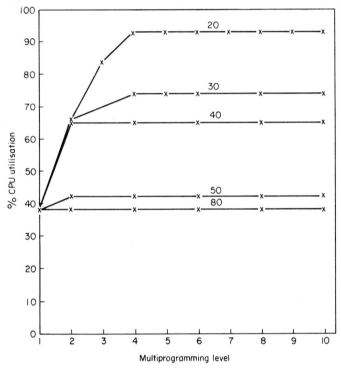

Figure 10. Lynch's Algorithm. Variation of CPU utilization with multiprogramming level for various working set sizes. 1st July, 1971.

We noted when discussing the workload that when uniprogramming we would expect to obtain a CPU utilization of 50%, further when discussing Lynch's algorithm we observed that due to the drain we would expect to depress the utilization of the top priority job by no more than 25%. We see that when multiprogramming level = 1 we obtain a utilization of 38%, 75% of that obtainable when not employing the drain.

It is instructive to compare the results of Lynch's algorithm with those for Wharton's algorithm. We observe that for working sets of 20 and 40, in which an integral number of jobs each with their full working set just occupy the whole of core, Lynch's algorithm is superior to Wharton's algorithm. Also, in these cases the loss of CPU utilization due to the drain is very small. However, in all other cases

Lynch's algorithm is inferior. This is because there is no significant gain to be made by squeezing only half of a job's working set into core and, moreover, in order to allow this we have drained pages from other jobs so depressing their CPU utilization. Thus we cause a loss of overall CPU utilization by draining in these situations. We also see that in those cases in which the core would be under-utilized (low multi-programming level), draining also incurs a loss. This is because the drain depresses the CPU utilization of the jobs in core and no further jobs are available to utilize the free page frames.

CONCLUSION

The present paper attempts to document some of the findings of a continuing series of experiments concerning the problem of thrashing. Although much remains to be investigated we consider that we have considerably extended our knowledge of thrashing and also of some simple mechanisms which have achieved some measure of success in avoiding the problem. It is hoped to obtain analytical confirmation of some of these results in the near future.

It is our intention to attempt to provide further validation of the parameters of the simulator, in particular, those concerned with the modelling of paging behaviour based on the workload of the 360/67 at Newcastle. We also hope to investigate some further inter-related aspects of the scheduling of multiprogrammed paging systems.

One by-product of our work has been to increase our already keen awareness of the ease with which one can fall into the trap of developing an algorithm whose behaviour cannot in practice be successfully predicted. The reasoning that was used to justify the Horning algorithm was accepted by *all* of us until experiments showed how inadequate this reasoning was. Yet the typical operating system contains many algorithms whose behaviour is far more impenetrable than this comparatively simple scheduling algorithm!

ACKNOWLEDGEMENTS

The work described in this paper has benefited greatly from conversations with our colleagues, in particular Jim Horning of the University of Toronto, who spent the autumn term of 1970 at the University of Newcastle-upon-Tyne, and Hugh Lauer, who provided a great number of helpful criticisms and suggestions.

REFERENCES

[1]   Randell, B. and Kuehner, C. J., "Demand paging in perspective". *Proc. AFIPS 1968 Fall Joint Comput. Conf., Vol. 33, Part 2*. Spartan Books, New York, pp. 1011–1018.

[2]   Denning, P. J., "Thrashing: its causes and prevention". *Proc. AFIPS 1968 Fall Joint Comput. Conf., Vol. 33, Part 1*. Spartan Books, New York, pp. 915–922.

[3] Shils, A. J., *The Load Leveller.* Report RC 2233, IBM T. J. Watson Research Center, Yorktown Heights, N.Y. (7 October 1968).

[4] Brawn, B. S. and Gustavson, F. G., "Program behaviour in a paging environment". *Proc. AFIPS 1968 Fall Joint Comput. Conf., Vol. 33, Part 2.* Spartan Books, New York, pp. 1019–1032.
and
An Evaluation of Program Performance on the M44/44X System. Reports RC 2083, 2275, and 2276. IBM T. J. Watson Research Center, Yorktown Heights, N.Y. (1968–1969).

[5] Wharton, R. M., "A page replacement strategy for multiprogramming systems", *Topics in Operating Systems* (Ed. T. Tsichritzis). Technical Report No. 23, January 1971, Department of Computer Science, University of Toronto, pp. 23–34.

ALLOCATION OF VIRTUAL STORE IN THE T.H.E. MULTIPROGRAMMING SYSTEM

C. Bron

Technological University,
Eindhoven, The Netherlands

INTRODUCTION

One of the objectives in the design of the T.H.E. multiprogramming system [1] has been the creation of a system which was easy to handle, both by the operator and by the programmer.

The operator aspect has, among other things, given rise to an organization of the tapereaders which presents itself very smoothly to the operators.

The implementation of that scheme, however, has been rather cumbersome and, in retrospect, is not as elegant as one would like a piece of systems programming to be.

An important user aspect can be derived from the virtual absence of "job control (language)". The only specification the programmer is asked to supply is the number of plotters and tape punchers that his program might need simultaneously. These numbers will play a role in the application of the "banker's algorithm" (p. 177). In particular, the programmer is not asked to specify the program's storage requirements. In relation to this aspect the following points seem of relevance:

1. The user is not required to supply an (implementation dependent) estimate that he cannot reasonably make.
2. The storage requirements for one particular program may vary widely depending on the particular job to be done. This remark holds very true for standard programs that are used frequently for both large and small problems.
3. Whenever a system requires a storage estimate as a job parameter it will take this estimate into account in its job scheduling algorithms. Now it is very hard to envisage how one can prevent "overestimates" from having a detrimental effect on system performance as a whole.
4. The absence of any knowledge of the (dynamic) storage requirements of the jobs being processed may bring the system to a point where the total requirement is larger than the amount of storage available. Once this point has been reached the operator will have to apply the axe. This method may appear very crude, but it will be shown – and this is one of the objectives of this paper – how, whenever possible, the "point of no return" can be circumnavigated.
5. Operating experience over the past 4 years has shown that the simultaneous execution of programs of which the total storage requirement exceeds the total storage capacity (where each of the programs separately might fit into store) occurs with a frequency of appr. 5 times a year. Whenever at other times the axe has been

168

used it has functioned to catch program errors like outrageous array growth (exceeding virtual store) or uncontrolled recursion (the stack outgrowing core store).

6. The flexibility of "allocating whatever is available whenever it is requested" is also reflected by the fact that users are only aware of the total amount of virtual store available. Of course, if they want to use it all their programs can only be executed in uniprogramming fashion. But as long as they stay away from the limit by, say, 20% such programs can usually be run in normal fashion without any scheduling to be applied.

1. GENERAL SYSTEM CHARACTERISTICS AND ALLOCATION PRINCIPLES

The T.H.E. Multiprogramming System was implemented on an EL–X8 Computer, having 48K of 27 bit words of core memory and, as a backing store, a drum of 512K words.

The drum is the medium onto which the existent part of virtual store is laid out. The adjective "existent" is used because the virtual address space created may be much larger than the amount of data contained in that address space. This is the case for example when an array has been declared but not yet used. As a happy consequence the penalty incurred in "overdeclaration" of arrays is only very slight.

There is an analogy in the allocation of core and drum storage. Of both media a certain part is reserved for permanent information. The remainder is treated as a pool from which store can be allocated pagewise and into which pages of store can be absorbed as circumstances demand. For neither of these media have we imposed requirements of consecutivity. More attention to the stack-in-pages will be devoted on p. 170.

2. CORE ALLOCATION

Core storage is roughly laid out as follows: The operating system, tabulatory material and subroutines extending the instruction set of the machine to facilitate the ALGOL implementation occupy roughly 10K of core memory. Five pages of 512 words each form the permanent stack-bottoms of the 5 slots that can process user programs. (As an afterthought we realize that we would have done better by having the system create these slots when the need arises, instead of having them permanently available.)

The remainder of core is divided into page frames. Of the total amount available a minimal number is reserved in order to guarantee that a process can never be blocked on account of the non-availability of core store. To be more specific, for each of the 5 slots we guarantee the availability of 2 core page frames, one to hold the current page of program text, and one to hold the current array page. Note that these reservations only apply to the total number of page frames and not to specific physical page frames. The remaining number of page frames is now available for the allocation of stack pages. Whenever the stack need of a process exceeds a certain limit (presently 3 stack pages) the operator receives a program generated request to grant the process more stack pages. He may now either grant the request or find that all of available core is already tied up in stack pages. At this point a number of alternatives is open:

(1) the job is aborted; this is the usual case when uncontrolled recursion or excessive overdeclaration of arrays is caught by the operator,
(2*a*) the job may be left slumbering until more stack space becomes available when another job terminates,
(2*b*) situation (2*a*) may be forced by aborting another job.

As an aside we remark that "stack page request" is a very infrequent occurrence. We should also add that having too much core tied up in stack pages (which are not part of virtual store) will tend to degrade system performance since the amount of core to grant access to pages of virtual memory will be too small (be it logically sufficient).

3. THE NON-CONSECUTIVE STACK

Although this subject falls outside the scope of actual allocation of store, it is nevertheless considered worthwhile to spend some attention to the implementation of a stack in a paged memory.

As we have seen already the stack is cut up in pages of the unit size of 512 words. Each stack page occupies a fixed core page frame for the extent of its life. This enables us to address the contents of the stack, whenever possible, in terms of physical addresses. The following type of data will be found in the stack:

(1) scalar variables
(2) array mapping tables
(3) descriptors of array pages
(4) display vectors
(5) anonymous working space, further subdivided in:
    (5.1) intermediate results
    (5.2) parameter descriptions, created in the calling sequence of a procedure
    (5.3) procedure return information
(6) stack page linking information to cater for stack breakdown, as required in "wild" gotos and dynamic errors.

Now if one analyses where consecutivity is a requirement then it turns out that the stack may be split into smaller sections corresponding to groupings (1) through (6). Whenever such a consecutive stack section is needed (and such points are well marked as we shall see) a corresponding routine is called which checks if sufficient space is available in the current (top) stack page, if so, it allocates the space, otherwise it calls for a next stack page, links it on the previous one, and allocates the requested space in the new one. Now we will indicate the points where space of types (1) through (5) may be requested.

(1) Upon block entry sufficient space is requested to accommodate all scalars of the current block consecutively, in order to allow "additive interpretation" of the second half of the ALGOL address couple (blockheight, local index).

(2) In each array declaration a mapping table is created allowing for later mapping of the index value(s) onto the virtual address of the array element.

(3) The second part of the array declaration introduces the list of descriptors. Consecutivity of the descriptors is a requirement to allow the mapping process to be "direct". If the size of the array forces the list of descriptors to be spread out over more than one stack page, subscription in that array will be slightly slowed down. One descriptor (of size one word) caters for 512 words of array data. Upon introduction a descriptor possesses the value "empty" and no store is yet reserved for the corresponding array page.

(4) Upon procedure entry space is reserved for the display vector of the new context. The length of that vector has been established beforehand by the compiler to be equal to the maximum inner blockheight of the procedure.

(5) As in (1) and (4) the compiler will have kept a count of the amount of anonymous stack space necessary for the execution of the statements in a block (not counting space used by procedures to be called). The space will be reserved after the declarations, but before the first statement of a block. As a result the stack pointer will be initialized either pointing in the old stack page, or at the bottom of one now chained on.

The inverse operations of the ones named above take place in block exit, procedure exit and "wild" goto. Not only may one or more stack pages be returned to the pool, but also the array pages of the block(s) being left will be returned to the virtual storage pool (p-decrease, see p. 174).

In summary: this section was devoted to demonstrating that even in a paged memory a stock of a priori unknown length can be implemented. Analysis shows that the requirement of consecutivity only holds for small sections of information in the stack, therefore the need to allocate a contiguous address space (be it real or virtual in some sense) disappears.

It is also shown that the growth and shrinking property of a stack it owes to the nested lifetimes of data can be very well reconciled with the storage demand in a multiprogramming system, where allocated storage does not have these decent lifetime properties.

4. INFORMATION STREAMS AND PERIPHERALS

Before turning our attention to virtual storage allocation we have to be more explicit as to the way in which input — output buffering is realized in the T.H.E. system. We make a distinction between two types of loosely connected processes inside the system.

On the one hand we have slots, that may execute user programs, the so-called PMs (for *programmable machines*). On the other hand we have the processes driving the physical peripherals. These processes are named CMs (for *constant machines*), since the program texts executed by these processes is constant. Associated with each peripheral (magnetic tape units are left out of consideration altogether) we have one dedicated CM.

For output processing we have:

one line printer CM
tapepunch CMs
plotter CMs

In the following, the latter two will frequently be termed "pluncher CMs" since their internal structure is so similar.
And for input processing we have:

tapereader CMs

Each PM possesses communication channels with the peripherals of the different types. To the user they present themselves as if they were the actual peripherals to which their program was directly connected. To the system the information streams represent buffering facilities. To be more specific a PM has at its disposal one line printer stream, and a fixed number of tape puncher streams, plotter streams and tapereader streams.

Note that we have not defined the information stream as a communication channel between a PM and a CM. From the viewpoint of a PM it is immaterial on which puncher output its is going to be punched, or on which tapereader its input tape will be read.

Clearly the existence of CM's and information streams (flexible I/O buffers) is motivated by the irreconcilable speed ratio's when comparing consumption/production of I/O by a PM and physical processing by one of the peripherals. We would like to stress the point that buffering does not only take place because the speed of a peripheral may be much slower than the corresponding speed, of the PM. Of more importance is the inverse possibility where the PM processes the information piecemeal. If we did not have extensive buffering facilities the peripherals might be tied up to a PM for too long a period of time. And peripherals are a scarce resource! We now have to determine when and for how long a CM will be tied up to a specific task. How do we see it, that CMs, once tied up, proceed as rapidly as physical limitations allow?

Such considerations have given rise to the concept of a "document". A document is a physically coherent piece of I/O information. Simple examples of a document are: a plotter picture, an input tape. For pluncher output we require the program to specify the end of a document. If such a specification is dynamically lacking, the end of the program will mark the end of the pluncher documents built up. For the line printer it has been decided that one form of printer output would make up a printer document. Document selection strategies should see to it that the line printer should, whenever possible, print consecutive forms from the same program.

The concept of "document" has served two purposes. It defined clearly the task assigned to an I/O CM, namely the processing of a document. It enables the system to tie up a CM to a specific task for as short a time as possible, viz. by not starting an output CM on the processing of an output document that has not been completely specified, and by not reserving a tape reader CM until a tape is requested and the operator is willing to supply it.

Naturally this general strategy cannot under all circumstances be applied because the I/O buffering capacity of the system is bounded. As a consequence tapereaders may halt while inputting a tape and pluncher CMs may be forced to select an unfinished (i.e. not completely specified) document. For the line printer we are not faced with this problem since the size of a lineprinter document (a form) is limited and small. Much of the following will be devoted to the treatment of the complications indicated above.

5. VIRTUAL STORE AND THE RELEVANT QUANTITIES

We define the most important quantities with which we will deal in the sequel. All quantities will be expressed in "number of pages" since no smaller units of virtual store are ever allocated.

tot   = total number of pages of virtual store (drum) available for dynamic
(constant)   allocation. Part of the drum (appr. 100 pages) is permanently reserved
              for the code of library routines, among which is the ALGOL compiler.
transp   = upper limit for the number of I/O pages constituting the information
(constant)   streams. This number is determined by the number of words
              permanently reserved in core to contain the descriptors of I/O pages.
              Since the lifetime of I/O pages is not nicely nested within the
              program producing or consuming the I/O clearly the descriptors of
              these pages cannot be allocated in the program's stack. Furthermore
              this wild lifetime behaviour of individual I/O pages would severely
              complicate dynamic allocation of their descriptors.

The pages residing in virtual store belong to one of three categories, their numbers being denoted by:

i = number of pages in input streams (buffered by an input CM, but not yet
     unbuffered by a PM)
o = number of pages residing in output streams (output specified and buffered by a
     PM, but not yet processed by the corresponding output CM)
p = number of private pages belonging to a PM. This number is made up of all pages
     of compiled object code and all array pages.

We may now describe the task of virtual storage allocation as trying to appease the following conflicting interests:

(1) When necessary we want to be able to allocate almost all of virtual store to private PM requirements as to not impose an unnecessarily low upperlimit on the size programs and their data may take.
(2) We want to be able to buffer sufficient input in order not to tie up tapereaders in the middle of processing a tape.
(3) We want to be able to buffer sufficient output in order to prevent plunchers from having to start on an unfinished document (thereby tieing up these plunchers for an indefinite period of time).

To this end it has been decided to set aside a portion of transp for output buffering only:

reso   = number of pages *re*served for *o*utput buffering only.
(constant)

    It is only the remaining transp—reso pages that may be shared among p, i and o (see p. 174).

It will be clear that the requirements of the points (1), (2) and (3) will not be met in an optimal manner if we simply divide virtual store in three areas, each of a fixed size, therefore the mechanisms to be described cater for the elastic allocation of virtual store.

6. THE STATE OF VIRTUAL STORE AND ITS TRANSITIONS

Since three (more or less) independent quantities play a role in describing the distribution of virtual store, the state of the system (with regard to storage allocation) can be described by a point in a three-dimensional state-space. State transitions are described by movements of that point. The state transitions that may take place are easily listed:

(1) i-increase: when an input CM chains on a (full) page of input information to an input stream. Note that the buffer page currently being processed by a CM is not part of the count. For each CM we have a permanent reservation of one (buffer) page which is kept out of the dynamic allocation schemes.

(2) o-decrease: when an output CM unchains a page from an output stream. The line printer CM unchains all pages of a form in a single shot. The fixed reservation for the line printer CM is therefore = maximum size of a form = maxpor.

(3) i→p transition: when a PM unchains an input page from an input stream. Note that the current PM buffer pages are considered to be array pages.

(4) p→o transition: when a PM chains on an output page to an output stream.

(5) p-increase: increase of the number of array pages. When the compiler generates object code it does so by filling an array with the compiled instructions. The actual p-increase takes place on assignment to an array element when the descriptor of the corresponding page is marked: "page empty" (see the remark in 1).

(6) p-decrease: the discarding of arrays in block exit, and processing of the last datum on an input segment.

We may draw these potential state transitions in the state diagram:

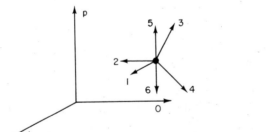

1	:	i — Increase
2	:	o — Decrease
3	:	i — p transition
4	:	p — o transition
5	:	p — Increase
6	:	p — Decrease

Figure 1

The problem of virtual storage allocation can now be expressed in terms of:

7. THE VITAL RESTRICTIONS OF VIRTUAL STORE

The following restrictions follow in a natural manner from the quantities introduced on p. 173:

(1) $i + o + p \leqslant tot$

This relation describes the limitation of total storage capacity.

(2) $i + o \leqslant$ transp,

    expressing the restriction imposed by the amount of core space permanently
    reserved for descriptors of I/O pages. Obviously : transp $<$ tot

(3) $i + p \leqslant$ tot $-$ reso,

    expressing the restriction imposed by the requirement that a minimal amount
    of output buffering can be guaranteed.

(4) $i \leqslant$ transp $-$ reso,

    expressing that (3) is not a sufficient condition to guarantee the buffering of at
    least reso output pages. Condition (3) only caters for the presence of storage.
    This condition guarantees the allocation of the descriptors in "transput area".

These four linear inequalities lend themselves to a very nice pictorial representation
in the following state diagram:

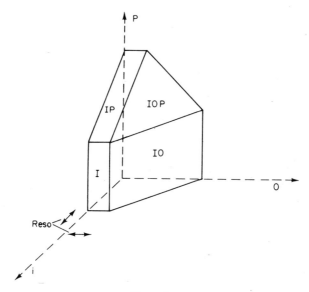

Figure 2

Obviously it is the task of the storage allocation mechanisms to keep the state within
the confines sketched in figure 2.

    We now note a striking distinction between faces I and IP on the one hand, and
faces IO and IOP on the other, i.e. when the state of store lies on face I or IP we
cannot guarantee any further progress. In order for i to decrease we need PM-activity
and then the state moves in direction 3 : i→p. This may bring relief if we are on face I,
but not on face IP. However, the crucial point is that further PM activity implies
the possibility of further p-increase and that clearly may crack the ceiling. From
these considerations we derive that holding up a process on the I or IP boundary
makes no sense because we are not certain of future relief. Breaking through the
I or IP boundary means: "disaster", and we should therefore carefully try to stay
away from these boundaries. For PMs this implies that sometime before the IP

boundary is to be hit the operator will be notified of the tight store situation and is given a chance to act accordingly.

Faces IO and IOP are of an entirely different nature. We may indeed let these boundaries be reached and hold up processes on the boundary, because we may expect relief from o-decrease by output CMs that do not make any further storage demands. This is only true, of course, when there will be at least one active output CM. To this end we force output CM activity as soon as

$$o > reso.$$

This may be printer activity, but it may also be activity of a pluncher CM, which for lack of a more attractive alternative had to start on an unfinished document. So we see that processes (PMs and input CMs) may be temporarily suspended on the IO and IOP boundaries. Since we can be certain of output activity we delegate the task of waking up suspended processes to transition 2 (o-decrease) taking place in output CMs.

Two additional benefits are derived from this scheme:

(1) Inspection of waking up obligations is not delegated to p-decrease (the state may move away from the IOP boundary), where p-decrease is expected to be a frequent occurrence, since o-decrease will in due time detect a waking up obligation.
(2) In p-increase (an equally frequent occurrence) when the IOP boundary is reached we can let the PM safely go to sleep, without having to inspect if now an output CM has to be activated for future relief, since active output will already be running.

8. THE OVERALL OUTPUT STRATEGY. PASSIVE OUTPUT

In the previous section it was shown that the consumption of output by output CMs plays a foremost role in the allocation of virtual store. Now we will examine more closely the consequences of decisions like:

(1) reserving part of transp for output solely,
(2) trying to prevent plunchers from having to start on unfinished documents,
(3) trying to prevent the line printer from printing forms from different programs in a wildly interlaced manner. (This point will be discussed in more detail in 10. For the moment we only remark that even wild behaviour of the printer CM has no detrimental effect on the performance of the system but only on the people faced with the task of sorting out the output.)

We recognize that output may belong in one of two categories, each with rather different characteristics. We distinguish between:

Active output: finished documents in streams for which there is a corresponding piece of equipment available, and unfinished documents the processing of which is currently taking place. In this respect a piece of equipment is considered *available* when it is not tied up for an indefinite period of time in the processing of an unfinished document. Obviously all line printer output is active output.

Passive output is made up of all output that we may not be able to get rid of under all circumstances. There may be two reasons for this (and with it two types of passive output):

(1) unfinished (pluncher) documents not currently being processed. We either need PM activity to finish specification of the document, which may result in a transfer from passive to active output. Or we may have to tie up a corresponding output CM to this document, which implies the risk of a deadly embrace and is therefore subject to the banker's approval (see p. 178).

(2) finished (pluncher) documents for which no corresponding equipment is available. Here we need further PM activity to finish specification of a document currently being processed, in order to make the equipment once more available.

The concepts just introduced may be described by the relation:

$$\text{paso} + \text{acto} = \text{o}.$$

As we have seen we want to be able to guarantee output activity when o $>$ reso. So we must put an upper limit to passive output, say "maxpas", where reso $-$ maxpas should be sufficient to keep active output trickling through. It follows that maxpas has been chosen such that reso $-$ maxpas = maximum size of an output portion to pass through the buffer. Since pluncher information is buffered pagewise, but line printer information is buffered form-wise the above maximum is taken as the maximum number of pages used to buffer a fully filled printer form (maxpor).

$$\text{reso} - \text{maxpas} = \text{maxpor}$$

Note: if printer information was not buffered form-wise it would have given rise to passive output in printer streams.

To end this section we list the occurrences that may influence the value of paso:

(*a*) increase of paso in a p→o transition when a next page is added to an unfinished document not currently being processed,

(*b*) decrease of paso when the banker decides to tie up a pluncher to an unfinished document. The pages constituting the document now move from passive output to active output,

(*c*) decrease of paso when a PM specifies "end of pluncher document". This decrease may take place in two ways:

(*c*1) if the document now finished was not being processed by a pluncher CM, this document itself moves to active output, provided a corresponding pluncher is "available". Note that the inverse transition (finished documents moving from active to passive output when the last available pluncher of the right kind is tied up to an unfinished document) will not take place because we do not allow unfinished documents to be selected in the presence of finished ones.

(*c*2) The document now finished was currently being processed and the pluncher CM now becomes "available". If previously no plunchers were available all finished documents of that kind move from passive to active output.

9. DOCUMENT SELECTION AND THE BANKER

By document selection we denote the complex of actions that takes place whenever a CM may have to start the processing of a document. It involves inspection of whether starting on a document is either necessary or attractive and allowed. It does not necessarily imply the start of physical processing.

Document selection for the line printer (printer selection) is called by a PM when it adds a form to its lineprinter stream. If the form previously processed by the line printer was from the same stream printer selection will certainly give rise to printer activity, otherwise it may not. Similarly, printer selection will be called by the line printer CM upon finishing the processing of a form, but the printer CM may or may not find something to do.

Tape reader selection may take place either in a PM, when the program requests a new input tape, by the operator when he wants to enter a program tape, or by a tapereader CM when it finishes processing of a tape and looks for a new job (a taperequest that could not be granted because of the unavailability of a tape reader).

Pluncher selection of unfinished documents is more complicated as it has been decided to apply the banker's algorithm to prevent deadly embrace whenever a pluncher CM is to be tied up to an unfinished document. At this point we say: the banker grants a loan to a PM. Each PM has specified beforehand its claim, i.e. the maximal numbers of plotterstreams and puncherstreams it might want to use simultaneously. A new loan will only be granted if the banker has enough in cash and if granting of the loan leaves the situation "*safe*".

A situation is "safe" when all processes can be ordered in a "stack of processes" that can be *emptied* by repeatedly applying the following two steps:

(1) there should be enough cash left to be able to grant the process on top its total claim
(2) when the process on top is finished it returns all of its claim to the banker's cash reserve. This process is now removed from the top of the stack. The cash should now be sufficient to apply step (1).

For details of the banker's algorithm see [2].

It should be borne in mind that although the full algorithm may seem complicated, the implementation in the case where the maximum number of puncher streams = 2 and the maximum number of plotterstreams = 1 is straightforward. Application of the algorithm is only called for when an unfinished pluncher document is considered for selection. The term banker has come into use for "unfinished pluncher document selection". We see that the banker will come into action when

(a) tentative p→o transition in a PM that would result in paso > maxpas. If the banker does not allow document selection the PM will be held up.
(b) finish pluncher document is performed by a PM. If a CM was tied up to this document this ends the loan. The banker might now be able to complete a successful document selection which was previously prohibited by the banker's algorithm.
(c) a pluncher CM finishes processing of a document. The storage situation might be such as to necessitate selection of an unfinished document.

Whenever an unfinished document is selected it moves from passive output to active output. The resulting decrease of paso now enables the banker to inspect if now PMs can be waked up that were suspended on account of not being able to effectuate a p→o transition (blocked on the "paso barrier").

One might wonder why document selection for printer and tapereader is not subject to banker's approval. For the line printer we have already seen that output is only produced in portions of "finished documents" (forms), therefore the line printer is never tied up for an indefinite period of time. By defining a line printer document to be similar to a pluncher document (e.g. all printer output of one program to be one document) we could have guaranteed consecutive output from the same program. However, since we had only one line printer and it could be expected that printer output would be the most common type of output, extending the scope of the banker to approval of the "loan" of the line printer might have become impractically restrictive.

For the tapereaders the following reasoning has been applied. On the one hand tape readers only process finished documents (each input tape has two ends), on the other hand we cannot guarantee tapereaders to buffer a complete tape since there is an upper limit on i. Whether a tapereader will be tied up for an indefinite period of time will depend on: (1) the length of the tape to be input, and (2) the storage situation as the tape is being input.

The danger of deadly embrace (if the banker bypasses tapereaders) obviously exists. Application of the banker to tapereaders could even be attractive if we could ask the user to specify in his program at which point the claim of the tapereader(s) could be withdrawn, in particular since there is a large class of programs that only read some input in the beginning. We decided against this extra burden on the unaware programmer.

The alternative, maintaining the claim over the lifetime of the program is equally unattractive as now the banker might become so restrictive that multiprogramming would be endangered. The solution that was adopted may appear very crude but has performed extremely satisfactorily over a number of years. Tapereaders will tend to keep the information stream to which they are connected "reasonably" filled, depending on the distance from the limiting boundaries and on the length of the stream. If, however, there is a request for a new input and no readers available then both readers will read full speed until one becomes free. In doing so a deliberate risk of storage exhaustion is taken. Thanks to the fact that "transp–reso" is sufficiently large the disaster sketched above has only occurred when we forced it during testing or demonstrations, but never during normal operation of the system.

10. REGULATION OF LINE PRINTER ACTIVITY

In the previous chapters we have already paid some attention to circumstances that may cause "printer selection". Also we have defined all pages residing in printer streams to be active output. Finally we have imposed the requirement that output should be actively processed whenever o > reso. How do we combine this requirement with a strategy of preferably having the lineprinter print a number of consecutive forms from the same stream (program)?

Let's make a distinction between attractive reasons for the line printer CM to go to work and unattractive ones.

If we assume the line printer CM to "know" the stream from which it printed the previous form, clearly this stream being non-empty is an attractive reason. Processing of the final form of a program (marked as such) will make the line printer CM "forget" the previous stream. Another attractive reason is a stream in which (at least) one such final form has been inserted, because now all output in that stream including the final form can be processed consecutively.

As an aside we should mention the only strategic decision that had to be revised after the system became operational. Originally when there was no need for printer activity on account of o > reso the printer CM would prefer to wait for a next form in the previous stream, rather than to select a new stream containing a final document. Consecutivity benefited from this strategy but as an unpleasant side-effect finished line printer output might remain in the system for a considerable time after the program that produced it had terminated.

Now we will look at the unattractive reasons for line printer activity, i.e. when the line printer is forced on account of o > reso. We introduce "sump" as the sum of all pages residing in printer streams. Now active output consists of:

$$\text{sump} + \text{active pluncher output.}$$

If pluncher selection is such that a pluncher CM is urged to activity whenever there is active pluncher output (i.e. equipment available (see p. 176) and finished documents present) we can be sure of output activity when active pluncher output > 0. When active pluncher output = 0, we have acto = sump, and then when acto + paso = sump + paso > reso we have to urge the line printer to activity.

So in the absence of attractive reasons the condition sump + paso > reso will set the line printer to work. From this analysis we derive that line printer selection is not only the task of p→o transition in a PM for line printer forms (increase of sump), but also of p→o transition for pluncher streams (when the transition gives rise to an increase of paso).

In fact we have exploited the relation sump + paso > reso in printer selection independent of further pluncher activity on the assumption that even when active pluncher output goes down to zero we will still need printer activity to get o ⩽ reso.

In writing this manuscript it occurred to us that the urging of printer activity on sump + paso > reso is somewhat precocious. Parallel with pluncher activity two things may occur:

(1) a PM may specify the end of a pluncher document and thereby cause a decrease of paso,
(2) a PM may specify the final form in a printer stream, printer selection will now find an attractive reason for printer activity, eventually causing a decrease of sump.

An improved condition for urging printer activity should now read:

$$\text{sump} + \text{paso} > \text{reso } and \text{ active pluncher output} = 0.$$

The suggested refinement is very illuminating of the increased complexity that may be incurred. With the improved condition printer selection must also be delegated to a pluncher CM when it finishes processing of a document for now active pluncher output may have gone down to zero. Also the quantity "active pluncher output" would have to be separately updated, both in o-decrease by a pluncher CM and in p→o transition in a PM.

The above description is still incomplete. When the storage situation is very tight a requested increase of sump which will bring o > reso may not be allowed. The requesting PM is held up in the p→o transition and the printer will not go to work since o ≤ reso. In order to be certain that a p→o transition can in due time be accomplished we have to create a hole of size maxpor, i.e. we urge the printer to work slightly sooner, in order to allow a PM to put in a next printer portion in the "hole". A slight change in the criterion follows the lines of section 8 when "maxpas" was introduced. The modified criterion for printer activity should read:

$$\text{sump} + \text{paso} > \text{reso} - \text{maxpor}.$$

If now the printer is urged to activity we are sure that in due time "sump + paso ≤ reso − maxpor" will hold and it will be possible to allow a requesting PM to add a next portion. Note that the criterion for printer activity may be written as "sump + paso > maxpas", in other words: we are willing to consider printer output as "pseudo passive output" as long as total (pseudo) passive output does not exceed the upper bound maxpas. But when that bound is exceeded the primary candidate for selection is printer output.

11. STRATEGIES OF CHOICE

In sections 4 through 10 we have only payed attention to the logical structure of dynamic storage allocation. No mention at all has been made of the strategies employed when a choice has to be made among a number of logically equivalent alternatives. Although this subject, we feel, falls outside the scope of this paper, questions might be raised on the subject so we will describe very roughly some of the strategies involved.

For document selection the remaining question is: if an output CM has to be activated, which will be the document to be processed next? We will distinguish the strategy for the line printer on the one hand, and for plunchers on the other. Part of the line printer strategy has been discussed in the previous chapter. We have been guided by two principles:

(1) try to print consecutively as many forms from the same program as possible,
(2) prevent the possibility of monopolization of the line printer by one program.

As for (1) we have already seen that the line printer CM "knows" from which stream it printed the previous form and goes to work whenever a next form in that stream is present. Criterion (1) is also responsible for the strategy of selecting the longest stream when a choice has to be made among logically equivalent streams. Both aspects of this strategy are in conflict with criterion (2). The following "balancing" strategy was applied:

(2.1) Make the line printer CM "forget" its knowledge of the previous stream after
      a sufficient number of consecutive forms from that stream have been printed,
      unless the stream already contains a final form.
(2.2) Do not simply select the longest stream, but take into account the "age" of
      the information in the stream as determined by the "time" elapsed since the
      last addition to the stream. The selection criterion now reads "length + age",
      where age is expressed in suitable units.

For the plunchers somewhat similar considerations hold, in particular where
selection of finished documents is involved. Our strategies should, however, see to
it that the following situation is avoided: a pluncher tied up to an unfinished
document, the stream empty, and the PM to fill that stream held up in its p→o
transition when all available bufferspace is used by other streams. A strategy that
would tend to keep all streams equally long was employed to avoid that situation.
It implies that in selection of an unfinished document the longest stream will be
favoured, in reactivation of a PM held up in a p→o transition we favour the one with
the shortest stream.

For the tapereaders we specify the criterion for an input stream to be "reasonably
filled", this criterion has been implemented as:

length of stream $\geq 1/2$ * minimum of distances to IO and IOP boundary.

We see that this is a rather conservative criterion. If the storage situation is tight we
accept a smaller amount of input buffering. The criterion does not prevent a disaster
on the I or IP boundary (when o is small). It will be hard to give a justification of
this choice, but it has performed very satisfactorily.

12. DIMENSIONING OF THE RELEVANT QUANTITIES

A few words should be devoted to the actual values of the quantities discussed in
the previous chapters and their influence on system performance.

12.1. The size of core store

During the design phase of the system we had no idea whether the bottleneck
would be the central processor or the drum channel. To counter the first possibility
one tries to design routines that operate efficiently, an ordinary practice. However,
the drum channel cannot be made more effective. It is a well known fact that by
providing more primary storage the number of drum transfers can be brought down.
Our original configuration with 32K of core memory did not behave satisfactorily.
One commonly used program (viz. the ALGOL compiler) did not fit well in the paged
part of core memory. A subsequent extension with 16K, raising the number of core
pages from 40 to 70 was not only sufficient, but we feel, — and this seems important —
that no significant increase in system performance may be expected from further
extension of core memory. We stress this point because so often the performance
of a multiprogramming system is a (linearly?) increasing function with the size of

primary storage. Adapting the size of core memory to the requirements of extremely demanding programs (high vagrancy in page references) would not only be economically injustifiable, but clearly without any limit.

12.2. The distribution of virtual store

The total size of virtual store should be considered as an upper limit on the capacity of the system and cannot be subjected to discussion. Important values are "reso" and "transp". Out of approximately 1000 pages, 256 were part of "transput area". This figure seems reasonable. It does not give rise to excessive I/O buffering which in turn might impede the storage allotments of running programs. On the other hand, it was sufficient to cater for the buffering of over a full reel of paper tape (300,000 octades).

If transp had been considerably smaller the main impact would have been on the speed of tapereading. The occurrences of "forced reading" and with it, the danger of storage exhaustion would have increased.

The value of "reso" was set to 64 ($\frac{1}{4}$ of transp), with a buffering capacity of appr. 20 lineprinter forms of average printing density, or $\frac{1}{3}$ of a reel of paper tape. Increasing reso would have had a beneficial effect on the selection of unfinished documents and the application of the banker's algorithm. At the same time (as can be seen from figure 2), it would have increased the I and IP surfaces at the expense of the IO and IOP surfaces, so the danger of storage exhaustion would have grown.

A next parameter of relevance is the degree of multiprogramming to be allowed. Our objectives were twofold:

(1) to provide for a large uniform virtual store, in which the programmer was to be unaware of the implementation in two levels of storage. In order to utilize the processor time lost during drum transfers a sufficient number of executable programs should be eligible for processor time.

(2) to provide for rapid access to the machine during processing of the batch of user programs.

These purposes were well served by setting the (maximum) degree of multiprogramming at 5 (PMs). Having to allow for a much higher degree of multiprogramming, without adjusting the size of virtual store or the amount of equipment would have been logically simple, but the performance of the system might soon have degraded.

Operating experience over more than 3 years has proved the system to be robust, and to provide for smooth operation. (Illustrative of the effect of our flexible buffering schemes is the fact that the T.H.E. system is particularly preferred over the EL X-8 uniprogramming system (which also makes use of the drum for buffering) when plotting programs have to be processed.) The pathology and the disaster situations, so extensively dealt with in this paper are virtually unknown to the operator.

The addition of magnetic tape units has certainly relieved the tape punchers and readers of some of the bigger documents. Maybe they should also be commended for their role, although their exact influence is difficult to judge.

In retrospect we feel that the relevant parameter values have been very well chosen (and never revised). But we would like to pose an open question: how much do we owe to sound judgement, and how much to mere luck?

13. CONCLUDING REMARKS

We hope this paper has served two goals:

(1) It may have shed some light on an aspect of the T.H.E. Multiprogramming System, of which so little appears on the outside.
(2) It may have demonstrated that the major problem in designing a multiprogramming system is not the sharing of the processor. Since time is the only unlimited resource this sharing presents no problem. A graver problem presents itself as soon as one tries to share the other resources in an optimal manner, viz. without imposing strong restrictions.

Resource sharing can be done with beneficial effect both for the user and for system performance. Sharing should, however, not be carried to extremes. Two examples of deliberate non-sharing were: (1) setting aside sufficient core pages as to never let the availability of core become a blocking factor in the progress of a PM. (2) setting apart a number of pages in virtual store for output buffering only, to prevent the banker from coming into action too frequently.

In deciding how far sharing should be carried through one should have a keen eye on: (1) danger of increased overall complexity, and (2) external behaviour of the system. Several refinements of sharing strategies have been discussed and it has been shown how additional refinements greatly increase the overall complexity of the system, and how additional securities may influence the external behaviour in an inacceptable manner.

The degree of structural complexity involved in the virtual memory allocation schemes designed by our five man team seems pretty close to the limit of what can be convincingly conceived. It is not likely that increasing the size of the design team would allow for the design of significantly more complex structures.

14. ACKNOWLEDGEMENT

The author is greatly indebted to Prof. Dr. E. W. Dijkstra, above all for being the spiritual father of virtually all of the material presented in this paper.

15. REFERENCES

[1]   Dijkstra, E. W., "The Structure of the T.H.E. Multiprogramming System". *Comm. ACM*, **11** (1968), 341.
[2]   Habermann, A. N., "Prevention of System Deadlocks". *Comm. ACM*, **12** (1969), 373.

DISCUSSION

McKEAG: Our paper examines a number of store management techniques that have been used with success, and tries to relate them to the environments for which they are best suited. We suggest that for each technique there is a range of circumstances for which it is quite adequate, and that the designer of a software system should select the simplest such technique that is suitable rather than try to choose the most general one.

The first part of the paper examines seven relatively simple techniques that have been found to be perfectly adequate for many purposes. These range from the empty machine — with no operating system and no store management system, but with the undoubted advantages of not requiring special hardware, of maximum flexibility, of greatest simplicity and of minimum cost — through to the use of sequential or uniprogramming supervisors, simple multiprogramming using partitions, swapping schemes such as the MIT Onion Skin Algorithm and Irons' Minimum Overlay technique, to the Delayed Swap technique.

The second part of the paper examines some of the more complicated schemes that in the first part of the paper we've shown are not always necessary. The use of paging techniques arises from the inflexibility of the simpler techniques which constrain programs to use contiguous regions of core. There are three consequences of this: thrashing can occur quite unnecessarily when there is other core lying idle; material cannot be shared if programs have to use contiguous regions of core; and programs are limited to fit the size of the machine or less. Our survey of paging techniques describes some of the bread and butter housekeeping mechanisms used, and then discusses three main problems involved in the administration of a paging system. Firstly we look at page replacement algorithms; secondly latency reduction strategies; and thirdly load shedding schemes.

The cost of using many page replacement algorithms such as the Atlas Loop Detection method and Least Recently Used, is exorbitant; yet systems designers have been loth to forsake them and their variants and adopt more simple-minded techniques like First In First Out. Burroughs have taken the plunge with surprising success. A technique which has been proposed, which combines much of the simplicity of First In First Out with much of the predictive power of Least Recently Used, is the Second Chance algorithm.

The latency delay caused by a page fault is the real cost of paging, and under heavy loads latency delays rise very rapidly unless some form of drum scheduling is used; an example of this is the one used in the Michigan Terminal System on the IBM 360/67. Other latency delay control techniques include the use of pre-paging; but this can aggravate the problem rather than alleviate it. An extreme case of pre-paging can, however, be useful — that is the blocking together of pages currently being used by a program when it has to be suspended for a relatively long time, for example between multi-access interactions or when load-shedding is required. An ingenious method of reducing latency delays is by chaining together those (small) pages of a program, which constitute some logical region or segment. When a fault occurs for one page of such a region all the other pages of the same region can be brought into core at the same time on the assumption that they also will be required shortly. This form of pre-paging seems more likely to be used effectively by a programmer than one involving explicit transfers.

However well designed any paging system is, whatever load it is designed to support, there must be times when that load is exceeded. For example, when a number of programs change phase about the same time and the pressure on the core is much higher than the system can stand. Therefore there must be some mechanism for detecting such peaks and for load shedding by temporarily suspending some job, or jobs. We discuss several such techniques, and one of the simplest and most effective is by monitoring the rate at which page faults occur. As Fenton has said, Burroughs are considering the use of such a technique described by Wulf [13].

The final problem we considered was page size. Recently we have been studying the B5500 and its use of variable length pages and rather reluctantly have come to the conclusion that they appear to have little to offer over the use of small fixed length pages with chaining to reduce the latency delays.

We sum up, not by coming up with a "Which?" best buy, but by trying to point out a number of considerations which should be applied in the design and evaluation of a paging system. Firstly, there are three main savings that a paging system achieves: it does not allocate store that is never used, it delays the allocation of storage that is not required until late in the execution of a program, and it saves on storage that is required early in the program but never again; so long as a paging system makes the most of these savings it isn't too important if it fails to take into account any other savings. The second point is that a paging system should be able to support a high paging rate; this implies that the latency delays must be kept from rising when the system is heavily loaded. The third point is that some form of load shedding must be available for dealing with those occasions when the paging rate that the system is designed to support is exceeded. Fourthly, it is desirable that the page replacement algorithm must be discerning, so that the paging rate is not unnecessarily inflated by throwing out pages that are going to have to be brought back in again shortly afterwards. The final point we make on paging is that whatever techniques are used they should be simple enough to explain to a software writer or the designer of a large program, as better results will always be obtained with a modicum of human assistance. If these five considerations have been taken into account adequately, the other decision will be far less critical than is generally imagined.
VINCE: The most disturbing aspect of the paper is the lack of a proper relationship between segmentation and paging. One of the best ways to organize one's store is to have a two-level store organization, i.e. segmentation to look after those things that are logically related, and paging below that whose only function is to alleviate the embarrassing problem of store fragmentation. Then if a page fault occurs within a segment, the whole segment is fetched, and similarly, a whole segment is discarded at a time.

I agree that pre-paging is not feasible, but when one is looking for pages to reject to bring other pages in, I would suggest that a system pool of available pages should be used. The first thing one does is to take space from the system pool and initiate the segment fetch, because this is something that can't be done in parallel with the process for which the segment fault or page fault has occurred. Once that's initiated, select a segment for rejection, since the rejection can be done in parallel with the process that has faulted. One further idea might be to give each user a real partition of the store to start off with, not necessarily contiguous but contiguous at the page level, and again to leave a system pool. This has the advantage that when we come to select a segment for rejection the first place we look is in the user's quota. If such a segment can't be found then space can be taken away from the system pool and the fact recorded, and the segment fetch can be initiated into that space. Then on a subsequent fault when a segment can be found for rejection from that quota, the space can be returned to the system pool, so one's got a sort of knock for knock situation which, in the end, will more or less even out.

If the hardware were available to have "use" bits both at segment level and at page level, then to find a page for rejection you look at the "use" bits at segment level (which are cleared periodically, perhaps by the second chance algorithm), to find segments that haven't been used for a fair time. Of these segments you start looking for the one with the least number of "write" bits set at page level and that means you've only got to write a minimum amount out to the drum.

I agree with drum scheduling to take the first sector in terms of rotation. In fact now that one's got rotational position sensing on IBM 370 devices this can be done quite effectively. In fact some controllers will actually do the sector optimization for you.

I find it disappointing that this is just looking at things that are possible with backing store equipment that we've got now, and that consideration hasn't been given to devices like, for example, large MOS shift register stores which have very much better performance than drums, where probably quite a different approach may have to be taken.

McKEAG: You mentioned a technique using segment bits and page bits. What we were trying to emphasize was the use of techniques that have low overheads, the overheads would increase considerably using such a technique and the resulting algorithm might not be more discriminating. The second chance algorithm uses "use" bits, but very simply; it doesn't have to do a scan of all the segments to see whether or not they have been used.

VINCE: The computing overhead might not be as important as the advantage gained from minimizing channel traffic. Without investigation you can't say which is the better trade-off.

BRINCH HANSEN: I read a paper last year which started with the words "Paging is a sound concept". It's roughly like saying a jumbo-jet is an excellent means of transportation, however one would hesitate to use it for city traffic. We ought to congratulate McKeag and Hoare for making explicit that techniques of resource allocation can only be meaningfully discussed and understood in economic terms, and they have succeeded in presenting a set of techniques in increasing order of cost and complexity.

They have a certain amount of courage to go against the current, popular trend of paging and segmentation, in exposing a somewhat ambivalent attitude towards various techniques — what I would call praying to two Gods. You are praying to one God but you are not quite sure that this God will be the favourite one, so you pray to another one without telling the first one. I would regard, for example, falling into the temptation of introducing variable length pages as praying to two Gods; that is, on the one hand you have the original aim of simplifying the allocation of main and secondary store by partitioning your store into fixed length units, but on the other hand you now destroy that aim as you somehow don't feel confident about whether this is the right God or not. Also, the economy

gained by dynamic storage allocation should make the further gain of program
sharing negligible and not worth the complexity of segmentation, and the paper
clearly brings out that point.

The main weakness of the paper is that it gives an ordered set of techniques,
like characterizing cars as mini-cars, medium cars and prestige cars, but the dealer
of these cars refuses to tell you precisely what they cost. He will tell you that
one is more expensive than the other, and you now have to make up your mind
which one you are going to buy. So although the paper presents the logical
complexities of addressing and swapping around of information there is a lack of
performance analysis.

NEWELL: This paper gives a very nice list of possibilities but I found it very
unsatisfactory because it was not possible for the evaluations to be quantitative.
If you can't be quantitative at least you can discuss what you mean by "expensive".

I don't think you've discussed store management, you've discussed various store
topographies that the various store management systems aim to end up with.

RANDELL: But there are one or two conclusions and there are one or two
numbers, and in fact the paper worries me more when it gives numbers. There's
the one, for example, that says that external fragmentation costs you 20% of the
store; certainly my own attempt at investigating that by simulation would not
have made me give that number. Then there's the conclusion that variable length
pages don't seem worthwhile; again, the paper didn't make out a sufficiently
convincing case.

Our work on thrashing came about because I suggested that we look at an
operating system as being a servo-mechanism with several feedback loops. What
is described in the paper concentrated simply on one feedback control loop,
the feedback concerned with the problem of thrashing and the level of multiprogramming. Thrashing we regard as a very nice, simple and important example
of the dangers of positive feedback in an operating system. Many people have
achieved the design of paging systems in which they've built in nice, simple, positive
feedback so that if there are too many jobs in core store the result is that the
operating system will bring in another one. We were interested in finding algorithms
which would, by definition, avoid positive feedback. We knew of Denning's [2]
work but it seemed a rather complicated way of going around the problem,
involving a priori judgement on a whole set of parameters, which looked strange to us.

Our investigation was done using a simulator that did not go down to the level
of address traces and did not keep account of which pages a given program had
in working store at a given moment but which kept track of just the number of
pages that each program had in core, adjusting these numbers up or down as we
modelled the acquisition or the loss of pages. The simulated machine used a
sector-queued drum for backing store, it had a limited size core store, and it had
independent input/output channels and facilities for each job. We started with a
simulation which involved an attempt to characterize the load that we believed was
being processed on the MTS system at Newcastle. This is a mixture of very small
jobs which modelled things like APL interactions, somewhat larger jobs: the smaller
compilations and small student runs, and then the much bigger, luckily less
frequent, jobs that are occasionally thrust down our throats by people who, for
example, insist on using the PL/1 F-level compiler, which is great on a demand
paging system!

Figure 1 in the paper shows the effect of core size when using this model workload. The immediate thing that this shows is that all of these algorithms, and many more, are quite capable of doing very well if they've got enough core storage; a fairly obvious point but one that tends to be forgotten. We soon realized that a much more instructive way of comparing algorithms was to fix the core size and vary the constraint on multiprogramming level to see the extent to which the algorithm imposes its own restraint on multiprogramming level (figure 2). The only one that doesn't do this very well dies very badly. That's all very well, but why do the various algorithms do this and why do they vary so considerably? Figure 3 shows the technique we used to try to understand what was going on in the simulation: each line of the core map indicates how many pages each program had in core. The purpose of these core maps is to enable us to gain an insight into the algorithms by seeing how they perform in severe conditions. My own belief in simulation as a tool is not that it gives you surprising results so that you can then say "Oh good, now I know what happens." Rather, I believe quite the opposite, that the main advantages are, firstly, the psychological point that it spurs designers to understand their designs a bit more because they know that by to-morrow morning there'll be some results; and, secondly, it keeps them a bit more honest because very often, if they are challenged to say in advance what their algorithms will do, even very good designers find that their skill in this is not as high as they had hoped.

In the paper we use a very much simpler workload with a set of identical jobs and describe just three anti-thrashing algorithms. The first is by Wharton, who suggested that you give an essentially fixed priority to each job and steal pages from the lowest priority job with pages. He correctly predicted that this certainly could never cause thrashing. What does happen, of course, is that a job, as it gradually uses more and more of its different pages, will eventually drive out more and more of the programs below it until perhaps, if there's somebody still above it, it too starts to suffer the treatment that it's been meting out to others. Figure 4 shows this happening, with job number 4 and job number 5 gradually being driven out. Figure 5 shows Wharton's algorithm varying with multiprogramming level in an 80-page machine. Essentially it's a very nice algorithm because as you increase the constraint on multiprogramming level the algorithm gives you a monotonically increasing CPU utilization. It constrains itself very nicely for exactly the reasons that led to its design. However, it's not necessarily making the best use of core memory; it's avoiding thrashing by being far too conservative.

Figure 6 shows the reasoning behind the next algorithm: one can imagine some sort of graph of CPU utilization against multiprogramming level as having a shape such that up to a certain level further multiprogramming is good, beyond that level it is bad and soon becomes disastrous. This is an advertising agency type of graph — there are no scales. There is also a graph of the number of drum reads against multiprogramming level. The idea was that we wanted some sort of feedback mechanism that would tend, if one got into region B, to drive you to the left, and, if you were in region A, to drive you to the right. We wanted what I would describe as implicit feedback rather than the explicit feedback which characterizes the Denning working set mechanism and, for that matter, the Burroughs 6700 working set mechanism. The suggestion of Horning was to take the Wharton algorithm, with the jobs in the mix being scheduled according to fixed priority and with pages being queued for the drum according to this same fixed priority, but if a page was stolen it would be stolen at random from the pages in memory. If you are in region B of the graph, the number of drum reads would be so high that the drum queue would have a lot of items in it; therefore jobs which are low down in priority would perhaps never get their drum reads performed. Jobs with high priority would get favoured treatment and they would tend to grow and push out the low priority jobs, so there would be a tendency to drift towards region A. You can reverse the argument and say that if you are in region A there is a tendency to drift the other way. This was a very appealing argument to the point where we all believed it, but the simulation showed that it didn't work like that. In fact the Horning algorithm very neatly equi-partitions memory, and this is the last thing you want to do if you have too many jobs competing for memory (figure 7). The paper describes in more detail why this happens. Basically it was possible to have too many jobs in memory and still not have the queueing discipline coming into effect. So we had somewhat red faces over the Horning algorithm but we predicted the exact graph in figure 8 and were then very pleased when we actually got it out by simulation, just to show that sometimes we won. The algorithms we like are the ones that we can show to be monotonically increasing with multiprogramming level, although figure 2 shows that this condition is not necessarily a sufficient one for judging algorithms.

Lynch attempted to improve on the Wharton algorithm by finding some way of taking pages away from a job, and this was the very simple idea of a fixed drain. At quite regular intervals – every second logical revolution of the drum – a page was stolen from every job that was not in page wait status, whether it was on the CPU or waiting for I/O. It was possible to set this so that one could calculate the badness of the effect on a program that had its exact working set in core. This was 25%, and clearly this was a figure we could have adjusted. In figure 9 you see how different the picture is from the Horning algorithm. Figure 10 looks like the graph for the Wharton algorithm except that the lines are moved up a bit. What we now have to do is to find a feedback mechanism that controls the stealing rate in order to get as much CPU utilization as possible without running into the danger of thrashing.

We also tried to impose a CPU–I/O balance on top of this mechanism to ensure that the feedback loops are disconnected from each other. These three algorithms all use a priority which is fixed or, at least, whose rate of change is slow compared to the phenomenon we have been talking about here. One can investigate the value of shuffling these priorities within the set of programs in core; or alternatively, causing migrations into and out of this set. But these changes should be at a rate sufficiently slow that they can be regarded as a second order effect. Whether you should do so can be argued, but certainly from the way I've seen some automatic paging systems go, that thrashing is a first level effect to worry about.

The other important lesson from this research is the demonstration of how easily even somebody of the calibre of Horning could fool himself and us by a plausible argument as to the behaviour of a very simple algorithm. This leads one to have very grave worries about the danger of adding complicated algorithms to operating systems. You can think of an operating system as a set of servo-mechanisms; alternatively you can think of it as being a set of interconnected queues. You can think of any given queue and argue fairly intelligently about treating this queue as FIFO or LIFO or priority or whatever. You can argue about what effect that might have on the overall behaviour of the system. The question that is very difficult is whether the queue will in fact have enough items in it normally for that discipline to have any effect.

VINCE: You've looked at one sharing aspect, that is sharing the resource of core store, but you haven't taken into account the sharing of other resources in the system. For example: a low priority job has opened a file which it only wants to keep open for a short while; it is interrupted and then paged out by a high priority job which then wants to share the file which the low priority job is now unable to close. I would suggest that the interaction with the rest of the system is not just the sharing of files but is more involved and complex.

RANDELL: We don't say that one should directly take these algorithms and mindlessly put them into an operating system without regard for any of the other interactions. What we were trying to do was analyse the consequence, which in the past has often been quite disastrous, of ignoring one particular feedback loop.

VINCE: Dijkstra has proposed that operating system software should be built up in layers. What you're saying now is that to make your algorithm work you've got to have very close and intricate interaction between the software that is managing page rejection and the software that is looking after resource control. In other words, you're not achieving any separation of these levels of abstraction at all because they're so closely interrelated.

RANDELL: Agreed, and Dijkstra's system does suffer from thrashing. So here is a case where the T.H.E. system's levels of abstraction are not adequate. I'm not trying to preach against levels of abstraction — I like God, Love and Motherhood too.

VINCE: There are systems in which one wants some sort of architectural and engineering principles; unless one has these one ends up with an operating system that doesn't work because all the modules are so interrelated and the interfaces are so complicated. One might be paying for adopting a very close attachment between the level at which paging is looked after and the level at which resource control is looked after, by ending up with an operating system that you can't get into the field until a few years later than you might otherwise have done.

RANDELL: When phenomena are interrelated then you'd better know about it in designing your operating system.

HOARE: One of the purposes of writing down a survey of techniques and making a few remarks about how one might choose between them is to try to see whether the time has come when we can get some agreement among experts that the important things have been isolated, and that at least the lines along which solutions are being sought are the right ones.

So I would like the audience, in reference to our paper, to state whether they think the conclusions are trivial, boring, obvious, which I hope they are, or contentious, highly subject to doubt. Whenever I give advice as a consultant, I always recall the lines of Hilaire Belloc who, in one of his poems, said that

> "Scientists, who ought to know, assure us that it must be so.
> Oh, let us never, never doubt what nobody is sure about."

I would like to be sure about some things, therefore I would like to ask Randell, who has some doubts about some of the remarks made in our paper, to make those doubts explicit and say what is wrong with sector queueing and what is wrong with Least Recently Used, for example.

RANDELL: On sector queueing I was specifically thinking of the remark about MTS. The MTS sector queueing involves trying to schedule two or three complete revolutions of the drum, and one of the results of doing this is that there is an increase in latency over and beyond what might be necessary, since the fact that a page has arrived is not immediately reported back to the program waiting to use it. This relates to the fact that the paging was put in underneath the non-paged system; it was a system which was first run on the model 50 and then on the model 67 used as a 65; so the "paging drum processor" is not integrated as fully into the lower parts of the system as would otherwise be the case.

There are some fairly simple queueing theory results which show that you've really got to have a very high demand rate from the drum before you start to benefit from your sector queueing. Sector queueing is so obviously marvellous until you actually look at some of the numbers. Now if we're really going to talk about sector queueing and about very high data rates from a drum then there is a store management technique which I think should have been surveyed, and that is the one in the BCC 1 system.[1] This uses a very small and very fast mini-computer, very closely tied to the drum, which not only schedules but also allocates space on the drum; it is a system that puts its money on the drum and drum channel and saves its money on the core store, and that gives a very different view of the world.

HOARE: Not to report back to the program immediately its page has come in obviously nullifies all the advantage of sector queueing.

I regard LRU as a page discard technique, not a load shedding technique.

ALDERSON: We found with MTS that when we got into an overload condition, LRU pulled more and more jobs down to try to build up the multiprogramming level to cover up the paging delays. When that was realized we put in FIFO instead.

HOARE: How does FIFO cure the situation? Is it because FIFO ensures that each page spends a reasonably long time in core store; and prevents the paging rate from escalating? Every page is now going to reside a fixed length of time in store at least. That's really the thing that's important.

BRINCH HANSEN: That couldn't prevent thrashing. What is bad about LRU is not at all in conflict with your paper, because Randell is talking about using LRU without load shedding, and you are correctly pointing out that the effect of load shedding is the major problem; and once you have done that the choice of replacement algorithm is almost completely of secondary importance.

FENTON: It's not clear to me how a paging algorithm such as, LRU or FIFO, actually schedules more jobs.

RANDELL: LRU without any explicit control on multiprogramming level would thrash like many other algorithms, but not all other algorithms without an explicit control.

FENTON: So what you were really testing your algorithms against was being overscheduled by whoever was really supposed to be doing the multiprogramming?

RANDELL: That was part of it, the other was that we were testing the extent to which they were underscheduled by avoiding thrashing but also not getting high CPU utilization.

When we were arguing about the relative merits of explicit and implicit feedback we realized that implicit feedback had the great merit of not having a parameter to

[1] Greenberg, M. L., "An algorithm for drum storage requirements in time-sharing systems". *Third ACM Symposium on Operating Systems Principles,* Palo Alto (Oct. 1971).

set. The working set algorithm in the B6700 has eight parameters associated with it, which the installation manager or the systems programmer has to set, and it wasn't clear to me either (1) that these parameters were independent of each other or (2) in the case of many of the parameters how I would go about finding out what their numbers were. At first I was worried about algorithms that didn't have any parameters because there's nothing left to adjust to make them any better.

JOB SCHEDULING TECHNIQUES

Panellists: G. Newell and B. A. Wichmann

PANEL DISCUSSION

WICHMANN: Low level scheduling is the technique for scheduling processes or activities which have already been loaded into core. These can be of a number of different types. At one extreme, an interrupt process does not need to be scheduled, because it is a piece of non-interruptable code. The problem is to decide how long to make that piece of code, and when to delegate its task to another process, to be scheduled at a later stage. In a real time system the total length of non-interruptable code is a significant system parameter.

On the KDF9 we maintain a strict priority system for the low level scheduler. The advantage of this is that you know exactly what is happening; you can put processor bound programs at the bottom and soak up the processor time. You know, for instance, what size buffers it's reasonable to allocate to the peripheral transfers at every level, because you know the scheduling process characteristics at that level.

But there are a number of distinct disadvantages. We have to maintain a process scheduler within a level of the supervisor. Also, the service for the lower levels of the priority chain depend on the behaviour at high levels. We have, for example, programs which only require 10 minutes processor time sticking in the machine for over an hour; this is just a characteristic of the load conditions. In many ways a round robin system would be more satisfactory, but then you can't give a priority to functions that have low CPU overhead and small core utilization.

It is important that the amount of processor time used by the low level scheduler should be extremely small. We tried to make modifications on the KDF9 to remove the restrictions on the number of multiprogramming levels to increase the capability of scheduling, but because of the CPU overhead in changing it just wasn't acceptable.

One can see the necessity for having several levels of scheduling corresponding to the different types of jobs; for instance supervisor functions and user jobs, (1) which may or may not be interactive, and fast batch.

With batch systems you need to process the jobs as quickly as possible. Strict limits have got to be enforced on the processor time and the peripheral transfers used by such programs.

(2) With both supervisor functions and certain user jobs, you must maintain some degree of response predictability. What one wants is some cheap method, in terms of processor time, of controlling what's going on. For example, if a user is sitting at a terminal for any length of time it should be only because he is using a significant amount of a system resource.

(3) At a higher level we have remote job entry systems. If you consider a system like the Atlas, which contains nothing but batches, you can see that processor

194

utilization and gross turnaround are good criteria for organizing job scheduling, and we know how to do that. There are problems like core thrashing even with remote job entry systems, but one can detect and prevent this within the time scale which is insignificant compared with the sort of turnaround time one is considering.

IBM OS 360 deals with each class differently: this is not necessary on the 1900 series, where a dynamic core division can be arranged. A reasonable management decision is to have a fast batch system, and ensure that it runs efficiently and allow a certain degree of activity in the multiaccess system; but it mustn't be allowed to degrade the other systems. But obviously these decisions will have ramifications all the way through the operating system.

NEWELL: In George 3 we have four schedulers; a high level scheduler, a low level scheduler, a time sharer and a co-ordinator. The low level scheduler, or process dispatcher, is given a list of programs to run by the high level scheduler and runs the highest priority program. The interface consists of numbers called c.p.i's, i.e. computing power index. We foolishly thought you could communicate between these two routines in terms of this single number. You can't integrate the two schedulers into an overall process scheduler because one handles processes in system phase and time shares them, whereas the other time shares processes that are in program phase. The reason Hartley can separate them is because processes in system phase genuinely are in that phase for such a short period it doesn't matter; they don't cause any blocking problems. For various reasons in George this won't do.

Most of the names involved with the job scheduler are self-descriptive, for example job limit; when a job is put in a card reader or someone logs in, it checks whether the job can enter the system. It's a dynamic limit on the number of jobs, and the operators can change it during the day; they find that the operating system isn't making a very good job of the overload conditions. Other parameters which are given to the job scheduler are the object and chapter quota; they are not partitions in the physical or conceptual sense, i.e. they are not hard upper and lower bounds.

In writing operating systems, particularly ones with complex dynamic core allocation you can never assess what the true situation is. What you do is stick your finger in the air to see which way the wind is blowing and make a decision, and return at regular intervals to see how things are going; you make no assumptions about the correctness of future predictions. You seem always to be looking backwards and trying to sort out the neglected jobs. Object quota indicates when to swap a program in, and since you haven't got a simple test like "Is the partition vacant and will the program fit in?" you swap and see if it works; if it does you try and swap another one in until the limit is reached. Once reached, you don't stop there because a major principle of the system is that every bit of core should be used for the currently best purpose, so you continue to try and swap in. What is different is the way you react to failures; if you haven't met the object quota, you go into the various thresholds of core unjamming. This is an installation parameter, because we didn't know how to do it so we passed the buck to the user. Operating systems tend to be too willing when asked to do the impossible, and end up thrashing themselves to death instead of saying "go away" and flagging out. This is mainly because they don't know how to discern that condition. Load shedding has a similar quota, and when you want space for further overlays to the operating system you keep trying even though you've met the quota. The core allocation system can remove chapters down to the chapter quota; this is not a hard lower limit. If you are really stuck and get a certain threshold of core jam you can go below the chapter quota; but again, as with all servo-mechanisms, it can stray back.

The servo-mechanism analogy is relevant because core unjammers say "Right, this is a mess, everybody out!" and the low level scheduler says "My job in life is to pack this core with paying programs" and the situation tends to oscillate between these two extremes. If you overdamp the oscillation the system gets into a core jam; it knows how to get out of it but it takes ten minutes to do so. Anybody who designs a thermostat knows that you mustn't make it switch on on the way up at the same temperature as it switches off on the way down, because it would then just remain at that temperature clicking like mad until it breaks itself. We avoid this problem because we cross our boundaries in discrete steps; so it's safer than the thermostat design but still observes the servo-mechanism principle.

In an operating system you can't afford to discern accurately what the situation is because that would take longer than the potential saving would justify. In the Mark V version of George the user could rewrite the scheduler, and access a very large amount of information. The time taken to do the sums on this information in any useful way would outweigh any savings made. The information provided is: what jobs are on the machine, their characteristics, whether they're MOP or background jobs, what the load is on backing store. Presently, we're being asked for the mean response time on all the MOP consoles, and which should be loadshed? It's difficult to defer jobs that have shared files open; you've got to leave information in core, if the file control block is to stop other people who wish to write to this file. This is certainly the hardest and most interesting part of the job scheduler to design. We have a very rudimentary algorithm which checks and sets c.p.i.'s for the various jobs. Not many of the users have re-written their schedulers, so we cannot judge whether they can do any better than us.

There is one other handle called the MOP c.p.i., which indicates to the low level scheduler, in the absence of the high level scheduler, what the division in time should be between the background and MOP jobs, e.g. during the day it might be 90% while at night it is set to 10%.

Overall, we have been using the crudest mechanism we can get away with to do the job.

HUXTABLE: We've got two quite distinct situations; (1) the integrated system dealing with jobs coming in on a very wide basis, and (2) the system built up of sub-systems, each of which has its own individual access point, its own individual control system. The sub-system situation is simplest from a high level scheduling point of view, the users do it themselves; they group themselves and form a queue to get their required service. We have different problems with a mixed set of people, all of whom have to be sorted into separate queues, the length of the queue is then weighed and judged against priorities. I'm surprised, we have been able to survive without a high level scheduler for so long. Have the operators and general system managers been doing this?

NEWELL: The situation can be more complicated when you introduce remote job entry in a significant way. It depends how you present your remote job entry situation to your users; if it looks like a mini-computer then you need more and more parameters when a job's introduced. The trouble with these installation parameters is that you're moving towards the largest unstructured programming language in the world.

RANDELL: There is a distinction between the mechanisms used inside the system to maximize the amount of work that goes through the system and the mechanisms used to ensure a certain user, or class of users, gets priority at the expense of the rest of the users. You might be willing to have the rest of the users suffer far more than the privileged ones have gained. You can make this distinction if (i) you don't allow it to go too far, and (ii) the amount of work that is being presented to your system is such that there are not too many different ways of taking a sub-set and still run your system at full blast.

In a sense the more unbalanced your system is, the easier it is to tell whether you're running it with 100% efficiency or not. If you've got an agreed indication of the efficiency of the system, then the distinction between maintaining full blast operation and favouring a group is a good way of giving some philosophical meaning to the two different scheduling techniques.

NEWELL: The only difference between these two approaches is, what happens when the favoured users aren't using the resources and how then can you let the other users have the use of those resources, rather than leave them idle?

RANDELL: I'm assuming the system moves amongst a set of strategies which equally maximize throughput. When there are no really important users, your system works calmly. Once you've got everybody as a high priority user you've got problems.

HOARE: A normal generous philosophy would be to give any spare time available, when the batch system is rather lightly loaded, to the multiaccess users. But this leads to a serious difficulty. What multiaccess users want more than anything else is predictability of response; they don't like random variations, which would occur if there was a sudden upsurge in batch users. There seems to be psychological grounds for fixed allocations of core and time to multiaccess users, although a "generous" man would allow variable allocations. Have you any experience of this? Have you found customers wanting to adjust their scheduler to take some cognizance of this fact?

NEWELL: Well users complain their response times are bad anyway. You should certainly never load the system so that Hartley's principle is invalid, namely that the time spent in system processes is so insignificant that it wouldn't degrade performance. It depends what you are responding to. One of the troubles with having a command language that's got a macro facility is that users don't notice the difference between built-in commands and macros. They don't realize the time difference involved because they don't know what they're asking the operating system to do; it's something they should be made conscious of.

FENTON: One way of making the users aware of this is for the operating system always to respond to the steps in the macro, even though you know they're coming from the macro rather than from the man putting it in.

HARTLEY: It is unreasonable to expect a good system to respond similarly to a simple edit as to a FORTRAN compilation. This is what people tend to regard as response time.

FENTON: An awful lot of work has been done in the field of response times in radar displays, where they do very carefully engineer what information they're going to present to the user and how often, rather than depending on which way the wind is blowing.

VINCE: The salesman ought to quote on the basis of rate of performance rather than on a particular response, and the same is true at hardware level. He should quote

the rate of performance of the virtual machine rather than the fact you multiply in
1·6 microseconds.

WICHMANN: What I'd like to see is response predictability for a fixed task. Take
the edit function, for instance, on the KDF9, if you do a simple edit the response
you get will be anything from 2 seconds to 20 seconds. Response prediction is well
nigh impossible, as jobs get processed on a first in first out basis, because of the
way in which the machine is structured. It's impossible to get the normal supervisor
functions to allow more reasonable scheduling, but this has got to happen if the
user isn't satisfied with what he's getting.

NEWELL: I'd like to ask Needham was response predictability the reason why you
put in the feature whereby a terminal user can enquire how many people are on at
one time?

NEEDHAM: No. It's used to enquire whether particular people are on if you wish
to converse with them.

There's one very important point in considering the feasibility of job scheduling
and that is the time scale at which its objectives have got to be achieved. Particularly,
if one is talking of the proportion of machine resources which go to the background
jobs. This can be achieved by manipulating the number of people who are allowed to
log in simultaneously, because this will even out the utilization over a long time. We
do this over the period of a day on Titan; any shorter period would be much more
difficult. In a number of cases the difficulties of job scheduling arise because you're
trying to satisfy ridiculous short-term objectives.

NEWELL: That's true, but let's take your example of averaging over a day. How do
you decide when to start getting worried about meeting the objective? When does the
scheduler decide to run the job to meet the deadline?

NEEDHAM: You count the proportion of time that goes to background jobs so
that you can say on a certain number of days last week it was rather low so we had
better change the limit on the number of people logging in from 24 to 23 say.

BRINCH HANSEN: You can do a lot of reasonable prediction for background and
foreground jobs, by considering the limits imposed by human impatience. With
foreground jobs you've got to keep pace with the rate at which users can type things.
You can make more reasonable predictions with background jobs where the users can
make sensible estimates of the time required. At the recent IFIP Congress[1] I described
a method called the highest response ratio, by which you make a reasonable estimate
of the execution time of your program and measure its waiting time; the ratio is then
a measure of how much slower the machine appears to the user compared to the
situation in which he owned the whole machine. The response time is simply the run
time you get in a shared computer environment. The algorithm takes the job which
has the highest response ratio, that is the job for which the machine appears to be
slowest at the moment. A variation is to calculate the scheduling of all jobs each
time a user makes a request and if the introduction of a new job makes the machine
slower than a factor decided by the installation the job will be rejected. Then you
get a system which has the property that all systems should have, in that you can
predict response times. It's like the shop where you enter and say "How long will it
be before I can be shaved?" and the barber says "It will take anywhere between one
and two hours".

[1] Brinch Hansen, P., "An analysis of Response Ratio Scheduling". IFIP Congress, Ljubljana,
1971.

You can achieve a balance between foreground and background jobs so that foreground jobs will occupy a certain percentage of processor time. Given the highest priority you know that they will delay other jobs by 10 per cent, so you can predict response on background jobs. You can at the same time give high response to foreground jobs, but when they exceed the limit you refuse to let a new user log in.

VINCE: What you're doing is establishing a rate of execution for each type of job and based on that rate you have at least some predictability.

BRINCH HANSEN: Yes.

RANDELL: That depends on the extent to which you know what the future is going to do, and you could spend more time calculating the future than you could ever gain back.

BRINCH HANSEN: Any form of scheduling is nothing more than a political rule based on the assumption that for all customers waiting time is equally expensive, and therefore you try to minimize the overall sum. The highest response ratio is based on the assumption that all users should see a machine with roughly the same speed because they pay the same for it. Therefore one has to define the political objective before one can talk in logical technical terms.

Hoare suggested that the purpose of an operating system is to make the unpredictable predictable, and that must take place at a certain cost. If you want to be predictable then you will either lose resources or have idle resources. In the case of a storage allocation system you can give reasonable examples of techniques which allow background processing at an acceptable cost. It's the customers who care about predictable performance and that is where the compromise has to be made. An operating system should give you a prediction of turnaround time which is within the limits of human patience. This is not true of Dijkstra's banker's algorithm, which provides the kind of bank where you go in and say "To-day I am eight years old and I would very much like to buy a house" and the banker says "Well, we will lend you the money. We can't say whether we will do it when you are forty years old or when you are one hundred and twenty seven years, but we'll certainly do it within a finite time".

HOARE: There is a technique operating at this University which gives a certain degree of predictability. We run a certain class of service at certain fixed times of the day, and the user knows that if he gives his job in by twenty-five past the hour he will always get it back by the hour, i.e. within thirty-five minutes. He wants fixed turnaround, he doesn't want to leave his program in the machine for longer than thirty-five minutes; at least not if he's got a compile time error. He may be prepared to leave it longer if he gets past the compiler, and with this predictability he schedules his own time in an effective manner to co-operate with the planning of the installation and this is good in many ways. The only way in which it is bad is that he is going to rush his error corrections to get in on the next batch.

BRINCH HANSEN: It would seem to be very strongly related to the principle of load shedding in that to achieve predictable performance we had better not uncritically mix programs with highly varying requirements of response times. What users demand is predictability within a certain range of time and not over twenty-four hours a day.

HUXTABLE: This is easily done if people come into a centre; but how do we achieve the same effect with remote teletypes where you just don't know what the user is going to do before he actually logs in?

VINCE: That's not always true; for example, we're told that we get a service at a particular time of day, at any other time the service is unpredictable.

NEEDHAM: It might be worth pointing out one or two dangers in simple minded approaches to these things which in the interests of apparently maximizing physical resources is liable to have unfortunate feedback effects to the users. For example, if you roll object programs in and out, it is convenient for the machine to give as much processor time as possible to the physically largest program, and this encourages users to write large programs.

Secondly, we suffered from a shortage of tape units, so we tried to maximize the utilization of tape units. In particular, we reduce the interval between the tape being mounted and running the job requiring it. This had the unfortunate effect that a user could get a better turnaround for his off-line job by requiring a tape to be mounted to which he never referred.

HOARE: These principles are best used as a guide to the technique rather than the technique itself. Whatever technique you adopt, it should be positively correlated with the effects of equalizing the response ratio. It shouldn't necessarily use the calculation as its strategy, and this is even more true at the process dispatching level.

BRINCH HANSEN: The analogy to the operating system where you can initiate jobs of any length would seem to be the kind of shopping centre where they don't make any distinction between counters where you can buy candies and counters where you can have your suit tailormade; there's just one huge pool of assistants and they will serve any customer who comes in. Now try to predict when you get your candies.

NEWELL: I don't know why we're so apologetic. The exhaust fell off my car on the way to work the other morning and there was a garage which advertised "Exhausts fixed while you wait". So I drove in, handed over the keys, and the man said "Come back at 4 o'clock", and I said "What about the advertisement out front?" and he said "Well, sure you can wait till 4 o'clock!"

PROCESS DISPATCHING TECHNIQUES

Panellists: P. Brinch Hansen, G. Goss and D. F. Hartley

PANEL DISCUSSION

GOOS: Firstly, a few points about our system. Our low level scheduler has the equivalent function of the high level scheduler in the George 3 system. Also we have a two-processor system. The dispatcher works on a list containing the process name and state ordered according to their priorities.

We distinguish between system and user processes with the former having the highest priority, ordered according to their level. The user processes come next, and the number of these is variable. This means the low level scheduler has the power to change the level of multiprogramming. One of the difficulties in designing the dispatcher was in deciding how frequently to allow a change of program. With a single processor system you simply compare the priority of any new process with the currently running process and switch if necessary. In a multiprocessor system you have to consider all the processors, and this requires one or more interruptions. After carrying out some simulation experiments we decide to change the program only in the cases of error and in connection with I/O. Normally we let a process run on a processor as long as it wants, despite the fact there may be processes of a higher priority in the system. The delay caused to a high priority process does not substantially reduce overall system performance.

The main task of the low level scheduler is to periodically re-order the priorities for the dispatcher. It considers the amount of processor and I/O time used since last examined, also how many page frames in core are free, how many page faults for each program and the number of I/O requests handled. The processes are ordered in three queues; (1) the shortest expectation of processor usage, (2) the processor and I/O usage is fairly evenly balanced, and (3) the processor bound processes.

VINCE: In what sort of time period is the expectation computed?

GOOS: It depends on the way the user enters the system, whether he comes from a console in interactive or remote batch mode or whether in batch mode.

HUXTABLE: Did you use simulation to look at the problem of changing priorities, and high priority jobs being held up by low priority jobs being given the system?

GOOS: The simulations indicated a slight deterioration in system performance. What we found was that after an interrupt, to switch to another processor took from 1 to 5 millisecs., which seemed to be unreasonable.

BRINCH HANSEN: You implied that it's more difficult to use a priority concept with a multiprocessor than with a single processor. The ideal solution, when you have an event such as an interrupt, and which activates a process, is to preempt the running process with the lowest priority. In a dynamic system the identity of the processor on which the job of lowest priority is run changes all the time. So you need a hardware mechanism for each processor indicating the priority of the job it's executing, and any interrupt must then automatically be directed to the machine with the lowest priority.

GOOS: This is not sufficient since it could be a software generated interrupt.

BRINCH HANSEN: There is, of course, a simpler method which in the long run has the same effect: whenever one process activates another, compare the priorities of the former process and the first process in the ready queue and schedule the most urgent one.

GOOS: We can expect interactive users to use the CPU for about half a second and so we get enough processes terminating and going into waiting state. The processor has then become free to execute the process with the highest priority. If we had a batch system we would adopt a different strategy.

NEEDHAM: This is analogous to the rate at which core store becomes free. If core store becomes free at a fast enough rate you needn't trouble about destructive devices to make it become free, and if you have enough CPU's the same becomes true.

PATEL: Surely the number of interrupts arising from outside is sufficient to reschedule the processor frequently enough not to require preemption of the other processor.

GOOS: The usual interrupt handling takes about half a millisecond and therefore it might happen that for a long period (long meaning a hundred millisecs) one processor is not interrupted.

VINCE: What would you do in the case where the interrupt rate was higher than you wished? If, for example, you have 2000 peripheral terminations per second, on some occasions you'll resume the process that you interrupted. Rescheduling is expensive inasmuch as you've got a lot of register reloading to do.

GOOS: I have to reload the registers anyway, and the scheduling is not too expensive. What has to be expected is that a system process will be ready to run only for a very short period of time.

ALDERSON: On the point about high interrupt rates, we did some measurements before we got our last core box and the figure was in the range one every 10 ms, and we rescheduled a job every time an interrupt occurs.

GOOS: That's exactly what we do. Perhaps I should explain another minor detail in our structure. One of our processors has access to the priority list but after the dispatcher has found out which process has highest priority it must not be interrupted as this would give a misleading result, not only for the process itself but also for the interrupts on the other processor. So either the dispatcher runs as an indivisible action by disabling interrupts, or we have to know if the dispatcher is interrupted and the priority scheme has changed. It must then start again at the beginning since it can't resume action at the point where it was preempted.

VINCE: I agree that when you have to wait, you go to another processor, but there's no logical necessity to reschedule if you have a high interrupt rate. Using a slaved machine since processes have separate address spaces, there is an extra overhead in going to another process, whereas going back to the process you were running has the advantage of still having the slaves usefully populated.

GOOS: We have to interrupt the second processor if it is idle and we have a process in the ready state. We avoid using the dispatcher if we haven't any process ready after serving an interrupt or if the process which is set ready is of too low a priority. The computation of priorities is made when the process is put on the ready list.

HARTLEY: Both with job scheduling and dispatching one has an algorithm to determine priority; the algorithm is one thing and the mechanism quite another, it is the algorithm that you use to adjust the environment within which the mechanism operates. In the Titan system we have taken account of the known factors about certain processes, and these were built into the mechanism; and the part that wasn't known became tactical, i.e. could be plugged in and taken out or changed.

The question of dispatching user processes isn't strategic and has to be tactical, because you don't know what the user process is going to be like when you design the system; it's a function of the environment. So we had a mechanism which would take the user processes given to it, in some order of priority, and we separated the idea of who was going to decide and what that order should be. So the coordinator simply has the user processes in some order at any one moment in time, on a chain. The rule is simply that the first process which is free to go is the process which runs. Independent of this, there are strategic decisions that supervisor and interrupt processes are always at higher priority. If we have a process running which is not at the top of the queue and one higher up becomes unblocked, the rule is to switch immediately and run it till it in turn is blocked. If it becomes blocked then review the situation and find the first one which is not. This is what we put into our system saying one day we'll design ourselves an algorithm when we know what it ought to be.

Our algorithm was designed for batch jobs, which like the Atlas system never communicated directly with the outside world. Input/output was all spooled, and the only connection with the outside world was either to the disc for spooled information or to magnetic tapes. We were very concerned about magnetic tape jobs because of our shortage of tape decks. We therefore needed an algorithm which gave preference to magnetic tape jobs. If we put magnetic tape jobs at the top of the queue, these jobs will not use their magnetic tapes all the time, so we want the algorithm to order the jobs according to their actual current use of the tapes. Secondly, if we just had a few jobs in the machine, we wanted to do them on a round robin basis.

We decided that jobs which communicated with the outside world would, by definition, be communicating with slower devices and therefore not be wanting much processor time, because they would frequently be waiting for I/O. This was the basis of the algorithm; to try and detect those jobs which were using little processor time and keep them at the top. We had a one second interrupt program which looked at the jobs which were running and found which had used the most processor time in that last second, and that job is moved to the bottom of the queue. If a job interacts with the outside world it will float to the top, and of course as a job changes its characteristics this mechanism is automatic. If all the jobs are otherwise equal, and there is no interaction with tapes, then it degenerates into a straight round robin.

When we introduced multiple access to our system we found that the original algorithm was still working rather well. It had been thought out on the principle that jobs which communicate with the outside world generally don't want much computing time anyway, and this is still true in a multiple access environment. So we were able to keep the same algorithm for about three years.

We have actually changed it two ways since then. One is a very *ad hoc* change. In our filing system the File Master is a user process; and therefore not subject to this mechanism. The File Master never does much work; opening and closing files is a disc bound activity, so it's unlikely to use much processor time anyway: the process will stay at the top of the queue, and indeed it did until one day it didn't. One day there was a jam in the system; all the user processes were trying to open files and the disc was too busy. In that situation the filing system was the only job that could do any work for a second, so it went to the bottom of the queue. In that extreme situation it took a long time for the File Master to get back to the top again. We therefore changed the algorithm so that the File Master is fixed at the top of the queue regardless.

The other change was due to the fact that foreground jobs were getting a bit too much CPU time compared with background jobs. Now we classify jobs into two categories, interactive and not interactive, and calculate not only the amount of time used in the last second but also the previous seconds, with a delay factor thrown in. Then on the basis of some threshold figure the jobs greater than this are classed as non-interactive and those less as interactive. The interactive jobs are all given higher priority. So we have a list in two parts and the jobs move around within the parts.

To have planned our present scheduling algorithm originally would, with hindsight, have been a mistake. We went to a more elaborate algorithm because of a second order rather than a first order effect.

HOARE: I suggest you went to it because in an already existing system it happened to be the part that you could change easiest. If you started from scratch now perhaps you would go back to your original algorithm and decide to combat second order effects by means of second order algorithms, which is a better structured way of doing it.

NEEDHAM: That isn't quite so. The new algorithm is very like the old one but there's a blister on it, which might be a better structured method but a less clean way of programming it. The effect we tried to produce was that while the terminal job was being highly interactive it got the best processor service it could, but if it enters a phase where it makes extensive use of the processor it's actually treated rather worse than a background job.

HOARE: My objection was a philosophical one: the success of splitting an operating system into levels is really dependent on the fact that decisions made at a certain level (either the process dispatching or the core management level) can be made on considerations which, very largely, are relevant only at that level.

GOOS: In job scheduling we can take into account that there exists a thrashing problem. We cannot take into account that there exists such a thing as reponse time, we have to do this in dispatching. From a practical system point of view I would disagree that at every level we can make decisions based only on the knowledge about what has happened from the hardware up to that level. This is simply wrong.

RANDELL: For example, the set of jobs that the dispatcher was working on should change slowly enough so that it won't interfere with what the dispatcher was doing, but fast enough so that it would achieve whatever balance you want between terminals and batch processing. It is only by this difference in time gain that you manage to get a clear conceptual separation. It's no use bandying the word level about unless you know what you want on which level, and the question of thrashing is a very nice example of a partial inadequacy even in the very nicely argued set of levels which Dijkstra has established.

NEEDHAM: There aren't any system processes which run once a month and have sufficient information available to them to make the automatic adjustment to parameters at the lower level which will be required in this case.

RANDELL: The development of the Titan scheduler reminds me of a story. Two teams have been building a railway line, one started from the west and the other from the east and they didn't exactly match up (figure 1(a)). In an academic

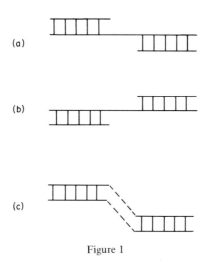

Figure 1

environment you might think of some good axiom which was to be taken if they didn't exactly match up. If you weren't careful you might have told each team to build their rails left-handedly and they'd both go back and start up again and you end up with the reverse picture (figure 1(b)). The next level of sophistication is to arbitrarily decide that one team should start all over again. A more realistic picture is to decide how long it is going to be before the first express comes thundering down and decide how far back you can go and put in a "glitch" (figure 1(c)). With any luck you can go far enough back so that the glitch doesn't become apparent. It may well be there isn't time to do anything really sufficient about it so you put in a warning notice about two miles out.

HANSEN: I would like to describe a series of seemingly innocent design decisions which lead from one disaster to another — how we converted a machine executing a quarter of a million instructions/sec into a system able to respond to about ten events/sec — the speed of a mechanical device.

I find that even at the lowest level of scheduling there is a policy rule invoked; that is, you decide which process should use a given resource next, and, since you can only choose one of them, you are even at that very low level favouring one customer against another. As a well known example: if you have a semaphore queue and you perform a V-operation, you can only activate one process and the one you choose is definitely favoured over the others. So from that point of view there is no conceptual difference between short-term and medium-term scheduling. There is only a difference in political aims, and I therefore feel it is unfortunate to use two different words for the same thing; to talk about *dispatching* at one level and *scheduling* at another. I shall use *short-term scheduling* instead of *process dispatching*.

The partitioning of scheduling into decisions made at lower and higher levels is necessary because human beings are only capable of considering large problems in a stepwise manner. The danger is that at a certain point the abstractions achieved by the scheduling rules at the short-term level break down. I'd like to explain what I mean abstraction breaking down.

An abstraction is a partial description of a system which enables you to ignore certain phenomena inside that system. A paging system enables you to ignore the difference between two levels of store. But if, at a later stage, you find out that you have ignored precisely those features of the system which you are now desperately trying to control again, that is where the abstraction breaks down. As another example: P- and V-operations on semaphores enable you to ignore details of how waiting processes are scheduled — in fact you can't even find out. But the moment you find out that you must indeed control scheduling of individual processes you are in trouble. This breakdown of abstractions, especially for short-term scheduling, happens much sooner than one would expect; namely when the response time is observed at higher levels is of the same order of magnitude, or even larger than the intervals of time you are trying to control at the higher levels.

In the RC4000 we started with the idea of implementing the abstraction of a message system and converting interrupts into answers from peripheral devices; that is, you send a message to a peripheral device which appears like a process and produces an answer instead of an interrupt. This abstraction enables you to ignore interrupts. However, on a machine with a 4 microsecond operation time the production of such an answer took about half a millisec, which means you have slowed down your machine from an ability to answer interrupts within say 50 microseconds to 500 microseconds. This didn't worry us too much because we had an environment in which the requirements were determined by human response and impatience.

We also wanted a mechanism for changing priorities dynamically and the simplest idea we could think of was round robin time slicing among active processes. We decided not to tolerate more than about 2 per cent of the processor time to be wasted on answering clock interrupts and changing priorities. So, at this level of abstraction we selected a time slice of 20 milliseconds; every 20 millisecs the running process is interrupted and put at the end of the queue. When a waiting process was activated by a message or an answer it was decided to put it at the end of the round robin queue to prevent it from monopolizing the processor. In a real time system there might perhaps be about ten processes ready to run, so we now had a response to an interrupt of ten times 20 millisecs, converting a fast computer into one with a guaranteed response of five events per second; any respectable mechanical device could do better than this.

To improve the situation we invented an algorithm which accumulated the amount of processor time used by a process, and whenever a process was delayed, remembered how much it had used last time. When the process was activated again it went to the front of the queue if this amount was less than 20 millisecs, otherwise to the end. This algorithm gave beautiful average real time response, but unfortunately we didn't know when we got it.

The next thing we did was to invent a different kind of process called an interrupt process. In contrast to a computational process, it could not be created dynamically but only at assembly time when the whole system nucleus was translated. We now got excellent response to interrupts; the only difficulty was that in order to program such a process one had to stop and assemble the system. Even though they were often part of the user's problem interrupt processes had to be part of the RC4000 basic monitor because there was no protection inside that nucleus, so it grew and grew, all because the innocent assumption was made that in practice round robin would often turn out to be a suitable algorithm. As Hoare said earlier; for scheduling one cannot maintain built-in abstractions very long; one must face the problem that scheduling has to be controlled at a much higher level than you normally think. The dilemma is that the highest levels of software must be in control of response times at the lowest level. But it is intolerable that every decision requires transfer of control to an algorithm at the top level. When you delegate authority to the lower levels it shouldn't be evident to the upper levels what takes place in detail at the lower levels.

FENTON: Do you think that the fact the low level scheduler doesn't have enough information most of the time can be got round by being able to explicitly say "My abstractions are breaking down" to the high level scheduler?

BRINCH HANSEN: There must be a certain amount of interaction between various levels of scheduling: the high level scheduler issues commands like "Run these jobs according to these simple rules", on the other hand the short-term level accumulates measurements which are periodically inspected by the higher levels.

The ideal short-term scheduling algorithm is one which after every instruction scans the entire ready queue, evaluates the priority for each of them and selects the one with the highest priority. But this is unrealistic of course at the short-term level of scheduling, decisions are made so fast and the time range is so short that it's reasonable to assume that priorities remain constant at that level and keep queues ordered accordingly. All that is needed then is for the machine, is, after each instruction, to examine the priority of its currently running process and the most urgent one in the ready queue. But even this requires more storage cycles than required to execute the next instruction. So you start to look for the simplest algorithm in the world – the examination of a single bit in which the environment indicates that "things have changed, so you'd better look at the ready queue". One can therefore regard an interrupt as the world's simplest form of low level scheduling.

RESOURCE ALLOCATION TECHNIQUES

Panellists: D. J. Howarth, R. M. Needham and D. F. Hartley

PANEL DISCUSSION

HOWARTH: The Atlas 1 was one of the first paged computers, which had a built-in method of converting virtual to real addresses. The primary store was the core store and the secondary store was the drum. The term "one-level store" was coined to describe this, but it was really a two-level store with one addressing mechanism; a user program was split dynamically between core and drum.The first replacement algorithm implemented was the least recently used. But, in the case of a program cycling through blocks of data, this is the worst algorithm possible because every block needs to be brought in for each loop. Consequently this algorithm was replaced by an elaborate "learning" algorithm, which not only used the time since last accessed but also kept a record of the previous on-off period of the block. It decided that if a block had been idle for a longer period than it was idle last time, including the time on backing store, then it had fallen out of cyclic use; otherwise it was waiting to be used.

While testing this algorithm we were guided by events, because the drum had some logic faults in it and use of it was delayed for about six months. During this period we implemented the same system using magnetic tapes instead. The effect was disastrous as far as speed was concerned, but it was very good from the point of view of tuning the system, because the designer could watch the magnetic tape move up and down simulating a drum and could see when the algorithm locked onto two blocks and produced a tape oscillation. We therefore removed the design errors in the sytem by this very *ad hoc* method. We ran a number of matrix calculations and showed that the system did a good job in these cases. But then we started to run real jobs, the first one being a production of a Mercury Autocode Compiler using compiler-compiler. Mercury Autocode worked perfectly well on Mercury itself but not on the Atlas system, and this was because compiler-compiler tended to scatter text all over the virtual store, and did not keep commonly used areas together. When this was remedied the compiler used less than 16K words of core store, which was the store size of the first Atlas.

We then started to add multiprogramming regarding the job mix as one system program, treating all the core store on an equal footing. However, this system worked rather badly, so we put in various parameters whereby one could adjust the idle time of a store block, so that certain jobs were given priority whilst others could be regarded as background jobs. When the system first became functional we found that the processor utilization was rather bad; it turned out that all the wasted time could be eliminated by sensible high-level scheduling, and we eventually achieved processor utilization which was typically 70 to 85%.

Next we measured the efficiency of the paging system by using techniques which did not degrade the machine by more than about 1% and applied these over a two or three shift operation on the London Atlas. Various learning algorithms were tried, not because we were concerned about the amount of processor time used, but to try to measure what was going on. We tried the old faithful algorithm of "least recently used" which we proved previously could not possibly work, and it turned out to give about 10% better performance than our more complex algorithm. Also we tried an algorithm which chooses a block at random for overwriting and that was not too bad — something like 30% worse than the standard algorithm we were using. This gives an example of the dangers of over-design; we could have saved ourselves a great deal of effort on Atlas and had a system which in practice worked equally well.

We found also that adjusting the multiprogramming parameters, did not make any difference to the one-level store. The reason for that is that the total amount of virtual store available to programmers is limited to something between 3 and 6 times the core store size. Namely, we have a system where there is a fair amount of core store compared with the total amount of virtual store available. We built complex algorithms for packing the virtual store to capacity, and found that we had adequate core store to allow it to act almost as a straight slave of the total one-level store. The system was a typical batch system with fairly static characteristics, and this simplified our problems.

Whilst one can produce a plausible theory, there is also much to be learnt from simply trying something and measuring what happens, because the amount of actual information you can get is quite substantial. We found from measurements on a university job mix (which included commercial-type jobs, a lot of short jobs and a few long jobs) that a lot of the pre-conceived ideas of what programs were doing in fact seem to get smoothed out over a short space of time. If one averaged over twenty minutes, the choice of low-level algorithms was fairly irrelevant and a reasonably static state emerged where simple algorithms give adequate results. I admit the Atlas 1 is a simple case, but as an example of what happens in system design it has some significance. The results of our measurements were published in the IFIPS Congress of 1968.[1]

NEWELL: You found one page replacement algorithm 10% better than another, was this due to the time spent in the more complex algorithm?

HOWARTH: No, the percentages I quoted were concerned with the idle time spent waiting for drum transfers.

FRASER: You first described a manipulation of the low-level strategy without the high-level strategy, then a manipulation of the high-level strategy without the low-level strategy, finally changing the low-level strategy again without the high-level strategy. Are these two very closely interlocked? Your final result indicated that adjusting the low-level strategy has no great effect. Does this mean you have a static high-level strategy?

HOWARTH: I'm convinced that the high- and low-level strategies ought to be interlocked very considerably. This happened without our knowing on Atlas 1 because of the limitation on the real size of the one-level store. Given that limitation the low-level strategy is unimportant because there isn't the high degree of freedom that you would find if the backing to core store ratio was raised from 3 up to 100. With a higher ratio it pays to integrate your high-level and low-level strategies.

[1] Baylis, M. H., Fletcher, D. G. and Howarth, D. J., "Paging Studies made on the ICT Atlas Computer". IFIP Congress 1968, Edinburgh, D. 113–118.

FRASER: Are you suggesting that a high-level strategy which determines how many jobs to load based on their total core demand is a good strategy?

HOWARTH: Yes; but bearing in mind the unpredictability of core demands, some feedback is needed.

RANDELL: Surely the high-level strategy should order the jobs by external priorities and other slow changing factors such as the allocation of peripheral devices, whilst the low-level strategy should decide how many jobs to run at any one moment based on such things as core storage contention?

HOWARTH: It doesn't make much difference whether the low-level scheduler is regarded as a relatively unintelligent object which runs what it is told to run, or whether it transmits advice back up to the high-level scheduler.

HOARE: How do you detect core contention, and what criterion would you recommend for load-shedding in such circumstances?

HOWARTH: If you count the number of page transfers per program or per process and and if this is uniformly high it indicates core contention. The problem arises if one program has a very high page rate and the rest are reasonable. At one time we had an algorithm which examined the total paging rate and if this was exceptionally high it stopped one program after another until the paging rate reduced to a reasonable level. Immediately we ran it we locked back on to a drum limited job, i.e. we threw off everything until we reached the program causing the trouble. So we took the algorithm out because it did not have any effect. We found it impossible to deduce whether it is the level of multiprogramming that is causing the trouble or the characteristics of that one job.

VINCE: Isn't the problem keeping the virtual-real ratio right for each program, which takes you back to the uniprogramming case of keeping the amount of real store required for the working set steady?

HOWARTH: Certainly you have got to ensure that the core store is adequate to take the working sets of the jobs you are trying to run.

VINCE: So if the paging rate was very high on one particular program you might take that program off and run one with a smaller working set.

HOWARTH: You might but then there is the risk of having an essentially core limited program which never gets run.

HARTLEY: In Titan if we detect a core jam we throw all the programs out and bring them back into the same place as required. It is just a matter or re-arranging the workload.

NEEDHAM: The point is that having thrown all the user programs out the entire store is free for non-resident parts of the operating system and bufferage, and probably the reason why you were in trouble was that you had no room for these. So you bring back one of the programs in the hope that you won't have to bring it all back.

FRASER: There are two characteristics of the Titan system that are relevant here. One is that input/output buffering is done in two different stages, so that when you throw a program out you don't necessarily have to throw its data out. Secondly, the core allocation is done on a per-phase basis, each phase requiring a different amount of core. With the particular job load this produces a very active market place for space, so that if you cause a sufficiently large disturbance the nature of the market has changed by the time things settle down again.

NEEDHAM: One of the most important parameters in any core allocation system is the rate at which space becomes disused. The only reason you remove material from core is that you want the space and it won't become available of its own accord. If people do not die fast enough you are going to have to shoot them for population control. The Titan system tries to keep the core on the move, and in one set of measurements we found that object program core was becoming relinquished at the rate of about 2000 words per second.

RANDELL: The M44 starts throwing out jobs if there is contention, starting with jobs which gave least evidence of activity in the hope that the terminal user has gone to coffee.

HARTLEY: The mechanism on Titan is a crude one and works on the assumption that it does not happen very often, because if it happened a lot the efficiency would drop enormously.

NEWELL: The easiest thing to do in the case of core contention is to throw away all the file-read buffer blocks; and if that does not work you start writing away file-write buffer blocks.

NEEDHAM: We don't do that because by the time you get into this contentious situation you have probably started writing file output buffers already, and you want to give it a chance for the output to be completed.

NEWELL: Normally when a process wants to acquire space it has to make a mandatory "get-core" request, but in the case of user programs the low-level scheduler sees if it can get the program in. If you have a fragmented core try an optional "get-core" so that if that program does not fit you can try another. Now it is very difficult to use these optional requests in the feedback mechanism to decide whether you have passed a core jam threshold.

NEEDHAM: Our system allocates space to user programs without taking any account of what actually is already there; it relies on the level underneath to remove whatever is in the way.

HOARE: Are there any further simple techniques for load shedding which have appeared to work in spite of being rather crude and simple?

FENTON: In the B6700 we try to detect the existence of working sets by watching the page faulting level, and then fit the working sets into the physical core, removing the program with the highest paging rate if it can't fit them all in. We have found that this method works and throws off the right jobs.

HOARE: That is a very sophisticated scheme. Any scheme which attempts to estimate for the separate jobs in the current mix is usually based on Denning's theory about the behaviour of paging systems and is liable to counter-productive effects.

FENTON: I accept that, but we only draw on Denning's theory to the extent that we accept his behaviour curve for programs.

RANDELL: There is a simple and crude mechanism which detects pages that have really gone to sleep by throwing a random one out every now and again.

HOARE: It is a very good algorithm, but the "second chance" algorithm is one better. The second chance method tentatively takes away a page and allows it back immediately if it is used in a short time. My theory about effectively random removal of pages is that when you are moving towards a heavy load condition, the cascade effect of throwing out pages which are in use is going to tend to move you closer to the undesirable overload condition.

RANDELL: Yes, but remember that ours is not an uncontrolled environment.

HOARE: I agree that you have an adequate load control on top, but you should try to delay your approach to the need to use load shedding as long as possible.

VINCE: If you have a high-level scheduler which is trying to keep the estimated virtual/real ratio right, you need measurements of page faulting in order to indicate that a particular working set is smaller than first thought.

HOARE: I disagree. There is a tendency in operating system design to use far too many controls to provide far too much data in the operating system tables. One forgets the amount of effort and synchronization needed to keep this information up-to-date. You are writing hundreds of words of code just to keep this information up-to-date; and even worse, once the information is there, clever people try to use it.

VINCE: Depending on the hardware you have got, it is either difficult to keep such records or it is not.

HOARE: There is a tendency to keep information on the off-chance that you may be able to include it in some feedback loop.

VINCE: I don't think it would be worth keeping if the overhead of keeping it is going to degrade the performance more than the improvement the information would give.

RANDELL: Very often people gather all sorts of "good numbers" in the design stage without knowing what they are going to do with them. Whatever you guess beforehand they are usually not the ones you want.

FRASER: There is a general point here about redundancy in the system. Redundancy has three uses: it can allow you (1) to detect errors, (2) to repair errors, and (3) to optimize. There is an elaborate and hidden cost associated with keeping redundancy. It is very easy to specify in the design stage that you will keep a count as well as a set of table entries, and then find that all the routines which add things to the table have to do two operations instead of just one. When eventually you come to determine the cost of this extra facility it is impossible because there are disruptions all over the place.

HOWARTH: Basically, I favour producing a system that you enlarge, not necessarily to make it more complex but to do a better job. We proved this in Atlas, where we had three major stepping stones in Supervisor development apart from the inevitable minor modifications. They were of incalculable value because you were at least treading on solid ground when you did the next rather more sophisticated type of thing. From that point of view, I am in favour of putting in enough redundancy in a simple system, if you are going to use it in your more complex system, which you are going to produce. What I am not in favour of is producing redundancy to satisfy, for example, a salesman.

VINCE: Do you think accounts should be kept per process for page faulting?

HOWARTH: Yes, because it is a very easy thing to do, and is meaningful.

GOOS: We use the "second chance" algorithm and control the speed at which the pointer is moving round; if it is too fast we have contention, and if it is too slow then we can perhaps increase the level of multiprogramming.

NEEDHAM: Commonly, the only way you can be certain of not getting knotted is to waste something. In Titan we are usually short of disc store, which is required for spooling and many other purposes. All the on-line and off-line jobs require space from this pool and nobody knows how much they are going to use. If we were to fix a large upper limit for each program (say a thousand blocks) and make sure that that is available for each of 30 programs running, then we would need a new disc because this is bigger than the disc capacity.

But if we start new programs with too little disc space available, there is a risk of a deadly embrace, i.e. a situation where all programs have requested more disc space, and all of them are waiting for it to become available. If this occurs, it was obviously foolish to start so many programs, but by then it is too late to do anything except restart the whole system. There is a well-known way of preventing this situation (the banker's algorithm), but this is very complicated in the presence of multiple resources, and often prevents programs from running when in practice the risk of deadlock is negligibly small.

We have tried an empirical approach to this and it works very well. For all the resources of this kind you keep a count of how much is available and how much you have used up, and this is the basis of the allocation system. You find that the average job will require x units of resource A and y units of resource B, and ensure that these amounts are available at the start of each job. Now these amounts probably won't stay available; and if several large requests arrive shortly afterwards the system will become deadlocked. So we don't apply any intellect to find out what these numbers x and y should be; we simply make a rule and then the jobs are started if the unused figure of the resource is less than x. To discover x we simply decrease its value until the operating system stops working and then increase it slightly. This is something we need to do once or twice, because with a large number of processes the law of averages works in our favour. If you are dealing with multiprogramming level of two the processes' requirements are unpredictable but when you reach the level 20 or 30 it all smooths out, and you can set the parameters and leave them for months at a time. It is worth having another look now and then because the characteristics of your workload may change. For example, somebody may introduce a popular compiler which uses an immense amount of disc so you may have to alter your parameters for a few days until you can get the compiler writer to mend his ways. This approach, we called "regulation", works rather well and has been applied in a number of places, and anyone faced with a situation like this should seriously consider the crude and simple approach before attempting anything more sophisticated.

HOARE: You must have at least N words of disc and M words of main store before you start running a program irrespective of what the program is. This is simpler than the Burroughs compiler estimates of core utilization.

NEEDHAM: I would not believe anything a compiler told me.

HOARE: That is very wise. Could I suggest dividing the disc space in use by the number of users N and make sure there is an 1/Nth of its space left free before loading the Nth program.

NEEDHAM: I don't think you would gain very much because the numbers tend to vary and the average would not help. Looking at the current position of the jobs in the system is not much good because jobs change their nature. You don't know when this is going to happen, because all the user tells you is the largest amount of store he needs, and this does not tell you how he is actually going to behave.

RANDELL: In many installations one can see cyclic differences in average characteristics at different times of the day or week, and it might be so steady that you can deal with it.

NEEDHAM: In this context we considered how much we could over-allocate the disc. We knew that user file allocations would exceed the total amount of disc available, otherwise we would be wasting expensive disc surfaces because they would be allocated but empty. Finally, we decided that if there weren't 2000 blocks free at the beginning of the day we are liable to get into trouble. So, when somebody requests file space we look to see how much we had free at the beginning of the day, and if we had say 2500 blocks free we have 500 blocks to give away. We don't know how much we have already allocated; we work purely on the basis of the state of affairs at the beginning of the day.

FRASER: This also works because there is a high turnover in the University in which students are coming and going all the time; there is a fairly steady market place for disc space.

LIPPS: As far as disc space is concerned we at CERN are living on the same dangerous ground. But, rather than check how much disc space is available before we start the job, we keep a record of how much space we have currently and give an indication if we are getting short of space. You allocate most of your space to the user files whereas for us the ratio between user and temporary files is fifty-fifty. We therefore have more room to manoeuvre, and if necessary we can dump some of our disc information, which is destined for say the printer, to magnetic tape.

Have you other limitations on starting jobs which mean that only in extreme cases do you reach the disc space limit, or are you usually close to that limit?

NEEDHAM: The limitation is normally the level of multiprogramming; the disc space limit arises if we have accidentally allocated too much file space or if one or two programs have been extremely large. The disc limit may delay a person's log-in or affect the beginning of an off-line job, but it does not happen very often.

LIPPS: Can you really be sure that it is this additional limitation that saves you, and not the fact that you are far from the limit in the normal situation?

NEEDHAM: Yes. If we remove the limitation altogether we get deadlocked of the order of two or three times a week.

HOARE: Do you then reduce this limit until you get more deadlocks than you can stand, and then turn it up a bit until your deadlock rate goes down to say one a month?

NEEDHAM: In practice it is a very sudden effect; the deadlock rate drops from once an hour to virtually never.

HOARE: What do you tell your users when it happens?

NEEDHAM: We tell them that the system has crashed, and then restart. The balls fall down in different places and it works. You don't have to change the parameter necessarily before restarting, because the person who knows how to do it may not be there. The restart takes about two minutes.

LIPPS: What do you do in the exceptional case where a user really uses all the disc space he can grab?

NEEDHAM: There is an absolute limit of 1000 blocks on the amount of disc space and the system will allow one user only to do that.

NEWELL: What happens if, on a restart after deadlock, the balls fall back into the same place and you have the same situation again?

NEEDHAM: It's unlikely to happen, because on a restart the first thing to be restarted is the peripheral output, so that by the time user jobs are resumed a lot of the peripheral output will have drained off the disc.

Deadlock does not come automatically if somebody puts in a request for disc space and there isn't any; the reaction is to block him until space becomes available. You have a real deadlock only if everybody gets into this situation. So we adjust the parameters so that faulting for this particular reason is unusual.

HUXTABLE: You said earlier that with a large number of users the statistics favour you. How much statistical variation can you allow?

NEEDHAM: Clearly if you have very wide oscillations you will be in trouble. It is necessary to be able to accept enough jobs for multiprogramming to keep the processor busy. If you reach the limit before this happens you have got to manufacture or buy some more of the resource.

HUXTABLE: You are thinking of the situation where you have a much more mixed batch of multiprogramming and console activity?

NEEDHAM: Yes, if you are in that situation, all you can do is to set your limits drastically high so that you are wasting a lot of the resource most of the time, ensuring that you do not run out.

VINCE: Could you not have two categories of job, each with its own constant limit? If you are not able to run another big batch job, you might be able to fit another couple of small output jobs in.

NEEDHAM: Obviously one could do this, but I distrust any information about the category of a job, because the most innocent terminal user may suddenly decide he wants to take a copy of the Fortran library.

HARTLEY: My theme is that of allocating time to the users. In our system we are particularly short of terminal time and file space, and we have a user population of about one thousand, of which around 75% are officially authorized to use the terminals. There are about 60–70 terminals, permitting around twenty people to be logged on simultaneously, so there is going to be some congestion. Earlier systems such as CTSS had this problem, so they had the idea of priority lines whereby each user is either a normal user or a priority user. This broke down very quickly, because so many people had different reasons for becoming priority users, and it got to the stage where you could not get on unless you were a priority user. The trouble was that you were either a priority user or not a priority user and there was nothing in between; there was no possibility of having priority for a particular day or an hour. We started off by trying to regulate not so much the time that the users used but the rate at which they used it. Each user was given an allocation per day; this allocation had to cope with his busiest day and so you immediately completely over-allocate the system.

We then implemented a much more general and complicated system. It was influenced by the general purpose security mechanism in the filing system in which conditions of security can be programmed. The general mechanism determined the conditions on which people could have time and was open ended so that you could introduce new reasons for giving time. This allows the administration to allocate resources to users and tailor-make them to the user's needs. We have four levels of priority – low, medium, high and top; the top is in fact never used. Resources are allocated at the priority levels in shifts because night time is cheaper than day time. The normal day user has medium priority in all shifts with an occasional small amount of high priority; a student would have a low priority. A user is given a monthly allocation, but controls and conditions of use may be imposed upon this allocation. For example you can control (1) how much allocation he may use in a day or a shift; (2) how much time he can have each time he logs in; (3) which terminal he logs in on; (4) the mode of access he can have when he does log in; and finally (5) you can give him a pair of dates saying that he can only log in during this period.

To avoid users being thrown off the system because they had used up their allocation even when the machine was lightly loaded, we added an overtime facility. If some of the controls were violated you would still be able to log in, but at very low priority. It was a simple way of allowing you to use more than your allocation but with the condition that you were the one who was thrown off if resources became short.

When someone requires high priority, it is not necessarily because he is important, and he certainly does not want it for ever. Someone may want high priority because he has booked the graphics equipment at a given time and he would clearly need the machine time to coincide with his booking time. A user may tell us that he needs to get results out in order to finish his thesis by next week, so we give him high priority time for next week and put a date control on it. Another example is the person being visited by his sponsor requires high priority time to demonstrate his work; again we could enforce a date control and possibly a time control as well.

We have been giving some thought to this problem in preparing for our new machine. What one really needs to control is not how much high priority is used, but the rate at which it is used. This is linked with turn-round, because the faster turn-round becomes the faster you use up your resources. A user can have good turn-round at say twice the cost of poor turn-round, irrespective of how much time he uses over the year. Consequently, if a person wants to do a project we give him an allocation and if he finds it is not good enough we will give him more.

One problem in our environment is not so much controlling the big user as dealing with the person who starts off as a small user and becomes a big user. Once a person is committed to a project it is very difficult to stop him half way through because he has now become a big user. We are hoping that by controlling turn-round rather than total allocation we will solve the problem.

RANDELL: The APL 360 system had a simple technique for regulating terminal usage. They had about 2000 users and 50 terminal ports, and everybody entered the system by dialling one of various telephone numbers. One or two of these lines were made express lines on which you were only allowed to stay for five minutes before being thrown off. You could dial in again, but that was an annoyance. There was a tremendous change in ability to get onto the system, merely because of this simple express line technique.

HARTLEY: We did a similar thing recently. We inserted a mechanism that gave the first five minutes of any session in edit mode free, and the load went down marvellously.

RANDELL: Did you not find that people were logging in and out every five minutes?

HARTLEY: We put in a constraint which limited logging-in to three times per day.

LIPPS: What has been the reaction of your user population to your efforts?

HARTLEY: The high priority mechanism seems to work quite nicely. People come along and ask for it and we give it to them very quickly provided it is a small amount.

LIPPS: At what rate do people ask for high priority?

HARTLEY: A few each week.

HOARE: There are two ways of exercising this sort of control. One is to have a routine which looks up filed constraints for each user trying to enter the system in order to determine whether he is entitled to or not. If you have a very large number of very small jobs this could be expensive. The second method is to keep a log of jobs run in the system and to analyse this by a program afterwards to see whether anyone has broken the rules. Do you have any feeling about the relative merits of these two ways of enforcing limits?

HARTLEY: Catching rule-breakers after the event does not work in our experience. We have a large number of users and it would be an enormous task to search out and reprimand the guilty ones. Although we check our on-line jobs in an on-line way, this does not include the off-line jobs; we always intended to do it for off-line work but we were concerned about the efficiency aspect.

NEWELL: In George 3 this mechanism causes a bottleneck as a number of processes need the file on which the information is stored. The trouble is that you need to write to the file as well as read from it in order to register changes, e.g. a user has logged in twice to-day.

HARTLEY: We keep the current shift information in core so that we can see who has logged in this shift, how many times and how much time they have had. We only update the file three times a day. Consequently, we only need to read the file when a user logs on, rather than read and write to it.

NEEDHAM: The overheads in our system are caused by users trying to log on and being told they can't. When this was carefully observed over a period of forty minutes we found that an unsuccessful attempt was made every six seconds, and every one of these required an access to the main file to make sure that the person should be refused. It amounted to about ten per cent of the total capacity of the machine.

INPUT/OUTPUT CONTROL TECHNIQUES

Panellists: D. P. Fenton and H. Lipps

PANEL DISCUSSION

FENTON: In the Burroughs 6700 system, there were several layers of input/output routines. The innermost layer was concerned with organizing and checking that transfers have been successfully completed; this layer was used by other operating system routines but was not visible to the user because it has to choose its own disc addresses. There were two layers visible to the user: one was a commercial-type record blocking layer, and the other accepted lists of characters and variables with formats which it applied to the variables before calling the middle layer.

In the original version only the two top layers were available to the user and we found disappointed customers who wanted to program the peripheral units themselves. For example they wanted to get better control over tape positioning, to do their own buffering and their own overlapping, to implement their own variable length blocking structures, and, not least, to share a file between several co-operating processes.

So we eventually decided to implement direct input/output so the user has the option of controlling his own blocking, positioning, tape handling and buffering, and can initiate several transfers to the same unit. There were three things we learnt from this exercise.

Firstly we tried unsuccessfully to make the innermost layer of input/output available to the user, so we were forced to implement a proper intrinsic for direct input/output. Now all the operating system routines that do transfers use it and their performance is improved. This illustrates a general point: unless a facility that is provided in an operating system is actually used by other operating system routines it's unlikely to be any good.

Secondly we had to provide a method for the users to access and possibly update operating system tables, tables which you wouldn't normally let users access. Therefore we had to provide a set of checks to control these accesses.

The third point concerned the accounting for the input/output sub-system. Previously we had only one transfer going for each file at any time, so we were able to do the accounting in the tables that corresponded to that file. Now we have to do the accounting in the block that controls the transfer, and this could give rise to a user being charged for fifteen seconds of input/output time when he's only on the machine for three seconds.

HOARE: As access to system tables is controlled by going through an intrinsic, you have to enter executive just to find out the content of a single location. Surely this is at least a factor of fifty overhead, and could be crippling if used by other operating system routines?

FENTON: Obviously operating system writers have facilities to avoid checks. But there are many programs inside an operating system that are really user programs

218

except that they're supplied by the manufacturer and have only this one extra facility.

VINCE: You allow direct input/output for co-operating processes but do you allow direct input/output for contentious processes, not necessarily sharing the same file but sharing the same device? If so, how do you provide protection between these contentious processes?

FENTON: We don't allow it except on the disc. With the disc a user can, under the supervision of the intrinsic, see what addresses he has been given, but he is never allowed to generate addresses. Although a user can indicate a preference for a particular bank of discs it's up to the system to find legally available space.

RANDELL: Does this protection mechanism benefit from the feature in the 6700 whereby you can access what you think is a word in memory and find yourself unexpectedly obeying a subroutine which eventually gives you the piece of data you thought was in the word?

FENTON: The facility exists but it's not used at the moment, although it will be when a more detailed file security system is implemented.

HOARE: The business of operating systems is not to create virtual machines that are easier to use. Often the closer a virtual machine is to the actual hardware, the simpler and more flexible is its use. The difference between your original and present approaches is that your original approach was attempting to create a virtual machine which (for perhaps 99% of your users) was more convenient in that they have record and character oriented input/output, but your new approach has the advantage that it makes no attempt to abstract from the hardware, or only just the right amount to prevent the ill effects of sharing.

FENTON: Yes, I agree, but rather than arriving at this result by introspection we did it as a result of feedback from a user community.

HOARE: Thus your machine-oriented interface is more successful as an operating system interface than the runtime library was. This fits in reasonably well with my idea of where the division of labour between an operating system designer and a run time library designer should be.

FENTON: We do have a number of commercial users and these people would be very unhappy if the operating system didn't do their blocking for them.

The record-oriented input/output has not changed in its appearance to the users nor in its implementation structure. We have not just added it to the direct input/output intrinsics; rather we've made trap doors in the record formatted input/output intrinsic and labelled them "direct input/output".

GOOS: We designed a basic input/output handler and, based on that, one which is record-oriented. There is one module in between which handles sharing of files in order to allow the sharing of information inside a file without writing it to disc, and users seemed to be satisfied at first. Later on we detected some important cases in which we had to open the direct input/output facility to the user.

About 98% of the input/output is done on a record basis and about 2% on a direct basis; but that 2% is essential. It's not that the user *likes* the machine-oriented facility, but sometimes he has to rely on it.

WARWICK: How does Hoare's definition of an operating system, that sharing was its principal characteristic, deal with the situation where sharing comes in at various levels. There must be sharing at the level of direct input/output; there must equally be sharing at the record level. Surely on your definition both are operating systems?

BRINCH HANSEN: One possible answer is that the principles of resource sharing repeat themselves at every level of programming. It is convenient at the very lowest level to identify a particular program which we call *the* operating system, But the principle of sharing repeats itself recursively and cannot meaningfully be identified with a single managing program.

FENTON: The point at which programs end and the operating system begins is where you have two financially independent users and you have to arbitrate between them.

HOARE: Another criterion is unpredictability — the fact that user programs are no longer co-operating on the same task, and therefore there's no predictability of their mutual demands; they become contentious. In Algol where you've got the same store used for different purposes in different blocks at different times, you have a storage allocation problem; it is not an operating system problem because there is co-operation between the two parts as to when they're going to use it and when they're not.

LIPPS: On the CDC machines the central processor has access to two levels of central memory, but no access to any of the peripherals. Instead, the peripherals are driven by a number of peripheral processors (usually ten) each of which has a 4K 12-bit words of private memory, and access to the main memory, and all of the (usually twelve) data channels of the machine. This enables the CPU to process the user jobs whilst most of the operating system and all of the input/output organization can be done by these small but relatively fast processors.

A Fortran user program would call upon input/output library routines which collect data and place it in a circular buffer in the user's area. Once there is enough information in the buffer the library routines, which form part of the user program, request the operating system to output the information. A request is made by inserting it in a location within the user program which is regularly (every 100 microseconds) examined by the peripheral processor zero, usually called "Monitor". Monitor analyses the Supervisor call and passes the task of transferring the data to one of the other peripheral processors. From the systems point of view there are several levels of implementation. A set of peripheral processor routines (which are overlays) are concerned with the physical transfer of individual blocks of data between the device and central memory. Above that we have a layer of peripheral processor routines, which perform the necessary logical checks, changing logical into physical addresses and determining which device is involved. Finally, the peripheral processor routines report to the Monitor that the task has either been completed or has failed, by means of a set of control words in central memory.

We have found it necessary to ensure that the user has a considerable degree of freedom in what he can do in the case of exception conditions such as parity error on tape, end of tape, etc. We do not allow the user to write his own peripheral processor routines; this would be disastrous because peripheral processors have no memory protection and have access to the whole of main memory. Instead, we allow a diversity of requests to the peripheral processors within the framework of the interface between the central processor program and the operating system.

There is a problem when the central processor is considerably faster than the peripherals. The recent CDC 7600 approach is to provide high data rates for the discs and tapes, and transfer as much information as is reasonable at one time. This is satisfactory when you are dealing with sequential data, but rather different when you are dealing with random data, for example, when you need many accesses to pick out a number of small routines from a library. On the CDC 7600 even the tapes are too slow to transfer data fast enough to keep the processor busy, and the handling of magnetic tape has been relegated to the same category as card readers and printers, namely, the information is transferred to disc before the user program is run. This means that users have no control over their tapes in the case of parity and other errors. At the high performance end of a machine range this is inevitable until a faster device closes the gap between disc storage and magnetic tape.

HUXTABLE: I have often wondered which view to take of the CDC peripheral processors, whether they are very intelligent controllers or whether there is an operating system distributed around several machines.

LIPPS: On the 6000 series peripheral processors were provided as a set of intelligent and interchangeable controllers; but on the 7600 there are several layers of PPU's and you can interconnect them, each one having a number of channels of its own. It is more economical to build a set of fast but simple CPU's and if necessary use some of them as low-level controllers which normally form part of an individual device. For example, behind the tape controller you may have a further controller which you would otherwise call a computer.

From our experience, the use of peripheral processors in place of channels has been found to be quite efficient. But they are not really suited to handle a large number of different devices which all have different characteristics. It seems unreasonable to interface a large number of terminals of different speeds and characteristics to a single peripheral processor or even a pair of them. We have done something similar in running all our printers, card readers, punches, plotter and paper tape equipment with one single peripheral processor, and by careful design and tuning we have arranged to get a reasonable level of efficiency out of this part of the input/output system; but this would not be possible in a system intended to be extensible. The answer is to have various small machines which all take part of the load in the system.

VINCE: Having issued an input/output transfer request, how does a central processor program know when it is able to request a further input/output?

LIPPS: The central processor program must wait until the location in which it placed its request is cleared by the Monitor. It then knows that the transfer has been accepted.

VINCE: How does the Monitor start the appropriate peripheral processor when it has decided which one to nominate?

LIPPS: The idle peripheral processor is running in a 125 microsecond loop monitoring a particular location in main core.

VINCE: So once again there is no interrupt?

LIPPS: No interrupt whatsoever. The time taken in the loop is negligible in comparison to the amount of time you spend on any transfer to a peripheral device. Also, the time taken for the peripheral processor to collect information from the main memory is only about five microseconds — a negligible amount.

VINCE: Is this true when you are transferring to a faster memory, for example, extended core store (ECS).

LIPPS: This is one of the reasons why CDC and ourselves have found it difficult to incorporate the extended core store into the system.

VINCE: If you had extended core storage would you drive it through a PPU or directly by the CPU?

LIPPS: We would drive it through a peripheral processor as this is simpler. But you would not get the true performance out of the ECS, which is one 60-bit word every hundred nanoseconds.

VINCE: So it seems you want to try to run the ECS directly from the CPU.

LIPPS: The 6600 was not built that way, but the 7600, which has included extended core storage, is restructured so that the basic monitor is now a CPU program.

VINCE: Can input/output go directly to ECS rather than into the main memory?

LIPPS: As far as the 7600 is concerned, all input/output goes into small core memory (fast core) and from there goes out to large core memory (LCM) under the control of the CPU. The 6000 series CDC have recently announced a back-door entry through which the peripheral processors can get direct access to the ECS controller. One of the problems here is that the ECS was designed for a very high transfer rate once the transfer has been initiated, and is used rather inefficiently if a large number of short transfers are made.

HUXTABLE: There appears to be a master-slave relationship between the monitor and the central processor. Is this not the source of a problem when one comes to connect up many machines to a single centralized disc system?

LIPPS: The master-slave relationship is one way of solving the communication problem between the peripheral processors and the central processor. At the time this was designed, few people thought of connecting several main frames to the same disc.

HUXTABLE: I was not intending to comment on the design of the machine, but to look at the logical situation where one sets up a master-slave relationship, then tries to bring several masters together merging some of their slaves and then tries to treat them as a single entity. It creates a situation which to me seems rather horrific.

LIPPS: You have simply two different problems: one is that if you look at the performance within one main frame you have one way of organizing your sequence; if you now want to connect several main frames to the same set of peripherals you have a different problem. The two problems do not really interfere with each other, and should be solved separately.

BRINCH HANSEN: If you think in terms of a message-oriented system, one approach is to camouflage physical input/output as messages. However, in practice there is a great difference between the ability to simulate input/output by physical copying of ten words at a time, as we did in the RC4000 system, and the ability to pass messages between virtual machines data structures of arbitrary size and complexity using pointers alone. This extension of the message concept has a very strong influence on the kind of storage addressing you can have and the kind of language features which are desirable. Is this sort of extension a desirable and practical in the kind of systems you are familiar with?

FENTON: We have provided a mechanism whereby the user program does not know whether his file is a file of records or a file of messages, but this does require the existence of another program to sort out the difference.

GOOS: It is more important to design storage so that we can input or output a complete list including the list pointers. The interpretation of this as a message transfer would then follow automatically. For example the B6700 is stack oriented, but as soon as you try to implement a list or a string manipulation language you lose many advantageous features of the machine.

LIPPS: It is more practical to look for a communication method that is adequate for a particular situation rather than a more general solution. A method which is good for communication between peripheral processors may not be any good for communication between different main frames, and I fail to see the point in trying to get uniformity. It is much more satisfying and interesting when you come to implementation to be influenced by the available hardware.

BRINCH HANSEN: One can simplify a machine by taking advantage of the physical attributes of an input/output device. But I have seen people struggle to implement an operating system because they could not properly transfer large amounts of data internally between processes. This may be treated as two different problems, but any respectable message switching facility should be prepared to deal with messages of arbitrary complexity.

LIPPS: You may have message sizes of different orders of magnitude, but it is dangerous to generalize rather than consider the best course for the current hardware environment.

GOOS: It is useful in every particular situation to search for the best method for that situation, but rather than use an inferior method it might be better to use a generalized method that is useful for all the other applications. Also, it is not good to have twenty or thirty different methods all occupying storage merely because each method is useful in certain circumstances.

FILING SYSTEM TECHNIQUES

Speaker: A. G. Fraser: "File integrity in a disc-based multi-access systems"

Repliers: B. Randell, J. Warne.

FILE INTEGRITY IN A DISC-BASED MULTI-ACCESS SYSTEM

A. G. FRASER

Bell Laboratories, Murray Hill,
New Jersey*

INTRODUCTION

The operating system that is used on the Titan computer† at Cambridge University includes procedures for the organization and maintenance of file storage. About 10,000 files, belonging to some 700 users, are held on a magnetic disc that has a total capacity of 128 million characters. For the past 4½ years this system has been used on a scheduled 20-hour day to provide job-shop and multiple-access facilities to a total user population of about 1500 persons. The file management software is described here in some detail. An overview of the system will be found in reference [1], and further details will be found in references [2] and [3].

Under the heading of file management we include these procedures which are concerned with file identification, file privacy, space allocation and file integrity. In this context a file may be any ordered string of data and it is of no interest to the file management software to know what that data represents. In practice each file is held as a string of blocks (one block can accommodate 4096 characters). A quite distinct set of data handling routines provide the user with convenient means of processing the contents of a file.

The file management software consists of complete programs that operate under supervisor control in the manner normally associated with other users of the system. One of these programs, the File Master, receives special recognition from the supervisor and it is around this program that the file management system revolves. The File Master contains five main functional parts.

1. Routines that service calls made by the supervisor itself.
2. Routines that service enquiries and demands that come direct from a user program.
3. Routines that provide special functions for the other programs in the set of file management software.
4. A routine that is entered at the start of day and after a system failure.
5. Routines that investigate or alter a user's entitlement to perform a requested activity.

The special status of the File Master stems from two facts.

1. The supervisor knows about and relies upon the File Master to provide it with certain services.

---

* This work was done at the University of Cambridge, England.
† The Titan is the prototype for the I.C.T. Atlas 2 computer.

2. The File Master uses information on disc to decide what disc accesses the supervisor should allow and determines which area of the disc it should access.

The File Master program is set in operation before any other program is allowed to run and it does not terminate itself until the operating system closes itself down. The program is activated whenever its services are requested and each activation services just one request; a queue of outstanding requests is held by the supervisor. The File Master is the only program that has direct access to the disc and it has certain other special privileges that allow it to communicate with the supervisor in order to obtain a few specialized services.

There is a substantial number of distinct programs in the total set of file management software and they fall into the following five categories.

A. Programs that use magnetic tape as additional file storage space and as an insurance against loss of filed data.
B. Programs that provide the user with convenient facilities connected with file management, such as printing a list of file titles.
C. Programs that provide the installation management with necessary statistics and allows him to exercise necessary control over the use of various file system resources and functions.
D. Programs that facilitate inspection and maintenance of the file system data base both on disc and magnetic tape.
E. Programs that provide an artificial environment in which to test new versions of the file system.

In this paper I deal only with the operations of the File Master and the programs in category A. Programs falling into the other four categories represent a substantial part of the whole but are often somewhat parochial in nature.

THE FILE DIRECTORIES

Lists of file titles and related information are maintained on disc. The lists, known as file directories, are maintained by the File Master and are the key to its operation.

Each file is a separate entity. Although some files may have similar titles, they are each preserved and protected separately. For administrative purposes we form collections of files, and one directory contains the names of all the files in one collection. In many cases the file directory bears the name of one user and the collection of files will usually be his own private property. Other directories contain collections of more general interest. A group of users may choose to share together and the library of publically available programs provides an extreme example of the communal use of a file directory.

Certain administrative controls are linked to the file directory. Space accounting is an example. Each directory is given an allocation that is an upper limit to the volume of filed information that is permitted on disc. There are three classes of file and for each class there is a separate allocation. The classes are:

1. Permanent
Files in this class reside permanently on disc. The file support software automatically makes spare copies of these files on magnetic tape so that there is some protection against loss.

2. Temporary

Files in this class reside on disc during the day on which they are created; temporary files are flushed out at the start of each day. No spare copies are made on magnetic tape.

3. Archive

Files in this class reside permanently on magnetic tape and are not available for processing until they have been re-classified as permanent.

The file space allocations are checked by the File Master whenever it services a request to change a file or create a new one. Before a file can be processed, the user must OPEN it, and when he has finished it must be CLOSED. When opening a file the user must specify the way in which he intends to use it and, once access has been granted, the program will be held to its stated intention. The actions which take place when a user opens or closes a file are two-fold.

1. The supervisor calls upon the File Master to check the validity of the requested action, to verify that no privacy restrictions are being violated and, in the case of file access, to obtain the disc address of the file.
2. The data handling routines that will be used to manipulate the content of the file are initiated, or terminated, as appropriate.

The three recognized modes of file use are READ, EXECUTE and UPDATE.

File creation is treated specially but for most practical purposes is rather like updating a previously null file. We allow any number of users to use one file simultaneously providing that none of them wishes to update it; only one user is allowed access to a file if it is being updated. In consequence, one of the reasons that a request to open a file may fail is that someone else is using it. A request to open a file may also fail because the specified file title is not listed in the file directory, because there is a privacy restriction on the file in question or because the file is in archive storage and not on disc.

FILE DIRECTORY STRUCTURE

The file directory serves three main purposes.

(*a*) To contain a list of file titles with some information about each.
(*b*) To contain a list of privacy arrangements.
(*c*) To contain certain administrative data that affects all the files collected into the one directory.

Each file has a name, such as /x/mk. 1, which contains two components separated by solidus. Each component is the arbitrary choice of the author but no component may contain more than 8 characters. A file directory also has a name, such as D, which prefixes the file name to give the full file title, D/x/mk. 1. For convenience, the user may omit the directory name if the default setting will suffice. The default value may be set arbitrarily by the user but it is normally set to his own name.

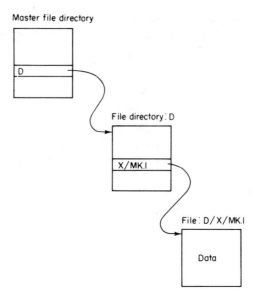

Figure 1. File directory hierarchy.

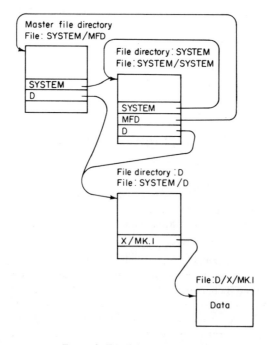

Figure 2. File directory structure.

With the name of each file, the directory contains the disc address of the data that is the file. The disc address of the directory is itself held in another list, the MASTER FILE DIRECTORY (see figure 1).

The directories are all held as files in their own right and in this capacity they are associated with a file directory named SYSTEM (figure 2). By this means we have arranged that all of the standard data handling facilities provided by the supervisory software are available to the system programs that manipulate the file directories themselves. In consequence we have made an important contribution towards simplicity in the file management software.

In principle it would have been possible to make the file directory SYSTEM serve a dual role and thereby avoid a separate main file directory. But, by using a separate main file directory with a compact internal structure, we have been able to reduce directory search time appreciably.

STORE SPACE MAP

A file may occupy more than one block and these will not usually be located in consecutive positions on the disc. To link the several blocks of one file together we use a store space map in which there is one entry for each block position on disc (figure 3). Each entry contains two fields.

(*a*) The block address of the next block in the file.
(*b*) A flag to identify the first block of a completed file.

The unused blocks are linked together as if they formed two large files; the significance of using two rather than one free store list is discussed later in this paper.

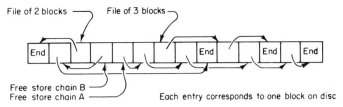

Figure 3. Disc space map.

PRIVACY

The control system that safeguards the privacy of filed material operates, for the most part, on the basis that nothing is permitted unless it has been authorized. For convenience, of course, default settings exist for most controls so that it is usually unnecessary for a user to be continuously aware of these controls.

There are two distinct mechanisms. One mechanism exists to prevent one user from masquerading as another (without, at least, the cooperation of the other). The second mechanism concerns the right of access to filed data and the use of special file system functions.

USER IDENTITY CHECK

As a means of preventing one user from masquerading as another, each person has a password which is chosen by him and can be changed by him whenever he chooses. The user must quote his password when seeking access to the system through an on-line console and he may optionally quote it from within a program that is run through the job-shop system.

The passwords are held in scrambled form. The mechanics of the process used to scramble a password are not kept a secret since there is no known economic way of performing the reverse operation. Whenever a user attempts to quote his password, the quoted word is first scrambled and then compared with the stored original. If the scrambled forms are identical then it is assumed that he has quoted correctly.

From time to time a user will forget his password and appeal to the administration for help. For this reason there is a privileged system function that allows a password to be set to a new value by someone other than its proper owner. It would also be necessary to use this device if, through some system malfunction, the password file becomes corrupt.

It is assumed that each user keeps his password secret. As a means of policing this arrangement the system records the date and time whenever a password is changed or quoted correctly. When a user successfully quotes his password he is told the date and time of the previous occasion on which this was done. By this means a user can detect an infringement although the evidence may not always be sufficient to identify the offender. Of course, the user can choose a new password immediately after detecting an infringement.

RESTRAINT ON USER ACTIVITY

The controls that prevent unauthorized access to data can also give protection against accidental misuse. In a university environment it is the latter that is the more common requirement although privacy controls are essential for the accounting files and other central facilities.

Control over user activity is exercised in two stages.

1. The authority of the user is calculated. This is, in effect, a list of the activities that he is entitled to perform.
2. The authority is compared with the requested activity and, where an existing file is involved, it is also compared with the particular restrictions associated with that file.

Before it is possible to describe either of these two steps it is necessary to explain the method by which activities are identified for control purposes.

For control purposes, activities fall into two distinct classes. They are as follows:

1. Activities that involve existing files.
    These are: EXECUTE, READ, DELETE, UPDATE and CHANGE STATUS.
2. Activities that do not involve existing files.
    These fall into two groups for efficiency reasons only. In group A are those that

are more generally useful: FILE CREATION, and CREATION or DELETION OF A PRIVACY ARRANGEMENT.

In group B are special activities reserved, usually, for system programs and the administration. Some of these are:

(*a*) Creation or deletion of a privacy arrangement that authorizes a special activity.
(*b*) The use of system calls that are ordinarily reserved for use by dump system programs.
(*c*) The act of overriding all file access controls.
(*d*) The use of a system call that permits one person to masquerade as another.
(*e*) The act of reloading a file from a system dump tape.
(*f*) Creation of a new file directory.
(*g*) Interference with the schedule of dump and reload activities.
(*h*) Alteration to file space accounting controls.

In order to be able to perform calculations about activities and the authorities that are necessarily associated with them, we use the following internal representation.

1. Activities that involve existing files

Each activity in this class is represented by a 4 by 5 array of one-bit elements. For the ith activity the ith column of the array contains non-zero elements whereas all other columns contain zero elements. For example, READ, which is the second activity, is represented by the following array:

$$
\begin{array}{ccccc}
0 & 1 & 0 & 0 & 0 \\
0 & 1 & 0 & 0 & 0 \\
0 & 1 & 0 & 0 & 0 \\
0 & 1 & 0 & 0 & 0 \\
\end{array}
$$

The reason for adopting this particular representation will become apparent in due course.

2. Activities that do not involve existing files

Each activity in this class is represented by a 26 element vector of one-bit elements. The ith activity is represented by a vector that has zero elements in all but the ith position. Thus, file creation, which is the first activity in this class, is represented by

$$10000000000 \ldots 000$$

It will be immediately apparent that we are able to represent composite activities by the logical sum of the representations of the separate activities involved.

RESTRAINTS ON FILE USE

It has already been stated that, where a requested activity involves an existing file, the authority of the user is compared with the specific act requested and with the particular restrictions associated with the file involved. Whenever a file is created, the creator must specify a list of the actions that are to be permitted for that file. The internal representation of this list is the 4 by 5 array that is the logical sum of the representations for the permitted activities. Thus, for a file that is generally available for reading (activity 2) and execution (activity 1) the representation would be

$$
\begin{array}{ccccc}
1 & 1 & 0 & 0 & 0 \\
1 & 1 & 0 & 0 & 0 \\
1 & 1 & 0 & 0 & 0 \\
1 & 1 & 0 & 0 & 0
\end{array}
$$

Now, it is convenient to be selective in the issue of permits to act on a file. For example, the owner will usually wish to retain the right to delete the file whereas he may not usually wish others to be able to do the same. This facility is provided by identifying four categories of file use.

The activity READ, is subdivided into four component activities:

READ in category 1
READ in category 2
READ in category 3
READ in category 4

The representation for READ in category 1 is a 4 by 5 array with zeros in all elements except the ith row of the second column (READ is activity number 2). Thus the total action called READ is a composition of four primitives and the representation of the composite activity is the logical sum of the representations of the primitives.

We allow a file creator to list the primitive actions that he wishes to authorize for his file and we represent this list by the logical sum of the representations of each of the primitives. Thus, for example, a file may be available to every possible category 1 activity, it may be restricted to reading and execution in category 2, and not available at all in the other two categories. The representation for this would be:

$$
\begin{array}{ccccc}
1 & 1 & 1 & 1 & 1 \\
1 & 1 & 0 & 0 & 0 \\
0 & 0 & 0 & 0 & 0 \\
0 & 0 & 0 & 0 & 0
\end{array}
$$

In practice, the user describes his privacy requirements by quoting four letters, one for each category. The situation described in the above example would ordinarily be described by the four letters

F   R   N   N

Each letter specifies the set of actions permitted in one category and a sequence of four letters completely describes the total permitted activity. Each letter must be chosen from the following list:

F Free access. Allow all activities including UPDATE.
D Allow DELETE, READ, EXECUTE and CHANGE STATUS.
C Allow READ, EXECUTE and CHANGE STATUS.

R Allow READ and EXECUTE.
L Allow EXECUTE only.
N No access.

The default value, which is used if the creater does not specify any privacy requirement, is

F F R R

That is, free access in categories 1 and 2, and read or execute in categories 3 and 4. As will be seen later, category 1 activities are normally only authorized to the file owner and category 4 activities are available to all users without restriction. The default value, FFRR, therefore gives free access to the file owner whereas members of the general public are restricted to reading and execution.

AUTHORITY TO ACT

A user's total authority is a list of all the activities in which he is entitled to indulge. The representation for this authority is the logical sum of the representations of the individual actions that are allowed. This is computed in two parts which correspond to the two classes of activity identified earlier. For example, the file access authority for a user who is allowed to perform all actions in categories 2 and 4, and is allowed to read or execute in category 3, is represented as

$$0 \ 0 \ 0 \ 0 \ 0$$
$$1 \ 1 \ 1 \ 1 \ 1$$
$$1 \ 1 \ 0 \ 0 \ 0$$
$$1 \ 1 \ 1 \ 1 \ 1$$

The same user may be able to create new files and his authority for class 2 activities would be represented as

$$1000000 \ldots 000$$

To discover whether a user may create files we need only check that the first element in his class 2 authority is non-zero. In general, if we need to decide whether he can perform some class 2 action, r, we need compare the representation for r with the class 2 authority of the user and if these two have a non-zero element in common the requested action is allowed. In practice, this means that we require the logical product of r and the user's class 2 authority to be non-zero.

When reference to a file is requested, we also need to check the privacy arrangements for the particular file in question. The request is allowed if the logical product of r, the file privacy and the user's class 1 authority yields a non-zero result.

CALCULATION OF USER AUTHORITY

A user's total authority is made up of his basic entitlement together with any additional authority that has been vested in him by explicit statements made to that effect.

Every user has a basic entitlement that allows him to perform all category 4 actions when referencing a file. This will be his total basic entitlement unless his name is the same as that of the file directory being used.

The file directory contains two marker digits that determine the basic entitlement of a user whose name is the same as that of the directory. The presence of either of these markers places an additional requirement on this user. If the additional requirement is met, or if the marker digits are not set, then his basic entitlement will allow all activities in classes 1 and 4, and in addition he will be permitted to create new files or privacy arrangements. The extra requirements that may be made are:

(*a*) The user must have quoted his own password correctly, and
(*b*) The user must be sitting at an on-line console.

The user's additional authority is determined by scanning the list of statements of authority held within each file directory. Each entry in this list contains a condition and an authority. The authority, which may be a composite activity, is given to any user that satisfies the specified condition. To compute the total additional authority we look for conditions that are met by the user in question and we accumulate the logical sum of the associated authorities. Where the requested activity involves a particular file, we scan the directory in which that file is listed. Where the activity does not involve any particular file, we scan the one particular file directory that is set aside just for this purpose.

In the interests of speed and space economy, the condition contained in one directory entry has a rather limited structure. There are four parts to this condition all of which must be satisfied (or null) before the condition is said to have been satisfied. The four parts are as follows.

Part 1   If not null, this requires that the user be sitting at an on-line console.
Part 2   If not null, this requires that the user should have quoted his own password correctly.
Parts 3   Each contain expressions of the form F(X) which must either be null or
and 4   true. The choice of function F is as follows:

(i) User name is X.
(ii) User has quoted key X.
(iii) User is obeying command program X.
(iv) User is using a file in group X.

Typically, a file owner will create a number of partners each of which is allowed to indulge in some category 2 activity and create new files. To do this he creates a directory entry with the associated condition:

User name is FRED

The authority that he gives to FRED is specified in the same notation as is the privacy requirement for a file. Thus, the authority to act freely in category 2 is written as NFNN and represented within the machine as

0 0 0 0 0
1 1 1 1 1
0 0 0 0 0
0 0 0 0 0

ARCHIVES

It is convenient to use magnetic tape to provide storage space for files that are not in regular use. There are at least two attitudes that one can adopt towards the use of this second level of file storage.

(*a*) One can attempt to integrate the two storage levels so that the user is unaware of the division and one can seek to find an operating strategy that minimizes the overheads involved in the management of the slower store. To do this one needs to find an effective means of deciding which material to keep in the faster store. This approach is analogous to the use of a paging technique between core and drum.

(*b*) One can seek to use the slower store in a way that does not conceal its existence from the user yet gives him convenient means of exploiting its extra capacity. In this case the user's view of the system is more elaborate but the onus of deciding which material to keep in the faster store is left in the hands of the user, who is better placed to make the necessary assessment of relative priorities.

It is the latter approach that has been adopted at Cambridge, and the second level store is known to the user as the archive store.

The user is required to assign each of his files to one of three classes: Permanent, Temporary, and Archive. Material with long-term value will be classified as Permanent if it is to be held on disc, and as Archive if it should be held on tape. It is by classification and re-classification of filed data that the user makes use of the archive store. However, he is subject to certain restraints that make him aware of the different characteristics of the storage media involved.

(*a*) Files must normally be transferred from archive store to permanent store before they can be used and this operation takes time (there is a delay of up to one hour). The user is thus aware that re-classification involves substantial system overheads and should not be undertaken without due consideration.

(*b*) Each file directory has associated with it a space account in which Permanent, Temporary and Archive files are each accounted for separately. Within each class, there is an upper limit on the permitted volume of filed material and this limit is set individually for each directory.

(*c*) The maximum number of file directory entries that can be accommodated in one file directory is set individually for each directory by the installation management. This reflects the fact that system overheads increase with the number of files handled as well as the volume of material filed.

ARCHIVE TAPE SYSTEM

For the purposes of tape management, file directories are assembled into archive groups; each directory is assigned to one group. For each group there is a distinct set of magnetic tapes that provide secondary storage for filed material.

The groups are chosen such that the total of the Permanent and Archive space allocations is not greater than the capacity of one magnetic tape. All files in these two classes and belonging to one archive group can therefore be accommodated on one magnetic tape. A set of tapes (usually four) is assigned to each group and these are used in rotation. At each update, one tape is completely re-written to contain the up-to-date material for all members of one archive group (figure 4). The three

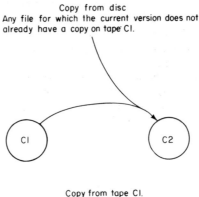

Copy from disc
Any file for which the current version does not
already have a copy on tape CI.

Copy from tape CI.
All files that have neither been deleted nor
updated on the disc

Figure 4. Archive update.

previous generations are kept for back-up purposes and to allow limited facilities for retrieval of 'deleted' files. The tapes are used and re-used on a cyclic basis so that, for a cycle of four tapes, the father and grandfather are always available. The fourth tape, the great grandfather, will also be available until the start of the next update run. Under normal circumstances there is one update for each group each week but a user may request an unscheduled archive update when necessary in order to clear a backlog of material from the disc.

Archive files are held on disc until they have been transferred to the archive tapes. Once an archive file has been preserved in this way it is removed from the disc leaving only the file directory entry as a link with the copy on magnetic tape. In view of the fact that permanent files are also copied on to archive tapes, it will usually be the case that there is little or no delay between the change to archive status and the subsequent release of disc space. If subsequently a file is re-classified as permanent, the copy on archive tape continues to be maintained so that further disc to tape transfers are avoided.

File recovery is initiated by re-classifying an archive file as permanent. When this act takes place a flag is set in the directory entry for the file in question. At hourly intervals, the directory is scanned and a batch of reload jobs is initiated. The directory entry contains enough information to allow the system to identify the magnetic tape from which the file may be reloaded. This operation together with the mechanics of the archive tape update program are discussed in greater detail later in this article.

INTEGRITY

The integrity of a disc-based file system is put at risk by the possibility of hardware failure, software malfunction, mismanagement by the operating staff and misplaced user activity. To minimise loss and corruption in the face of these hazards, we have taken some trouble to incorporate error detection and correction procedures at a number of levels throughout the file management software. In practice these procedures account for a very substantial part of the software involved.

It is convenient to describe the system in two parts. First, there are those actions that are taken in order to detect, prevent or repair file corruption within the confines of the disc store itself. Secondly, there are the procedures that use magnetic tape to hold redundant copies of filed data.

FILE INTEGRITY ON DISC

Error detection relies upon the existence of redundancy in the data base. However, it may be noted that this is not the only function of redundancy and, in particular, we use redundancy in a number of ways to obtain increased operating speed. In the first instance we sought a basic data structure that was simple in the sense that it contained little redundancy. The file management process was then defined in terms of manipulations upon this structure and it was this process and this structure that were used to assess the effects of hardware malfunction. Using this as a design base, we have added redundancy both as a means of enhancing the error detection capability and as a means of increasing run-time speed.

We have found that it is possible to obtain a high level of integrity and yet retain simplicity of design by persistent and meticulous attention to detail during the early design stage. There are three questions which must be asked when evaluating a design proposal.

1. How would the data base look after a system failure? To answer this question one must have a knowledge of hardware (and low-level software) failure characteristics. With this knowledge one can determine the effect of a failure at critical points in the run-time process.
2. Is it possible to deduce a valid and self-consistent data base from that which is left after a failure? It is quite possible to produce a system that fails in such a way that it is not possible to decide upon a data configuration that can be reliably used as the basis for a system restart. It is desirable to design the system so that the more likely configurations into which it falls after system failure are those from which a satisfactory restart configuration can most readily be obtained.
3. What is the cost of the search for inconsistency within the data base? Since the search must usually be conducted on every restart, it is desirable to avoid data base designs for which a thorough check is ruled out on economic grounds.

This method of evaluation can be applied to some advantage even at the earliest design stages. I shall give two examples.

It is necessary to choose some means of associating the several blocks of a file with the file directory entry for that file. One way of doing this is to link each block to the next by a pointer contained in the block itself. The file directory entry would point to the first block and the last block would contain a null pointer. But consider the effect of a central processor stop while a file is being copied to the disc. It is most likely that some, but not all, of the data will actually have reached the disc. As a result the chain of pointers that link these blocks will end by pointing to a block with arbitrary content. A loop may result or two files may appear to have some data in common. The restart program must therefore be able to detect this type of corruption in the data base and it is more than likely that the most effective solution to this and allied problems would be to make a full check of all inter-block links. But this would involve reading every block of disc store and could be prohibitively expensive in consequence. At Cambridge we use a map of disc space, as described earlier, and this particular aspect of the restart process is consequently a thoroughly practical proposition.

One of the possible erroneous configurations that could result from an untimely central processor stop results in one, apparently legitimate file obtaining data that belonged to a file that was deleted just before the system failed. This effect is one consequence of the fact that file directories and the disc map are updated in core store and then transferred to disc separately. It is the information on disc that forms the basis for restart. Rather than try to make it possible for the restart program to detect erroneous configurations of this type, we chose to adopt a run-time procedure that minimizes the likelihood of the error occurring in a not-easily identifiable form. Three actions are required.

1. We use two free store chains (see figure 3). When a file is deleted the space that it used is added to free store chain B but when a file is created it uses space from free store chain A. Only when the disc map has been safely written on to disc does the free space in chain B become part of that on chain A.
2. When a file has been deleted we refuse to construct the directory entry for a new file until the directory entry for the deleted file has been successfully written to disc.
3. The last act taken on behalf of a newly created file is to set a marker in the disc map entry for the first block of the file. When a file is deleted this marker is removed. On restart, we discard any filed data for which the disc map entry is unmarked.

RESTART FROM DISC

The operating system must be restarted after any serious failure and after a period of scheduled down-time. When this happens, the system calls the file restart program. It is the task of this program to make maximum use of information held on disc, to check it as thoroughly as possible and to re-establish the file management system with a sound data base. There is no attempt to utilize information left in the core store at the end of the previous session.

The checks made by the restart program are as thorough as we can make them in the direction of ensuring that there is no inconsistency within the file control information. We emphasize the need for consistency in this area because it is a property of this type of system that minor errors in the control information can provoke wholesale corruption throughout the data base. For this reason we read and check the disc map and every file directory. Whenever errors are found we chose to abandon data on disc rather than risk an apparent corruption to the content of a file. For example, we abandon any file that is in the course of being created since we are uncertain whether it actually reached the disc before the system failed.

When all checks have been made and when corruptions have been cut out, the redundant control information is re-computed; totals of space used, the free space chains and the cross-reference from file directory to master file directory, are all re-set to their correct values. The entire restart process takes about one minute and part of this is time-shared with the normal computing load.

Finally, the restart program notes the absence of any file directory. If one or more directories are missing a suitable directory reload job is automatically inserted into the job queue and this job is run before any other jobs are permitted to proceed. The job obtains copies of the missing directories from the magnetic tape most recently written by the incremental file dumper.

THE INCREMENTAL DUMPER

At regular intervals new and recently updated files are copied from disc on to magnetic tape. This is a purely precautionary measure that avoids complete dependence upon the integrity of the disc system. The material copied on to the dump tapes is only used when the original is lost or corrupted.

The dumper is a program that is automatically inserted into the job queue at regular intervals. The appropriate choice of interval depends upon the reliability of the disc hardware and on the overhead involved in running the program. In practice the interval has been as short as 20 minutes but is currently set at 3 hours.

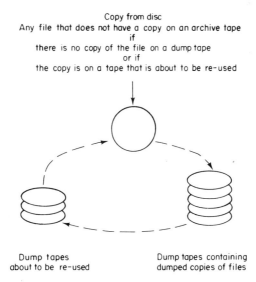

Copy from disc
Any file that does not have a copy on an archive tape
if
there is no copy of the file on a dump tape
or if
the copy is on a tape that is about to be re-used

Dump tapes
about to be re-used

Dump tapes containing
dumped copies of files

Figure 5. Incremental dump.

The dumper uses a set of about 15 magnetic tapes in rotation (see figure 5). At
any instant one of these tapes is known as the current dump tape. When the dumper
runs it copies material on to this tape starting at the position reached at the end of
the previous dump run. Gradually the tape is filled and when a tape is full the next
in the cycle is used. We count the number of reels of tape that have been filled and
this number, the series number, is used to identify the content of the current dump
tape. When a file is dumped the series number and tape position are written into the
file directory. The combination of series number and tape position is known as the
dump name. The dump name uniquely identifies a dumped version of a file and serves
to distinguish between successive sets of data to which the user has assigned identical
file titles. It is relevant to note that the dump name increases in numeric value
with each successive dump activity. The significance of this becomes clear when one
considers the controls that are required in order to ensure integrity within the dump
system itself.

From time to time it is necessary to re-dump a file. The fact that the dump tapes
are used in rotation implies that we risk over-writing a valuable copy of a file when
the tape containing it is re-used. To avoid this, we automatically request a re-dump
of a file that is threatened in this way. We periodically compare the dump name of
every file with the series number of the current dump tape. If the difference between
these two values exceeds a pre-set limit, the dumper is asked to re-dump the file
in question. A similar problem arises if the system fails while dumper is running.
After restart we need to compare the dump name of every file with the position
and series number of the current dump tape. It is necessary to re-dump any file with
dump name that is beyond the point from which dumper will resume operations.

When dumper finds a file that needs dumping, it copies the file on to tape and
then writes the dump name into the file directory. The directory itself is also
copied on to magnetic tape when a file is dumped or when the directory contains
a marker indicating that a significant change has been made to its content. We
also dump one copy of every file directory on to the beginning of every dump tape
in order to facilitate restart when a directory has been lost from the disc.

TWO TIER DUMP SYSTEM

Two systems which copy files on to magnetic tape have now been described. The
archive system maintains copies of all permanent and archive files on magnetic
tape in an orderly fashion and this is done on a weekly basis. The dump system,
on the other hand, writes material to tape in no particular order but with minimum
delay. In practice, the two systems are made to work together to provide a uniform
system providing magnetic tape back-up as well as archive storage. The archive
system provides long-term storage in an efficient and orderly fashion, and the
incremental dumper gives protection between the time of file creation and the next
archive update. In consequence of its dual role, the archive system is also known as
the secondary dump system.

Coordination of dumping is effected by a subroutine that is entered whenever a
new file is created, an existing one is altered or when a dumper requests access to a
file directory. The routine checks and, if necessary, resets a number of flags which

in turn control dumper action. The five flags and two dump names, which are held in the file directory entry for each file, are used as follows:

1. Incremental dump name.
This is the series number and tape position of the file on the incremental dump tape. It is re-set only when the file is copied from disc on to tape.
2. Archive dump name.
This is the series number and archive group for the archive tape on which the file is held. It is re-set only when the file is copied from disc on to tape.
3. Incremental dump request.
If this flag is set the incremental dumper will copy the file at the earliest opportunity. It is set when a file is created or updated. It is also set when the "archive current" flag is not set but the "Incremental dump name" is less than the series number of the current tape minus some constant (5 at present).
4. Incremental dump made.
This flag indicates that the current version of the file is also to be found on an incremental dump tape.
5. Archive dump request.
If this flag is set the file will be copied from disc to the appropriate archive tape at the next update. It is set whenever "Incremental dump made" is set and "Archive dump made" is not set.
6. Archive dump made.
This flag indicates that the current version of the file is also to be found on the latest tape of the appropriate archive group.
7. Archive dump in trouble.
This flag is set when magnetic tape failure or some other hazard leads to abandonment of the archive copy of a file.

The overheads of file dumping are reduced substantially by keeping, in core store, a vector in which there is one element for each file directory. One flag per directory signals the need for attention by the incremental dumper. By this means we can avoid reading every directory from disc.

MANAGEMENT OF MAGNETIC TAPES

It is desirable to take whatever steps one can to ensure continuity of file dumping in spite of hardware failure or injudicious operator action; the dump system will be expected to run automatically and unattended. Thus, for example, a bad patch on one magnetic tape should not be allowed to bring all progress to a halt. Another consequence of the absence of supervision is that there will be no frequent check on the integrity of the dump process. Errors in this part of the system will only be found when attempting to restart the file management system after some failure and on these occasions one is rarely equipped to deal with unwanted complications. To avoid this, it is necessary to incorporate consistency checks into the dump system itself. Time spent in this way will rarely be wasted. In addition to the usual device of checking tape identity by program, we include identity and consistency checks on each section of dumped material. If bad sections of tape are found we

ignore them, and if corruptions are detected the system automatically backs up
to the last good position. However, we have found it essential to make sure that
all errors and corrective actions are reported on paper so that events can be
traced manually should the system knot itself.

As added protection against loss, we write all incremental dump tapes in
duplicate. The duplicate copy is written at the same time as the original. This
system has the disadvantage that both copies are on the machine and being
written at the same time. In an earlier system the copy was made after the
original was written but the need to skip over bad sections of tape is then
inconsistent with the almost essential aim of obtaining exact duplication. Without
exact duplication, errors encountered during the recovery process become more
complex to handle.

FILE RECOVERY

Permanent files that are not on disc will be reloaded automatically from magnetic
tape. At regular intervals (currently once per hour) the file directories are inspected
and a list of missing files is assembled. Each entry in this list contains a file title
together with a dump name or archive name. When the list has been completed file
reload jobs are inserted into the job queue; each job uses one dump or archive
tape. When a reload job reaches the execution stage it scans the list of missing files
and copies to disc as many of the missing files as it can.

The effect of this strategy is to batch file reloads and so avoid excessive tape
handling. However, it does mean that a user may have to wait for some time before
a missing file is replaced. The list of missing files is not strictly necessary but it
does serve to reduce system overheads. Without it, each reload program would
need to search the file directories and this would involve a substantial number of
disc transfers. System overheads are further reduced by holding. In core store, a
vector in which there is one entry per file directory. A single flag per directory
signals the need to search that directory for missing files.

It is essential to arrange that failure to reload one file does not halt progress with
other reload activity. If magnetic tape or other failure means that a file cannot be
reloaded the system sets a flag in the file directory, prints a warning message, and
then proceeds to reload other files. The flag is inspected by several system programs
which issue warning messages to both management and the user.

There is usually more than one copy of a file on magnetic tape; dump tapes are
written in duplicate and it is a property of the archive system that a new copy of a
file is made each week. During its first week, a file is held by the incremental dump
system and on one archive tape. Thereafter there will be copies on at least two
archive tapes. At present, there is no automatic mechanism that makes the system
try to find the second copy of a file when reload fails. Such a mechanism would make
a worthwhile improvement if it could be designed to distinguish sensibly between
transient, avoidable and intransient failures since it would further reduce the need
for human supervision.

The mechanics of file reload are very similar to file creation. There are two main
differences. When a file is reloaded we insist on using an existing file directory entry
for the file instead of creating a new entry. If the reload fails the file directory

entry is not deleted, as could be the case when file creation fails, but is reset to its initial state. We take particular notice of failures that result when the file space allocation is exceeded. Reload tasks for such files will not be scheduled until the necessary space becomes available.

APPENDIX

Information held in a file directory

1. The directory heading

1.1 The name of the directory.
1.2 The size of the directory.
1.3 The total volume of disc space occupied by files associated with this directory. There are separate totals of space occupied by Permanent, Temporary and Archive files respectively.
1.4 The maximum volume of disc space allowed to files associated with this directory. There are separate allocations of space for Permanent, Temporary and Archive files respectively.
1.5 The name of the archive group to which the directory is assigned.
1.6 The total volume of space occupied on the latest archive tape.
1.7 The position of the master file directory entry that contains the name of this directory.
1.8 Dump control markers. There are three flags.
    (*a*) Indicates that the directory should be written to tape as soon as possible.
    (*b*) Indicates that incremental dumping has started and has not been interrupted by a further change to the directory.
    (*c*) Indicates that this directory should be deleted from the disc. Deletion actually takes place when a final copy of the directory has been dumped.
1.9 A flag to indicate that files associated with this directory can be read or executed but new information may not be added. This flag will usually be set prior to final deletion.
1.10 Conditions for directory ownership.
    If a user should have the same name as the directory itself then he will be treated as the "owner" if he satisfies the conditions demanded by the following two flags.
    (*a*) If this flag is set the user must have quoted his password correctly.
    (*b*) If this flag is set the user must be sitting at an on-line console.

2. A file description entry

2.1 The name of the file.
2.2 The size of the file.
2.3 The access status. This is a 4 by 5 array of one-bit entries. Each of the four rows describes permitted activity for one category of user. Associated with each column is one possible activity and a one-bit indicates that the activity is permitted.

2.4   An interlock that indicates the number of people using the file and the manner of use. If positive, it is the number of people reading the file and, if negative, the file is being written.

2.5   The position of the file on disc. Zero if there is no copy of the file on disc.

2.6   The class of the file. Files are classed as Permanent, Temporary or Archive.

2.7   A flag to identify a file that forms an essential part of the system software and which should therefore be present on disc before normal service jobs can be expected to run properly.

2.8   A flag to identify the "preferred" version of a group of files that all have similar names. This flag is consulted whenever the user asks to use the "preferred" version and it is this version of a system program that is normally used.

2.9   Control information for the incremental dumper.
   (*a*) A flag to indicate that a copy of the latest version is held on the incremental dump tape.
   (*b*) A flag to indicate the file should be copied on to an incremental dump tape.
   (*c*) A flag to indicate that dumping has started. This flag is cleared if the file is updated during the dump process.
   (*d*) The dump name. This is the series number and position of the dump tape when the file was dumped.

2.10 Control information for the archive dumper.
   (*a*) A flag to indicate that a copy of the latest version of the file is held on the latest archive tape.
   (*b*) A flag to indicate that the file should be copied on to the archive tape.
   (*c*) A flag to indicate that an archive update has started. This flag is cleared if the file is updated while the update is proceeding.
   (*d*) The archive name. This is the name of the archive group and the series number of the tape on to which the file was first copied.
   (*e*) A flag to indicate that, through some system malfunction, the copy held on tape may have been corrupted.

2.11 Control information for the file reloader. This consists of three flags.
   (*a*) A flag to indicate that the file should be reloaded from an archive tape.
   (*b*) A flag to indicate that the file should be reloaded from an incremental dump tape.
   (*c*) A flag to indicate that the reload system failed to recover the file from tape. This was probably due to a system malfunction.

2.12 The date and time of file creation.

3. *An authority description entry*

3.1   An integer that uniquely identifies the directory entry.

3.2   A marker to distinguish the type of activity that is authorized. There are two types:
   (*a*) File access (see 3.3 below).
   (*b*) Special file system function (see 3.4 below).

3.3   A description of authorized file system actions:
   (*a*) A flag to indicate that file creation is permitted.
   (*b*) A flag to indicate that new statements of authority can be created.

(*c*) A 4 by 5 array of one-bit entries.
The four rows correspond to the four categories of file use. The five columns refer to the five ways of using a file. If the entry is non-zero then the activity is permitted.

3.4 A description of authorized special file system activities. This is a 24-bit array in which each one-bit entry denotes permission to perform one special activity. Some of these are:

(*a*) Ability to use the system calls that create and destroy statements of authority that allow special file system activities.

(*b*) Ability to use the system calls that are normally reserved only for dump system programs.

(*c*) Ability to override all file access controls.

(*d*) Ability to use a system call that permits one person to masquerade as another.

(*e*) Ability to reload a file from a system dump tape.

(*f*) Ability to create a new file directory entry.

(*g*) Ability to interfere with the schedule of dump and reload activities.

3.5 A description of the conditions under which authority is granted. There are four parts to the condition all of which must be satisfied before the condition is said to have been satisfied:

(*a*) A flag to indicate that the user must have quoted his own password correctly.

(*b*) A flag to indicate that the user must be sitting at an on-line console.

(*c*) A function $F(X)$. The function F must be chosen from the following list:
User name is X.
User has quoted key X.
User is executing the command program X.
User is using a file from group X.

(*d*) A second function plus parameter chosen from the same list as for (*c*).

3.6 The date and time when the statement of authority was added to the file directory.

ACKNOWLEDGEMENTS

The work described in this paper is part of the program of research and development being carried out at the University Mathematical Laboratory, Cambridge, under the direction of Professor M. V. Wilkes. The entire operating system has been the co-operative effort of many people but is mainly due to Professor D. W. Barron, Dr. D. F. Hartley, Mr. B. Landy, Dr. R. M. Needham and the author. The early stages of the basic supervisor work were carried out in collaboration with International Computers and Tabulators Ltd., and subsequently the project has been supported by the Science Research Council.

REFERENCES

[1] Barron *et al.*, "File Handling at Cambridge University". *AFIPS Conf. Proc.* **30** (SJCC 1967), 163.

[2]   "An introduction to the Cambridge multiple-access system". University
       Mathematical Laboratory, Cambridge (1968).
[3]   "Cambridge multi-access system manual". University Mathematical Laboratory,
       Cambridge (1968).

DISCUSSION

FRASER: The nature of the work load of the Titan installation is biased towards
jobs with small data sets. The system is therefore geared to handle small files, the
average being around six thousand characters. Many of the files contain a program
which is developed by means of an editor, usually from a console. The large files
associated with commercial data processing or scientific matrix manipulation would
be unsuitable for this file system.

One notable feature of the Titan computer is its distinct unreliability. This has
obvious disadvantages, but also has the advantage that it forces one to study the
requirements for building a high integrity system on low integrity hardware. It
gave us an environment to test out ideas for overcoming hardware unreliability and
produce a more dependable system.

It was anticipated that the disc space available would probably not be enough
to handle all the files that might naturally arise in practice. Consequently, the file
system was required to make good use of the disc store. Rationing and accounting
mechanisms were necessary in order to encourage users to use the disc sensibly. We
were also forced to consider the use of magnetic tape as auxiliary storage for files.

These were the main characteristics of the system which determined the design.
In order to obtain reasonable performance, care had to be taken in distributing data
on the disc; in particular, chaining through blocks on the disc itself was avoided.
Also, at the time the system was designed, the machine did not have a generous
allowance of core store, and to make sure that the cost of the file system, in terms
of core store, was not very great, a number of economies were made.

Although not a requirement of the environment, we also wanted the inclusion
of a system of privacy controls, which would be completely secure, but still retain
flexibility. This was the second of the more successful aspects of the system
(integrity being the first).

The file system was designed in 1966 and brought into service in March 1967.
At that time there were very few file systems designed for on-line use available,
the most influential at the time being the Multics proposal[1].

The Multics design was not particularly well suited to the Titan space-time
constraints. Also in Multics there was a very close correspondence between the
notion of a directory structure and the notion of protection and privacy control. I
believe this correspondence to be fallacious and misleading, although it has turned
up in a number of other file systems since then. In the Titan file system the correspondence does not exist.

Except for a small fixed-arm disc, the disc hardware contains a separate moving
arm for each disc plate. The disc capacity is 128 million characters, something like
80 per cent of which is available for use by the file system. The rest of the disc is used

[1] Daley, R. C. and Neumann, P. G. "A general purpose file system for secondary storage".
Proc. AFIPS FJCC, pp. 213–229, 1965.

for Supervisor working space and Supervisor program. A file in the system is an integral number of blocks containing about 4000 characters each. The maximum length of a file is 100 blocks.

Briefly, there is a one block Master File Directory which contains 1½ word entries which point to the User File Directories. There are about 350 User File Directories which contain an entry of six words for each file, including the privacy controls. The directories themselves, including the Master File Directory, are each files in the system. A further directory, called the system directory, is used as a universal mechanism for accessing both directory and data files.

The file system is composed of user programs running under the Supervisor. Only the File Master has privileges with respect to the Supervisor to enable it to manage the file directories. All the other file management programs, such as the dumper, work in the normal environment for an object program. However, they are controlled by the privacy mechanism. It is clearly necessary for the dumper to be able to read every file on the disc, and the privacy mechanism was made flexible enough. By using the system directory, any user program with adequate privacy privilege can open and read the Master File Directory. There are, of course, interlocks on all files to prevent timing troubles.

In normal running mode, the File Master occupies 2K of 48-bit words and is divided into four equal areas. (1) a fixed program; (2) an overlay area used to hold one of three overlays; (3) a buffer area; (4) a copy of the Control block, which contains absolute disc addresses of the Master File Directory etc. The File Master is used by the Supervisor whenever (1) a user wishes to open or close a file; (2) a user wants to create or alter a privacy arrangement; (3) a system program, such as the archive or dump program requires to establish interlocks. Basically, it handles all the extracodes (i.e. system calls) for the file system. In addition, the File Master executes small functions, such as checking the password of a user, although they are not logically part of its role. To reduce the number of disc accesses by the File Master a number of tables in a working store hold information obtained from file directories. For example, when a user opens a file for reading, an interlock is established, which specifies that the file can not be subsequently opened for writing. This interlock is stored in the User File Directory. This would require reading and possibly writing the User File Directory each time the file is opened or closed. Instead there is an area in working store to hold the names and interlock values for up to N files. Providing there is an available slot, we can store a short identifier for the file and its interlock information. Then, whenever another user attempts to open the file, the working store is scanned first and the validity of the request is checked and the working store updated if necessary. When the file is closed, the working store slot can be re-used for another file. Using tricks of this nature we can get away with using only a small amount of core store for the file system.

Some of the programs of the file system are associated with integrity and are periodically scheduled to do such things as dump files, see if a file needs reloading onto disc and so on. The file system keeps a list of jobs which need to be scheduled on a long term basis, and initiates them at the appropriate time. A typical program is the file dumper which is scheduled to run every three hours. When the file system initiates this job, it then waits to make sure that the job is in fact run to completion and does not die as a result of machine failure. When the job is complete the run is recorded and the job is scheduled again for running after an appropriate interval.

A number of file system utilities can be invoked by using the command system, either on-line or off-line. Commands can be used to enquire about the status of a file, to list the user's file titles, to set up privacy relationships and to perform various operations on the files. Most of these commands are interpreted in terms of extracodes (i.e. Supervisor calls) for File Master operations.

An essential part of the file system is the set of programs which aid file maintenance (e.g. scan a dump tape for errors or other information), and the management aids which facilitate changes to the accounting information and gather statistics of usage.

A test environment was also provided, so that changes to the system could be tested out without risk of corrupting existing files. A reserved area of the disc was used for test files which could be updated and the existing files could be used in a mode which did not permit writing. Sets of tapes of commands exist which can drive the test environment automatically. This gives you an alternative approach to running the file system under itself.

It is difficult to separate the procedure for dumping files to magnetic tape for security purposes, from the use of magnetic tape as auxiliary storage for files, so in practice they became integrated into one.

Incremental dumping is now done once every three hours, and if the incremental dump tapes are allowed to accumulate indefinitely they will nearly all contain a large amount of garbage. In order to overcome this problem, a second mechanism was invented, similar to doing a complete disc dump one a week, it also avoids turning off the filing system whilst the dump is going on and using a scarce resource at a particular time during the week. A little extra complexity allows you to time share it with the rest of the workload by doing the complete disc dump a little at a time. The disc is divided up into twelve sections, and have twelve jobs which are scheduled throughout the week. This allows flexibility in the scheduling of the dumping operations. In order that complete dumps can be postponed, an interlock is required between the incremental dump system and the longer term dump system to ensure that a copy of a file is kept by the incremental dump system until a complete dump is eventually done.

The weekly dump system is also incremental in the sense that we only dump from disc the files which have changed since the last weekly dump, the other files being obtained from the previous tape. We therefore have two incremental dumps, one slow and one fast, making use of almost the same software. There is extra software in the second level system to enable us to read from tape. Also, most of the data transfer in this system is from tape to tape and does not cause undue load on the disc store. The only unattractive part of this dual system is that the archive system knows nothing about the dump system. This means that the archive system cannot pick something off the daily incremental dump tapes if it turns out that the disc copy of a file has become corrupted. In this situation, we must postpone the archiving of this file until next week when it will have been reloaded from the dump tape.

With archiving we have a problem in predicting when a file is going to be required. The solution is to call upon the user for advice on this question, and then bring archived files back on demand. We put a control into the systems, which allows the user to specify whether, for the coming time period, he wants the file on disc or tape, and it is then up to the user to manage his files so that he does not have too much on disc at any one time. In fact, we optimize the system around his instructions, and sometimes write a file to magnetic tape before the user specifies it. Whenever an archived file is required back on disc, the recovery is done as soon as possible after the request.

To complete the archiving process all we need do is erase the file from the disc. The recovery of an archived file is much the same as the recovery of a corrupted file under the file integrity scheme. We now see how interwoven the file integrity and the file archiving can be in practice.

The problem of making a file system reliable is difficult, but can be solved using only a small amount of code. One overlay of the File Master contains the restart process, which is brought in on initial system loading and also on a restart. Its job is to check the disc for ambiguities and to make changes to the disc in order to remove any ambiguities that might exist. This may involve the reloading of information from magnetic tape.

The first action which Restart takes is to check that the chains linking blocks of a file, and the chain linking free blocks, are all properly formed. To avoid reading every block on disc a map is used in which there is one small field for each block. Then instead of storing the pointers in the blocks on the disc itself, you can store them in this map.

An entry in the map which is at the head of a chain is marked accordingly for file integrity purposes.

Suppose that a file owner deletes a given file causing all the blocks of the file to be passed to the free block chain. Another user then comes along and creates a file, taking blocks off the free block chain and by chance gets the same initial block. If the machine fails before the map is written to disc, the user who created a file appears to have a file which uses all the blocks of the previously deleted file. This is a timing problem involving the interlocking actions of the File Master and the routine which writes the map to disc. We circumvent this situation by withholding the head block of a deleted file from the free block chain until after the map has been written up to the disc successfully. It is first written to a "dummy" free chain, whose elements are all transferred to the proper free chain when the map has been written to disc successfully. This procedure does not take very much code and it certainly makes the restart program easier to write.

Writing a system that is restartable, consists of a number of tricks like this, which account for very little code and merely require a certain amount of forethought. Problems such as these probably account for the difficulty one experiences when an attempt is made to superimpose a dumping or file integrity system onto an existing file system. For example, when the incremental dump system was added to CTSS (Compatible Time Sharing System of Project Mac), they took an incredibly long time to get it to work. I would not know how to write a restart system if the system for file updates did not co-operate.

WARNE: This is a very thorough paper, so precise in detail that it is almost a guide to implementation. Even if one does not wish to emulate the Cambridge Titan system, it can still be used as a guide.

However, there are several points I would like to comment on:

Firstly, the separation of the File Master from the Supervisor is a good example of the construction of a more advanced operating system within the framework of a simpler one.

Secondly, many modern operating systems are moving towards trouble when they structure the filing system to give them some form of protection and also to reflect the management system of the organization. A two-level nomenclature is about all that a user should normally expect and if he wants deeper levels this must be achieved by specially designed techniques. The potential inefficiency of such techniques should not be imposed on standard users. For example, most of the multi-level filing systems try to reflect certain budgetary controls, which can be done quite separately by having a file in the filing system which shows the relationships between different directories. We are thus superimposing on the basic structure, a more complex structure through which we can deal with the problem of budgetary controls. It has been illustrated by the Cambridge filing system that you can have a number of controls in the system without necessarily reflecting them at user level.

Finally, in the Cambridge system the user is aware of the two-level storage regime. A decision was made that the user should know when he does not want a file, and that he should, therefore, make the decision to move it from one storage medium to another. If the designers had been working with a greater variety of storage media, they might have needed to solve the problem of automatic migration of less frequently used information.

HARTLEY: This was discussed a great deal, and it was decided that the file owner was in the best position to decide whether a file should be on tape or disc, and any automatic mechanism either did the wrong thing or could be beaten by the user in some way.

WARNE: If one includes large data bases in a filing system, I think that one would prefer to have removable media, such as exchangeable disc stores, in order to achieve the kind of security required. This would seem to call for different methods for obtaining integrity from the ones used in the Cambridge system.

The principle of "prevention is better than cure" is a good one, and it seems to have been used in the Cambridge system. it is a good idea to take action before an event rather than be involved in a difficult reconstruction after the event has occurred. The idea of withholding certain blocks from the free list until after the map has been written to disc is an example of this principle. The technique of maintaining a disc map outside the files is also good, because it does cut down the reconstruction time. Another point is the technique of using markers to indicate partially updated files, so that in the event of corruption we know which files to discard.

RANDELL: I would have liked to hear more about the extent to which you and other people have learnt about filing systems during the period 1967–1971. How many of the decisions, which are incorporated in the present system, were made at the design stage, and how many have been included as a result of user and operational feedback?

Files are not the only things which can be corrupted and then become the concern of the restart system. Consequently, in a separate design, you will either have rather different dump and restart facilities or you will find that they will become tied together, despite the separate design, as one side realizes that it can use the other side's facilities. The Multics situation is an example of the alternative approach.

When a large number of people are co-operating in modifications on a large data base there is a definite dump and restart problem. In order to dump we have to essentially stop the world at a consistent point for at least one particular user, record the situation, and then if a restart is required we must enable the users to get back to this situation.

FRASER: First of all a comment on the separation of the filing system and the Supervisor. Somebody once said that software is structured to reflect the management structure which produced it. My job was to implement a filing system under the already constructed basic Supervisor.

There are no substantial advantages and in fact certain disadvantages in integrating budgetary control structures into the file directory structure. The system performance is very sensitive to file directory structure, and one ought to be very careful when seeking to integrate it. There are ways of making budgetary control structures of an elaborate nature which are not so central and not so influential on the system performance.

I regard auto-migration between storage levels as being a specific engineering solution to a specific problem. I would not dream of suggesting that this specific solution should be used in a different environment. However, my past experience indicates that the abdication of control to a pseudo learning program is a very expensive way of dodging the question. You should rather strike a nice balance between what the user regards as a control and what the system takes to be a control. Now, in the case of archives, the user can specify when something ought to be in archive storage and when it ought to be on disc, but the timing is the responsibility of the system. We can provide an almost equivalent performance from the point of view of the user, without substantial overheads to the system, by not taking the user's controls at face value.

FRASER: It is unfortunate that there has been very little progress of an intellectual nature in the design of file systems in the last five years. This may be because designers have been more concerned with the bread-and-butter problems. But I feel that in the specific engineering problem that Cambridge addressed itself to, there were no important factors left out. Of course there are plenty of things which one could do to improve the performance. The most significant of these improvements were probably not realized at Cambridge because of the division between the File Master and the Supervisor. For example, it is very difficult to engineer a system so that it schedules jobs on the basis of which files are open and which files are closed. This would be useful in situations where we would like a job to run after another job has finished updating a specific file.

The design of the file system went through a number of rewrites. The original system did not incorporate a restart facility, and when this was looked at, I realized that the file system had better be reconstructed. The privacy mechanism also had to be rewritten twice. The important feature about the filing system is that it is small and I was able to replace the entire thing every time I changed it.

The dumping mechanism does not provide the user with the ability to specify that at a particular state he requires everything to be dumped. However, knowledge of the system would allow him to refrain from working on the system whilst the dumper was running so that he could have a complete set dump. If a user has a file open for updating when his files are dumped, this file is dumped but a marker is set in the directory to indicate that the dump of this file should be ignored. We have organized dumping in this way so that the user is not interfered with when the two processes are running at the same time. We could probably have stopped the user's "world" in a consistent state when we wished to dump his files, but the pressures to engineer this did not exist.

The dumping of other operating system material has been circumnavigated. The accounting routines, for example, make files which are dumped by the dumper. Other material does not go out directly through the dumper, but takes a contorted route to get there. This area of the system could have been made cleaner.

NEEDHAM: As the File Master is a user program it remains in a halted state until the Supervisor wakes it up to deal with a request. Having been woken up, the File Master receives the message, services it and then looks for a further message; if there are no more messages, it halts. This could probably have been improved upon if the File Master could receive more than one message at once instead of taking messages from a queue one at a time.

Regarding the question of map management, the file storage is divided into 16 parts, each file residing exclusively in one part, so that the maps are kept to a reasonable size. The required maps are kept in core whilst they are being used. If you have a very large disc store, the management of the maps themselves becomes tedious and the desirability of a map system is questionable.

WARNE: One alternative is to construct smaller maps out of the larger maps. For instance, you could take the tracks which are essentially part of a file being used, to form a smaller map.

NEEDHAM: Yes, but the more you fragment the more difficulty you have in keeping up to date and consistent, and it is quite hard enough anyway.

Finally, the question of very large files. One approach to this which has turned out by accident to be taken at Cambridge is to provide suitable utilities for the user to look after his own integrity problems. He can mark his file so that the incremental dumper takes no notice of it, and then use utility programs to perform his own integrity operations.

NEWELL: Rather than the map system we use a block list system on George 3, and using this we have designed high integrity of the disc blocks through head crashes. We are careful, when we update a file, to keep parallel copies of blocks which are changed. If a disc crash occurs, even during a transfer, we are able to recover by reverting to the correct blocks.

One of our problems is that when the dumper comes in we have to freeze the file directories in order to take a snapshot. I am surprised that your system does not suffer from the same deficiency; perhaps you are not getting a consistent picture of the file store by taking only one twelfth of the disc at a time.

FRASER: We aim for an accurate picture of the file store over a period of time, rather than a consistent picture. When a file is dumped, we store with it the time at which that copy was last written to. The onus is then on the user to determine whether he has got a consistent picture or whether one of his files has been retraced further back than another.

NEWELL: How does he know there has been a fatality causing files to be backed up?

FRASER: There are some mechanisms in the system which allow the file system to send messages to the users, but this has not been implemented in practice. One tries to put out bulletins or send messages to people in cases of breaks which cause file back-up.

MISCELLANEOUS TOPICS

Panellists: R. M. Needham, B. Randell and J. Warne

PANEL DISCUSSION

NEEDHAM: I should like to talk about instrumentation, which I regard as just a fashionable word for counting things. It's extremely important to be able to count things, not so much for the purpose of setting up models of one's system, but in order to find out why it does not work properly and how it can be improved. What one wants is some sort of fairly general mechanism, so that the process of having to count something new and implementing one's decision is straightforward. At Cambridge we have two ways in which numbers are brought out of the system. A few lines of numbers are produced every minute by a piece of program which takes the numbers, which have accumulated in certain cells, and prints them with a name attached. Another program, every quarter of an hour or so, looks at these and other numbers, and adds them on to incremental totals which appear either on demand or at worst once a day. To count something new arrange that the numbers of interest are deposited in an appropriate cell. The kind of thing one counts are passes through various routines, the number of disc transfers done, classified according to the reason, the amount of idle time, etc. Some of the things one wants to count don't derive from the supervisor, they come from user programs or user level programs, e.g. compilers. There is a very simple mechanism for doing this by using an extracode which says count one, in the count specified in the argument; it has a very rudimentary security mechanism which can be corrupted by anyone. User level programs can include this extracode for counting something if they want to.

To count things in the Supervisor, you've got to change the Supervisor, and this brings me on to my next topic of maintenance and improvement.

When people say that it's difficult to record what's going on inside the system, what they really mean is that it's difficult to put the program there to do it, because it's difficult to maintain the improved system. If you solve that problem you've solved the other one. The procedures we adopted have been described in [1]. Essentially all the text of the supervisor is held on files, and to count something all that's necessary is to edit the appropriate record: there are about 200 records which constitute the supervisor. If you then call for the supervisor to be compiled you get a new absolute binary copy which needs to be brought into service, and you then get your statistics kept.

Which brings me to the other aspect of improvement — how do you install another version? We keep four absolute binary versions of the supervisor on the disc, and you select a version by a key when you're doing the bootstrap operation. So if you wish to get some statistics, you make your version and next time you are doing a warmstart, use it. So the ability to do one's counting depends on the ability to bring the new version into use easily. We place great emphasis on being able to do warmstarts with different versions of the system while retaining all the information which needs

to be retained, and this is an exceedingly important aspect of the whole business.
To maintain and improve your system, while giving reasonable continuity of service,
you must recognize that, exhaustively though you have tried to test your new
facilities, they may be wrong and you must be able to fall back on something reliable,
quickly and easily. This presents no particular difficulty except in the case where
the very information which is preserved over warmstart is what you are improving.
Now the situation is such that you have some data which has to be preserved over a
warmstart being made by a program, say A, to be consumed after the warmstart by
a program, say B. First we must replace A by A', which makes both the old and
new data. We must then replace B by B', which consumes the new data. We can always
fall back on one version because the old data which is being produced as well can be
consumed by the old version. This process must trickle through all the versions
of the systems which are kept in order that you should be safe at all times. If other
development is going on at the same time this means it's a very slow process and
updates of the warmstart system itself, typically, take several weeks to do even if
they involve only changing two or three bits. The warmstart procedure itself, the
part which is strictly to do with the supervisor, preserves the input job queue or
output which is going to be completely produced, but not yet printed. So one's got
a sufficient set of facilities which make the keeping of instrumentation easy.

I've gone through the process in this way to show that if you want to discuss how
an operating system is implemented, you can't do this on its own; you'll have the
greatest difficulty unless the rest of the environment into which it fits is reasonably
co-operative. If the environment is unfriendly making small changes is going to be
extremely difficult, otherwise they will be very easy.

FRASER: It is extremely difficult to make changes to a file system. A file system
has to do with continuity of information over a long period of time, and nearly
every change you make has to do with the sort of action Needham has been describing in relation to programs which effect the warmstart. It is extremely difficult,
once you have a file system working, to make any significant changes on the directory
structure, particularly if you have an archive system which gives you a history
which may add up to several months.

NEWELL: More interesting are the problems of format change and reversion. Your
A' and B' solution doesn't work for the filing system because you can't produce the
complete file store in the new and old formats. If you revert, the mark N restart
routines can pick up the appropriate one. But if you want to change the directory
format, the restart routines in mark N and mark N + 1 have to deal with either
format and you have a self-descriptive data format.

NEEDHAM: Yes, there's only some information that you physically duplicate, and
then you have to make it label itself.

FRASER: But where you have an incremental dumper, duplications exist. You
can't duplicate the information on the rapid access store.

NEEDHAM: Yes, you don't want to duplicate all your archive store as well, you'd
have twice as many tapes.

NEWELL: If you do a dump process operation going back over increments which
may be in quite a lot of different formats, do you get trouble with the dumper
process?

NEEDHAM: It is very much more difficult to get the complete solution for a
filing system. To test the supervisor requires the co-operation of the filing system.

Before you have an historical filing system you can load your new Supervisor into the empty machine and see if it does what it's supposed to do; but an historical element in the system precludes that. Any realistic testing needs care. At Cambridge a certain amount of the disc is dedicated to testing purposes. A particular console key, when engaged at bootstrap time, causes the system to be loaded in testing mode. The file system collaborates by making all ordinary files read only and if it creates any files they go in this disc area. Also no directories are permanently updated and no disc maps are dumped. Effectively, you have an insulated system which is nevertheless capable of having people log in from a restricted number of terminals, the only difference being that nothing you do will last. This means most changes can be exercised pretty thoroughly in testing mode, and this is the class of facility which often ought to be present in any system which has an historical file store.

NEWELL: It depends on whether you have another machine to test the changes on. Although this is being done during a testing session, you presumably want to use your regular file store as test data.

NEEDHAM: You want to be able to (say) run a Fortran program and the Fortran compiler is in the file store. This applies much more in the design of dedicated real-time systems, of which there is only one. It's not relevant in the manufacturer's situation because he can surround himself with computers which are only used for testing purposes. But it's a very good discipline to have available the facilities that in the case of a dedicated real time are absolutely required.

RANDELL: I'd like to describe, an abortive attempt to benefit from some of the work done by Lynch in attempting to schedule the users at Case Western Reserve. They soon realized that there was no single good scheduling algorithm. As soon as they set up the system to favour a certain class of user they soon found this type of user create themselves, over perhaps even a day, and they'd be back where they started. At first they made it easy for the users by posting the details of each new scheduling algorithm on one of the notice boards. After a bit they found this wasn't necessary; the user population reacted irrespective of whether the scheduling algorithm was known explicitly or implicitly from its effects. From all this experimentation they soon realized that this wasn't really part of an operating system. It was very much dependent on, e.g. what part of the university term they were in, sometimes on what day of the week. These strategic signals were not part of the operating system but rather the responsibility of the operations supervisor. So they decided to provide the various hooks that the operations supervisor might need to try various scheduling algorithms and find out their effect on the normal workload.

Since they received their first 1107 they had been logging data about every job that had gone through the system. It was self-identifying so that processing this data could deal with different periods of the past use of the system. This data was sufficient for testing a new scheduling algorithm, though not, of course, the full psychological effects. It became a standard tool to the operations supervisor; he could program a scheduler and go back a year and re-run the world at high speed and find out what it would have done.

FRASER: While Lynch was logging user behaviour did he try a sufficient variety of scheduling algorithms so that all configurations of user behaviour had in fact been logged? It's my experience that past user behaviour is nullified in response to a new scheduling algorithm. It's like strategy and anti-strategy.

RANDELL: To a large extent the logging was used for the first level of debugging of the scheduling algorithm. The second level involved a two or three day feed-back, while the users got accustomed to it; and the only way to debug that was by common sense.

HARTLEY: Since December 1969 we have logged every log-in, every log-out, and whenever someone gets chucked off because someone else has logged in. It does not log how many people failed to log in as that might be too large. We haven't used this information except to try and find out what the chances of getting in are, because we are very concerned about the overloading problem.

RANDELL: The sort of information we get out of MTS is either at too high or too low a level to be useful. We need something more detailed than just a log-in.

NEWELL: How do you use this data?

NEEDHAM: It's obviously all right for the first level of debugging, to make sure you're not about to do something which will refuse to run any jobs after, say, the seventeenth!

NEWELL: I wonder whether it's useful, if it's as crude as that.

RANDELL: Some of the scheduling was very complicated; it wasn't just a fixed decision such that small terminal users were treated better than big batch users. To a large extent it was a continuing battle by the operations supervisor, aided by these tools, to use the system in a way which was best for the system and, at least in his opinion, best for the users.

NEEDHAM: Another alternative is that you try the new scheduling algorithm and arrange that it is very easy, even automatic, to fall back to an earlier one.

FRASER: If you want to obtain measurement information for the purpose of running an operating system, it is difficult to know in advance what measurements you need. What we did, was get the compiler to compile the operating system and accumulate a large amount of trace information. Then we wrote several models of the complier from different points of view; we simulated its chapter swapping characteristics, data flow, procedure calls, etc. We ran the trace against our various models and metered the models. This allowed us to discover a great deal about the compiler's behaviour, without having to wait a long time, and consequently we made substantial improvements in the compiler's design.

NEEDHAM: For a substantial operating system it's very complicated to perform simulation tests, for the users learn to accommodate themselves very quickly to changes, and you end up having to simulate the users as well which is even more difficult.

RANDELL: One of the tools we have available at Newcastle was built into the Algol W compiler. It produces as a standard by-product what is called the "profile" of a program. With the listing of the program you get with each line of text a count of the number of times that line was obeyed. The clever part is to be able to do it as the standard mode of running Algol W. The large counts on lines, indicate where perhaps you should be more careful, and zero counts on lines indicate where you have absolutely no reason to believe the code is even partly debugged.

HARTLEY: There are two sorts of trace one might want; one where the trace tells you what's just been happening when you come to a dead stop or you think you might have to stop, and the other where you don't know where you are going to stop. I once designed a tracing mechanism which switches itself off after the program established a nice pattern. When the program settles down you have no output, but when it suddenly changes its activity (which might well be a sign of something going wrong) it would automatically switch on again.

RANDELL: Our system does not try to detect patterns. Each straight line segment of Algol W code is compiled with one extra instruction. The first and second time you hit that instruction it causes an interrupt which gives a source language trace of the straight line segment. All other times it just counts rather than causing an interruption.

HUXTABLE: I would like to ask Needham what measurement aids he has in fact used for tuning the Titan, particularly in the class of hardware resources and also in the class of human resources.

NEEDHAM: It was done by counting the interrupts to central system routines to see which were worth further examination. We measure about 150 quantities of one sort or another which just get looked at when somebody feels unease or we receive an explicit request.

HUXTABLE: But this only works when you are able to find monitoring points which would, in a sense, quantify the user's reactions or emotions, like e.g. testing his strength by hitting the return button.

NEEDHAM: We have a command, in connection with the file system, called PROTEST. You type this followed by any message you like and it gets sent to the operating system people together with a little bit of diagnostic information.

WARNE: I wish to speak on the subject of programmed interfaces.

One of the major difficulties of operating system design is that quite often the operating system is built after much of the software which it has to control has been built; and thus the operating system designer is faced with the non-trivial problem of interfacing existing software with the operating system. In seeking a solution to this problem, the designer can either employ *ad hoc* techniques or centralize the problem by designing a job control language. The latter solution consists of running a sequence of software or user programs and using the job control language to determine the actions that should be taken when certain conditions are met. In terms of efficiency, this solution is perfectly reasonable providing that for each job the number of controlled actions, and therefore the corresponding number of job control language statements, is small. In practice, this is very often not the case and consequently the execution of the job control language becomes a serious source of operating system overhead.

Some years ago I joined an operating system design team to work on the problem of compiler interfaces. I discovered that it was necessary to have a large number of job control language statements in order to describe the actions required to control the compilers. Thus, even for very small jobs, the number of job control language statements executed by the operating system had to be quite large. I was particularly concerned with the interactions between the controlled program and the operating system, in that many of these interactions were fairly trivial and therefore justified a fast response.

For example, a halted condition in a program, would normally demand operator action, but because we were now running the program under an operating system an attempt would be made to take this action automatically. When working on the Qube operating system here at Queen's, instead of using the command language, in the conventional sense we used a table structure and a set of small routines. We found, with success, that this kind of mechanism worked exceedingly well for controlling efficiently different sequences of programs. Having looked at the latest version of the George operating system, my impression is that job descriptions are becoming larger and larger; and the operating system is more and more like a compiler, having to run through the job description and interpret each statement. We ought to attempt to compile the job description into a unit of code which can be interfaced with a program or a phase of a job, and this should be used to control those aspects which are best left to it. The operating system should be primarily concerned with resource allocation and linking such interfaces to the correct phase of the job. Running large job descriptions to control large numbers of student jobs is the kind of inefficiency which should be avoided.

HOARE: This fits in very well with my philosophy that the actual control of what the user wants to do is part of the user's program. He can say that he wishes to have a certain environment set up for him and it's up to the operating system to do this. This may include a little bit of code to run through a number of job steps and it may or may not include a compiler. The operating system responsibility is the other side of the job control language. Now the design of a job control language can be safely left to a competent designer of high-level procedure-oriented programming languages.

FRASER: I have met systems where it is possible to do things by job control language which it is not possible to do by extracode or system call. The ability to create a job from within the machine seems to me to be important. The ability to seize a scarce resource requires some control. These functions should be available not just through the job submission mechanism, but also (under control) to the programs.

HOARE: What about resource limits? Could you ignore my programmer's demand that he is not going to pay for more than two hours of machine time on this run? The programmer has set a limit to protect himself against his program going wrong, and then his program goes wrong in such a way as to change this limit. This is one thing you must not be able to do from within your program.

FRASER: I'd like to distinguish between the exercising of control of jobs, and privacy controls for the availability of functions.

HOARE: This is exactly the right solution. Procedural aspects and the moving of jobs through a number of steps are functions which should be under the control of the programmer from within his program or a program written on his behalf. Even the predictions about how long the program will run and how much resources it will consume, the claiming and releasing of resources, can and must be dynamic, because very often the programmer does not know this at the time he writes his program. The settling of political and managerial control over the environment — these are a form of declaration, and are not procedural at all. The setting of these political limits, which are quite independent of the prediction of the actual behaviour of the program, can and should be part of the operating system and not the running program.

NEEDHAM: It's much easier to design a system so that all the functions which should be part of the running program are so. It is more difficult to write a system in such a way that they can only be called by the job description interpreter. Apart from anything else the system has to know when it's obeying the job description interpreter.

RANDELL: Yet sometimes knowing that a certain type of action can only have come from, say, somebody sitting at a terminal rather than having been generated from inside an actual program, can allow you to gain advantage. For example, the giving of passwords. Sometimes you can rely on the fact that a programmer is going to lose patience, trying passwords. If he can write a program which can generate passwords then perhaps you would feel a bit insecure and want to put in a little extra mechanism which would say that nobody is allowed to try more than five passwords. An example affecting performance rather than security arises from the APL [2] system, where the designers were worried about the extent to which backing store and disc transfers were going to be a bottlerteck. They knew transfers arose from two different sources. One was the roll-in, roll-out mechanism, and this was quite easily predicted and controlled by the operating system. The other was transfers which are caused by people sitting at their terminals. They decided to only have a certain type of time sharing; desk calculator plus single interpretive language. To reduce the load on their disc, transfers to and from backing store were available only to somebody typing the command at a terminal, but not as something generated inside a loop by a program.

FENTON: But should a user be able to find out his own time limit? He might decide to either do a detailed analysis on a batch of data or decide to do a more limited analysis on some different data depending on how much of his specified resource is left.

NEEDHAM: It's possible in Titan to write programs to look and see how much time is left, and either start another iteration or come to a tidy conclusion.

GOOS: Our system interface is two-level, supported by hardware. A user program can only enter a private operating system which contains all such information you need. When in special mode, i.e. the mode in which the private operating systems run, you can enter the general supervisor. If the interpreter, for lack of command language, acts like a normal user program in normal mode. it requires its own private operating system. So the job description has two parts; a part which can be accessed from inside a program and the other for implementation of commands from a terminal. The command language interpreter, as well as the private operating system, takes into account from which input stream you receive your programs. The calls you make in the private operating system are interpreted differently depending whether you enter from a terminal, a remote job entry or normal batch processing.

WARNE: I agree with you that the idea of a private interface is a very good one, because you can tailor an interface to a particular environment and you can have rather elaborate interfaces for elaborate types of systems program. You are not imposing a penalty on other users because it's not actually built into the operating system. But what I'm primarily concerned with in designing these monitors or interfaces etc. is reducing the job description language down from about 40 statements to 2. In Titan each command essentially is a macro; it does a lot more than just a simple operation, it possibly does a whole set of housekeeping operations. What I'm against is the operating systems that are asking the user to specify the form of the macro, which consists of a whole series of micro steps that must be taken in order to control a single program. This ought to be compiled on efficiency grounds, because if you interpret macros in the form of source text, you have to expand the macro in the core of the machine and that gives rise to the problems mentioned earlier as well as requiring a larger number of blocks stranded throughout core containing source texts, which you are going to interpret at some later time.

GOOS: If you reduce the number of commands you increase the number of parameters. What's the good of this?

WARNE: For instance, most users just want standard types of action. In a university environment most people are content to write the smallest possible job descriptions because the system's programmers have probably made the decisions that they want to take.

NEWELL: It does not affect the user interface because all he has to do is call the macro anyway. What tends to happen is that most macros that are issued as standard have about ten parameters, most of which are default. There is a second kind of statement which caters from the dynamic peripheral requirements. That's not satisfactory because of the overhead of blocks in core; it is better for a program to have the ability to issue commands directly. The trouble is that the languages we use are standard, and have no means of invoking such operating system functions.

On the question of translation versus interpretation, the reason for interpretation is that you have to interpret for the on-line case. However it would not be difficult to change the interpreter to a translator. The reason why not, is that you have to involve people in a compilation process storing the translated job control language. You treat the matter as procedure calls but you've still got a link edit problem. We know the job control language is a programming language but I don't think we want to carry this view to extremes. The overheads of the other approach appear to be negligible.

WARNE: But it's serious in terms of the amount of core storage it occupies if you start using macros.

NEWELL: I think not.

VINCE: Surely you can go half-way and have a decision table.

WARNE: If you take the Fortran compiler, for instance, and have a look at the job description language, and if you are going to run it every day, then it is far better to have a binary program rather than interpret it as a source text each time.

RANDELL: That's a standard question — is the amount of machine time that it would take me to run the translator greater than the amount of machine time saved by having the translator?

GOOS: In our system the command language allows for the definition of macros, which are contained in a file, so you can forget about what the command language should be.

FRASER: I would like to change the subject slightly and consider the type of availability and non-availability of information. Often one has information available and chooses to lose it, and subsequently has need of it. For example, to determine whether a password has been submitted on- or off-line, the information was presumably available at some point and ended up being delivered to the password decoder. Other examples concern system performance characteristics, like job description statements which may or may not be protected from the user. Programmers tend to protect the users too much, hiding information from them unnecessarily, e.g. correspondence between real and actual objects in the system.

NEEDHAM: In Titan we are generous towards the user and on one or two occasions proved to be overgenerous, when the information was mis-used. At one time it was convenient for a particular user's program to know on which tape unit their tapes were mounted. We decided the best way was to let them read the core area where this information is kept, which unfortunately also enabled them to read other people's passwords. So one reason for being so secretive is that you are not sure whether you haven't given away too much.

HARTLEY: Also there is the cost of making such information available. In Titan, because in the early days we had a very small store, we decided to have only an abridged rather than a complete job listing in core. This means certain job information would not be available in core and it would be very expensive to make it available.
HOARE: The reason for including this session was to, at least, pay lip service to the fact that the design of operating systems is not all philosophy, structures and techniques, but that a very large amount of attention must also go into the detail.

REFERENCES

[1]   Landy, B. "Development of scheduling strategies in the Titan operating system", *Software, Practice and Experience,* **1** (1971), 279–297.
[2]   Falkoff, A. D. and Iverson, K. E., "The APL/360 terminal system", *Interactive Systems for Experimental Applied Mathematics* (Eds. K. Klerer and J. Reinfelds). Academic Press, New York (1968), 22 37.

THE USER'S PROBLEM

HOARE: In seminars of this kind, a number of distinguished and experienced experts talk about problem solutions that they have found, and a number of practitioners or observers are very interested in these solutions but somehow they don't seem to fit their own problems. I thought we could spare a session in which users could explain some problems that are currently exercising them but for which no solutions seem to be forthcoming.

For example, the problem of having to live with an operating system that is not as decently engineered as one would like: are there any techniques of general interest which could be brought to bear to solve this problem in the short or long term? This is a very serious problem, and it will always tend to divide the experts from those who would like to use the results of their expertise but who are faced with problems of an altogether different nature.

RIMMER: I agree that this has been a conference of people who are writing operating systems, while the vast majority of people in the business are at the receiving end. The situation that is facing a lot of people is that you have a machine — in our case IBM with OS/360 — and you are stuck with it. What do you do in order to get proper value out of it?

If you have a fairly simple system you can rely on the advice of the manufacturer's systems engineers, but if you have a rather complex system you can run beyond their knowledge. They usually suggest that you train some of your own people to deal with your particular situation.

HOARE: If a supplier of jet engines were incapable of conveying to an airline's main frame manufacturer the necessary information for the proper use and maintenance of his equipment he would go bankrupt. If any engineering concern makes products that they cannot understand and their customers cannot use effectively the normal effect of competition should be that the sales of that manufacturer go down.

RANDELL: Any aircraft designer who was as naive about aircraft engines as some buyers of computers are about the systems for which they pay hard cash is also likely to go bankrupt.

HARTLEY: The solution is to have your own experts who are as good as the manufacturer's software engineers. I can think of no successful installation that hasn't got its own experts and this isn't necessarily the fault of the manufacturer's; it's as much a matter of what the environment is like as of what the basic system is like.

PATEL: One thing that keeps puzzling me is that we hear quite a lot of bad reports about OS/360, and yet this has no effect on their market. One has to conclude that OS/360 must have some features that the customers consider to be good and on which they make their decision to buy that system. What are those features that enable IBM to take 80% of the world market?

RIMMER: We have built up a fair amount of experience with IBM and have an enormous number of programs which we have acquired over the years. Machines such as the 704, 709 and 7090 did the job they said they were going to do, and were well supported by software by the standards of the day. It's simply that as the hardware is becoming more and more complex, their software is starting to run behind a bit.

If you want to do standard work such as running a batch processing Fortran or Cobol installation then it will cope extremely well. But if you have 160 teletypes attached by two peripheral processors and fast data links to about 20 computers around your site and you want to extend the system, then this is not what they are thoroughly familiar with and you start running into trouble.

I'd better put the record straight on the fact that we are getting an enormous amount of good work out of the 360 and probably we've made the right decision to be using this system , but we're terribly near the edge of what is viable.

The other point is that my own proposed solution − to train up our own experts in the field − is of course self defeating because as soon as we produce a real expert he disappears off somewhere else.

FRASER: A related problem concerns the competence of engineers to maintain software and give advice, and the distribution of information and carrying out tests. There are very few people who can chase down a bug in a large system. I am reminded of my current employer who has a great deal of complicated − mostly electronic − equipment, and has the problem of maintaining this, and also of educating the customers, and also has great difficulty in recruiting engineers that are capable of understanding how it works. This resolves itself as two problems: first of all the problem of handling a vast amount of documentation in such a way that a relatively unskilled engineer can find his way around it; and secondly, as engineers come to be in short supply, there is the problem of remote diagnosis by automatic or by remote human-driven systems for testing equipment.

HOARE: The main reason why people like Rimmer get so little help from academic conferences is because their problems can so easily be initially diagnosed as management or political or commercial problems, but Fraser has pointed out two technical points that might be helpful.

RIMMER: OS/360 is apparently documented extremely well, and IBM offer full training facilities for people who buy their computers. We have stacks and stacks of manuals and the courses come flying fast, but still we have to have five or six really competent people who are permanently learning about the system to keep abreast of it.

BRINCH HANSEN: There has been a good deal of talk about the structure of operating systems; and it seems evident that structure is solely for the purpose of human understanding; the machine couldn't care less about the upper levels of abstraction, all it cares about is the detailed program.

To give one example of how structured documentation has been done in practice consider the RC4000 system. There is a paper in the communications of the ACM[1] of about ten pages describing the overall structure, intentions and limitations of the system. The first fifty or so pages of the manual repeat the same story in slightly greater detail which can be understood without any specific

---

[1] Bruich Hansen, P. "The nucleus of a multiprogramming system". *Comm. ACM*, **13**, 4 (April 1970), 238–250.

reference to the RC4000. If you go to the next level of documentation you find
fifty more pages describing precisely all the supervisor calls without any reference
whatsoever to how they are carried out; and should you be interested in the implementation details you can go to an appendix. One might well suggest that the success
of this system was that the documentation was actually written in that order.
We regard the documentation as part of the program design.
HOARE: I should like to ask Fraser to amplify his remarks about documentation
management, and remote diagnosis and test, because I think that programmers can
very probably learn from problems and solutions which have been adopted in other
fields.
FRASER: It's dangerous of course to take an analogy too far. However the matter
of maintaining equipment is not new, and the matter of understanding it and selling
it and adapting it for different environments is not new.

At least as far as engineering documentation is concerned, the Bell system does
benefit from a standard notation; and this arises from standard specifications for
circuits. You get quite a complicated circuit on one chip and the logic diagrams
just contain a reference to that chip whose detailed specification can be found in a
book. Also most of the circuitry we put together is inefficient in the sense that
we use complex circuits in environments where simple circuits would do; for example
when we just need an "add one" function we might use a chip with a complete adder
on it.

Perhaps this technique can be applied to programming, where by using unnecessarily powerful modules, some degree of efficiency is sacrificed for the benefit of
those who have to understand the program. The point about Bell and about IBM is
that their systems operate on a scale that is several orders of magnitude different
from the scale Brinch Hansen was talking about. If you want to have one individual
cope with a very large system you have to have more and more levels of abstraction
inside it. There may be a technology here, which we haven't developed, which deals
with making information retrievable.

Going back to the test business: Bell equipment is more expensive than equipment with the same function and capability that you can buy elsewhere. The
difference is that Bell has to maintain what it produces and finds it worth making
expensive equipment which doesn't fail so often and when it fails it does so in known
ways. This calls for a high level of engineering, a style of engineering that we are not
used to in programming. Another reason why telephone equipment in general seems
to be much too elaborate is that test equipment is invariably built into it. For
example, in the telephone exchanges that are run by computers, a little more than
half the program sitting in the computer deals with restarts and error diagnosis and
a little less than half deals with the main telephone business.
HOARE: The characteristic of software errors is that they are design errors; and that
when a failure occurs it will always occur in an unknown way.
PATEL: I don't think one would tolerate a lower error detection rate or a lower
error correction rate from a micro-programming CPU or from a programmed
peripheral controller than one would from a hardware peripheral controller or CPU
In either case one would expect the error detection and correction to be done by
software, by micro-programs in the case of CPU or actual programs in the case of
peripheral controllers. Therefore the same techniques could be extended further
into the software of operating systems.

FRASER: An example of software which is relatively impervious to hardware failure, is the Cambridge filing system. The sequence of events that takes place when you delete a file was specially chosen so that if the machine fails at any point there is only a certain subset of all possible configurations the system can fall into.

NEEDHAM: Designing hardware systems to that the software can have the desirable property of being able to cater for its own errors is a big challenge in computer architecture at the moment.

HOARE: My own view of the technological challenge which was posed by the original question from Rimmer, and that it is primarily a matter of documentation. The techniques for writing documentation have been standardized, but, apparently unsuccessfully — even by those who spend very large amounts of money upon it. One of the reasons is that documentation has to be designed for human consumption and no set of documentation standards is going to force people to write prose that is readable or even relevant. The development of conceptual frameworks, philosophies, terminologies and techniques for documentation both at the user level and at the system design and maintenance level, pose a major challenge for academic research and which may, in the long run, produce an approach to the solution of the original problem. Standards of documentation will have to be significantly better than the present techniques in order to have any effect. They will have to document not only the details of how things are done but also why they were done; the design decisions will have to be documented because these are the things that the modifier of the program needs to know. The attempt to provide documentation at this level of excellence may indeed affect the economic characteristics of the software in the sense that it will not always be the most efficient software that you can produce. I would like to see it accepted, as in the telephone engineering field, that software may contain redundancies and expensive items due, not to the need for self-diagnosis of faults, but to the need to explain and justify all the decisions that went into the design of the software and the techniques that are being used.

Another possible approach to the problem is the wider use of installation parameters and modularity. These techniques have been pursued beyond their logical limits by manufacturers and designers of software. I do not think they have been wholly successful. The number of installation parameters is so large that no user can control them effectively; and, furthermore, most changes that he wants to make cannot be achieved by changes to the installation parameters. Similarly with modules: the first difficult thing that the customer wants to do cannot be catered for at all by plugging in an alternative module.

However I think that all three of these topics are susceptible of research and technological development, but much remains to be done. Installation parameters and modules can be used to a certain limited extent; but in the last resort your ability to adapt, correct and modify a system must depend on the excellence of the documentation.

TITAN OPERATING SYSTEM

Speakers: D. F. Hartley: "Techniques in the Titan Operating System."
R. M. Needham: "Tuning the Tital Operating System."

Repliers: A. G. Fraser, R. Wilson.

TECHNIQUES IN THE TITAN
OPERATING SYSTEM

D. F. Hartley

Computer Laboratory,
University of Cambridge,
England

INTRODUCTION

Titan is the prototype Atlas II which was developed jointly by Ferranti Ltd and the University of Cambridge in the early 1960's initially to provide the University with a new service machine. Shortly after work had begun on both hardware and software, Ferranti Ltd then decided to market the computer. The central hardware is basically that of Atlas 1 with the paging mechanism and drum removed, and replaced by datum and limit registers. Peripheral and backing-store channels are different but essentially similar. There are enough important differences between Titan and Atlas to make it necessary for a completely new supervisor to be developed. The Atlas supervisor took advantage of the "one-level store" concept, but many of its techniques, in particular the process structure, were relevant and much was learnt from the parent system. Consequently, Titan was to have its own supervisor, and in the initial stages this was developed jointly by Ferranti (later ICT) and the University, although much of the later development was done by the University alone. Many significant developments took place in these latter days, notably the replacement of the magnetic-tape well by a disc well (spooling), and the addition of both a filing system and multiple-access facilities. In addition, of course, the system has undergone an extensive program of extension refinement and tuning.

The purpose of this paper is *not* to attempt an overview of the Titan supervisor, but to consider in detail two particular areas of the system. The first area considered is the fundamental process structure which is described in sufficient detail to show why it was designed in the way it was, and from this certain principles of process control are then highlighted. The second area is, as it were, at the other end of the scale and can be summarized as the job control part of the system. Here various features are described in the order in which they were developed, and some attempt is made to consider whether a better system could, in theory, have been designed given the benefits of hindsight.

Thus, two quite different areas are described, and each subjected to a somewhat personal commentary. I hope that in each case something of general application to the design and implementation of operating systems emerges.

PROCESSES

At first glance the Titan supervisor harbours three distinct types of process, which are known as *Interrupt Routines* (IR's), *Supervisor Extracode Routines* (SER's) and *Object Programs* (OP's). (Since this terminology is immediately confusing, only the abbreviations are used from hereon.)

First, I shall define IR's. As their name implies, these are processes that arise directly from interruptions. Since an IR runs in a state where further interruptions are held off by the hardware, only one IR can be *active* at a time, no IR can ever be suspended, and there is thus no need for IR's to have process bases and a software co-ordinator. An IR always has precedence over other processes except in the brief periods when the current process (in fact an SER, never an OP) sets the hardware to inhibit interruptions. One purpose for doing this is to permit synchronization between IR's and other processes. IR's themselves are always written to run for a very short period of time, and if they wish to initiate more lengthy work they must arrange for another process to do it for them.

SER's are effectively supervisor processes, they have the free run of the machine, and are generally short in duration but are not subject to time limits. SER's are controlled by the *co-ordinator* and each is characterized by an *SER base* which holds relevant information about the process, for example:

A resumption address and index register values when not in execution.

Pointers to process code.

Pointers to the process working space.

The state of the process.

An SER is either *dormant* (i.e. not currently in use) or *active*. If it is active then it is either *halted* or *free*. Halted means that it has decided to wait for some future action to occur, which it does by entering the co-ordinator with a statement of the reason for which it is halting. For example, waiting for space to become available. Each reason for an SER halting is characterized by a *halt-queue* and the bases of all SER's currently halted for that reason are chained to this queue in chronological order of halting. An SER that is free is either *waiting* or *running*. In the waiting state the SER is placed on one of three *free queues* depending upon whether it is a priority SER (associated with fast peripherals), and ordinary SER, or an SER associated with an OP (see later). If an SER is either halted or free and waiting then its resumption address and values of index registers are stored in the SER base. Of the free SER's (if any) just one will be running; i.e. it is executing under the CPU. It is still said to be running even if it becomes interrupted by an IR, since the latter uses different hardware control and index registers.

When a running SER halts itself or has finished its job (in both cases this is done by entering the co-ordinator), the co-ordinator chooses a further free SER to run by taking the free queues in order and, within a queue, a first-in first-out system is operated. SER's may also enter the co-ordinator (as a subroutine) either to free another SER (i.e. move an SER base from a halt queue to a free queue), or to activate another SER (i.e. to put it onto a free queue); in either case the current SER continues to run. In addition, an IR may activate a dormant SER, but in fact is not allowed to free a halted one. If no SER is currently running when an IR does this (i.e. an OP is running instead), the OP is suspended and the SER is entered immediately.

Note that no SER is ever "interrupted" by another SER, and all SER's run either to completion or until halted. This is an important attribute of SER's, and is deliberately exploited. Whenever the co-ordinator finds no free SER's to run, attention is turned to the OP's and normally this results in control returning to the OP that was last running before the recent supervisor activity. OP's run until either

(*a*) an IR takes control, which may result in an SER being called, or
(*b*) the OP itself "enters the supervisor".

The latter occurs when the OP requests some activity (e.g. a disc transfer) which must be done "in supervisor". For this purpose, there is $1-1$ correspondence between OP's and certain SER's (known as OP SER's), and entering supervisor is a call to the co-ordinator to activate the relevant OP SER. If the OP SER runs to completion and, in the meantime, no SER (either itself or another) frees another OP SER which is halted, then the co-ordinator returns control to that OP. If the OP SER halts then the OP is also said to be halted, and the co-ordinator will choose some other OP to run. If another OP SER becomes free, then the associated OP is said to be free, and then the co-ordinator may choose to resume execution of a different OP according to the relevant priorities of OP's. Note therefore that OP's are freed or halted according to the freeing and halting of their associated OP SER's, and so this only occurs within an SER.

Note that OP's are always lower in priority than SER's which in turn are lower than IR's. The co-ordinator work space for an OP (i.e. the register dump etc.) is an extension of the OP SER's base. The scheduling of SER's is basically very simple as described above; OP scheduling is necessarily more complicated since it is necessary to provide time slicing with a dynamic priority allocation system to ensure that OP's communicating with the outside world get higher priority than the others. This mechanism is described elsewhere.

By way of commentary, the following observations can be made about this system.

1. Direct advantage is taken of the three types of process (IR, SER and OP) being organized strictly in a hierarchical fashion. In particular, communication between processes can be affected largely without semaphores and other devices. Working space is normally constrained by convention to be used or changed by a particular type of process. In particular, SER's only need to worry about communication with other SER's when they halt (i.e. at explicit places). OP's in general do not communicate with each other, and OP's communicate with SER's in well-defined ways designed to minimize the usual problems. Similar conventions exist to enable IR's to communicate with SER's and so on.

2. Elaborate time slicing mechanisms are confined to OP's (where they are needed) and not used for IR's (where they are not relevant) or SER's (where they are unnecessary).

3. When an SER or an OP halts, it does so by an SER base being placed on a particular halt queue and each queue is associated with some particular reason for halting. In most situations this is perfectly adequate, but in practice we have found

a number of situations in which it is desirable for a process to halt until either one of two events occurs; that is, it is required to halt for two reasons. A typical example is where an OP associated with an on-line user wishes to halt until either the user has typed some more input on the console, or until a certain time has expired. The co-ordinator mechanisms do not lend themselves to dealing with this kind of situation, and to get round this SER's tend to make their own arrangements.

4. It is usual to think of an OP and its associated OP SER as being two separate processes. I firmly believe that this is wrong and gives rise to confusion. The OP SER is simply a part of the object program process run in supervisor mode. When it is in this mode it is a supervisor process and subject to the same scheduling as other SER's; when not, it is subject to the time slicing of object programs. In other words, SER's and OP's are really examples of one type of process controlled by one co-ordinator, and the difference being the various details about how the process is handled. Some processes always run in supervisor state (i.e. a process for controlling the line printer), others (for "controlling" user programs) transfer from one state to another as required, and as they do this they become subject to different scheduling, work space conventions and protection regimes.

5. One problem caused at least partially, by the distinction between the three types of process is the difficulty of developing system routines. The conventions for handling storage and inter-process communication are different at different levels, so that, for example, it is very awkward to develop an SER as an OP. Since OP's are the only store protected part of the system, the ability to do this would clearly have been an advantage.

JOB CONTROL

In the early stages of planning the system, job control was the name given to those parts not concerned with process co-ordination and space allocation, peripheral control or the well (spooling system). In some senses, this area was sadly neglected with the result that the initial features were designed and implemented both last and in something of a rush, and they have undergone considerable development ever since.

In the first instance, jobs were all off-line being input entirely from paper tape and/or cards buffered on disc, all output buffered to disc and then disposed of out of the machine. Each job was introduced by a *job description* specifying the following information

User Identifier

Time Limit

Input Documents

Output Documents

Compiler

Store Size

Private Magnetic Tapes

Thus a typical job would specify the source language used by the program, what input documents were associated with the job, which were data and which were program and what stream numbers they were to be referred to by the program and the compilers, how much store space was required by the object program, which output streams would be written and to where they were to be sent.

In the initial planning, the requirements of compilers were to be somehow known to the system, so that it and the supervisor could arrange to compile and load the program; it was naively assumed that all jobs were of the form: compile in some language, load and execute. On the other hand, the designers were of the opinion that compilers etc. should not need to be heavily interfaced to the supervisor, at least to enable maximum freedom in developing and installing new compilers.

The initial job control system was both very simple and designed and implemented very much at the last minute. It is unfortunate that the idea of a command language (job control language) had neither occurred nor got through to us at that time. The scheme devised, which is also the basis of today's system, is as follows.

A job is divided into *phases,* the idea being that each phase is either a compilation, the running of a users object program, or some other system program. The first phase of a job is specified in the job description (normally this would be the name of a compiler), and any phase has the option of either terminating the job or causing a new phase to be started. In the latter case, the core store occupied by the program (i.e. the current phase of the program) is thrown away and a new piece of store, just the size needed for the next phase, is requested from the system. Note that other information associated with the program (the values of central registers and the state of input/output streams) is retained.

In this way, compilers can call for loaders, and user programmers can either call for a further part of itself, or for a further compilation of some other system program. Use of this mechanism was extended when editing programs and the like were developed for making amendments to the source forms of the program and data (note we are still in the days of a pure off-line system, and the idea of editing documents was in use before multiple-access techniques were adopted). An editor would include a command to enable the programmer to cause editing to cease and a new phase to be entered; typically this would be a compilation. Thus, job steps (which is what phases essentially are) occurred sequentially with the next phase always being specified by the previous one.

Disadvantages of this approach were realized in two quite separate contexts. Firstly, when multiple access working was introduced, there was clearly a need for a command system, and it seemed obvious that a command should somehow correspond to a phase in some way. Second, the advent of proper programming language systems (which came late in our case) that enabled independent compilation of programs and the loading of pre-compiled routines brought about the need for some form of control system to provide some of the features commonly provided in JCL type systems.

The command system eventually developed now provides most of the modern features normally expected in operating systems. This was essentially done by a simple glitch to the supervisor. The command system runs as a phase of the user program — typically it is called (automatically) after log-in by on-line users, or (optionally) by specifying a desire to use the command language in an off-line job. The command system (which has some privileged access to the supervisor) informs the supervisor that the program is running under command control, which in turn causes both the job termination instruction and the job abort mechanism to change phase to the command program instead of cancelling the job. The command program is trusted to tell the supervisor when the job has terminated by a further special mechanism. The command program causes a command to be executed by changing phase into it. Thus, the effect is produced of a nested command system by the use of the change phase mechanism, with the one small effect that a return to command status necessarily causes the current command to be cancelled and no record to be kept of its core store. (Thus, there is no concept of a temporary excursion of a program to command status and back again.)

There is one important problem with the job control mechanism of the Titan system, which is a result of developing from an essentially simple concept of a job consisting of compiling and running a program, to the idea of a job being a sequence of commands. This is in connection with input and output. All user programs and system utilities communicate with input and output through the mechanism of input and output streams. Each stream is known to the program by a number, and facilities are provided whereby actual input can be associated with a numbered input stream in various ways. Input can originate from reels of paper tape or packs of punch cards or can be a file on disc or magnetic tape, or can be an on-line terminal. The association between the input material and the input stream which is referenced by the program can be achieved in a job description, in the command language or can be set up by programs themselves. Similar facilities are available for dealing with output. The problem arises with the fact that input and output streams are referred to by numbers. Although a wide range of numbers is available, rather poor conventions were adopted for deciding which number should be used for which purpose. For example, compilers were written which assumed that the source program was contained in the lowest numbered input stream existing at the time of entering the compiler. When document editors began to adopt similar conventions it was difficult for the programmers to select the proper input stream number to use in certain cases. In other words, input stream numbers were global names and there was no concept of locality of name as one finds to great advantage in modern programming languages.

Also it was found that there were certain basic facilities lacking in the system. For example, it is often convenient to arrange that the source program to be presented to compiler is organized on more than one input stream, whereas the compiler ideally simply requires to process a single stream of information. To provide this facility, it was necessary for all sub-systems to make their own arrangements for enabling the programmer to specify that this was being done, whereas a common mechanism in the supervisor would have had considerable simplifications.

The system that is in use today, however, successfully hides much of this unfortunate history. Most sub-systems (e.g. editors, compiler etc.) can be called through the command system with a standard set of parameters specifying what information is to be processed, and in general this can usually be from more than one source.

In conclusion, one can claim that most of the early design deficiencies have been dealt with in adequate if not ideal ways. On the other hand, it is difficult to speculate what would emerge if one was to begin again; hopefully this would be for the better.

TUNING THE TITAN OPERATING SYSTEM

R. M. Needham

Computer Laboratory,
University of Cambridge,
England

The objective of this paper is to discuss the topic of tuning operating systems with reference to specific examples from the Titan case, rather than to go into a great many technical details about the specific Titan operation. It is, however, expedient to say briefly what the Titan is and what it is used for.

The Titan Computer was brought into operation in 1964 to furnish a general computing service for Cambridge University. It has been run with the operating system under discussion from early 1966 to the present time, a major change occurring in the middle of 1967 when terminals first began to be supported. The machine executes an instruction about every four micro-seconds, has 128K of 48-bit words, a fixed disc file, and in addition to the ordinary machinery and peripherals a multiple-access to which are attached something over sixty teletypes. At the present time some two dozen of these teletypes are supported simultaneously, on a round the clock basis. That is to say, the terminal service is available whenever the machine is running.

As a general proposition, one can assert that the tuning of an operating system consists of so adjusting it as to maximize the utilization of some resource or another. On this basis one would be tempted to regard all tuning as an essentially similar activity, but I believe it is convenient to divide the activity into two according to whether the resources to be well utilized are mechanical or human. Human resources for this purpose include both machine-room operators and the ordinary terminal user. Whether it is more important to optimize the use of mechanical resources or human ones depends essentially on the economic climate; mechanical resources can, however, rarely be totally neglected.

Within the context of mechanical resources, there are of course a number of different and sometimes almost independent types of resource, which one might wish to tune up. In an old-fashioned machine like the Titan, and possibly some more modern ones, there is no doubt that the utilization of the central processor must come first. The effect of this is that one first tries to tune up processor utilization, more or less regardless of anything else, and having achieved the satisfactory result then varies the tuning of other items subject to the condition that processor utilization shall not be impacted.

If we now look at processor utilization, we find that there are some questions to be asked before we can make much progress in tuning to maximize it. Presumably what we want to do is to maximize a percentage of the CPU's time which is engaged in doing work which is directly conducive to the manufacture of results for users, and to ensure that in so far as it is under our control, these calculations are done efficiently. The extent to which this last point is under our control is not very large, though how large it actually is depends on points about system structure. For example, in the Titan system, a good deal of input/output formatting and conversion is done within the operating system in circumstances where it often is done outside it, and thus the program associated with this which enters into almost all work the machine does is susceptible of being made efficient in tuning the system. It is in this area that we can hope to make gains in circumstances such that there is no doubt whatever about their reality. If we can rewrite these user service routines in such a way that they work more quickly without getting any bigger, or, if they are not resident, without passing the threshold of the natural transfer unit of the backing store device, we know that the results will be good. Simple statistical investigation may be expected to yield a knowledge of which these routines are most commonly employed, and it is then quite obvious what to do.

Pieces of the operating system whose purpose is not of direct service to the user are typically concerned with scheduling and accounting functions. These should not consume a great deal of the machine's processor time, though they can easily contribute serious holdups. We shall return to this point later. Turning now to the avoidance of idling time in the processor, in the system we are considering this is what happens when, of those activities present in the machine, none is able to proceed. There are two different reasons why this can happen. Firstly, since only activities for which the program is in the core store are in a position to proceed, there may be insufficient space to contain enough activities to ensure that the probability of all being held up at once waiting for something is acceptably low. Secondly, the probability of an individual activity being held up for some reason is unacceptably high, resulting in an unacceptably high probability that they are all held up. Fairly clearly, there are two approaches to our problem, though unfortunately they are not completely de-coupled from one another. Firstly, we can try to find more space to put the activities in, and secondly we can try to reduce the probability that an activity will be held up. Considering the first strategy, in the Titan case, we first look at what occupies the core store. There are essentially a fairly short list of different things; firstly the fixed part of the supervisor, secondly space occupied by user programs, thirdly space occupied by input/output bufferage, and fourthly space occupied by non-resident pieces of the supervisor. With the exception of the fixed part of the supervisor, all of these things are thoroughly interchangeable, and much of them dynamically shiftable if need be. That the fixed part of the supervisor ought to be as small as convenient goes without saying. With the other things there is a certain freedom of manoeuvre. A piece of non-resident supervisor is not automatically flushed out when the activity using it is completed; this is an efficiency point concerned with avoiding delays caused by reading it back in again. Fairly clearly, we can make a trade-off between the amount of non-resident supervisor held in store and the amount of activity provoked in bringing non-resident supervisor in on demand. Our observation has been, not surprisingly, that the amount of retrieval activity increases very markedly indeed if one oversteps the mark. A second thing that can be manipulated is the amount of bufferage. The Titan system works entirely in terms of dynamically allocated buffers, which behave very similarly for different peripherals. The system is prepared to overwrite material in core if copies exist on the disc, so that sometimes a user's output may get read from the disc several times before it succeeds in getting put out, though this is not regarded as a good thing and is avoided if possible. Substantial core savings

were made by tailoring the amount of bufferage consumed by peripherals to
their effective output rate. Naturally enough, the savings were most noticeable in the
case of very slow peripherals.

At least as importantly as anything else, one may influence the size of programs
which are used. In a system like the Titan where the individual steps of a job are
processed quite independently except that they are done in the correct order, so that
having done a Fortran compilation for a user, there is no commitment to do
associated load and enter next and, *a fortiori*, not in the same space, a great gain
can be made by getting to work on the people who write user level software which
is in heavy demand. Notice that this is the kind of tuning which can only be done in a
very fixed environment. It is not easy to measure its effects, but we believe them to
be substantial.

The other approach to this problem is to lessen the likelihood of individual
activities getting held up. With one or two very minor exceptions, the only reason
why work gets held up in this kind of system is waiting for channel transfers. Clearly,
we want therefore to lessen the number of these that are performed, but once again
as usual the situation divides into two. We must divide our channel activity into two
sorts according to whether or not it lies on the critical path. To be able to hive off
channel-intensive activities to work as separate and parallel processes is an elementary
design feature of one's system; to recognize that by the proper organization of
the work possibly more of it can thus be hived off, is sometimes a piece of tuning.
There are some channel transfers however, which essentially cannot be hived off
because they are done when they are done for reasons of interlock either in
connection with a file system or to ensure system integrity on restart. These are the
ones which it is very important to optimize from the point of view of disc accesses
if at all possible. In the case of the Titan, when the amount of disc involved in this
sort of activity became uncomfortably large by comparison with the rather small
amount which was available with fixed heads (so that there was no arm movement
delay) a decision was taken to move out from this ready access area pieces of non-
resident supervisor, to avoid serious holdups in serially interlocked operations. I
believe that this point about the avoidance of serialization delays deserves to be
strongly laboured, particularly in that kind of serialization which tends to turn up in
filing systems where it affects more than one process. The absolute numbers of
disc transfers performed by the system is, perhaps paradoxically, not so important.
This is because unless the system is behaving in a very eccentric manner the flow
down the channels is dominated by material which is at any rate nominally of some
value to the user. One can achieve more in return for ones tuning and optimizing
efforts by inducing the people responsible for the popular compilers to behave in a
sensible manner as regards their overlays if any, the files they repeatedly pass through
when scanning pre-compiled libraries, and the verbosity of the format of their
intermediate code, than by a reasonable amount of tidying-up of the operating
system itself.

If we assume that after considering all the previous set of points the CPU
efficiency is reasonably high, we can now direct our attention to tuning up other
parts of the system. The channels have of course received a considerable amount of
attention, but mostly from a point of view of how much they are used rather than
how they are used. All that is required on the subject of optimizing channel use
is to comment that it can be done at leisure and independently of everything else,

provided that the overall system design is such that general requests need not be executed in the order in which they are presented.

Notice that there has been no mention of the size of the unit of space and allocation for bufferage and similar purposes either in core or on disc. This is quite deliberate, because it is a matter of initial design and one that is hardly subject to tuning. It is worth remarking, nevertheless, in this context that in designing the system we severely over-estimated the amount of character stream material which would come in from peripherals and go out to peripherals, and under-estimated the amount of essentially similar material that would be involved in purely within-machine transactions such as being passed from one phase of the compiler to another, or from a compiler to a loader. Since the mechanisms by which all of these things are handled are virtually identical, the mis-estimation made no practical difference.

In our context, the other major physical resource which required to be tuned was the utilization of tape drives. The scheduling of tape drives, and indeed the scheduling of other things, have been described in a paper by Landy [1]. Readers are referred to that paper for the history of tape scheduling, where it is made clear that if tape drives are a scarce resource the consequence of ignoring their utilization is unreasonable penalizing of those jobs which happen to use private tapes. From the present point of view, tape scheduling is more interesting for the way in which it shows the tuning process moving from the pure optimization of physical resources to something else. When we were dealing with optimizing the use of the CPU, there would be little doubt about the general desirability of keeping it gainfully employed all the time. As soon as we move to operations like tape scheduling, and even more some others to be mentioned later, questions may be asked as to the extent to which it is worthwhile or justifiable to interfere with the natural order of events, to favour one job or class of jobs as against another, when we are not affecting the total throughput of the system. An example of the way this happens with tape scheduling is that a particular job may get promoted from a very lowly place on the queue right to the front, merely because the particular tape it requires is already mounted on the machine, and has just become free. Someone has to take a judgement whether efforts saved to the operators in removing and subsequently remounting the tape is or is not commensurate with the apparent or even actual inequity caused among users by moving a job three hours up the queue. What our attitude should be on this point is a matter of management decision, and it is perhaps reasonable to say that most subsequent tuning-up, that is, to attempting to ensure full utilization of the processor, is concerned with improving the freedom of action given to the management, or with better implementation of policies which the management has already stated. Examples of this are furnished by considering the question of response to on-line commands. In the Titan system, the typical terminal user can call directly from his terminal for the execution of any program, subject to the condition that any input to it must be obtained from a file, though sometimes an anonymous file, and that output from it will be buffered to his terminal via the disc. This is to be distinguished from typical remote job entry, which is also provided, in that the time scale is usually one of seconds rather than minutes, and that output from the program appears on the terminal without any further intervention from the user. Typically, the response to commands of this nature is almost wholly determined by how long it takes to find a piece of core to put them in. Because of the constraints on the way they run, programs like this are no more subject to hold-ups than pieces of ordinary off-line jobs are. While they are running they are disconnected from the terminal and therefore cannot get involved in really protracted input/output waits. They have the practical characteristic, however, that they involve a fair amount of IO, and are very rarely processor limited for any substantial period. The interests of response are clearly served by giving such programs high priority for available space. One has to decide what this priority should be, and also to be alert as to unexpected consequences of giving it. Landy gives a history in his paper already referred to; it is more appropriate here to look at the cycle of observations and actions which brought the system to its present state. In a rather schematic form it was as follows:

Observation	Action
Generally insufficient response to commands needing core store	Increase priority of on-line store requests
Still great delays in circumstances where there were large off-line jobs running	Dedicate some memory to on-line small store requests and improve waiting strategy
Everything apparently O.K.	Congratulate oneself
Insufficient background throughput	Change time scheduling to bias it *against* on-line work

Notice that the last step is a little unusual. Not many systems bias the time scheduling against terminal work, the opposite being perhaps more usual. The general rationale is as follows. In order to run, any job needs core space and CPU time. Before the final change to time scheduling, the priority for store given to terminal work meant that a high proportion of the jobs currently in possession of store were of that sort, and thus since all jobs in core were treated *pari passu* they took a high proportion of the CPU time. The time scheduling system previously kept jobs which only ran in short spurts near the head of the queue, and a job which began to compute hard would soon find itself removed to lower down. In the current system a terminal job which begins to compute hard will be demoted sooner than an off-line job. This preserves rapidity of response to small commands but gets some time back for off-line work. Again, essentially a turning process on human resources, not mechanical ones.

This paper has treated its topic in a discursive way — deliberately, because this is the kind of subject it is. I believe that tuning of systems is essentially an informal activity, or at any rate that it is so to a large extent. This is because as soon as the early hurdles are surmounted one is running the system for the benefit of people rather than of machines, and our formal models of the behaviour and needs of people is even less than our almost completely deficient models of the behaviour of systems.

REFERENCES

[1]   Landy, B., "Development of scheduling strategies in the Titan operating system". *Software, Practice and Experience*, 1 (1971) pp. 279–297.

DISCUSSION

HARTLEY: When we started development of Titan, there was no such word as a process, and so we invented what one now calls the process system. So briefly I shall describe our system as a process system using modern terminology.

There are three types of process in our system — *interrupt processes*; supervisor extracode routines (i.e. SER's), *supervisor processes*; and *user processes* sometimes termed object programs. Each type of process has a different purpose and a different set of characteristics, but they can communicate and interlock with one another.

The interrupt processes are routines which are entered when an interrupt occurs in the CPU. When this occurs the hardware flips a switch to inhibit other interrupts until the software issues a special instruction to allow them through. Interrupt processes therefore run until termination and do not require a scheduler or co-ordinator. The co-ordinator is in fact the hardware scheduling on a first come first served basis. It was necessary that the interrupt process be kept very short (limited to about 30 instructions), and if the process requires more work to be done calls upon a supervisor process to do this.

Each supervisor process has a *base* and is controlled by a software co-ordinator, which determines when a process can run, and deals with the halting (or blocking) and freeing of a process. A supervisor process has no time limit imposed on it, but as it will typically not have much to do it will not run for very long. Therefore, there is no point in having elaborate scheduling of supervisor processes. Once a supervisor process has gained control of the processor, another supervisor process cannot run until the first one halts itself or terminates. If a supervisor process has to pause to allow another process to run, this other process must be an interrupt process. There is a strict level of priority in which interrupt processes always enjoy a higher priority than supervisor processes.

A user process is only run when all the supervisor processes are dormant. It is controlled by a part of the same co-ordinator that deals with supervisor processes. However the scheduling of user processes is more elaborate than the run-to-completion rule for supervisor processes in order that the response at terminals is realistic and that important resources such as tapes are not held up for longer than is necessary.

A user process will wish to communicate with the supervisor when it requires certain supervisor functions to be executed. So for each user process there is a corresponding supervisor process (supervisor mate) arranged in a one-to-one correspondence. In addition there are other supervisor processes which control peripherals, the interval timer and so on. If a user process calls its supervisor mate to perform some function on its behalf and this has to halt, then automatically the user process is also halted and must wait until the supervisor process is finished. Consequently, we see that the user process and its supervisor process are not altogether separate, but have a special relationship. In other words when the user process actually calls the supervisor process then at that point the user process is halted. As the supervisor process has a higher priority, it takes over from the user process, and we should therefore think of the user process not as being halted, but as being suspended.

When we pass from one level to another, we do not need to dump information as we do on a process change, because the working space for different levels does not coincide. In fact we have a hierarchy of three distinct levels in which a process on a higher level can interrupt a lower level, and what happens at a particular level depends on that level. If we now think of a process as being a thread of control, we can see that two processes, on different levels, are essentially the same process. The process is merely changing its state and characteristics depending upon what it is doing. This does not apply to all supervisor calls; disc transfers, for example, are autonomous activities and the user process need not wait until they are finished.

This level structure has been used to achieve the necessary process synchronization in the absence of Dijkstra's P- and V-operations, which had not then been invented. Within the critical sections of a supervisor process, we cannot be interrupted by another supervisor process or by a user process, and are therefore quite safe. Communication between one level and another is a little more tricky because one may interrupt the other; in such circumstances one needs to program carefully and obey certain rules.

There remains the problem of halting and freeing. We always halt for a reason, which may be either global or local. An example of a global reason may be a request to the space routines for more space. The local reasons concern only the process which is halting, and therefore cause no problems. In the case of a global halt, several people may be halted for the same reason and their bases will be chained together. Halted processes may be freed by another process in three different ways: (1) all processes waiting for a certain reason; (2) the process that has been waiting the longest for a certain reason; (3) a particular named process, if it is waiting for that reason. All three ways are used in the system; there is no question of which is the best. However, the fact that we have chosen to halt a process for a given reason, causes a problem in one or two cases. For example, if we have a user process waiting for a man to type a line on his terminal, the process is halted on the particular queue waiting for input. The process could, of course, wait on that queue for ever, because that line may never get typed. On the other hand, the user's time limit might expire or alternatively the operator may wish to kill the job. Rather than remove this process one wishes to free the process from waiting, but not allow it to carry on with what it was doing. You could, of course, check every time a process is freed to see if certain things have happened, but this is very tedious. The problem is sometimes described as a requirement to free a process for more than one reason when it is halted for only one reason, the others being implicit. There seemed to be no easy way round the problem except by very *ad hoc* means.

The use of different levels on our machine created a problem: the fact that the working registers are different at different levels on our machine means that it is difficult to write a supervisor process and run it in a test environment as a user process. The communication methods being different at different levels also causes problems of a development nature. This was not the only reason why we had development problems — there were also hardware reasons — but it certainly contributed.

NEEDHAM: In general terms, tuning an operating system means changing it to make someone happier. Sometimes, one can make a distinction between tuning up mechanical and human resources. A more formal distinction concerns the method of tuning, which can involve either adjusting parameters or changing algorithms, or both. One could always object that these are really the same activity, but the point about adjusting parameters is that you are making changes in ways which you did foresee; you have chosen a class of algorithm which is fixed, and you are adjusting within this class. The only examples which have been useful, concern the tuning of the priorities for requesting space and for holding on to it. But, beyond this, it has always turned out to be the case that some more radical changes were needed. It is important, when designing one's operating system, to arrange that the pieces of program can be replaced altogether, rather than having parameters to be adjusted on the assumption that your algorithm is in the right class. For example, if you want to maximize the amount of processor time which is doing something useful for the customers, you achieve this not by fiddling with parameters, but by realizing that things are grossly wrong. In this case the cause of the problem is often unnecessary serialization, causing user processes to wait unnecessarily. This leads to the desirability of scheduling operations being done by independent processes. For example, suppose that a user program is being very co-operative and wishes to inform the system that it has finished with a certain tape drive in advance of the actual end of the job. The consequence of having given this information, is that we can execute some scheduling activity to decide what can be done with this valuable resource which has become free. If we enter a subroutine to do this, we do not merely have the problem of several processes trying to schedule the same resource at the same time, but also we are liable to cause a great delay to the user program, because the code which is used for scheduling tape units will not be resident. This seems most unfair; the user has done something for motives of social usefulness and your reply is to hold him up. We have here a good reason for separating out this sort of activity to be queued, so that we can execute the original activity whilst the code is being brought down. Now removing unnecessary serialization of this nature is obviously a matter of a greater change than fiddling with parameters.

A similar situation exists when a job ends and you wish to go on to another one. The job may end suddenly in a state where the system is still busily reading ahead for input, on its behalf, which will never be required. One wishes to abort the activity of buffer filling as quickly as possible, rather than wait for it to build up. Here again, we need a major change rather than a mere parameter change.

When you have finished this form of tuning, you have presumably got a fully utilized CPU, or as fully utilized as you are going to achieve. But there remain problems affecting the happiness of people. This again falls into two categories – the happiness of system operators and the happiness of users – and it is noticeable that tuning for this reason was done at a later stage. For example, keeping the processor fully utilized led to rules for the scheduling of tape units which were very sub-optimal. However, one now begins to encounter interaction with the management in the form of those people who either actually or hypothetically set the objectives for the whole installation. You do not need to ask the management whether you should maximize the utilization of the processor; this is regarded as obvious. But what you should do with tape units is a different matter. One can minimize the handling of tapes on and off drives, by promoting a job from the back of the job queue which in the ordinary way would get done in three hours time, but has one or more of its required tapes already mounted. Is it reasonable to promote it in the interest of keeping the operators suitably idle, or is it reasonable to leave it in the interest of predictability and regularity of the overall system response to the user? I have no doubt that the programs used for this sort of scheduling should be as isolated as possible, because they have subtle algorithms, and one needs to be able to change them without getting into a mess over the system interface. There are a number of modifications like this which are concerned with tuning up the use of the operators. As soon as you have a terminal system, you have also got to improve the use of the human resources to suit the terminals. This is usually described as improving their response times. One is at least as much occupied with attending to the ergonomics of what they do, rather than to the time it takes them to do it. In particular, great attention to the brevity of commands they type, is not required. It is very commonly said that only beginners are prepared to type out the full name of a command, and that one must have abbreviations for the more experienced user. If one uses long words like "rhododendron" as commands, this might be true, but as most of the words which naturally appear are quite short, it is not important.

Another way to improve the utilization of people, is to try to make the behaviour of the system predictable as far as they are concerned. You cannot achieve this completely, because if the system is lightly loaded it will work faster and nothing is going to change that. But, in general terms, the system should behave predictably, and this is something which has given us a great deal of trouble. The reason for this, is that the factor which dominates the user's response is usually core store allocation, and flexible though the core store allocation is, it is not indefinitely flexible. One can get into the situation on the Titan whereby, if a user calls for a program from his terminal which takes 32K of store, the amount of time it takes to obtain it will fluctuate wildly between one second and one and a half hours. We devote a lot of effort to changing the algorithms for core store management, with a view to trying to solve this problem. The time when this sort of tuning should be done is after you have established your proper base-line of processor utilization, because this then enables you to think about one thing at a time. If you do not then your operations begin to interact with each other in uncomfortable ways, and you then do not know what you are doing.

WILSON: When investigating the Titan system I found an operating system which is friendly towards the user, but, nevertheless, subjects him to a fairly strict discipline. It does not allow him to overrun the system as may happen in a free-for-all environment. There is a distinct management scheme for allowing an on-line user to log into the system, and this forces him to log-out if a higher priority user wishes to enter a heavily loaded system. Interactive use of the system is not encouraged and users requiring this facility have to log-in, in an "expensive" mode. The number of users working in this mode is restricted. Programs such as the editor are interactive, but do not require expensive mode because they are pure procedures within core, allowing several people to use them simultaneously.

Whilst there are these restrictions on the users, thought has also been put into helping the user without relaxing these restrictions. An example of this is the Queue-file facility, by which users with jobs requiring a large amount of core store, may not be able to run them during the day, and can enter a file for running under the operator's guidance during the night.

I think the Titan supervisor processes closely resemble the "activities" of George 3. The core management of the two systems has also got similarities, in that user programs lie in contiguous areas, and the supervisor chapters are manipulated by a different mechanism to the user programs. But certain decisions have been made on the core management of Titan, which contribute heavily to its efficiency. Firstly, user programs cannot swap in and out, and remain in core until the completion of a phase, and secondly, user space is not actually surrendered to the user until it is required for use and is available for use by the supervisor chapters and buffers until then. When the user program does come to need the space, the supervisor information is moved to a different area of core store, where it fills free space or overwrites supervisor information of lower priority. The priority of a chapter is a fixed amount calculated from statistics of use etc. Is this method of priority evaluation efficient, or would a more dynamic method of evaluating these priorities take better account of different modes of usage over a period of time?

NEEDHAM: I do not think that a dynamic method would have been worth the trouble, because experience shows that altering the numbers of the priorities makes remarkably little difference, provided that one does not do something absurd like arranging that different chapters in the same chain of control have widely varying priorities, or giving a chapter a much higher requesting priority than its live keeping priority. One should regard the priorities as a means for expressing commonsense about the system, rather than for making fine adjustments.

FRASER: It is now two and a half years since I was at Cambridge, and since then I have been working at Bell Laboratories, where there exists a variety of machines — specifically, three IBM 360/65s, a 360/50 and a GE 635 with Gecos. I have been appalled that these systems are so badly engineered in comparison to the Titan machine. Although the Titan does not allow certain types of interaction which are judged not to be common requirements, the responses are good, the commands that you would like most to have are there, and you do not have to fight your way through arbitrary fences placed in your way, as is the case in the Gecos system. A Gecos example of these arbitrary fences, is the use of very different Fortran compilers for on-line and off-line use; the error messages are different and they do not interpret the same language.

One of the reasons why the Cambridge system is so successful is that it is geared towards a specific environment. For example, this resulted in the decision not to allow interaction in large programs. The system gets its performance from the fact that the low-level co-ordination is built into the hardware. The lower levels of the system are very messy, at the user level, things are not too bad. The Titan system makes a very good case for building a system with heavy emphasis on speed, and a small emphasis on generality. The Titan system is written in a very low-level assembly language and is all woven together. I doubt if the system could have been made to handle a much larger task. It would be suicide to try to make a system like this to handle a wide range of installations and a wide range of peripherals etc. In order to obtain such flexibility one should compromise and pick a level, possibly extracode level, above which the system could be handled in a more organized fashion. But, as most of the high performance comes from the low level, one should try not to take the ideal of good discipline and good organization too far down.

This system grew over a substantial number of years and certainly grew through a whole lot of mistakes. The evolution of this system is evidence that one should not expect to be able to produce a system of large design and implement it to perfection overnight.

NEEDHAM: Because of the not-very-modern way in which our system has been written a good deal of high grade effort has been invested into software which aids the manufacture of the system. For example, if one wishes to make a change to the supervisor, the procedure is to use a terminal, edit the appropriate record and initiate an off-line job which will produce a supervisor ready for use at the expense of thirty-nine seconds CPU time, and an elapsed time which depends on the time it takes to acquire 24K of core store for compilation. This is easy and quick and requires only a small amount of paper work. The system can keep the paper work up-to-date for you, and prevent you from getting behind in the batching together of alterations. Much of the emphasis people put on writing systems in high level languages, comes from the desire to keep the paper work under control more easily; but some of the advantages are recaptured even for a very low-level language, by investing a lot of effort in software design to help you update and test things.

WICHMANN: Could you have used SAL?[1]

HARTLEY: Possibly, if it had existed at the time. This poses the question of what we would do now, if we were starting again. I would like to think we would do better, but whether it would be SAL or ALGOL or FORTRAN I do not know.

NEWELL: Within the George 3 system we have a built-in editor and this causes problems of process scheduling. As the editor is a system process, it can hold up user processes that are doing very little other than outputting. Do you have this problem and should you not have an overall process scheduler, rather than a co-ordinator for your supervisor processes, and another one for your user processes?

NEEDHAM: We work on the assumption that no supervisor process lasts very long, and if you had something which looks as if it is going to last for a long time, then it would just have to break itself in the middle.

NEWELL: Yes, but would that allow user program processes in, or merely other supervisor processes?

NEEDHAM: The point is that none of the supervisor processes lasts very long, and we would, under no circumstances, have a built-in editor, because this would violate an assumption upon which the whole system is based.

HARTLEY: One can have the problem the other way round, where one user program is really a system process and should get higher priority than other user programs because of this. We had this trouble with our File Master, until we made it permanently at the top of the user process queue.

LIPPS: Regarding the addition of further facilities to an operating system, we have found that we could easily add on facilities, providing that these facilities were not outside the scope of the initial design. For example, adding a number of control points to our CDC system was not a thing which caused us enormous concern, whereas the addition of a fast drum was clearly outside the original design. Because of this, there is probably a limiting size above which it is impossible for a given system to grow. It becomes impossible because you have not enough people, and also because of the logical complications which multiply as one's system gets larger. It should therefore be said in fairness to manufacturers, who have set out to build a large system from the outset, that they have a much larger problem than the Universities or ourselves, and we should not say, "Look, we have been doing much better with a smaller number of people."

HARTLEY: There is one guiding principle when designing and building an operating

[1] Lang, C. A., "SAL – Systems assembly language". *Proc. AFIPS–SJCC* (1969) p. 543.

system, and that is — do not bite off more than you can really chew at once. Certainly the "all singing, all dancing" idea does lead you into problems, mainly because it is a big step to take at this stage. It is not that it is impossible, but it is obviously very difficult. I rather like the idea of having the same system across a range of similar configurations rather than up and down a range of similar central processors. It would be a marvellous idea to have the same system for a CDC machine and an IBM machine and everything else. Of course, they cannot have certain parts the same, but there are some parts, such as the job control language and editor which could be the same. Obviously it could not be the same operating system in total. But one certainly needs to design one's system to run within a given range of equipment, and not expect it to run on absolutely any configuration.

NEEDHAM: It is worth mentioning a peripheral limitation in the Titan system. The core space allocation and the disc space allocation use blocks of the same size. They are this size because of the access rate and transfer size characteristics of the disc. If somebody gave us a disc of very much higher performance and different parameters to interface with Titan, we would have the greatest difficulty in using it properly, because the characteristics of our present disc run all the way through the software. It is because the general machine manufacturer cannot make any such assumption that his task is an order of magnitude more difficult.

HARTLEY: When you buy almost anything in this world, whether it is a bar of soap or a piece of hardware, it comes nicely packaged. Someone has spent time putting a nice cabinet on your computer and has added some switches which make it easy to use. In my opinion, we do not spend sufficent time on this sort of thing in the software field. In the design of an operating system, we let the interior design decisions such as word length, number of characters in a name etc., get in the way of improving how it looks to the user.

CDC OPERATING SYSTEMS

Speaker: H. Lipps: "Batch processing with 6000-series Scope."

Replier: R. Wilson.

BATCH PROCESSING WITH 6000-SERIES SCOPE

H. Lipps

CERN,
Data Handling Division,
Geneva, Switzerland

INTRODUCTION

CERN has operated a CDC 6600 computer since January 1965. In April 1967 a CDC 6400 was added; in October 1969 this machine received a second central processor ("CP") and was thus converted to a 6500. The 6600 and the 6500 each have ten peripheral processors ("PP's") and 128K words of main memory.

The first operating system for the 6600 was developed together with the 6600 by S. Cray and his collaborators. What was later called the Chippewa Operating System was in fact delivered to the customer together with the first 6600 in autumn 1964. It was then one of the most modern multiprogramming systems. "SCOPE" is the name CDC gave to later versions of their operating system. SCOPE Version 2.0 which became available from CDC in autumn 1966 has subsequently been developed independently at CERN. I shall report below only about the CERN developments since 1966. Although these developments have changed our system significantly, the reader will easily realize that the state of the art has improved no less. Moreover, I shall limit myself to the system requirements for batch processing in an installation which carries a heavy production load. Unlike the environment which is typical for computing at universities, CERN processes many large FORTRAN programs and uses at present some 30,000 reels of magnetic tape. But it might be mentioned here for the sake of completeness that the system supports also a number of real-time applications and a link to a Ferranti ARGUS 500 computer which is used for the development of interactive graphic display facilities. Two IBM 1130 computers and a number of Teletype and display consoles are connected to the main computers via a CDC 3100 in order to allow for remote job entry.

RESOURCE ALLOCATION

A monitor program, MTR, coordinates the activities of all jobs which are executed concurrently. In particular, MTR allocates all resources of the system. As the algorithms used are tailored to the particular resource involved, they will be discussed one by one. The reader should keep in mind that MTR is a PP program which resides permanently in PP O and thus executes concurrently with the central processors. Only in a few instances will MTR use a central processor to speed up a lengthy operation.

Job scheduling

The number of jobs which are executed concurrently depends on the number of active "control points" (sometimes also called initiators). The Chippewa Operating System had been designed for a fixed number of seven control points, but we found that this was not enough and have made the total number of control points a system parameter. At present we use 16 control points on either machine of which five are allocated to system activities. Not all the others need always be active. Even so we are happy that our method of storage protection does not limit us to a maximum of 15 initiators.

All user jobs are identified by a job type; i.e. a letter on the job card. Different types impose different limitations on the system resources which a job may claim and constitute different queues. Within each of these queues precedence is determined by job priority (a code, if any, on the job card) and by sequence of arrival.

The console operator may allocate one or more control points to execute jobs of a given type, one at a time. Once a job has reached a control point it will retain it until its completion, even in the extreme case where the operator decides to halt the job.

As usual, a job may consist of several steps (or main programs to be executed). Job steps are executed in strict sequence. A fairly straightforward job control language permits a limited degree of branching on errors, but no loops and no macros. No concurrent subtasks may be defined within a job step.

Allocation of main memory

As the hardware provides a single pair of "reference address" (or base) and "field length" registers, each job occupies a contiguous area of main memory. I/O buffers and system routines are part of each job.

When a program has been loaded, any space not required for execution will normally be returned to the system. User programs will not alter their space requirements during execution. Thus, a job changes its core requirements only a limited number of times during its life, and need not be moved around too often to make room for others.

Requests for a reduction of space are always granted immediately once peripheral processor activity for the job has reached a pause. In the absence of enough memory, requests for a space increase will eventually reach a high-level memory scheduler which will roll out any job of lower priority. The two levels of memory scheduling — implemented partly within MTR and ancillary CP routines, and partly within a scheduler which resides at its own control point — attempt to balance conflicting system requirements.

Allocation of central processors

MTR switches the one or two central processors (two for the 6500) between control points. A special system of priorities is used for this purpose which is independent of the job priority. These priorities are re-evaluated once every second on the basis of the amounts of CP and PP time consumed by each program. In this way I/O intensive programs have preference over programs which are compute-bound. An exception is made for a few real-time applications and some of the system programs which are given top priority.

Allocation of peripheral processors and channels

Programs obtain input, output, and other services of the operating system via requests to MTR. Most of the tasks thus initiated are not executed by MTR itself. MTR has a pool of eight PP's at its disposal to provide the services requested. When one of the pool PP's needs access to a data channel it will apply to MTR for permission.

This system has considerable advantages: The nucleus of the operating system which is responsible for the synchronization of different jobs and PP tasks can be kept very small and logically simple. Moreover, it is not, in essence, subject to timing constraints — all factors which certainly help to make the system both reliable and fairly easy to change. A difficulty arises because pool processors will be delayed when they queue for the same channel. In extreme situations an artificial shortage of pool processors will occur although PP's are not genuinely in short supply. We have therefore implemented a special algorithm to release, if necessary, a PP from its channel queue, so that it can proceed with a different task.

Allocation of tape units

Not every type of job may use magnetic tapes. Those which may, normally do so via the job control language. However, we have found it important that tapes may also be requested and released freely during program execution, especially for the benefit of long production runs. We have therefore provided this facility, and we take no precaution against possible dead-locks because they are, in fact, a very rare event. However, a program which waits for a reel of tape to be mounted is automatically rolled out by the memory scheduler until the reel has been mounted.

SYSTEM PERFORMANCE AND ACCOUNTING

CDC's very first operating system for the 6600 included already a centralized machine log, called the "dayfile". All system routines present messages about significant events to MTR: Execution of job control statements, error messages, operator commands, etc. MTR records all these messages in the dayfile in chronological order after having added the current time and the job name. To facilitate automatic evaluation of the dayfile we have added an identifying code to each message.

For accounting and in order to monitor system performance the dayfile includes e.g. CP, PP, channel, and memory usage of each job step. Other messages have been added at times, for instance to determine how frequently our library routines are used. The dayfile is also scanned regularly for tape errors.

The most powerful tool to gain detailed performance figures with little or no disturbance to the system is a PP routine specially programmed to survey the use of critical resources. We have used this tool to test whether changes to the operating system have the expected effect on throughput. Even the user may X-ray his CP program during execution to locate those sections in which the program spends most of its time.

OPERATOR COMMUNICATION

The system is controlled manually via a display console which has two screens and a
keyboard. System and operator communicate by means of a program, DSD, which
is executed continuously by PP 9. The operator thus has a very dynamic picture of
what happens, especially because the information on the screens is regenerated by
software; any important news may be flashed. The very high degree of independence
which DSD enjoys within the operating system is particularly advantageous in
emergency situations. For example, if an intermittent hardware error occurs in a
channel or a control unit and blocks the system, PP 9 is never affected, and therefore
the operator can diagnose the situation at once. In many cases the fault can then be
cleared from the console without execution of a system restart.

   The contents of the CP instruction counters, a real-time clock, the status of all
channels, the amount of unused memory, and any warnings in case of emergency
are always present on the screen. The display of other status information is selected
by operator commands independently for each screen. For example, details about
the jobs in execution, the most recently issued system messages, and the contents
of various system queues and tables may thus be monitored.

   One of the displays which DSD offers, shows the requests for any tape reels
which must be mounted by the operator. However, this display is only used when
our proper "Tape Reel Number Display System (TRNDS)" is not available. TRNDS
shows the number of the tape reel in large digits directly over the tape unit at
which the reel is needed; it also displays which density and protection status is
expected. We have used the TRNDS at CERN since we have had the 6600 and have
found it more convenient than the alternatives offered by computer manufacturers.

   One difficulty with tape handling is still present: It happens at times that a tape
reel which is used by one machine is also wanted on the other. The effort then
spent searching seems a waste and an irritation to operators.

SPOOLING OPERATIONS

The original version of the operating system included a number of independent, simple
input reader and output writer programs to control different unit record devices.
Their use involved considerable overheads, because they would monopolize several
peripheral processors, channels, and control points, especially if additional devices
(e.g. typewriter consoles, the Tape Reel Number Display System just mentioned,
paper tape and plotting equipment) should be incorporated along the same lines. We
were also unhappy about the operating conventions which were not sufficiently
streamlined for closed shop operation: Identification and separation of output
and any error recovery procedures should require the absolute minimum of attention
and time of the operator. To quote just one example: A mispunched card should
never stop the card reader. On the other hand, we were willing to accept some
restrictions which were not imposed by the initial system: We could live without
on-line usage of slow peripherals (typewriter consoles excluded), and we knew
that our machines would never need more than one card reader or more than one
plotter.

   These considerations led us to the development of a single CP program which
controls all our slow peripherals with a single PP.

ERROR PROCESSING

The early CDC systems relied far too much on operator intervention to overcome all kinds of error and left the programmer with insufficient controls. This was in fact one of the main reasons why we departed from CDC system development in 1966. Programs may now recover not only from "mathematical errors" such as the call of a square root routine with a negative argument, but also from a large variety of "input/output errors", e.g. format conversion errors, tape parity errors, or the reading of a file mark or the end-of-tape marker on magnetic tape. They may recover from arithmetic overflow and similar conditions, from the use of an out-of-range address, and from miscellaneous other peculiar events. Each FORTRAN program includes a table of all conceivable errors, and it is up to the programmer to decide which of these errors should give control to his own recovery routines. We have even found it desirable to provide program recovery once when the CP time allocated to the job has been exhausted: The programmer should be able to leave his data sets in a condition which suits him for further processing with other jobs. In general, an operating system should not interfere with a job which has made its requirements clear. If a genuine error does prevent further execution of the program, then the operating system should furnish a maximum of diagnostic information. In particular, it is not acceptable that any data remains in the output buffer because a program is terminated abnormally by the operating system.

USE OF PERIPHERAL STORAGE

I shall now turn to a number of topics which are all related to data management. This is the area in which at least the initial CDC system had its most fundamental shortcomings, and in which also our own experience has developed particularly slowly — in spite of much sweat.

Access methods
The very first CDC system offered already device independence for all data sets, but only sequential access. The I/O routines operate on circular buffers, but originally only one logical record was buffered at a time. As we decided anyway in 1966 to re-write the I/O system in order to let the programmer deal with all errors, the method of buffering was extended to several logical records at the same time. A limited facility for random access reads from disc and drum was added later which is perhaps adequate for our current needs, but certainly not for more.

Allocation of disc space
MTR allocates disc and drum space in units of fixed length ("half tracks"), one unit at a time. As a data set is written, its half-tracks are chained together in peripheral storage. Tables in main memory show which half-tracks are occupied, how they are chained together, where each data set starts, how it is currently positioned, and to whom it belongs. While the method is economic with regard to both space and access time, it offers no means of recovery after a breakdown. When CDC later added a warmstart procedure, it relied on the contents of main memory to obtain

the starting point of every data set. It may be an exaggeration, but not a gross one
to say, in retrospect, that the system was constructed for fast use in between
maintenance sessions rather than quick repair in the midst of continuous
production.

Permanent user files

We decided to implement a system of user files which could be recovered
independently of any contents of main memory as a first step in the direction of
system recovery. The catalogue has its own tree structure of directories, all
recoverable from a root in a fixed place on disc. It offers a fair range of facilities
to the user, including concurrent access from several jobs, space budget control,
and protection against unauthorized access. To obtain further security and to save
the information when the discs were required for maintenance — we have no
removable discs — the permanent user files and the catalogue were dumped on
magnetic tape twice per day. Elaborate checks were included, both for recovery on
disc and for all tape operations.

Unfortunately, we lacked the man-power, hardware, and experience (or foresight)
which would have been necessary to rectify all the other mistakes at the same time:
Tape reels may not be catalogued, there is still no "volume table of contents", unused
data is not removed from the discs were required for maintanance — we have no
for each machine. In short, we still use the permanent files as an occasional aid to
computing, and not our computers as occasional aids to manipulate a data base
which exists in its own right.

System recovery

Only when we had considerable operational experience with our permanent user
files did we include system data (jobs and output) in the scheme. Once e.g. a job
has been written to disk for execution, the data set which contains it is recorded in
the catalogue, so that it may be retrieved during a warmstart. A system program at
its own control point makes all the necessary changes to the catalogue.

In this context the system restart procedure has been revised completely.
Whereas the system library is still loaded from tape for every warmstart, all
catalogued data sets are traced on disc. The entire procedure is executed in less
than ten minutes.

CONCLUSION

Many requirements of large batch processing systems are fairly well understood by
now, and enough field experience has become available to identify adequate
solutions. It may be true that the solutions depend heavily on particular hardware
and are full of ad hoc conventions. Resource allocation, for instance, offers plenty
of pertinent examples. The methods are probably poor from a scientific point of
view, but in practice they satisfy a wide range of users.

On the other hand, there do exist problems which have not found their proper
solution yet. I venture to propose a list of such problems and suggest to consider them
as key questions for significant further progress:

1. The effective use of two levels of word-addressable memories, such as the main memory and the Extended Core Storage of the CDC 6000-series computers.
2. Continuous availability of a multi-computer complex, including on-line maintenance, run-down, and re-integration of all its modules.
3. Simultaneous access to a disc-based data storage system from any number of computers.
4. Automatic migration of infrequently used data between a large disc store and some archive.
5. Access to the equivalent of a large tape store without manual intervention, so that operating costs may be reduced for the very large computers.

ACKNOWLEDGEMENTS

The following present or former members of CERN, of the Control Data support group at CERN, and of ICL have contributed to the development of SCOPE:
M. Baechler, J. D. Blake, T. Bloch, R. Brody, C. Clayton, M. K. Downie, F. Ekman,
G. V. Frigo, J. Garratt, H. Comaa, B. Lautrup, P. Letts (ICL), F. C. Lowe,
P. J. Marcer, A. Maver, F. McIntosh, P. McWilliam (CDC), E. Mettler (CDC),
E. M. Palandri, R. A. Pocock, D. Rösner, P. Samson, W. Simon, M. Smith (CDC),
B. Trenel, C. Vandoni, H. von Eicken, P. Warn (CDC), A. Yule.

REFERENCES

"Control data 6400/6500/6600/6700 computer systems". *Reference Manual,* Pub. No. 6010–0000, Minneapolis.
CERN Computer 6000 Series SCOPE General Reference (loose-leaf), Geneva.
Lipps, H., "6000 Series SCOPE at CERN", Proceedings of the Summer School on the Use of Computers in Experimental Physics, Alushta, May 1968.
Maver, A., "An experimental filing system for a large scientific computer", Proceedings of the International Seminar on File Organization, Copenhagen, November 1968.
Blake, J. D., "Design of a core memory allocation scheme for a large multi-programming computer", Proceedings of the International Computer Symposium, Bonn, 1970.

DISCUSSION

LIPPS: We have reached the stage where there are operating systems for large and small machines, and if you compare two — say, for instance, for the CDC 6000 and for the PDP 8 — you can see that although some of the techniques used are similar the implementation problems are very different. Also, installations which require time-sharing are in quite a different situation from those like ourselves at CERN who include consoles, but only use them for a small part of the machine load. For example, memory management will differ depending on whether you run a large number of small jobs or a relatively small number of big jobs.

The system at CERN has a well defined machine configuration consisting of two very similar machines, a 6500 and a 6600, and also in many ways a special load. The development of our operating system could therefore be tailored to a specific configuration and work load, and we have exploited this fact to our advantage. For example, most of our programs are written in Fortran, and the remainder primarily in assembly language. The Algol compiler is almost never used and we don't have Cobol. Therefore much to the advantage of our memory scheduler, programs run within some fixed amount of storage.

When designing the initial system (the Chippewa Operating System) CDC consistently used the simplest techniques available which gave reasonable performance. For example, a store management certainly uses hardware relocation registers in a straightforward manner, but no attempt has been made to implement paging. Also, a single peripheral processor uses a program of less than 4K words of 12 bits to provide multiprogramming and synchronize the entire machine. The general design has not only given us a fairly efficient system from the outset – at a very rough guess, say, 20% below optimum – but it has also greatly helped our efforts as we developed the operating system further. We might have run into plenty of pitfalls had we had a more complicated system.

In my paper I have tried to identify a number of specific problems which can be discussed independently. I believe that many of these are now sufficiently well understood that, from a pragmatic point of view, it has almost become a matter of taste to choose one of several solutions. However, there are also a number of subjects, where one still does not have a satisfactory solution from a practical point of view, let alone a thorough analysis of the logical fundamentals. I have listed some of these unresolved questions at the end of my paper because I believe that further progress in operating systems will largely depend on progress in these particular areas. I would like to mention two of these problems here.

Firstly, the use of main memory. Here I mean core memories, plated wire memories, and other high-speed memories which do not depend on mechanical devices. CDC have followed their own way of handling a two-level core store since about 1965 when they announced their extended core storage; but the extended core storage for the 6600 was conceived after the operating system for the 6600 had been designed, and thus its integration into and efficient use within the existing operating system has proved difficult. In the case of the 7600, the two levels of core store have been designed into the overall system from the outset. This has led to other changes in machine organization; in particular, it has meant that on the 7600 we have a central monitor rather than a peripheral monitor. More generally, so very little experience is as yet available in the use of the two levels of non-mechanical memories that I would expect significant future progress in this area.

Secondly, on the question of access to very large amounts of data, which is of particular importance to our installation as we have about 30,000 reels of magnetic tape. There are almost thirty tape units for the two machines, and the number of reels being mounted each day is in the order of a thousand. The situation raises serious operational problems.

We are therefore looking forward to devices which can store a sufficiently large fraction of the data now held on tape to simplify operation and reduce the delays which our tape jobs now encounter almost inevitably. With faster computers it will become important for large data processing installations to replace tape by some on-line storage device with considerably higher data rates, because one is not able to afford the large amount of main memory required to keep many programs going from tape. WILSON: I am surprised how few installations are actually running on a pure Scope system. Everyone has modified the system in some way due to the fact that it has been constrained by the hardware to being written in a very modular way. The hardware consists of one or two central processors and ten peripheral processors. A piece of system software will be run in any of eight peripheral processors. This is done by having a resident piece of program within each peripheral processor, which loads a requested routine. This routine may have overlays which it brings in as required. Therefore modification can be quite simple and involves changing or adding an overlay. For instance, input/output is achieved by calling a general routine which brings down an overlay to deal with the required device; hence if we have a new exotic device on the machine we merely write a new overlay.

There is a trend for moving new software from the peripheral processors to the central processor. The original Scope system started off with merely the "storage move" program run in the central processor, and this was kept in fixed store all the time. The advantages of using the central processor are that it is a lot faster and has a greater repertoire of instructions than a peripheral processor. For instance, a peripheral processor has no floating point instructions.

Scope, unfortunately, has a built-in limit on the number of control points (i.e. on the number of programs which can multiprogram). In the standard version this limit is seven, although it is to be raised to fifteen in the next CDC version. The raising of this limit is not a trivial exercise, and means that the systems had to be modified to quite a large extent. The major cause of control point hang-up is waiting for a magnetic tape to be loaded, as this resource can be allocated dynamically The control point then remains idle from the time the request is posted until the operator completes the assignment. The Lawrence Radiation Laboratory in Berkeley, California, has a modified Scope in which they try to keep thirty-two control points occupied with no more than sixteen of them waiting for tape drives. With only seven control points Scope has little or no deadly embrace problems on magnetic tapes, but when you have a larger number of control points there is more likelihood of a deadly embrace occurring. To avoid this the Berkeley system loads all the tapes for one job at the same time, having scanned the job description for the necessary information at the first tape request. It is possible that a job may die after a tape request without using any of the other tapes that have been loaded. If sufficient tape drives are not available the job is rolled out onto mass storage and the core store can then be used for other jobs.

Another interesting enhancement of the Scope system is the Mace system at Purdue University, which has a maximum of 26 control points. Idle control points are dealt with by an automatic roll-out to mass storage, the reverse roll-in process not necessarily being to the same control point.

As far as magnetic tape scheduling is concerned the common use of a magnetic tape by a number of successive jobs is not anticipated. If jobs do use the same tapes it must be very irritating for an operator to unload a tape and then have to load it again a few minutes later. If this is the case, magnetic tape scheduling such as that in the Titan system could prove very useful here.

The use of permanent disc files seems to be very limited in all variations of Scope. It seems to be oriented more towards the input of batches of cards, either remotely or on site, rather than keeping them permanently in a disc file. Unlike the CERN system, temporary files in Scope are not catalogued on the disc, and recovery of these files after a system break depends upon tables such as the File Name Table and the Record Block Table still being intact in core. Furthermore, I know of few Scope installations that actually dump files to tape for security purposes; perhaps this is because corruption of the file tables and disc files is fairly rare.

LIPPS: There are two reasons for the apparent move from the use of the peripheral processors to the use of the central processor by the operating system itself. The first is that when you introduce a second level of core store, as in the case of the 6600, the whole organization changes (in particular the input/output and the core management); and if you look at this in detail it is not difficult to see that it becomes necessary to have a CPU monitor program, simply because the PPU monitor has not enough information at its fingertips and is not constructed in such a way as to handle two-level core store efficiently. So to make efficient use of the extended core store there is a tendency to move more of the basic operating system into the CPU as in the 7600. It would be difficult for an operating system such as ours to make good use of ECS without a great deal of modification. The second reason is the tendency to expand the system and provide additional facilities to the basic system, because these facilities usually have features very similar to a user program, which should be implemented in such a way that the nucleus of the system looks at them just like a user program.

At a relatively early stage we altered the system to allow ourselves more than the original seven control points, basically because we expected to add further facilities in the form of user programs. It was not because we felt our use of magnetic tape was such that we needed more control points to run more tape jobs at any one time. It depends on the number of tapes used by any one job and also on the number of tapes you have in the system;

HARTLEY: We have here a specific case of the creation of artificial resources. The control points of Scope are a resource and if you have not enough you need to schedule them. It often happens in the design stage of an operating system that a decision is made about the size of an important parameter which appears at the time to be sufficient; but at some later stage it becomes clear that it is not big enough.

In such a situation we have to take one of two courses; either go back and start again or do a fiddle and share one control point between all the on-line users. The second alternative is the one taken in Scope and it works out quite well, but I think it is unnatural and I'm sure can lead you into other scarcities and problems.

We have the same problem in hardware of course, because we did not buy enough core or we did not have sufficient channels, but we always hope that the software can be changed. We therefore have here a very good example of the general principle of the problem of scarcity of resources.

LIPPS: In 1963 when the first version of Scope was implemented nobody had practical experience of multiprogramming. This probably explains the under-estimation in the number of control points. Another reason is that it was in line with the operational design principles of the man who designed the machine and the operating system to go for something simple and straightforward and see what happens.

NEEDHAM: One could even say that a high proportion of scheduling problems one gets are scheduling of artificial resources rather than real resources.

HOARE: Could you give a few more examples?

NEEDHAM: In the dynamic allocation of working space where you may devise an addressing mechanism which might be conveniently packed into a small number of bits. Then addresses themselves may be a scarce resource which have to be scheduled.

The file directory is another example where the number increased to the limit allowed by the address field. We had to make a great managerial effort to schedule the application of this scarce resource, but nobody could say that when the decision was made it was not the right one. This does not correspond to anything physical in the sense of resources such as core store, physical pieces of disc, tape drives and so on, but a very considerable proportion of the scheduling activity which goes on in a system is concerned with resources of this nature.

FRASER: There are also limitations on the number of user file directories that can exist and also on the number of blocks you can have in a file directory. This limits the number of files and the number of file users that you can have. This may seem unreasonable, but the reason they exist is connected with the performance of the file system. In order to define a file, the file system has to search through a certain body of data, and provided that you could rely on the body of data residing completely in one block, a high level of performance could be expected; if it was more than one block the performance would drop substantially. The reason for this drop is that although the system's discs allow you to store more than one block on a track and therefore transfer a large volume of information with only one latency, this piece of knowledge was not built into the space management routines, as a deliberate simplification of the space control structure. Also, a very nice restart procedure was possible if physical contiguity of blocks is wholly ignored. This was a hard decision to make and it resulted in an equally hard decision about the file directories. I suspect it also affects the working of the dumper, as this is geared to the knowledge of the directory structure. Although the decisions may look arbitrary, I was governed by previous decisions and I was not in a position to guess the number of users that would be on the system.

NEEDHAM: The important thing is to realize you are creating a limitation. I am not objecting to artificial resources as such, but an awful lot of them came into being not by any conscious action of anybody, but by just doing something which turns out later to have created an artificial resource; and this is to be avoided at all costs.

HOARE: Presumably, the semaphore which protects critical regions is an example of an artificial resource, but one which is absolutely essential to the logical functioning of the system.

RANDELL: One can generalize the principle much further to say that there are only three good numbers in system design and they are zero, one and infinity. The point is that in software one can usually get nearer to something that can be disguised as infinity than in hardware.

Multiprogramming for covering up input/output delays to and from discs and drums is not necessarily the same thing as multiprogramming for dealing with people at on-line terminals. I think this is a point brought out in Lynch's paper, where multiprogramming was not aiming for infinity, but tried very hard to get back down to number one.

FRASER: If you try to engineer something (whether it's hard or soft) at some point you have to make a decision that you are not in a good position to make. It may concern equipment, or the number of bits to allocate for a specific purpose. Then you build a large edifice on top of this decision. This is therefore a hard decision to make, but nevertheless we should try to make these decisions to the best of our ability with the limited knowledge we have available. It is this difficulty which makes the task of the "all singing – all dancing" system designer almost impossible. He is in a very bad position to make even a first order stab at some of the numbers. I suggest that in the end we are going to have to get away from writing such general systems.

BRINCH HANSEN: I have been creating a number of artificial resources in the RC4000 system, which I found to be partly due to the mismanagement of storage and lack of understanding of how storage protection ought to be achieved. We were partitioning store into at least three kinds of artificial resource; namely, the store to be allocated to a process, the store to be allocated to a message process, and the store to be allocated to the description of concurrent processes. For protection reasons we decided to include the two latter kinds of store inside the system nucleus, which would have a fixed size determined at compile time. Therefore, the number of message processes and process descriptions would be fixed at compile time. But, if we had a programming language which would enable us to allocate these message buffers and process descriptions inside the operating systems as part of their normal stack, and could check at compile time that the rules of access to these buffers were kept, we would need only one kind of resource, namely the amount of store allocated to a given process. So I suggest that there are decisions, as Fraser says, which have to be taken at design time; but some artificial resources are also created by mismanagement.

FENTON: It is very important to put a lot of effort into devising ways whereby you can change your mind afterwards. For example, the upper limit of storage allocation may be contained in a macro, so that if you decide that it is going to be different you can recompile the operating system.

HOARE: Can I speak out against the implicit morally superior tone of that last comment. Of course it is a good idea to write flexible programs, but the decisions which have to be most firmly built into your software are far too all-pervasive to be changed by the alteration of a simple algorithm or a single field of a data structure. They are often built into the philosophical framework which provided the basis of all subsequent decisions, and when you change one of these early decisions, all the rest of your system is now based on an incorrect original assumption.

I notice in designing compilers and operating systems that one is constantly not so much deciding to do things, but deciding not to do things. This, in itself, can lead to problems. For example, we may consciously simplify a particular feature because we believe we know our program will be limited by a bottleneck elsewhere. However, if you then come to realize that the bottleneck will not occur, the whole emphasis of where you should have put the complex algorithms has changed.

Nevertheless, decisions of this fundamental nature should not be regarded as evil, but as the only method which enables us to concentrate our attention on the problems that matter and obtain adequate solutions for them. For example, the decision to write a single-pass compiler has a great effect on the language or subset of a language you choose to implement, on the structure of the compiler, and on the speed and quality success of the compiler in the field. To make an early decision of this kind limits you freedom of how to do the job, but it is the only way in which you can produce a successful system to fixed time scales, and it is to be welcomed.

RANDELL: There have been some systems which have caused conceptually trivial matters, such as the layout of a control block, to have such an all-pervasive effect on the system, in such a way that there is, in practice, no possible way of changing even these decisions.

NEWELL: That is a similar example to the CDC control point limitation. Surely the reason is because these systems were written in languages which did not enable them to parametrize easily.

HOARE: I suspect that in the CDC system the design of the whole of the rest of the system was greatly simplified on the basis of the assumption that there are only seven control points, and this was the very reason why it was so difficult to increase the number.

LIPPS: The decision in the original system to have seven control points did not influence the rest of the system very much. It was really a matter of simplicity to have seven control points. This was a mistake but I can assure you the designer of the CDC system, namely Seymour Cray who also designed the hardware, knew what he was doing when he decided to have a fixed number of control points other than zero, one or infinity; he exploited the fact that he had a fixed number. The number seven was probably chosen partly because when the system was written no assembler was available with a sufficiently powerful parameter mechanism, and also it is a reasonable number for a general operating system.

BURROUGHS OPERATING SYSTEMS

Speaker: D. P. Fenton: "B6700 'Working Set' memory allocation."

Replier: R. M. McKeag.

In absentia: D. J. Roche: "Burroughs B5500 MCP and time-sharing MCP."

BURROUGHS B5500 MCP AND TIME-SHARING MCP

D. J. Roche

Telecommunications Development Department,
G.P.O.,
London

COMPUTER EXPERIENCE PRIOR TO B5500

In-house scientific computing in the Post Office started in March 1961 with the
installation of an Elliot 803B with 4096 words of core store. This machine was
used on an open-shop principle, the users booked time and operated the machine
themselves. There was no operating system you either wrote your programs in machine
code or Elliot Autocode and, apart from the need to book time, the users were
very contented. In 1965 an Elliot 503 was installed, this had 60 times the power
of the 803B and a magnetic tape based operating system. Closed-shop operating was
introduced and demand for computer time grew rapidly due to the availability of
a lineprinter and magnetic tape. This combination gave trouble in terms of
relationships between users and computer management. Programmers had to use
forms to specify their requirements. Even when programmers described their
needs accurately the operators were adept at misunderstanding the written word.
The turn-round time became lengthy and in many cases it was a turn-round of spoilt
work. This was an embarrassing situation with a daily load of 300 small tasks.
Easement for large work was given by allowing open-shop operating during
uncongenial hours.

INSTALLATION OF B5500

It was against this background that a single processor Burroughs B5500 with 24K
words of 4 μsec core store, two disc modules of 9.6M characters each and two I/O
channels was installed in 1968. The effect on turn-round was dramatic. The 503 had
been loaded to 150 hours per week and turn-round could be as long as three days
for a small task. Now it was possible to obtain three turn-rounds between
9.00 am and 5.00 pm. The 503 was used without the operating system enabling it
to perform efficiently on the larger tasks such as simulation of telephone exchanges.
If the users had not previously experienced open-shop operating, and time-sharing
had not been invented, we were in the position of giving a highly satisfactory service.
However, within months of obtaining the B 5500 the first time-sharing terminals
from an external bureau were provided and there was soon pressure to give terminal
access to the B5500.

REMOTE JOB ENTRY

Terminals were connected in 1969 and service provided via Remote Edit. We would have been wiser to have withstood the pressure until such time that the machine was enhanced and the time-sharing master control program was available. The remote edit system was only of value for a small number of terminals. We misjudged and allowed eight to be installed. With hindsight we should have restricted the number to six. Facilities available from the terminals were extensive, basically the user had almost as much control of his own environment as the control console. He was able to reduce the core estimate generated by the compiler, thus increasing the chance of his job being transferred from the schedule to the mix. Additionally, he was permitted the use of the extended ALGOL compiler. This allows the use of stream procedures, a means of addressing, without checks, an absolute offset from his data area. Mis-use and abuse of these facilities by ill-informed or over-ambitious users could, and often did, wreck the system.

The status of Remote Editor was no greater than any other program in the mix. The task of time sharing between its users was its own responsibility. When a time slice was allocated by MCP to Remote Editor it in turn decided which of its active users should have control. Since the obvious overheads in such a system and the ultimate workload (and hence the frequency and length of Remote Editors time slice) depend on the number of users, these were restricted. MCP has a facility enabling programs to devolve the time-sharing responsibility to the system. Use of this facility requires a Program Reference Table for each user. As these cannot be overlaid core fragmentation occurs with quite a small number of users.

TIME-SHARING ON B5500

Remote job entry did not provide the service required by the majority of users and it was necessary to enhance the system to introduce time-sharing MCP (TSSMCP). Shortly after this decision was taken it was also decided to purchase a second B5500 system with 32K words of core, two processors, four I/O channels and four disc modules. This second machine was to be installed at our Research Station at Dollis Hill. At the stage of ordering the second machine we were assured by Burroughs that TSSMCP was a viable system and one of our representatives witnessed a demonstration in the U.S.A. Despite this, however, it was necessary to include in the contract terms a firm condition that the acceptance tests included a demonstration of time-sharing.

TEST CRITERIA

The terms of the contract included "satisfactory performance when operating in the time-sharing mode serving twenty-four simultaneous users". Due to the difficulty of mounting a suitable demonstration during the factory trial it was agreed that this test should be conducted on the existing B5500 installation when a comparable hardware configuration was available. As this demonstration was deemed to be a component of the acceptance trial the test procedure needed to be constructed with sufficient rigour to enable it to be repeated as an integral part of the final site trial.

DEVELOPMENT OF TEST

With the aim of repeatability, of reducing typing loads, and ensuring a quick build-up of load a test was designed in which all users input their programs from prepared paper tape. The test was a complete failure. Although the initial system response was satisfactory the response to normal editing commands was intolerable. The use of paper tape, to this degree, was a mistake. It was not a typical pattern of use and resulted in the excessive allocation of core buffers simply to accommodate paper tape inputs.

To assist in reappraising the test procedure the activities of fifteen terminal user sessions were examined. Terminal activity was categorized into four broad groups.

(a)	Thinking and typing	34%
(b)	System activity to create and edit files (CANDE)	12%
(c)	Compiling programs	27%
(d)	Running programs	27%
		100%

The sample was small and was taken on a lightly loaded machine (TSSMCP had only recently been introduced). Of the four categories only "thinking and typing" was controlled by the terminal user, machine response significantly effects the remainder. The following load was chosen with the aim of approaching the observed pattern:

Schedule A

(i) One user with three different tasks to be run consecutively; a program limited by I/O, a CPU bound program, and a large ALGOL compilation. Details in Appendix 1.

Schedule B

(i) Eight users running an ALGOL program; loading from paper tape. Details in Appendix 2.
(ii) Eight users running an ALGOL program; three loading from paper tape, five typing their program from the terminal keyboard. Details in Appendix 3.
(iii) Seven users running an interactive matrix inversion program written in BASIC. Details in Appendix 4.

This rearrangement of the load was expected to be realistic but the poor performance of the first test had also drawn attention to the core estimating algorithm. As the core estimates of all CANDE (Command and Edit) subsystems are produced by this algorithm these were examined and where possible, reduced. The factors used by the compiler to determine core estimates are:

(*a*) Number of arrays declared.

If number of arrays declared is between 1 and 4	2000 words
If number of arrays declared is between 5 and 8	3500 words
If number of arrays declared is greater than 8	5000 words

(*b*) Segment size.

If segment size is less than 1000	the size in words
If segment size is between 1000 and 2000	1000 words
If segment size is greater than 2000	size ÷ 2 words

(*c*) Stack and Program Reference Table (PRT)

512 words for Stack* plus size of **PRT**   words
(* unless overridden by STACK CARD)

(*d*) Number of files declared.

Five times the number of files declared   words

(*e*) Size and Number of I/O buffers.

All buffers when declared   words

The adjustments made to the core estimates for Command and Edit (CANDE) were:

CANDE Subsystem	Compiler Estimate	Adjusted Sizes
LOAD	4K words	2K words
QUICKLIST	4K words	2K words
REPLACE	5K words	4K words
All others	5K words	3K words

A compiler requests more core by counting the number of overlays it initiates. Factors affecting the number of overlays include the size of programs and the type of diagnostic routines required. Normally the initial core allocation for compilers is 12K to 13K words. These were adjusted to 8K, this was acceptable as it was found that the majority of our small user programs did not call for more than 8K words when compiling.

It was appreciated at the time that tuning in this fashion, by the trading of core against time, can only be of value if the overall system response is acceptable to the users.

DEMONSTRATIONS

The first demonstration served as a factory test and was performed on an existing installation at 2–12 Gresham St. on 3 November 1970. This demonstration proceeded for 90 minutes and was agreed, by all users participating, to be satisfactory. The second demonstration was performed with the purchased equipment, on site at Dollis Hill, on 17 March 1971. This demonstration was also agreed, by users, to be satisfactory.

TEST RESULTS

The average number of users connected during the Gresham St. test was 23.5 and for Dollis Hill test 20.5.

By analysis of the terminal logs "snapshots" of terminal usage were taken at 150 second intervals. Histograms of the activity categories are shown in figures 2 and 3. From these histograms the following percentage figures were obtained and are compared with the observed activity referred to in section 6:

	Gresham St.	*Dollis Hill*	*Observed*
Thinking and typing	32.25%	23.5%	(34%)
CANDE	31.25%	37.4%	(12%)
Compiling	17.75%	16.3%	(27%)
Running	18.75%	22.8%	(27%)

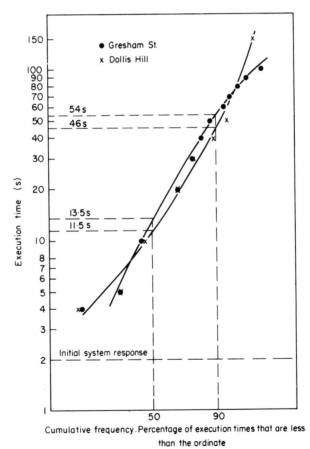

Figure 1. Log/normal plot of Schedule B execution times.

The correspondence with "thinking and typing" is reasonably good, the much higher CANDE activity reflects the additional load.

The times to affect the various CANDE tasks as detailed in the schedule are shown in tables 1 and 2 and have been interpreted in figure 1. Initial system response was always better than 2 seconds, 50% of the tasks were completed in less than 13.5 seconds and 90% were completed within 54 seconds. There would appear to be little significant difference between the results obtained from both tests. On one occasion during the Gresham St. demonstration the system reached a state of "no memory" and the response times increased. However, the system did not collapse and recovered itself in 90 seconds.

TABLE 1

Execution Times of Schedule B Commands – Gresham St. Test

CONTROL CYCLE No.	1	2	3	4	5	6	7	8
CANDE Command								
END	–	18.0	80.0	24.0	44.0	34.0	110.0	65.0
SAVE	5.0	4.5	5.0	8.0	5.0	8.0	11.0	25.0
DELETE	3.0	–	12.0	24.0	5.0	8.0	27.0	23.0
LOAD	14.0	12.0	18.0	12.0	9.0	35.0	30.0	36.0
SAVE	11.0	15.0	14.0	21.0	65.0	52.0	13.0	54.0
COMPILE	12.0	49.0	42.0	57.0	91.0	51.0	81.0	130.0
SCHEDULE	11.0	–	13.0	20.0	24.0	18.0	37.0	27.0
STOP	8.0	5.0	4.0	4.0	8.0	6.0	16.0	3.0
DELETE	5.0	7.0	4.0	5.0	–	6.0	7.0	19.0
REMOVE	3.0	6.0	5.0	5.0	25.0	5.0	11.0	7.0

All times shown are in seconds. The program running under Schedule A for Cycles 1 to 4 was the CPU bound program, for Cycles 5 to 7, the I/O bound program and for Cycle 8, the large compilation.

TABLE 2

Execution Times of Schedule B Commands – Dollis Hill Test

CONTROL CYCLE No.	1	2	3	4	5
CANDE Command					
? END	14.0	45.0	25.0	30.0	36.0
SAVE	4.8	5.0	5.0	4.8	7.0
DELETE	3.0	5.0	5.0	4.2	19.2
LOAD	8.8	11.0	13.0	12.5	38.0
SAVE	17.8	18.5	27.0	34.0	77.0
COMPILE	18.0	39.5	23.0	141.0	173.0
SCHEDULE	–	14.0	29.5	42.0	–
STOP	–	7.0	5.5	4.1	–
DELETE	7.0	8.0	12.0	10.0	–
REMOVE	3.0	12.0	9.0	8.0	–

All times shown are in seconds. The program running under Schedule A for Cycles 1 to 3 was the CPU bound program and for Cycles 4 and 5 the I/O bound program.

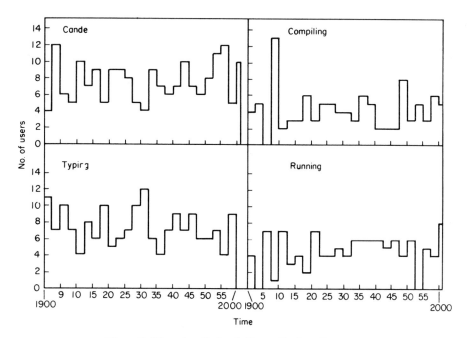

Figure 2. "Snapshots" of activities – Gresham St. test.

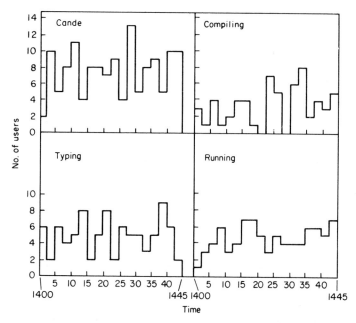

Figure 3. "Snapshots" of activities – Dollis Hill test.

The ratios of elapsed time/CPU time for the programs running under schedule A were:

CPU Bound Program

	Mean Value	Maximum Value
Gresham St.	1.47	2.9
Dollis Hill	1.38	4.58

I/O Bound Program

	Mean Value	Maximum Value
Gresham St.	28	60.2
Dollis Hill	47	105

The difference between the Gresham St. and Dollis Hill I/O bound figures is considered to be due to the 20% increase in the use of disc-resident CANDE sub-systems during the Dollis Hill tests (31.25%–37.4%). This greater CANDE activity would tend to "lock-out" the low priority background program. At the end of each demonstration one processor was switched off. The times to compile and execute were significantly affected. All other commands and edit response times, whilst being worsened, remained tolerable.

SUMMARY OF TESTS

A number of factors affect the consistency of the test results, these include:

(*a*) The original sample of terminal usage was small in size and was obtained by complete activity measurement on a lightly loaded system (between 5 and 10 users).

(*b*) The test results were obtained by coarse sampling of the hard copies recording terminal activity.

(*c*) The times for compiling, running, and CANDE are materially affected by the "System Waiting" time. This is dependent on:

   (i) Job mix
   (ii) Terminal load
   (iii) Core estimates of subsystems.

(*d*) The artificial load caused peaks of similar activity which were greater than those expected from a normal live load.

The demonstration confirmed that the system was robust enough to support 24 terminals and provide a service considered satisfactory by users experienced with time-sharing terminal services.

CONCLUSION

The need for purchasers to test the ability of multi-access computer systems will continue. The tests described here are concerned with only 24 terminals but the cost and effort required was high. In the future we will need to test systems involving hundreds of terminals and the use of another computer to provide the terminal environment will become essential. Although this form of mechanizing the test is quite feasible the accurate design of the load characteristics is crucial to the effectiveness of such tests. Our sample of user activity was too small and was taken on a lightly loaded system which allowed ample time for compiling and execution. The 34% "thinking and typing" time is possibly reliable as it is almost entirely user dependent. An environment can be specified by the number of connected terminals a typical work mix, plus a measure of time spent in "thinking and typing". From our present limited experience it appears that users are satisfied with systems where—

(*a*) initial system response time is less than 2 seconds.
(*b*) 50% of tasks are completed within 14 seconds.
(*c*) 90% of tasks are completed within one minute, and
(*d*) One-third of their logged-on time is spent "thinking and typing".

We have been unable to verify the results of our tests in a normal environment as, until additional disc is provided, the installations are being restricted to 12 terminals each. This disc should be available shortly and the connected terminals will be increased in steps up to 24. During this time the adjustment of core estimates will need close attention until experience is gained. When the system is being fully utilized user behaviour and reaction will be studied in preparation for larger scale tests of time-sharing systems.

APPENDIX 1

Schedule A

This schedule consisted of three programs designed to load the system either in I/O, CPU or a combination of both.

(*a*) The program limited by I/O randomly updated a very large matrix stored on disc and subsequently checked the updated matrix.
(*b*) The CPU bound program was a simple counting program which made no reference to any peripheral device apart from initiation and termination.
(*c*) To obtain a combination of both conditions the ALGOL compiler was compiled.

APPENDIX 2

B5500 TSS Test

Schedule B
Log-on procedure.

Dial...
On receipt of tone, operate the "data" button. System should respond with

B5500 TIME SHARING
ENTER USERCODE PLEASE

Type: ....
Response: AND YOUR PASSWORD

Type: 5500 ←

System will respond with your line number, usercode, date and time.

Type: MAKE TESTP ALGOL ←
Response: FILE: TESTP-TYPE: ALGOL —— CREATED

Load program tape into tape reader.

Type: TAPE ←
Response: OK

On receipt of OK, start paper tape reader. When tape has been read, turn off paper
tape reader and:—

Type: ? END ←
Response: #

Type: SAVE ←
Response: FILE: TESTP-TYPE: ALGOL —— SAVED

Type: DELETE ALL ←
Response: WAIT
                    #

Type: LOAD TESTP ←
Response: FILE: TESTP – TYPE: ALGOL ——LOADING
                    END LOADING n SEC

Edit the file by re-typing the complete lines containing the errors (see attached
sheet). Lines must be terminated by ←.

*Type: SAVE ←
Response: FILE: TESTP-TYPE: ALGOL ——SAVED

Type: COMPILE TESTP ←
Response: COMPILING
                    (Possible diagnostic information)
                    END COMPILE n SEC

[If for any reason the file is corrupt, diagnostic information will be included in the response. In these cases,

Type:	LIST ←
Response:	Program will be printed followed by:—
	END LIST n SEC.

Check program against the attached sheet. Edit by completely re-typing all lines that contain errors.

Restart test at *]

Type:	SCHEDULE TESTP TO DUMMY AFTER 1700 ←
Response:	END SCHEDULE n SEC.

Type:	STOP DUMMY ←
Response:	SCHEDULED

Type:	DELETE ALL ←
Response:	WAIT
	#

Type:	REMOVE TESTP, DUMMY ←
Response:	#

Type:	BYE ←
Response:	ON FOR n1 MIN n2 SEC.
	C&E USED n3 SEC
	OFF AT time
	GOODBYE

The above cycle should be repeated seven times during the test period.

```
100  BEGIN INTEGER J;
200  FORMAT F("THIS PROGRAM CHECKS THE DEPTH OF RECURSION
     POSSIBLE";
300  "WITH NORMAL STACK ALLOCATION");
400  FILE OUT REM REMOTE(1, 9);
500  INTEGER PROCEDURE SUM(J);
600  VALUE J;INTEER J;
700  SUM:=(IF J=1 THEN 1 ELSE J+SUM(J−1));
800  WRITE(LP, F);
900  FOR J:=1 STEP 1 UNTIL 200 DO WRITE(REM,/,J,SUM(J));
1000 END.
```

ERRORS . . . .
PLEASE CHANGE LINES 600 & 800 TO THE FOLLOWING

```
600  VALUE J;INTEGER J;
800  WRITE(REM,F);
```

APPENDIX 3

B5500 TSS Test

Schedule B (Amicable Pairs Test)

1 Dial......................................

On receipt of tone operate "DATA" button. System response

B5500 TIME SHARING
ENTER USERCODE PLEASE

2 Type   ....
  Response: AND YOUR PASSWORD

  Type: 5500 ←
  Response: line numbers, usercode, date and time

3 Type: MAKE TESTA ALGOL ←
  Response: FILE: TESTA-TYPE ALGOL —— CREATED

4 Type in the attached program invoking the "SAVE" and "LIST" commands at
  the points specified. When the complete program has been typed in and listed.

  Type: COMPILE ←
  Response: COMPILING
                  (possible diagnostic information)
                  END COMPILE on SEC

4a If there are errors comparison should be made between the final listing and the
  original and any errors corrected by completely re-typing the faulty line(s).
  Another "COMPILE" should then be attempted.

5 After successful compilation

  Type: RUN ←

  The program will produce 9 pairs of numbers

6 After the program has finished execution:—

  Type: DELETE ALL ←
  Response: WAIT
                  #

  Type: REMOVE TESTA ←
  Response: #

  Type: BYE ←
  Response: ON FOR n1 MIN n2 SEC
                  C&E USED n3 SEC
                  OFF AT <TIME>
                  GOODBYE

7 The above cycle should be repeated as many times as possible during the test
  period.

ALGOL AMICABLE PAIRS PROGRAM

```
100  BEGIN
200  INTEGER A,B,N;
300  FILE OUT REM REMOTE(2,15);
400  FORMAT F(216);
500  INTEGER PROCEDURE SUMFAC(N);
600  VALUE N; INTEGER N;
700  BEGIN
800  INTEGER PI,S,D,F,Q,T;
900  LABEL NEWF,NEXT;
1000 BOOLEAN NEWFAC;
1100 PI:=S:=D:=1; F:=2;Q:=N;
1200 NEWF;NEWFAC:=TRUE;
1300 NEXT : IF Q GEQ F THEN BEGIN Q:=N DIV F;
1400 IF N NEQ Q\F THEN BEGIN F:=F+D;
1500 D:=2; GO TO NEWF;END
1600 ELSE BEGIN IF NEWFAC THEN BEGIN
1700 NEWFAC:=FALSE;PI:=PI\S;S:=T:=1;END;
1800 T:=T\F;S:=S+T;N:=Q;GO TO NEXT;END;END;
1900 PI:=PI\S;
2000 SUMFAC:=IF N NEQ 1 THEN PI\(1+N) ELSE PI;
2100 END SUMFAC;
2200 FOR N:=1 STEP 1 UNTIL 10000 DO
2300 BEGIN B:=SUMFAC(N)-N;
2400 IF B GEQ N THEN BEGIN
2500 A:=SUMFAC(B)-B;
2600 IF A=N THEN WRITE(REM,F,A,B);
2700 END;END;END.
```

OPERATORS ARE ASKED TO "SAVE" AND "LIST" AFTER TYPING IN LINES 900, 1800 and 2700.

APPENDIX 4

B5500 TSS Test

Schedule B (Basic Program)

1 Dial ....

On receipt of tone press "DATA" button. System response:—

B5500 TIME SHARING
ENTER USERCODE PLEASE

Type: ....
Response: AND YOUR PASSWORD

Type: 5500 ←
Response: line number, usercode, date, time of day

2 Type: MAKE <filename> BASIC; COPY MATIN/P08; SAVE ←
   Response: . . . .
                            . . . .
                            FILE: <file name> – Type: BASIC – SAVED

   Type: RUN ←
   Response: . . . .
                            . . . .
              ②   RUNNING
                            DATA NOW . . .
                            ?

Immediately following the "?" type in 16 numbers separated by commas, the
last being followed by "←".

   Response: **HERES WHAT YOU TYPED**
                            <Copy of input data as a 4 x 4 matrix>
              ①
                            THE ANSWER IS
                            <Inverse of input matrix>

Provided the input data is good (i.e. not ill-conditioned since this will cause a
premature halt on an error condition at point ①) the program will return to
point ② and ask:–

                            DATA NOW . . .
                            ?

repeating the process until it has executed a total of 4 times.

3 The user, after completing 2, above, may then repeat the process or amend the
   program as he thinks fit (e.g. altering the Matrix sizes) and then re-run it.

4 This should be continued for the duration of the test period.

BASIC MATRIX INVERSION PROGRAM

```
1ØØ  DIM A(4,4), A(4,4)←
2ØØ  FOR I=Ø TO 3←
3ØØ  PRINT "DATA NOW . . . ."←
4ØØ  MAT INPUT A←
5ØØ  PRINT←
6ØØ  PRINT "HERES WHAT YOU TYPED"←
7ØØ  PRINT←
8ØØ  MAT PRINT A←
9ØØ  MAT B=INV(A)←
1ØØØ PRINT←
11ØØ PRINT "THE ANSWER IS"←
12ØØ MAT PRINT B←
13ØØ NEXT I←
14ØØ END←
```

B6700 "WORKING SET" MEMORY ALLOCATION

D. P. Fenton

Burroughs Machines Ltd.,
London

A. INTRODUCTION

The B6700 MCP memory allocation scheme known as "Working Sets" bears very
little relationship to that described under the same name Denning. He
postulates certain hardware, added to a fixed length by paged store. and discusses a
suitable operating system (not just a memory allocation scheme).

There is common ground between his and our approach, insofar as we both aim
to achieve memory/processor balance by (just) avoiding thrashing, and we accept
(tacitly) his model of program behaviour.

I will describe the model as a conceptual basis from which to discuss the
implementation.

B. PROGRAM MODEL

We assume the existence of an (undefined) memory allocation scheme, which will
overlay some of the programs own areas (copy the contents to head-per-track disc
and release the memory) when that program needs something else in core. This
scheme will accept a "core estimate" within which the program will subsequently
be *required* to work, causing the program to exhibit a certain turnover of items in
core.

We then suppose that programs behave according to figure 1 which shows how
their core turnover expressed as an overlay rate varies with their total permitted
space.

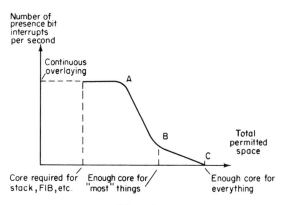

Figure 1

321

But are programs really like that? Well, if all areas of a program were referenced evenly in time, the graph would be linear between (A) and (C), with a slope which related the frequency of reference to a typical area to the time taken for disc accesses. However, some areas of a program will be referenced more often than others. If the memory allocation scheme overlays areas impartially within a program, then the frequently referenced areas will cluster into core because the program will ask for them back more often. This means that the average frequency of reference to the contents of core is higher if the total permitted space is less, which means that a second reduction of total permitted space will cause a proportionally higher number of presence bit interrupts than the first reduction, with a consequently higher increase in core turnover. Hence my suggested shape of the graph (A)–(B)–(C). Readers doubting this or charged with expanding the reasoning into a lecture, may consider the example of a man who is permitted to have use of only three out of four items:— left shoe, right shoe, watch, birth certificate. When he asks for the one he has not got, we randomly take away one that he has. Clearly, most of the time he will have the shoes and watch. If we reduce his allowance to two out of four, he will mostly have the shoes, and his frequency of exchanges will be much higher than twice the previous frequency.

C. IMPLEMENTATION

Returning to figure 1 we may state the objective of our "Working Set" implementation to be to assign the total permitted core so that the program is operated at a point such as (B), i.e. a place where "overlays happen, but not a lot".

Now the scale on the horizontal axis is not in general known, certainly varying from program to program and probably during programs.

However, the vertical scale does not vary, being bounded by a maximum overlay rate that a program cannot physically exceed, insofar as it cannot ask for more than one area simultaneously.

So we will specify a desired overlay rate for a program to operate at, and extract a suitable total permitted core (henceforth known as The Working Set — often WS). Figure 2 depicts this activity.

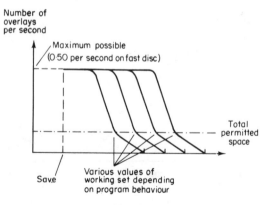

Figure 2

The fact that the graphs of figure 1 and 2 are not available to MCP is overcome by using a "cut and try" method. (That this is possible is fortunate indeed, since the form of the graphs is conjectural.) We hold, for each program, a current value of Working Set (WSSIZE'). (A prime (') on a variable indicates that there is one such variable per job. Unprimed variables are unique in the system.) When a program's core utilization (TOTAL') exceeds this, an independent runner which has been poised, like a vulture, swoops in in and starts overlaying areas belonging to that program until the TOTAL' falls below WSSIZE' again: the overlays so caused are counted in OLAYCOUNT'. This activity constitutes the "try"; the "cut" is done by GEORGE*, "every so often", by integrating OLAYCOUNT' to give OLAYFREQ', comparing that with OLAYGOAL (an operator defined system constant) and adjusting WSSIZE' if there is a serious discrepancy.

The overall picture so far is shown diagrammatically in figure 3. A detailed description of the key routines is at the end of this paper.

This figure also shows some additional features. The B6700 MCP allocates two kinds of core space — SAVE (not released till job termination and cannot be overlaid) and OVERLAYABLE (released at suitable times and capable of being overlaid). The discussion so far has assumed that sufficient of a working set is taken up by overlayable core that a reasonable turnover can be maintained. WSJUDGE (save) ensures this by preempting WSADJUSTER if $SAVECORE' > \frac{2}{3} WSSIZE'$.

WSADJUSTER provides three "byproducts" of its activities, which are available to a higher level scheduler. WSTOTAL is the sum of WSSIZE' for all active jobs (i.e. running, waiting I/O, or waiting for user events etc.). WSSCHED is the sum of WSSIZE' for all jobs in the mix (including those "ST'ed",† by operator or by the scheduler). WSINTEGRAL' is a time integral of WSSIZE': it is written back to segment zero at the end of the job (replacing the compiler core estimate) and used as a starting value for WSSIZE' next time the job is run.

An additional feature not represented in figure 3 is that, realizing that the pattern of memory accesses to program code is often very different from that to data, we organize separate WS variables and calculations for the two. (This is entirely compatible with B6700 hardware features supporting code re-entrancy.)

D. WS SCHEDULER

We now have all the programs in the mix hopefully running with just sufficient use of core to keep their overlaying to a reasonable level. However, since we did not know, when we allowed the jobs to start, how much core that would be, and we may easily reach a stage where the total of adjusted working sets (WSTOTAL) exceeds the available memory. This is readily detected by MCP (in the person of GEORGE) and suitable (low priority) jobs can be "WS-ed" (which is like being "ST' ed") until WSTOTAL falls to a satisfactory level. Similarly when WSTOTAL falls to a preset level, GEORGE will "OK"‡ jobs on a priority basis. (∗WSMAX and ∗WSMIN are required to be different (MAX>MIN) to avoid continual "jittering" by GEORGE.)

---

* The coordinating (i.e. stack switching) routine is the Master Control Program.

† Suspended by operator action.

‡ Reconsider for processor scheduling.

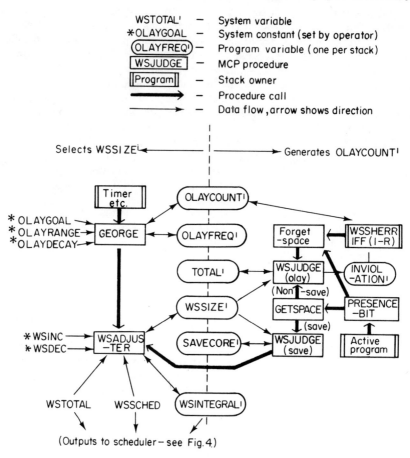

WSTOTAL' — System variable
*OLAYGOAL — System constant (set by operator)
(OLAYFREQ') — Program variable (one per stack)
WSJUDGE — MCP procedure
‖Program‖ — Stack owner
→ — Procedure call
→ — Data flow, arrow shows direction

Selects WSSIZE' ←——— | ———→ Generates OLAYCOUNT'

Figure 3

It is strongly recommended that advantage be taken of the facility of having
*WSMAX < 100% (say 95). This means that there will always be about 5% available
core, and that most (if not all) requests for core will be immediately granted, the user
not having to wait while core is cleared for him.

The scheduling system is shown in figure 4.

A virtue of this scheduler is that it will only run a high priority job if there is
genuinely enough core: to demonstrate this suppose we have the following mix
with core utilization being working set sizes as percentage of total core in the
system.

Job name	Processor priority	Core (%)
A	80	35
B	70	40
C	60	5
D	50	10

These are running well (total core <100). Then suppose we obtain (and want to run) another job J with priority 75 needing 47% of the core. SELECTION won't allow J to start because only 5% core is available, although we could force J in by using "CORE = 0;".

Using a standard MCP this would be ill advised, leading to thrashing, but using a

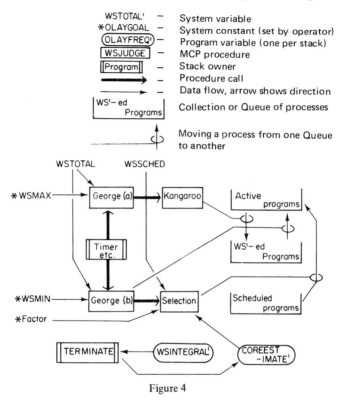

Figure 4

Working Set MCP the effect is exactly right, as the following narrative indicates, assuming *WSMAX = 95 and *WSMIN = 90.

J is scheduled with core estimate = 0 and starts running. Its adjusted working set quickly rises to 5%, when GEORGE suspends job D (lowest priority). The same thing happens for job C when J reaches 15% and job B when J reaches 20%. But when B has been removed there is room for C and D to return *and they do*. J now rises to 45% causing D to be removed, then continues to 47%. The final score is:

Name	Priority	Core (%)
A	80	35
J	75	47
C	60	5
B	70	40 (WS-ed)
D	50	10 (WS-ed)

The real advantage is not in the clever operation at the beginning of the job, although that in itself would be hard enough for a human operator, but in the fact that this automatic response to optimize first core, then processor utilization acts in sympathy with the dynamically changing composite job profile.

APPENDIX I

DETAILED LOGIC OF SELECTED ROUTINES
(drawn from release 1.10.0 of B6700 MCP)

WSJUDGE   (Called during Getspace/Forgetspace)

(a) Updates the core usage fields for the calling stack.

(b) If $SAVE' > \frac{2}{3}WSSIZE'$ then WSADJUSTER (SNR,0).

(c) If $TOTAL' > WSSIZE'$ then set INVIOLATION (SNR).

WSSHERRIFF   (Independent runner)

For each stack if INVIOLATION, searches core cyclically from location of last victim for this stack (OLAYLOC') until finds something to overlay, and does it, updating OLAYLOC'.

WSADJUSTER   (SNR, AM) Called from GEORGE and WSJUDGE

(a) AM is first vetted; and changed if necessary; first to ensure $SAVE' < \frac{2}{3}(WSSIZE' + AM)$, then to ensure $(WSSIZE' + AM) < WSMAXALLOWED'$.

(b) Update WSSIZE', WSSCHED, WSTOTAL (unless WS-ed) by AM.

(c) Set OLAYFREQ' to OLAYGOAL (until better data can be obtained).

GEORGE   (Contains housekeeping for process switching and idle loop). For the current stack (which may be leaving) and provided at least 90% of TIMESLOT' (a parameter for frequency of this calculation) has expired since we last did it to this stack, do:

1. $T := OLAYFREQ' := * \times OLAYDELAY + OLAYCOUNT'x$
(time since last computed).

$$\times (1 - OLAYDELAY);$$

2. If $|(T - OLAYGOAL)| > RANGE$ then call

$$WSADJUSTER \left(SNR, WSSIZE' \times \begin{Bmatrix} WSINC \\ \text{or} \\ WSDEC \end{Bmatrix} \times \frac{(T - OLAYGOAL)}{T + OLAYGOAL} \right.$$

Regardless of what stack we are in, examine system performance thus:

3. If $WSTOTAL > WSMAX$ and $WSVIOLATORS = 0$ then find lowest priority active non-sorting jobstack and "WS" it: i.e. say "PROGRAMMATICALLY STOPPED" and make it wait on an event WSRELAX. Its core will be lost by a process of attrition.

4. If WSTOTAL < WSMIN then if there were WS-ed stacks then cause WSRELAX, otherwise call SELECTION.

SELECTION   Moves jobs from schedule to mix. It will not do this, however, if either:

(*a*) Any stacks are WS violators, NOMEM-ed, WS-ed or ST-ed.

(*b*) (WSSCHED + COREESTIMATE$'$) x FACTOR > WSMAX.

REFERENCES

[1] *Burroughs B6700 Information Processing Systems Reference Manual* (1971), Burroughs Corporation, Detroit.

[2] Hauck, E. A. and Dent, B. A. (1968), "Burroughs B6500 stack mechanism." *Proceedings 1968 Spring Joint Computer Conference*, pp. 245–251, Thomson Book Company, Inc., Washington, D.C.

[3] Cleary, J. G. (1969), "Process handling on Burroughs B6500." *Proceedings of Fourth Australian Computer Conference 1969*, pp. 231–239, The Griffin Press, Adelaide, Australia.

[4] Creech, B. A. (1969), "Architecture of the B6500." COINS-69 Third International Symposium. (This contains many other references.)

[5] Creech, B. A. (1970), "Implementation of operating systems". *IEEE International Convention Digest*, pp. 118–119.

[6] Brooker, R. A. (1969), "Influence of high-level languages on computer design". *Proc. IEE*, **117**, 7 (July, 1970), 1219–1224.

[7] Denning, P. J., "The working set model for program behaviour". *Comm. ACM*, **11**, 5, 323–333.

[8] Wulf, W. A., "Performance monitors for multi-programming systems". *Second ACM Symposium on Operating Systems Principles*, Princeton University (October, 1969), pp. 175–181.

DISCUSSION

FENTON: Before presenting the paper on the B6700 working set I would like to mention some of the distinctive features of the B6500/B6700 operating system, particularly in connection with the use of the high level language Espol for implementation.

If you have a machine that executes Algol 60 – how do you organize a multi-programming/multiprocessing operating system on such a machine? What extensions would you find it necessary either to build into the machine or to simulate? The 5500 was a machine that executed reverse Polish using a hardware stack; it wasn't specifically an Algol machine, although it was built with Algol in mind. The redesigned 5500, which came out as the 6500, did actually execute Algol to all intents and purposes, but this was found afterwards to be inadequate *per se* for writing a multiprogramming operating system.

In order to execute Algol efficiently you need a hardware stack and each time you go through a block or procedure you need to mark the stack. These marked stack words are connected in two chains: one is the dynamic chain which shows you how to unwind the stack again when you exit from a block or a procedure; and the other is a static chain which shows you how to do the addressing. On the 6700 we have display registers which point to the relevant addressing bases. When you enter a block and declare any variable, the literal "zero" is pushed into the stack to save a word which can subsequently be used to hold whatever values you may assign to that variable; the variable is addressed relative to the display register just below it. Suppose we have a program in the outer block of which we have declared *real* x and *procedure* A, and in A we have declared *real* y (figure 1). The compiler will realize from its syntactic analysis that the outer block is at level 2 and that procedure A is at level 3 — levels 0 and 1 are needed to run the operating system. So, the compiler will know it has to generate (3, 1) as the address of y — in fact it's (3, 2). The hardware is as the first word is used for other purposes going to use display register 3 incremented by 2 as the address of y. Normally you have to allocate your own registers to do this, or perhaps shuffle numbers around at run time. The distinction here is that the display registers are special purpose and are automatically maintained when one enters or leaves a procedure.

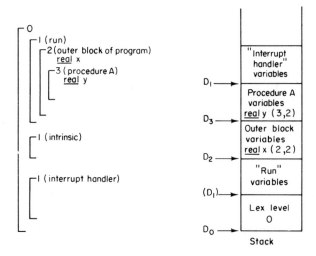

Figure 1. Program and stack structure.

So, given this machine, how do we run a multiprogramming operating system? Consider the uniprogramming case first. We have an outermost block, say zero, and within that at level 1 we have a procedure called "run" which chooses jobs to be run. Within that we have a user program at lex level 2 and this program branches out into as many lex levels as it feels is appropriate. Now this has the considerable advantage that all the user program has to do at the end of its run is to fall back, using exactly the same mechanisms, into "run" which then does the tidying up. Interrupts are handled by unscheduled procedure calls. If you are inside the user program and a hardware interrupt occurs, what actually happens is that a level 1 procedure, the "interrupt handler", is entered on an unscheduled basis so that the stack looks as figure 1. Also at level 1 are things like intrinsics — such things as mathematical subroutines, and subroutines used by the supervisor, including, of course, input/output — and for these to work correctly they must be able to see the level 0 global variables in order to do the sharing.

Suppose we want to get two programs running at once: we need to set up another stack for the other job to run in (figure 2). It has to have its own copy of "run" because "run" contains certain accounting information. However, this job's static link must point back from its own "run" to the same level zero as the first job, because when the intrinsics or "run" come to share things, or, indeed, if you start two copies of the interrupt handler running, then you've got to share the same location. Now, clearly, from the build-up of the stack that you get from the hardware you are not going to get that link pointing back as required so this, in fact, has to be forged by the software, and so you come to the first extension that we've needed: we have to have a facility for forging these control words.

The second facility that we need is the ability to initiate an input/output operation to complement the Algol machine, but the machine has been built so that the things required in the stack by that operation are Algol objects. One of them is the buffer which has to be implemented by an array in the user program. So, we

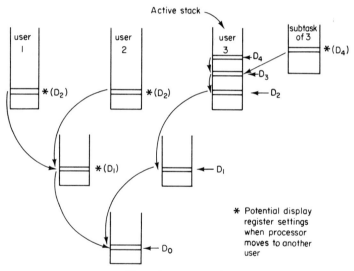

Figure 2. Cactus stack.

have in Espol something that looks like an intrinsic but which, in fact, generates a single operation, and we quote a physical unit number, which is a real, and an array, which is the buffer and which contains the operation code in its first word.

The third thing that we need is an instruction for transferring a processor from one stack to another in an organized manner. Two registers are saved in the bottom of the stack remaining: one that points to the top of the stack and one that points to the most recent marked stack word. The stack switch is performed by saving the two registers in the stack remaining and resetting them from the destination stack and performing an exit by the normal mechanism. This stack switching is done by a routine which would previously have been entered from the destination stack, so it looks as if control is being returned after an interminably long wait in the stack switching routine.

Memory management is the sort of thing an operating system has to do but which is not available in Algol. We have descriptors, or code words, and they have a base address (which points to the base of a memory area) and a limit count (which says how much of the area is theirs), and there are hardware operations for indexing and accessing words of what is obviously an array. What we do is arrange for an array that spans the whole memory to be made available to the operating system. It is declared in the outermost block and the rest of the memory allocation is programmed using Algol, with the one exception that we need to set protection tags on the two words outside the ends of an array. This is because the character handling instructions can scan the array until they hit a word that says "no"; this was felt to be a better design in the hardware than checking the limit count in the descriptor each time. The way we do this is by having a separate data type, *word,* with which we can do anything including setting the protection tags. In fact, the array for the whole of memory is a *word array,* in Algol-like terms.

McKEAG: One of the interesting things about the Burroughs machines, in particular the 6700, is that by using Algol or some other high-level language you can effectively force programs to behave themselves, look after their own protection, and, by having the intrinsics which look after the supervisor calls in an outer block of the Algol program, one can effectively pass the responsibility for the resource sharing from the conventional monolithic supervisor to the individual user programs. This could perhaps be used to make the programs co-operate along the lines of Dijkstra's T.H.E. system. In the B6700 just how much of the house-keeping of the resource sharing is put into these intrinsics in a user program and how much is in a separate level which is below the level 0 of each user program. How much monolithic supervisor is there underneath these user processes?

FENTON: There is no monolithic supervisor as such. There has to be a routine that honours the timer interrupts and says "Are things getting out of hand? I must schedule some jobs." Everything else is a matter of nested procedure calls.

The intrinsics that do any sharing, for instance the "get space" routine, use Boolean semaphores to co-ordinate the various copies of themselves, and they have to be written with this synchronization in mind. The writer of an intrinsic is allowed to say whether it can be hardware interrupted or not.

When we started writing the system we had only one processor; when we started running two processors we found that a lot of the coders had said "Well, we can't be interrupted so we don't need to set any locks". Now, in putting locks into an operating system like that, you start off by putting very gross locks in to solve your immediate problem; then you put in finer locks so that the other processor isn't held up for too long, and eventually you reach the point of diminishing returns.

Turning now to the problem of memory management. It's generally known that Burroughs use segments which contain something meaningful to the compiler, such as a data array or the code for a particular procedure. These can be loaded into core and then are accessed by the code word or descriptor. The advantage is that they can be loaded into core at any point and will automatically run at that point; this can be a disadvantage because it does make the choosing of space a little bit more difficult.

On the 5500 and in the early days of the 6500 we worked on the principle of first trying to load them into the smallest space that is available, and if that doesn't work, throwing out the segment that's been in core longest, and if that doesn't make enough space, throwing out its contiguous neighbours. Since the neighbours may be the most recently loaded pages, we found it a lot better just to have a round robin where a pointer works round the memory and throws out the next page. There is, of course, a problem with locked down store which we do make available for input/output buffers and for other purposes such as dope vectors. The top end of core contains all the locked down segments, declared as such when first allocated. This technique worked better than throwing out the oldest page and its contiguous neighbours, but it didn't totally cure the problem of thrashing when the system was overloaded or indeed of discovering when the system was overloaded.

Another technique has been implemented which Burroughs attribute to work done by Denning but which is also partly due to Wulf. For each process we establish an estimate of its tentative working set — how much memory it actually needs. There's a process, picturesquely entitled "working set sheriff", which checks whether anybody has more core than his declared or estimated working set, and, if so, throws a segment out on a round robin basis within that person's own memory. Obviously, this declared working set may not be right, and in adjusting it, our intention is to provide a fixed rate of page faulting for each process. So we have a "low-level loop" with each process demanding core and occasionally the sheriff taking it away again, thus providing an overlay frequency. There is a "medium-level loop", which runs about once a second, and which matches the actual overlay frequency of each process with the target. If necessary, it changes the process's working set estimate, and adjusts the total of working set numbers for the multiprogrammed mix, and preempts the "high-level loop". This can unschedule the processes with the lowest declared priorities until the total of the declared working sets comes down again to be slightly less than the physical core. The working set number is integrated over the run of the process and is stored back with the code file on disc so that it acts as a starting point next time. The first time a program is run we believe the compiler's estimate to start with, but the slack is very quickly taken up by the medium-level loop adjusting the working set number to get the overlay frequency right.

HOARE: Do you take any precautions against throwing out blocks that have been very recently used?

FENTON: No, we have no use detection as such. We try a little on the basis of the fact that we're doing a round robin for that process.

GOOS: Surely the effect of using a round robin scheme closely resembles that of throwing away the oldest segment, but with the advantage that the neighbours of the oldest segment are also old?

FENTON: Yes.

VINCE: One of the disadvantages of the stack organization is that space for the interrupt handler needs to be locked down and so the stack must be locked or else deadlocks may arise in the virtual store manipulation. If you adopt an overall policy that every stack has to be locked down, because there's a chance that some of it will at some time be locked down, than you might be penalizing somebody who is mill-bound and not having any interruptions and not needing the space to be locked down.

FENTON: All the stack spaces are locked down. We found on the same basis that we couldn't allow the dope vectors to move around the core. Apart from that, it does turn out that implementation is somewhat impure and the stacks do protect certain addresses, so we can't afford to lose them.

NEEDHAM: You said earlier that various cases of asking for resources were handled by different instances of the same program being activated at the same time and steering themselves through with interlocks. Our experience has been that this has lent itself either to very awkward scheduling problems or to not very good ones, because every program that has got to allocate resources has got to deal with all contingencies, and it can do this much better if it is able to consider the whole field of requests for those particular resources at the same time. Whereas, if you have a number of independent processes, which are all the same piece of code, trying to satisfy their individual customers, it's very difficult and unnatural to write them so that they survey the whole field because all they know about is the particular request they're handling.

FENTON: I accept this. I don't think we have any good answer to this at the moment.

HOARE: There's a short one – a monolithic monitor.

FENTON: Yes, it may be that we're losing something by not having this monolithic monitor. We try to put the entire system state in as a data structure so that any one of these instances can see what other requests are filed also. As a general principle, we file a request before trying to deal with it, but unfortunately this principle only evolved during the writing of the system.

NEEDHAM: I object to the mention of the monolithic monitor. All that is required is one independent process per resource to be allocated.

BRINCH HANSEN: But that's a monolithic monitor for that resource.

NEEDHAM: Yes, there's a monolithic process per particular resource.

HOARE: Monolithic, when applied to monitors, is a Homeric epithet.

RANDELL: Yes, that's my objection to it!

NEWELL: I expect in practice that these copies do not in fact run in parallel. Let's take the "get space" routine. Surely it has to block out the other copies straight away because it has to do a global assessment in order to do some kind of garbage collection; if it doesn't, it gets the schoolboy-at-both-ends effect which I'm sure Needham knew in the school photograph. The effect is that the "get space" routine is serially processing the requests.

FENTON: Yes, provided that the memory is available. If memory is not available the "get space" routine has to wait until the area that it's chosen has been emptied to disc. It's during this time that the routine must be unlocked and somebody else can ask for memory.

NEWELL: He may start organizing a clearance on his own account now.

FENTON: We can set a lock on each memory area. The first thing that "get space" does is to set the global lock and then look round the store. If it has to do some pushing out, it sets a lock on that area and then unlocks the global lock. Now somebody else can see what has happened, but the areas that are being pushed out are locked down and not available.

LIPPS: What do you think is the maximum number of users that can be concurrently in memory, and have you any figures for the system overheads, for example?

FENTON: The maximum and addressable store is a million 48-bit words. The installations that we've made in this country vary from 64K to 224K. As regards the number of users, this obviously varies tremendously on the workload and on the amount of memory. The 224K machine has two processors and we've never actually been able to start compilations fast enough to overload it while compiling. Obviously, it's not designed as a compilation machine − it's not balanced for that, it's got too much memory. On the 64K machine we can compile the operating system twice with itself before we run into thrashing, or we can get about 20 smaller student-type Algol compilations in at once. These are very inaccurate measurements from watching the console. In terms of actual processes a typical workload on the 64K machine will have between 10 and 20 stacks: some of them may be sleeping while waiting on occasional events. One of them is only supposed to wake up if there's trouble. These stacks belong to the five or six programs which would typically be sharing the single processor.

LIPPS: As a user, how much memory would I need in order to run the operating system?

FENTON: The operating system uses about 8K for its own devious purposes, but this does not include the various secret processes that it has to run, for instance, the working set sheriff, and one for organizing backing store disc (as opposed to the filing disc). As a trivial case, all the tables to control the units and the tables to control the stacks go in that 8K.

VINCE: If a user has a number of stacks and you have a multiprocessor installation, are you able to support a number of processes working on behalf of that user at once?

FENTON: Yes, we provide this feature in Algol as well. We allow you to adjust the task attributes of a process; for example, the priorities. You can find out its accounting information, and you can also see if it's in trouble. These things were originally developed for the operating system to use and we found that it was a very trivial matter to let the users use them in an organized manner by putting the array which controlled the task within their scope so that they can get at it.

VINCE: Can one process generate a software interrupt in another process?

FENTON: Yes, we have a variable type called *event* which can be used as a semaphore with wait and signal constructs. Also, you can declare an *interrupt procedure* and a construct for attaching it to an event so that it will be initiated by the event when it occurs.

VINCE: If there are a number of people waiting for an event, which is the first process to be notified, the one that first queued or the one with the highest priority?

FENTON: You get the best of both worlds. It's the one with the highest priority and if they have equal priorities then the first one in the queue.

FRASER: What happens when an operator types a command like "kill job"? What happens if there is a process waiting for results?

FENTON: The interrupt from the console brings an interrupt handler into either of the active stacks on the processors. The interrupt handler sees that this is a complex business and queues an independent process to deal with it so as not to interrupt the current user for too long. When this process is run it translates the job number into a stack number and examines the state of that stack. If it is blocked it must be rescued for the event wait queue; if it is running on the other processor an interrupt is sent to that processor to get the interrupt handler running.

FRASER: The user may be queued up waiting for a routine which is some way through allocating the resource and that the state of the user will reflect some unstable situation with respect to that resource.

FENTON: What actually happens is that the rescuing routine doesn't directly do a branch out. There is in the stack a marker where the user directly or indirectly called something in the operating system, say "get space". If the stack is waiting in an operating system routine it will not be woken up until the event is satisfied. If you kill a job that is demanding core, the job will not be killed until core is made available.

FRASER: Supposing you are waiting for something that is never going to happen and that's why the job has had to be killed?

FENTON: I suppose that could happen if the user had requested an impossible amount of memory. He's very unlikely to have done so because he could not have done it for a single dimensional array.

NEWELL: Surely all these waits are such that you have a multiple branch when you come back, one exit for success and the other for failure?

FENTON: This is done by waiting on two events: one is the event for the satisfaction of the request and the other is an emergency event. It may be that waiting for core is handled that way but I suspect not; that may be a loophole in the current system.

RANDELL: My understanding was that there were three distinct languages which I heard described as Espol, DC Algol, and Burroughs' overextended Algol. Assuming that I'm right, perhaps you could briefly describe the differences between these and indicate what's being used where?

FENTON: DC Algol — is Algol with one difference, that the job is recognized as a message control system. This means that it has a unique system number which can be put in messages either to be sent out to the data communications subsystem or to other message control systems. In all other ways it looks exactly like the overextended Algol.

When Espol and Algol were first produced on the 5500 they were very different. The Algol tried to be somewhere near Algol 60, whereas the Espol was pretty free because it was only for internal consumption. We're moving towards the point where Espol will be for external consumption, because the user will be allowed to write his own operating system intrinsics, and these will have to be written in Espol. Anything you can do in Algol you can do in Espol, so Espol is a superset, except that it doesn't contain all the clever formatting arrangements for input/output.

MISCELLANEOUS OPERATING SYSTEMS I

Speakers: A. L. Hillman and B. A. Wichmann: "Experience with the Eldon operating system for KDF9."

B. Randell (for W. C. Lynch): "An operating system designed for the computer utility environment."

Repliers: P. Brinch Hansen, R. M. McKeag, A. G. Fraser.

In absentia: J. R. Thomas: "The structure of a time-sharing system."

EXPERIENCE WITH THE ELDON OPERATING SYSTEM FOR KDF 9

A. L. Hillman and B. A. Wichmann

National Physical Laboratory,
Middlesex, England

The authors of the Eldon system from the University of Leeds have published an excellent short description of it [1], and so no attempt is made here to repeat that material. The Leeds system arose from three major additions to a very conventional multiprogramming system. These are: (1) Enhancement of the supervisor to allow more convenient and rapid access to the disc store, and to allow automatic job scheduling; (2) Provision of a multi-access program to control teletypes via a PDP8, to allow interactive editing and program preparation; (3) Integration of compilers and run-time systems into the new framework.

The system has been run at NPL since March 1970; but a number of modifications have been made as follows. The PDP8 software has been virtually rewritten for a larger core store, to allow the addition of further devices and provide a few extra facilities. Improvements have been made to the job accounting system to fall into line with the National Physical Laboratory accounting methods. Certain additional checks have been added to make the system more fool-proof.

The resulting system is very robust, in that it is terminated by software and operator errors no more frequently than hardware or suspected hardware faults. The mean time between failure is about twenty hours. This is in spite of the fact that there is no protection on the file-store, which means that by malice, a machine-code operator can easily wreck the system. The integrity of the file store is ensured largely by the use of special routines for reading and writing files, which do the necessary checking. These routines are built into the compilers and run-time systems, so that the user does not need to know the mechanisms used in machine-code for disc access. The main disadvantage of the one-level filing system is that users must have unique file-names. This means that mnemonic identifiers for files cannot be used.

The lack of job swapping means that users cannot converse with a running program — after initiating a job he must wait at the teletype for his output. The waiting time is typically two to three minutes, which the users seem happy to accept. Very few users appear to require interaction with the running program so the resulting simplification to the operating system and increased performance is very worthwhile.

Corresponding to each user who is logged into the system, there is a fixed work area of 760 words. Command processing is usually confined to work within this area, so that the disc access requirement is quite small. The code for each command is in a single segment area of just over 1000 words. This results in a very simple structure to the multi-access system. User jobs are not run within the multi-access

337

subsystem, but by means of two queues. The queues consist of fixed format job descriptions on a small area of disc. Foreground jobs are run on an extra level of the multiprogramming system when sufficient core and a program level is free. Output from such programs is ordinarily returned to the teletypes. The second queue is for background jobs, which are not processed until the user logs-out. A total of three minutes' processor time is allowed for background jobs whereas only 30 seconds is allowed for foreground jobs. As a concession, compilers are allowed to exceed these times on both queues, since the time taken for compilation rarely exceeds the limits by very much. This means that the user need only be concerned with time limits on those tasks over which he has direct control.

The majority of the user software is not "file oriented" so that very few programs write files to the disc. This largely solves the problem of protection on the disc, and also reduces disc accessing to a minimum. If all line-printer output went to the disc, for instance, it would very severely degrade the performance of the system.

PERFORMANCE MEASUREMENTS

Details of the system performance have been gathered by three means. Firstly a supervisor modification allows counts to be maintained for each supervisor call. Secondly a modification to the on-line multi-access program allows segment changes within this subsystem to be monitored. Thirdly, details of jobs executed are maintained by the ordinary accounting process.

The disc unit is a non-exchangeable device of 24 megabyte capacity, whose transfer time with typical block sizes is between 0.2 and 0.4 seconds. At peak times about 6000 reads and 2000 writes are performed per hour. This implies that a very heavy loading of the disc is almost certainly responsible for the degradation of the service at peak times. The disc file is allocated in "blocks" of 640 words, the available space consisting of 6144 blocks. About 4200 of these blocks are used for program texts, and since an average text file is about three blocks, this allows for 1400 programs. The practice is to dump the least used texts onto magnetic tape when there are about 1100 texts on the disc. The remaining disc area consists of about 850 blocks for system binary, 215 for library (kept in condensed text form), 400 blocks for users Algol binary programs, 200 blocks for machine code binary; 192 blocks reserved for scratch use.

The other significant input/output consists of about 10,000 lines of printer output per hour, and about 2000 PDP8 transfers per hour. The PDP8 transfers correspond roughly to a line of text on the teletype.

Analysis of the segment usage of the on-line subsystem reveals that only two of the 40 or so segments are very frequently required. These are the amender and the segment responsible for returning output from foreground jobs to the user. It appears worthwhile to put the small amount of code which does the return of output into the permanent part. The amender is called seven times a minute, and on four of those occasions it is already in the segment area. Hence the change suggested above would mean that the amender would for all practical purposes be core-resident (i.e. it would almost always be there). At the moment segments are called at a rate of about twenty per minute and on about 40% of the occasions the required segment is present.

The breakdown of both foreground and background jobs is roughly as follows, 27% load-and-go ALGOL, 18% assembly code translate, 17% printing of text files, 5% execution of previously translated ALGOL programs. The breakdown of the same jobs in terms of processor time is 27% load-and-go ALGOL, 31% ALGOL translate, 13% assembly code translate, 10% ALGOL execution and less than 5% for printing of files. Many ALGOL executions are done as operator jobs.

The breakdown of processor time between the various types of job is roughly as follows: 35% operator controlled jobs, 30% background jobs, 10 to 15% foreground jobs, 10 to 15% idle (in the supervisor) and 5% each in the supervisor and the on-line subsystem. The total number of all jobs processed per day is 400 to 500, but at peak periods the rate is one job per minute.

FUTURE DEVELOPMENTS

The Laboratory currently has two KDF9s. Only one is used for the on-line system, while the other is used for batch processing. The difficulty with this approach is that peak loads on the multi-access machine cause a poor response even though the machine provides a good service at other times of the day.

One technique for overcoming this problem is to link the two machines so that in peak conditions, the load can be shared. This looks a reasonable proposition since it is necessary only to move the job queue entry and the relevant files to the second machine. It is possible to consider this only because user jobs have a simple job description, and core swapping is not involved.

We should also like to connect the KDF9s to the NPL Data Network which is currently under development [2]. A simple connection is already in action for reading paper tape remotely at high speed into a KDF9. There would be considerable logical advantage in connecting all the teletype terminals via the Network. However, the existing PDP8 system exploits the fact that it works in duplex and inspects every character on input. Hence developments in this area are likely to be more difficult.

SUMMARY

Our main conclusions from extensive use of the system is given below as a list of advantages and disadvantages.

Advantages
1. The system has developed from a standard multiprogramming system without requiring substantial changes by the user.
2. No "core swapping" provides and efficient system with most of the facilities the user requires.
3. High processor utilization and integrity is provided.

Disadvantages
1. Users are annoyed by the pause (of about 5 seconds) on input of a line from the teletype. (This is caused by the slow disc, combined with a check on a line before the next one can be entered.)

2. New programmers find the editor hard to use due to a single-pass, context-only method of scanning the text.

3. Because of interpretive execution, the load-and-go ALGOL system does not process programs fast enough. This is not really part of the operating system but is very significant as far as the user is concerned. One NPL development could make a substantial improvement to this [3] .

4. Loading at peak times gives a poor response. Apart from the possibility of linking the two machines, we can encourage our users to program during the lunch breaks etc.

REFERENCES

[1]   Wells, M., Holdsworth, D. and McCann, A. P., "The Eldon 2 operating system for KDF9." *Computer Journal*, **14**, 1, 21–24.

[2]   Davies, D. W., "Communication networks to serve rapid-response computers." IFIP Congress, Edinburgh 1968.

[3]   Scowen, R. S., "Babel, a new general programming language." National Physical Laboratory Report CCU 7, October 1969.

AN OPERATING SYSTEM DESIGNED FOR
THE COMPUTER UTILITY ENVIRONMENT

W. C. Lynch

Computing Laboratory,
University of Newcastle-upon-Tyne

INTRODUCTION

The purpose of this paper is to relate the operating systems experience obtained over the past eight years at Case Western Reserve University (CWRU), with particular emphasis on strong and weak points of general significance, points which could form the basis of general operating systems principles. From 1963 until 1968 CWRU operated a Univac 1107 as a university computer utility, that is to say as a university computing centre. This system was operated under the Exec II and Exec III operating systems. The environment in which these systems operated has been previously described (Lynch [2]). Since 1968 Chi Corporation, wholly owned by Case Western Reserve University, has operated a Univac 1108 as a commercial computer utility, providing both commercial and university computer services. The 1108 has been operated under the Chios operating system. This system operates in a commercial computer utility environment to be described later in this paper.

The four operating systems, Exec II, Exec III, Exec IV and Chios form an evolutionary sequence of operating systems, the progression of which is well worth examining for strengths and weaknesses. Exec II was designed by Computer Sciences Corporation 1962, Exec III by CWRU in 1965, Exec IV by CWRU in 1968, and Chios by the Chi Corporation in 1971. Each has been based on the deficiencies of its predecessor in conjunction with changed requirements in the operational environment.

It is well worth examining the requirements for a commercial computer utility. The economic realities of time-sharing services have not, in my opinion, been widely appreciated. The original economic concept of a commercial time-sharing utility operating, say, a GE 265 or an XDS 940 fairly large numbers of customers, each representing a moderate sales of somewhere about $1000 a month would be serviced. Each of these customers require an overhead in terms of marketing and educational support. What was not generally realized in the beginning was that while the pool of customers remains stable in characteristics, individual customers flow through the system. That is, the typical customer of a time-sharing utility begins with relatively little knowledge of computers and relatively little use of the computer. The customer is sold the service by the time-sharing bureau, is educated by the time-sharing bureau, and gradually appreciates his usage from a nominal sum up to a sum of several thousand dollars per month. At this point this now large and profitable customer must leave the time-sharing bureau and seek out systems with a much greater capability. This is due to the fact that there are very few choices of systems which allow unified time-sharing and large-scale processing. Even the very successful Gecos III system still maintains a barrier between time-sharing and large-scale batch usage. Different compilers are employed and different filing systems are utilized for time-sharing and for batch processing. Conversion problems are necessarily non-trivial. Time-sharing bureaux with smaller machines do not have the processing power to economically accommodate customers whose usage exceeds a few thousand dollars a month.

As a result, large customers leave the time-sharing bureau and proceed to computer utilities operating with larger machines and a batch mode (those operated for example by University Computer Corporation or the Control Data Cybernet system) and are replaced at the time-sharing bureaux by very small customers representing a large marketing and education effort and overhead. As a result, time-sharing bureaux are in effect selling and educating customers for the large batch processing bureau. Time-sharing bureaux get the expense and batch-processing bureaux get the business.

Therefore, the computer utility, whether large or small requires a large scale processing capability so as to avoid losing the larger and more profitable customers. Likewise batch-processing bureaux do better if they also offer a concurrent time-sharing facility. The time-sharing facility may not be particularly profitable but it allows for customer development beginning with a much smaller base. It also allows the utility to provide total service to the customer rather than the customer having his computing needs serviced by several vendors. A computer utility, whether batch or time-sharing, will require a robust and well integrated system.

The second factor which was misestimated was the division of the market among time-sharing bureaux. It was initially felt that time-sharing bureaux markets would be divided more or less according to the cost of providing communication services. This has proved to be not entirely true and markets are tending to be more and more divided along application package lines rather than according to geographical distances. From a customer's point of view the tangible and intangible costs of inadequate support for particular application packages which he finds potentially valuable very much exceed any additional costs that might have to be paid for communication to a more distant bureau. Customers, very logically, would rather go a long distance to a bureau that adequately supports a useful package rather than go a short distance to a bureau that inadequately supports such a package.

To summarize then, a computer utility requires a system which is capable of dispensing a very wide range of services, from terminal services to very large computing services, all within the same integrated system. It must also be capable of doing a very excellent job of implementing certain specific packages. A further complicating factor is that the decision as to which packages to be supported can generally not be made until after the system is designed. Specifications for such a system sound very much like the specification for TSS.

EXEC II

The evolutionary history of Exec II, III, IV, and Chios and within the above environment provides an interesting case study. The systems adopted are quite different from those traditionally adopted in large general purpose time-sharing systems. For this reason a review of the history of these systems should prove to be worthwhile.

The Exec II operating systems was designed and implemented in 1962 by Computer Sciences Corporation under contract to Univac division of Sperry-Rand Corporation. The design point selected by CSC for Exec II was quite unusual. The basic design goal was to achieve as low a level of multiprogramming as possible. Such a low level of multiprogramming would allow a large amount of core store to be attached to the working programs. A low multiprogramming level together with high CPU utilization implies very little I/O wait time. This was to be achieved in the system by routing all important input/output to/from very fast drums.

The typical Univac 1107 configuration consisted of a CPU capable of executing 250,000 instructions per second together with two or more drums each containing four and a half million bytes, transferring at 300,000 bytes per second and rotating at 1800 RPM. The minimization of I/O time by routing all input/output through the drum necessarily implied the existence of a spooling system. Such a system was incorporated directly into the design of Exec II. Tape input/output, except for external recording purposes, was eliminated by also keeping all of the library materials and all of the intermediate files on the drums. As a final touch a large amount of effort was expended on the loader so as to make the absolute loader proceed at full drum rate the loss of drum revolutions at intermediate loading stages. With all of these techniques together it is possible to compile, link, and execute under the full JCS in approximately one second elapsed time. Very high CPU utilization, of the order of 90%, could be achieved provided the magnetic tapes were not used.

The Exec II design team fully believed in a low level of multiprogramming coupled with very low residence or dwelling time for the individual programs. Rather than run two one second jobs together with a 50% CPU utilization each, and an elapsed time for the two jobs of two seconds, they preferred to run the two jobs in series, each taking approximately one second, and again completing the sequence in two seconds. This provides for a somewhat better average response time and also allows essentially the full resources of the system to be deployed at the usage of each job. The alternative possible design, that of a high level of multi-programming together with a relatively smaller amount of core for each job, will of course necessarily lead to lower CPU utilization for each particular job. A high level of multiprogramming will be required in order to get a satisfactory CPU utilization. Each of the two designs, the low multiprogramming design and the high multiprogramming design, are self consistent. Whether or not either one of these forms a stable and useful configuration depends very much on additional factors.

One of the additional factors with the low multiprogramming design is the requirement for an extremely sophisticated scheduler. One might assume that with a multiprogram level of, say, one, scheduling would become extremely simple. This is not true. Maintenance of good turn around times (as described for example in Lynch [3]) depends rather critically on a sophisticated scheduler which certainly does not operate in a first come first served mode.

The low multiprogram system also depends upon spooling being carried out through fast drums rather than through slow disk units. This in turn depends upon the volume of input and output being kept small. This in turn depends upon the achievement of very low turn around times. Long turn around times means dumps and short turn around times mean interactive usage. A poor scheduler can make the low multiprogramming level mode of usage unstable and can lead to a breakdown in the operation of the system.

Several problems remain unsolved within the Exec II operating system and had to be avoided by one *ad hoc* means or another. The problem of deadlocks was not at all understood in 1962 when the system was designed. As a result several annoying deadlocks were programmed into the system. The security of the hardware left something to be desired. The 1107 was designed without a privileged instruction mode and as a result it was impossible to build good security into the system.

The use of tapes presented a problem for the system design. This was solved within the Exec II system by minimizing the tape usage. A heavy load of tape bound problems undoubtedly require a higher level of multiprogramming, thus attacking the basic design of the system. The usage of tapes has been minimized within the original system design by taking the most prominent use on second generation machines, that is the system library and scratch files, and placing these usages on a fast drum. As a result the primary mode of usage for tapes was as a file system medium since a disc based file system was not included in the system design. The inclusion of a conventional file system would have meant a higher level multiprogramming as one would certainly have had to keep the files on a physical medium other than on fixed drums.

EXEC III

The Exec III system was designed in 1965 to relieve the difficulties in Exec II caused by the deadlock and security problems. It was not intended to relieve the difficulties caused by tape bound programs or by the lack of a filing system. The 1107 at CWRU was modified by the inclusion of the now standard privileged instruction mode and the operating system was completely rewritten, making use of the new hardware, so as to completely eliminate all deadlock situations.

Exec III proved to be spectacularly successful in its approach to the deadlock and security difficulties. The system was for a long time considered to be unbreakable by user programs. This finally proved not to be the case. The system was finally broken by a group of undergraduates after they had studied the assembly language listings of Exec III for approximately 10 weeks. The level of protection provided by Exec III is, to my knowledge, unequalled by any other operating system.

This is not to say that Exec III did not have its difficulties. Certain problems appeared which were not apparent at the time the design was started. The absolute loader proved to be a nightmare. In any system, but particularly in a system which uses a low level of multiprogramming, a fast loader is essential. A loader which drops revolutions on rotating devices will prove to be impossible to live with. This requirement, coupled together with the requirement for absolute security, leads to an almost insoluble problem. Loading, of course, requires the data to be loaded together with directions as to where to load it. In any case, the addresses of the cells into which the data is to be loaded must be checked either by hardware or software for legitimacy. The requirement of not dropping revolutions on the recording medium means that a sufficient amount of buffering must be built into the loader so that the checking of the load addresses can be carried out in advance of the arrival of the information. If the load addresses are placed too near to the information to be loaded the timing constraints may become impossible.

The second set of problems were connected with deadlocks. The Exec III system was completely successful in eliminating deadlocks. However, as the system approached certain kinds of deadlock situations, the deadlock prevention mechanisms caused the system to slow down by several orders of magnitude. The approach to the filling up of the spooling areas is an example. Under certain conditions the system could be caused to slow down by a factor of 10,000. While the system had not reached deadlock and could in fact be shown never to reach deadlock, the practical effect was the same as deadlock. The only way in operational practice to remedy this situation was to stop the system and reboot it. In general one could not even afford to wait until a check point had been reached. A general lesson to be learnt from this is that very detailed, intricate and logical analysis assuring one that deadlocks can not be reached is, in general, more complicated than is required in practice and still insufficient to provide adequate practical operation. One must also very carefully analyse the operation of the system during facility shortage situations, so as to assure that the dynamic performance of the system still remains adequate. In fact, it is clear enough that assuring adequate dynamic performance in the neighbourhood of deadlocks will automatically prevent the deadlock situation from being reached. As a result of this practical experience, I now feel the detailed analysis and theories of deadlock prevention are not particularly useful in practice.

EXEC IV

The Exec IV operating system was written in 1968 as an evolutionary development of the Exec III operating system. It was designed to transfer the Exec III style of operation from the 1107 to a Univac 1108. At the same time we decided to increase the level of multiprogramming so as to be able to better accommodate tape-oriented jobs and so as to provide for an on-line filing system. The basic multiprogramming level of Exec IV was raised to two, requiring effectively a doubling of the amount of core on the 1108 over that on the 1107. This, however, allowed for the overlap of the transfer time from tape units and for the transfer time from the filing system. Afterwards, we were able to measure and observe that on Exec IV, operation with the multiprogramming level restricted to one would lead to a CPU utilization of approximately 70%. The remainder of the time would be involved in file system transfers. Raising the multiprogramming level to two together with the doubling of total core storage improves CPU utilization by approximately 30%.

The implementation of the file system was again not without its subtleties. Consistent with a low level of multiprogramming, the design called for keeping the level of multiprogramming within the disc file subsystem very low. When usage occurs the design attempts to devote most of the facilities to the handling of one job to the exclusion of competing jobs.

First, in order to maintain a low level of multiprogramming within the core storage it is still necessary to maintain most of the input/output on the fast drums rather than from slower devices such as the Fastrand II unit on which the file system storage was implemented. With the multiprogramming level limited to two this meant that there could be at most two jobs competing for the use of the file system at any given time. This in turn means that large areas of drum could be dedicated as holding areas for files during the execution of an individual job. Therefore a three-level system was introduced whereby, at the time that file accessing is initiated, an entire file structure called the Program Complex File (PCF) is transferred from the Fastrand II unit to the much faster drum units. Accessing of individual files and records then takes place on the fast fixed head drums. This means that, except for the initial loading and final unloading, all input/output still goes from the very fast drums.

This leaves the problem of optimizing the serial transfer to and from the file storage at the beginning and end of an individual run. This process is complicated by the fact that one may have up to two competing requests for file transfer operations. A system was devised whereby individual file transfers can proceed at between 70 and 85% of the instantaneous transfer rate of the Fastrand unit. This is accomplished by several techniques.

First, files are stored in physically sequential areas so that the records will follow one after another within a given cylinder on the device. Second, enough free space is left between successive blocks so that the time for "clean-up" computing at the end of reading one block and the time for "set-up" computing for the next block can be accomplished within the time which the Fastrand requires to rotate through the interblock free space. Thus, if two adjacent records are to be read this can be accomplished without losing a revolution between the record reads. This switching gap amounts to about 15% of the record length and is the main factor in determining the effective transfer rate. Thus, sequential records can be scanned off, one after another, at a rate which is approximately 85% of the instantaneous transfer rate of Fastrand.

All of this works very well provided that there is no competition for file transfers and that the only request is serial transfer request for a single job. In this case arm movement will only occur after entire cylinder of information has been read. The Fastrand requires approximately ten seconds to read a cylinder of 1.3 million bytes. The arm movement time involved in individual file transfers is thus small. Furthermore, since the cylinders are large, individual files rarely span a cylinder boundary.

If two competing file transfer requests occur simultaneously, and the Fastrand channel scheduling algorithm schedules the channel on a first come first served basis, we will observe one record being read for the first job followed by another record for the second job and then so on, alternating records between the two jobs. Since the two jobs will be accessing different PCFs it is extremely likely that these two PCFs will reside on different cylinders, leading to one arm movement for each record transmitted. This mode of operation reduces the total transfer capability of the Fastrand units by approximately one order of magnitude and is a very undesirable mode of operation.

The Fastrand channel allocation algorithm therefore was designed to give priority to that job which has last had the channel. If both jobs are doubled buffered this results in the Fastrand channel locking on to one of the jobs until it no longer issues requests for record transfers. The channel allocator then proceeds on to the competing job and services all of its record transfer requests. Thus each file is transferred at approximately 75% of the instantaneous transfer rate rather than at approximately 7% of the instantaneous transfer rate. This is again another illustration of keeping a low level of multiprogramming, performing tasks serially, and devoting all of the resources to the task at hand.

A word should also be said about scheduling with a multiprogramming level of two. Scheduling is even more of a problem than with a multiprogramming level of one. With a multiprogramming level of one priority should be given to shorter jobs so as to reduce the average turn around time. When a longer job is finally committed to execution one must wait until it is completed before a shorter job can commence. Otherwise some sort of roll-in roll-out facility is required. With a multiprogramming level of two, the system certainly has the capability of committing one long job to execution without blocking shorter jobs. The scheduler tries to avoid committing two long jobs simultaneously so that any shorter ones which may appear later are not blocked. The scheduler will, for example, hold one of the partitions open until a long job in the other partition nears completion on the speculation that perhaps a short job may enter the system. The scheduler will do this even if a long job is awaiting execution. The penalty for this reduction in the multiprogramming level from two to one is about 30% of the CPU. This case will only arise when the machine is lightly loaded. The resulting loss of computation time will thus be considerably less than 30%.

As explained in the Introduction in the 1108-Exec IV combination operates within the environment of a commercial computer utility. It is therefore desirable to allow both large and small customers to co-exist within the same system. This implies that many different terminals, both in kind and in number, are required on the system. The time-sharing type of usage requires low speed console-type terminals and, of course, a software system to support these. In particular, these terminals, due to their low input/output rate, must be operated in a very interactive mode in order to compensate for these low input/output rates. This, in turn, demands that, at least at the terminal level, a very high level of multiprogramming exist. If such terminals are to be accommodated within the system, an interfacing of the high level of terminal multiprogramming with the desired low level of execution multiprogramming must be accomplished. This is beyond the capability of the Exec IV design. Exec IV provides only spooling as a mechanism for this for interfacing requirement. Spooling alone is adequate for remote job entry (RJE) terminals but it is not adequate for very low speed teletype terminals.

For the larger users, RJE stations with their much higher capacity output devices are very desirable. Such remote card reader-printer combinations presumably would operate very nicely under spooling and could easily be accommodated within the Exec IV design. To an extent this has proven to be true but there have been difficulties. Spooling systems seem to operate rather smoothly with up to about sixteen medium speed terminals. By medium speed I mean terminals which communicate over a 2000 or 2400 baud telephone line. Beyond sixteen terminals things begin to get out of hand. First of all each remote RJE station requires a certain number of core buffers in which to carry out the remote transmissions. Obviously the amount of core required is proportional to the number of terminals hooked on. Likewise the number of accesses per second on the back-up spooling storage rises in proportion to the number of terminals. Since there is an upper limit on the number of access per second, this number must eventually be made a constant by making the blocking size proportional to the number of terminals.

That is to say, the increased transfer demands must be met by making the blocks larger and transferring them less often per line. The upshot of all this is that beyond approximately 16 terminals (on, for example, the 1108) the amount of buffering core required tends to go up quadratically with the number of terminals.

With this RJE problem one can pursue the other alternative. It is possible to increase the number of blocks per second that can be handled by the spooling drums by resorting to a sector queueing technique rather than to a first come first served technique. Analysis indicated that the potential of the 1108 drums in this respect is quite large. The system could require a modest amount of core storage (less than 1000 bytes) for maintaining the spooling system provided the system employed the sector queue technique. Such a technique, however, requires rapid (~100 microsec) response to interrupts and this in turn is prevented by the rather complicated Exec IV loader which is required in order to obtain high loading rates. The security of this loader demands that interrupts be locked out for a very long time, thus placing severe transients upon the spooling system and negating any possible good we might get out of the sector queue technique. An operating system with much better response time characteristics is clearly required.

CHIOS

It is clear enough that some of the difficulties within the Exec IV operating system are the result of pursuing an old operating system design. It is also clear that the effectiveness of Exec IV on the jobs that it is intended to do a direct result of this old design in which one desires to keep the level of multiprogramming very low and apply serial rather than parallel processing techniques. In designing the Chios system the question really was "How can we avoid throwing out the baby with the bathwater?" How can one introduce a higher level of terminal parallelism into the system while still retaining the very considerable benefits of serial processing.

The answer, of course, lies in the fact that there are different kinds of multi-programming. In a roll-in roll-out time-sharing system, for example, the level of multiprogramming viewed from the terminals might be 40 or 50 (that is, you might have 40 or 50 terminals on-line). On the other hand, the level of multiprogramming viewed from the processor or core may be only one, since, at any given time, there may be only one job in the core ready to compute. One can create the illusion (and often the substance) of large, slow multiprogramming by means of small fast serial processing. Let me illustrate just some of the ways that this is applied in the design of the Chios system.

First of all one can observe that processes, and particularly the processes that are a part of the software system, have the characteristic that their state word tends to be small when they are inactive and tends to be considerably larger when they are processing. A design should, therefore, avoid many levels of interruption (and the required saving of large state words) unless these levels serve some useful function. The purpose of interruptions, of course, is to improve the response time of certain processes at the expense of the response time of other processes. In many cases improved response time has no value. For example, there is no point giving 10 ms response to a person at a console since he will be absolutely unable to distinguish between 10 ms or 100 ms as a response time. To improve response in this case is valueless and if the degradation of terminal response time (say, from 10 ms to 100 ms) can be used to improve the system in other respects certainly that would be a valuable trade off.

Within the Chios system only four levels of parallel execution have been defined. Each of these has an associated order of magnitude response time. The highest priority level has an implied response time something on the order of 5 microsecs and is used primarily to implement command and data chaining within the I/O system. The next level of response has a characteristic response time of approximately 300 microsec and is used in the first level processing of interrupts. This level is particularly useful in maintaining the sector queueing on the drums. The next level of response is typically about 20 ms. This would be used, for example, in dealing with tape errors. Errors on the tape are relatively infrequent and it is not particularly important to have blocks reread and the errors corrected in a very small amount of elapsed time. The processing of tape errors by means of code overlaid from drum, a response time on the order of milliseconds, allows a great deal of core to be saved. The last level has a characteristic response time on the order of a few hundred milliseconds and is ordinarily used to respond to teletype terminals.

All parallel processes are sorted into one of these categories and a process is run to completion within a category before the next process of the category can begin. The level of active multiprogramming is restricted to the number of categories which is, in this case, just four. In addition to this, the categories dealing with the faster response times (command chaining and interrupt handling, for example) have small and well-controlled statewords. Even when they are interrupted they occupy only a very small amount of core. This low level of multiprogramming means that more facilities, such as core, can be allocated to an individual process at the time that it is computing. This results in much shorter execution times than might occur in a system with a higher level of multiprogramming.

This concept has also been applied to the filing system. A generalized three-level storage has been created with a software paging mechanism that is responsible for the transfer of data between the Fastrand storage and the fast drum storage. These transfers are to be generalizations of the file transfer mechanism successfully employed in the Exec IV design. The level of multiprogramming on the file storage channels and the level of multiprogramming on the drum are to be kept small, and a large amount of facility is to be devoted to each particular task. Only those jobs which are currently active should have their file space loaded from file storage onto the drums. Likewise, a file transfer channel is to be devoted to the transfer of a reasonably large quantity of information.

In solving the RJE spooling problem Chios utilizes drum sector queueing, blocking in place on the drum, and an on-line adaptive determination of the optimum core block size. The parameters of a model of the dynamics of the RJE terminal are determined adaptively and the optimum in-core block size is calculated. These blocks are transferred to/from the drum by a sector queue technique. Drum area is assigned so that these core blocks are automatically assembled into larger, sequential drum blocks suitable for transfer to the third level of storage.

WHY NOT TSS?

It was observed in the Introduction that the requirements for such a computer utility system were very closely matched by the descriptions of general purpose time sharing systems such as TSS.

The contrast of design philosophy between these systems and the CWRU/CHI systems seems to be rather great. It should also be noted that systems such as these have had, in the past, their difficulties in performing efficiently. There is in fact not such a wide difference between the Chios design and design of paged operating systems. They are, rather, two sides of the same coin. Time-sharing systems have evolved essentially from functional specifications. The Chios system has evolved essentially from performance specifications. The functional specifications of the Chios system are beginning to approach those of the paged time-sharing systems, and, hopefully, the performance specifications of the paged time-sharing systems should be approaching that of the Chios system.

There is every prospect of this happening. Consider, for example, the paper by Alderson, Lynch and Randell [1]. This paper illustrates the fact that thrashing problems in paged systems are due to an unstable positive feedback loop between the in-core level of multiprogramming, the amount of core allocated to each job and the loading placed upon the paging drum. Other examples of such instabilities are implicit in this paper. For example, the performance of the file transfer channel deteriorates as the level of multiprogramming on the channel is raised. Likewise a positive and potentially unstable feedback loop exists between the turn around time and the amount of output materials to be handled within the system (see Lynch [2]).

CONCLUSION

If there is a single lesson which the CWRU systems have illustrated over and over again over the past eight years, that lesson is that a serial, hence timewise asymmetric, allocation of facilities will lead to much higher system performance than a parallel or time-wise symmetric allocation of facilities. Serial allocation algorithms have proven to be much more difficult to construct than the corresponding parallel allocation algorithms but their results have amply rewarded their efforts. Such design efforts have required in the past and will continue to require in the future a more or less complete understanding of the dynamics of a proposed system. Perhaps operating systems design will soon become science rather than a black art.

REFERENCES

[1]   Alderson, Lynch and Randell [71], "Thrashing in a Multiprogrammed Paging System," *Proceedings of the International Seminar on Operating System Techniques,* Queen's University, Belfast, N. Ireland, September, 1971.
[2]   Lynch [67a], "Description of a High Capacity Fast Turnaround University Computer Center," *Proceedings of the 22nd National Conference of the ACM,* 22 (1967), 273–288.
[3]   Lynch [67b], "Evolution of Computer Operating Systems," *1967 IEEE International Convention Record,* 10 (1967), 18–22.

THE STRUCTURE OF A TIME-SHARING SYSTEM

J. R. Thomas

British Post Office
Telecommunications Headquarters,
London

INTRODUCTION

The Digital Equipment Corporation PDP 10 is a general purpose stored program computer that includes a central processor, a memory and a variety of peripheral devices. Several time-sharing supervisors are available for this machine, the one described here being the PDP10/50 Swapping Monitor, a version which uses random access discs and drums for both file storage and swapping use core images.

The supervisor is constructed from a number of distinct, relatively independent functional modules. It can be tailored for any particular hardware configuration by including only those modules which are required, and by the use of conditional compilation facilities with each module. The major parts of the monitor considered here are the command decoder, the interrupt and input/output system, the scheduler and the swapper, and the file handler. In order to appreciate some of the functions the monitor must perform it is as well to consider the system interface as seen by a user and his program.

THE USER VIRTUAL MACHINE

The monitor implements a virtual machine for the user programs to run under, and in which the address is divided into two separate and distinct areas (the high and low segments) which are mapped into physical memory by means of the two hardware relocation registers. Both segments are dynamic in size and are allocated memory in increments of 1024 words. Whilst the hardware is capable of operating on data or obeying instructions from either segment, user programs would normally make use of the shared program facility, in which the high segment is write protected and contains only pure code and constants, whilst the low segment is used for variable data. Thus if several users are executing the same sharable program the monitor arranges to map each of these users high segments into the same physical area, whilst allocating individual areas for the low segments (figure 1).

The first part of the low segment (the Job Data Area) is always reserved for storing specific information of interest to both the monitor and the user program.

COMMUNICATION WITH MONITOR

The usual method of communication between the user program and monitor is by means of a group of instructions (Unimplemented User Operations — UUO) which

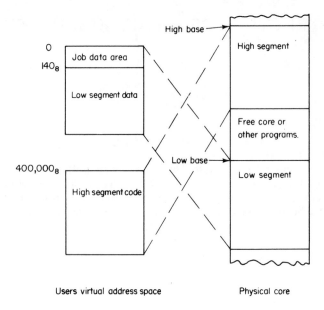

Figure 1. Mapping of logical to physical core.

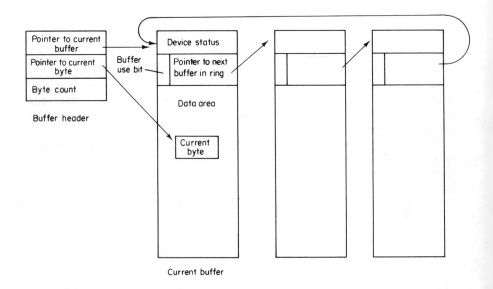

Figure 2. User input/output buffer header and buffer ring.

result in a hardware action similar to that of an interrupt. Under the present Monitor there are several types of UUO's, some have no valid meaning and are treated as illegal instructions, others are used to request some monitor action on behalf of the user program, whilst yet another group simply return control to a previously specified point in the users program, and can be used to implement a form of user specified extracode.

USER INPUT/OUTPUT

Under normal circumstances monitor will dispatch to a user program in such a way that the hardware will prevent it from issuing any explicit input/output instructions. All such operations are performed by monitor at the request of the user program and facilities are provided to assist the user in handling input/output buffers. On request monitor will set up a ring of buffers and a buffer header block which references the ring in the users low segment. The monitor service routines run asynchronously and in parallel with the users program, both using the individual buffer usage bits to synchronize and interlock (figure 2).

Provided the user request the monitor to set up his buffers his program need not be concerned with the peculiarities of any particular device, and input/output will be device independent for binary or character transmission.

USER TERMINAL FACILITIES

From the users point of view his console can be in one of two states — monitor mode or user mode. When in monitor mode, each line is treated as a monitor command, a command is terminated by a carriage return, whereupon the line of text is passed to the command decoder for analysis and action. Certain commands start or reactivate a users program, in which case the console is placed in user mode and is then available as an input/output device for communication with the users program. Whilst the console is in user mode monitor still examines input characters as they are received. One particular character (control C) suspends the user program and returns the console to monitor mode. A very useful feature is that any monitor command can optionally be abbreviated, and provided it is still unique will be correctly recognized by the command decoder.

RESOURCE ALLOCATION COMMANDS

The monitor allocates peripheral devices to users upon request, and these devices then remain allocated to the user until he explicitly returns them, or logs-off the system. When a user requests the allocation of a device he references it by its physical name, but at the same time he may assign it a logical name, which may then be used in all subsequent references to the device.

PROGRAM CONTROL COMMANDS

Facilities are provided which allow a user to copy an image of his core to any file
in the filing system, and also to load his core area from any such core image file.
The user has a choice of at most four entry points to a program. He may start the
program at its normal initial starting point, or re-enter it at its secondary entry
point where it would normally attempt some form of recovery and perform only
partial re-initialization. Alternatively he may continue its execution at the point
where it had been suspended if he had returned his console to monitor mode, and
finally he may activate a conversational debugging routine if it had previously been
loaded with his program.

BACKGROUND JOB COMMANDS

There is not necessarily a one-to-one relationship between jobs and consoles. Whilst
a console is always required to initiate the execution of a program a user may then
disconnect or detach his console from the job. The console is kept in monitor mode,
the user is free to run any other programs, whilst the detached job continues to
execute in parallel. Should a detached program attempt to communicate with
its non-existent console it is suspended until a console attaches to it. For security
reasons any user attempting to attach his console to a detached job must submit
the password of the originator.

THE INTERRUPT STRUCTURE

The PDP10 hardware incorporates seven priority interrupts levels, and any device
can be programmed to interrupt on any one of these levels. Whilst an interrupt is
being serviced a higher priority interrupt can occur and would be serviced immediately,
but interrupts occurring at equal or lower priority levels are delayed. The hardware
also provides the facility to switch on or off all or selected interrupt levels, and
artificially cause an interrupt to occur on any selected level. All the interrupt service
routines for devices on the same level are linked together, and when an interrupt
occurs each service routine for that level is activated in turn, until the device
causing the interrupt is detected by its own particular service routine. Before
proceeding further the interrupt service routine will initialize a stack pointer to a
data area, which is permanently reserved and unique for each level. Having saved
any necessary programmable registers on its stack the routine is then free to service
the interrupt using its stack for subroutine links and temporary or local variables.
Having performed the necessary service function the interrupt routine will always
restore the processor to the state existing at the time of the interrupt.

THE COMMAND DECODER

A command decoder is called from the clock interrupt routine every 20 milliseconds.
The routines responsible for accepting characters from consoles at the interrupt

level maintain a count of the number of monitor commands awaiting analysis and the command decoder only proceeds if this count is greater than zero.

The command decoder is divided into three main parts. The first part is responsible for scanning the console input buffers looking for any console which has input a monitor command, and sets up a byte pointer to the start of the command string. If the command passes some simple initial verification it is compared with a table of legitimate commands. Provided a single unique match is found some further validity checks particular to the command are performed, and a dispatch is made to the appropriate command routine.

The second part of the command decoder consists of a set of command routines, each routine being responsible for performing the functions associated with a single command. For certain types of commands the job may have to be in a suitable state (e.g. job in-core) and if necessary the command is delayed, and command processing for that job only resumed when it is in the correct state. Subroutines are available to scan the command string for various types of parameters which the command routine might require.

Having completed the function appropriate to the command, the third part of the command decoder performs certain clean-up functions such as setting the console to user or monitor mode, requeueing the job, and decrementing the "pending command" counter.

MONITOR INPUT/OUTPUT

For every physical device and for every active disc file monitor holds a Device Data Block (DDB), which describes the characteristics of the device and its status. All of the DDB's are linked together on a chain and monitor is only aware of the existence of a device by searching along the DDB chain for the required device by name — either physical or logical. In addition to the devices physical and logical names each DDB also contains the owners job number, pointers to the users buffers, the current device status and file name etc. (figure 3).

The input/output functions in monitor are in three distinct parts — a device independent section, device dependent routines and the interrupt service routines. An I/O request from a user program causes entry into monitor where the request is decoded and a dispatch made to the appropriate functional routine (e.g REWIND, READ, WRITE, etc.).

Having performed all the device independent functions, the DDB is located, either by scanning the DDB chain, or by indexing a table in the users job data area by the users logical channel number, and a pointer in the DDB is used to dispatch to the appropriate device dependent routine. This arrangement makes it possible for all similar devices to share the same dispatch table, or even for different devices to share a common functional routine.

In particular the READ and WRITE routines are responsible for advancing the user program buffer header to reference the next buffer in the ring, and inverting the buffer use interlock bit. If there are no more buffers available (as indicated by the use interlock bit) the job will be moved to the I/O Wait Queue, and if the device is inactive and there are sufficient buffers for it to transfer then it will be started.

An important feature of device independent is the way in which requests for device functions which are not available (as distinct from invalid requests) are ignored and a normal return to the users program. Thus if a user program attempts to make a directory entry for a file sent to the line printer, the request is ignored and the program continues correctly.

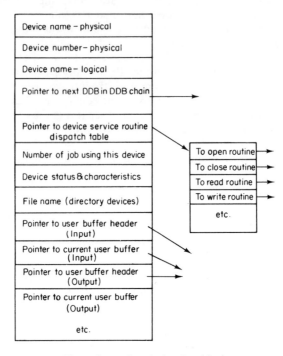

Figure 3. Monitor device data block.

The interrupt service routines are only concerned with responding to the device interrupt, checking for transmission errors, and in the case of character-oriented devices performing byte transfers between the users buffers and the device. After the successful completion of a buffer transfer the interrupt routine will stop the device if no more buffers are available and if the job was waiting to transfer it from the I/O wait queue to the I/O wait satisfied queue. In addition if more buffers are pending the routine will advance the buffer pointer in the DDB and initiate the next transfer, provided the job is not scheduled to be swapped out.

THE SCHEDULER

The primary function of the scheduler is the selection of the next job to be run — or more precisely the next user program which is to receive a quantum of processor time. In the PDP 10 Monitor the algorithms for processor allocation and physical core allocation are inextricably linked together — core space for a program is allocated or recovered as a function of the likelihood of its receiving processor time. Also incorporated in this module are the associated functions of core shuffling and job swapping.

The scheduler is normally activated at every clock interrupt (20 milliseconds), but may also be activated at any time by other monitor routines if the currently running program changes its state so that it becomes unrunnable. The monitor contains a number of job queues which together reflect the state of all jobs in the system. Each queue has a fixed priority in relation to other queues, and within any queue the position of a job determines its priority within that queue. The majority of the queues are used to hold jobs which are suspended waiting for some condition

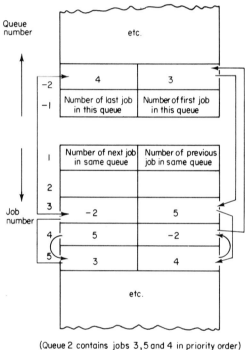

(Queue 2 contains jobs 3, 5 and 4 in priority order)

Figure 4. Monitor job queue table.

to occur — waiting for console input, waiting for disk storage etc.; but there are also three run queues which hold jobs waiting to receive processor time. The three run queues also have a priority order and each receives a different quantum of processor time (figure 4).

QUEUE TRANSFERS

If the scheduler was entered from a clock interrupt, then the quantum time for the current job is decremented, and if its time allocation has expired the job is moved to a different run queue of lower priority. When a job changes its state various factors influence which queue the job is transferred to.

A job entering a wait state is moved to the low priority end of the appropriate wait queue. A job having completed I/O is transferred to one of the run queues, the larger jobs being assigned to the lower priority run queues. A job leaving any other wait queue is usually placed at the head of the highest priority run queue, thus pre-empting all other runnable jobs. A highly computer bound job will receive a single quantum of processor time in the highest priority run queue, and from there it progresses to one of the lower priority run queues, where it receives longer quanta of time, but less frequently.

JOB SWAPPING

Jobs are moved in core, and between core and disc by three routines — the core shuffler, the swap-in routine and the swap-out routine. The swap-in routine is responsible for bringing jobs from disc into core, and depends upon the core shuffler. and the swap-out routines. At every clock interrupt the scheduler calls the swap-in routine, which scans the job queues in descending priority order looking for a job on disc which it could bring into core. Having found such a job it then compares the size of the job with the largest unused core area, and if sufficient room is available a transfer is initiated. If this attempt fails there may be sufficient unused core space but fragmented, in which case the core shuffling routine is called to combine the unused core areas by moving some of the in-core jobs.

To create sufficient space it may even be necessary to swap some other job out to disc. The swap-out routine scans the job queues in reverse order (lowest priority first), looking for a job or jobs of lower priority than the one to be swapped in, and giving preference to write protected segments.

To minimize the amount of swapping activity, each job when brought into core is given a minimum residency time as a function of its core size. These values are decremented for all in-core jobs and only those jobs which have exceeded their residency time are considered as candidates for swapping out.

Under certain circumstances a job may not be moved in core, nor swapped out to disc, if for example it is actively performing input/input. In this case the attempt is delayed, and a new attempt made when the swapping routine is next activated.

THE FILING SYSTEM

The file handler module of the monitor is responsible for maintaining the file structure of the disc system. A user may create any number of files, each file being of any size, and the file handler automatically allocates space for a file as it expands, without requiring an explicit user program request to do so. The structure maintained by the monitor are generally transparent to the user who addresses logical records within a file.

Disc space is allocated using a storage allocation table (SAT) which is a bit map indicating the free or in-use status of each physical block. The SAT is held as a system file and is available to any user as a "read only" file.

Directories are organized as a two-level tree, the Master File Directory (MFD) at the head of the tree acts as a directory for the individual Users File Directories (UFD), which themselves act as an index to the users files. The organization and access mechanisms for the MFD and UFD are identical, each entry consisting of a two part name and a pointer to further retrieval information for the file. This further information includes a repeat of the file name, the date and time of creation, the date last referenced, the mode or type of file, the number of blocks in the file and a protection key. In addition each block of the file is referenced by a pointer and is sum checked (figure 5). By organizing the directories in this

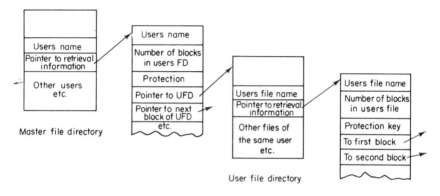

Figure 5. Monitor directory structure.

manner, and isolating the file names from the access information, directories are kept small and reasonably efficient directory look-ups can be performed without having to resort to hashing techniques. For file protection there are three categories of user recognized — the owner, other members of the project, and all other users. The protection key in a files directory entry allows the owner to specify the access modes available to each of the above user categories — read only, read and write, or change protection.

Any number of user programs may simultaneously be reading the same file, and there are three modes of writing a file. It is possible for a user to create an entirely new file, to create a new version of a file which will automatically supersede the old version when it is not in use, or to modify selected blocks of an existing file. This organization seems to be a good compromise between efficiency of storage and speed of access, and also permits a reasonably rapid reconstruction of the SAT should it be suspect.

THE ROTATING MEMORY HANDLER

This part of the monitor is responsible for all data transfers to drums and discs with both fixed and moving heads. It is used by the file handler and the swapper, is predominantly device independent, and primarily attempts to optimize on a queue of access requests. All requests for access to the rotating memories can pass through two queues, a position wait queue and a transfer wait queue. (There is also a controller wait queue which will not be considered here). The position wait queue is used for access requests which require head movement, and is bypassed for fixed head devices — they always appear to be "on track". The transfer wait queue is used for all requests which involve some access delay due to the rotation of the memories. Requests are selected from the queues to minimize head movement, and rotational delays. To provide a reasonable response to all users a request is not allowed to wait in a queue indefinitely, every so often the optimization algorithm is bypassed and the longest waiting request is selected. Requests made by the swapper are given the highest priority and they also bypass the optimization process.

SYSTEM RECOVERY

Any detectable processor fault causes an interrupt at the highest priority level, even if monitor was executing at some lower interrupt level. If monitor was running at the time of the error an attempt is made to recover which often results in the loss of a user job, or at worst halts the processor.

Whilst this is by no means complete or foolproof it is usually sufficient to detect and recover from the majority of errors that can occur when testing a new version of the monitor.

Should the monitor appear to be malfunctioning the operator can opt to halt the machine and restart via one of a number of re-entry points, some of which perform such minor re-initialization that they do not destroy all users core images; so that some useful recovery is possible in this manner.

BATCH FACILITIES

A "pseudo-teletype" facility is provided whereby any user program may open an input/output channel to such a device, and all communication is then treated by monitor as though coming from a normal user terminal. Thus any user program has available all the facilities offered to a user at his terminal, and this feature can be used for multi-tasking etc.

A Batch Control program can be initiated by the operator and runs as a "detached" user program. It will read job commands from various input devices which are assigned to it, and controls the execution of user programs via the pseudo-teletypes. Whilst this approach has some disadvantages, it does unify the job control language and guarantee compatibility between programs run under time-sharing and batch.

CONCLUSION

The design approach adopted by DEC has resulted in an operating system which is conservative in its use of core store, and in its demands on processor time. The interface presented to a user is simple and convenient to use, and terminal response is quite acceptable, probably as a result of the monitor being fully core resident.

REFERENCES

PDP 10 Reference Handbook.
Program Logic Manual for PDP 10 Time-Sharing Monitor. (DEC-10-MRZA-D).
PDP 10 Remote Batch Users Manual. (DEC-10-NUZA-D).

DISCUSSION

WICHMANN: The Eldon system is designed for a second generation machine and yet the user obtains from it facilities which I think more elaborate systems fail to provide. The reason is that the system has essentially grown up from the standard manufacturer's operating system for the KDF9 computer. This multiprogramming system allowed for four user programs and the enhancements made were the provision of more convenient disc accessing within the supervisory program, automatic job scheduling, the use of one of the multiprogramming slots for a multi-access system controlling teletypes and, unfortunately, the integration of the compilers and the run-time system to fit within this new framework. We have made a number of minor modifications but basically the overall system architecture remains unchanged; we envisage making further improvements in the future which would be extremely difficult with some of the more elaborate systems.

The KDF9 core store is partitioned into the Supervisor of about 3.6K, the on-line system of about 2.7K and then there is the possibility of three user programs. The Supervisor, which is not overlaid, is a grown-up version of the standard multiprogramming supervisor and provides facilities for the loading of programs, the allocation of core store, the allocation of peripherals and an off-line output system. Core allocation is done by core sliding; programs cannot increase in size but, can reduce the amount of core store they require. Because of a hardware protection feature peripherals can be accessed directly by user programs; the exception is the disc store which is used by all the programs. The off-line output system is mainly for the line printer output: lines are output from the user programs onto shared magnetic tape under Supervisor control and the tape is later transcribed by a user program; we find this to be very successful in that the time taken to transcribe the output (of the order of half an hour) is small in relation to the turnround time at NPL.

The on-line system consists of a fixed area, ten words to hold information on each of the thirty-two teletypes connected, an overlay area of about a thousand words, and a work area of seven hundred and sixty words. There is one overlay per

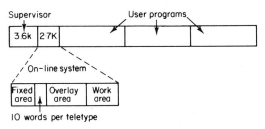

Figure 1. KDF9 core store layout.

command. The actual control of the teletypes is done by a PDP-8 computer which buffers the lines and does the code conversion. When the operating system receives a line it loads the correct overlay and processes the line until a hold-up occurs; the overlays are pure code and the required one may already be in the overlay area and so need not be reloaded — this happens very frequently with the editor.

The system is fairly robust in the sense that the rate of software error tends to be substantially smaller than the rate of hardware error. The basic Supervisor provides no protection on access to the disc store so we have some special routines and this gives adequate security: we've only once lost the contents of the disc as a result of lack of protection.

Within the on-line system the user can edit files and do a number of other simple tasks that can be managed in the 1000 words (2000 or so instructions) that are allowed to the overlays. Because of the original multiprogramming system we decided not to allow job swapping, so that if you want to compile and run a program you put the job into the "foreground queue" and you are unable to continue on-line until all your answers are written out to your teletype. This proves to be reasonably effective for program development which is the sort of work that we do at NPL. Since you can't have job swapping you must arrange a rigorous time schedule, so jobs in the foreground queue are done on a first come first served basis and are limited to thirty seconds of CPU time. For the compilation and execution of typical Algol programs of three or four pages you wait about two minutes at the teletype for your output; bearing in mind the speed of the machine this is very reasonable. We have also a "background queue" of batch jobs which are not so limited and whose output goes to the line printer.

Since this has been a development of a simple multiprogramming system the majority of the users' software is not file oriented; in other words users tend to output to the line printer rather than to files. This has the advantage that we don't have a file security problem. We are rather anxious to reduce file writing as much as possible as we have to keep disc accessing down to a very strict limit: at the moment when the system is running twenty teletypes the disc is running at 80% of its full capacity.

Our main conclusions are that one can provide quite a reasonable user facility by a relatively simple addition to a standard multiprogramming system; and that a lack of core swapping, although horrifying, does provide the user with quite substantial facilities. One does get; even with such a system, quite high processor utilization and reasonable integrity. A disadvantage: it's frustrating; the users are annoyed by a pause of typically five seconds on inputting a line through the teletype. The reasons for this are that there is a single-buffering system with the PDP-8 and the line is validated completely before you are allowed to type the next character; also the disc is very slow with an average access time of about 120 msec.

NEEDHAM: Could you explain that? Surely you don't write each line to the disc as it's received?

WICHMANN: No, you have to bring down an overlay to interpret the line, so there are about three transfers for each line.

HOARE: One way of getting over this annoyance is to send blank characters out to the teletypes while the machine is thinking. You come to the end of the line and it goes "blip blip blip blip blip" and then you're there.

WICHMANN: That was one of the first modifications we made to the foreground queue where a wait of two minutes is even more frustrating. In fact that was one of the modifications that caused the greatest increase in user happiness.

NEEDHAM: You said that inputting a line caused three disc transfers. This would suggest, according to the peak time figures given, that three-quarters of all the disc transfers are caused by handling individual lines of text. I should have thought that would be a place to change.

WICHMANN: Yes, there's an error in the system design in that the user isn't given any option but to get every line validated on input. Leeds have partly overcome this by batch processing a number of lines so as to reduce the number of transfers; it made a 30% improvement.

NEEDHAM: The original designers of the system may have made an inappropriate choice as to how they should have used the limited disc capability. It would have been preferable not to validate the material at all so that they would have had enough disc facility left in hand to be able to provide more of a filing system.

BRINCH HANSEN: I must say I like the paper very much; it's simple to read and understand and it brings out an important point: efficient sharing of equipment among a group of users requires a range of operating systems, each geared to a limited form of service in a most efficient and simple manner. As Wichmann pointed out, there is in this system a sensible division of jobs according to response time requirements. There is multi-access to a fixed set of programs for editing and job preparation where the response requirement is of the order of a few seconds; there is a foreground batch queue where the response time is of the order of minutes; and there is a background queue where I assume that the response time is of the order of hours.

I have recently seen a similar division of workload at the University of Waterloo where they have a range of operating systems on three different machines. One of these, a very simple batch system, takes care of about 1000 undergraduate students, and removes the majority of the load from the larger machines.

The attitude taken at the University of Waterloo, and by Wichmann and his colleagues, is that the only thing that a keyboard terminal is good for is precisely the same as an ordinary typewriter, namely typing pieces of text. The main thing from the user's point of view is to get fast and informal access to a machine with rapid response. The idea of computational artistry — inventing systematic ways of testing your programs — changing your mind about what the program ought to look like — at the speed at which the computer can execute instructions and you can type, is to my mind altogether ridiculous and is avoided in this system.

HARTLEY: How many potential users of the KDF9 are there, and how many of these do actually use it? What I'm trying to find out is how successfully your system caters for your users.

WICHMANN: I'm constantly trying to answer this question myself. We have about 200 people with log-on names, and each week about a hundred people use the computer, and the total user community is about four hundred. To a certain extent we are in open competition with commercial time-sharing systems which are available in the Laboratory. The problem is that some of our software is difficult to use.

HARTLEY: If you are getting 50% of your population to use it and 25% to use a bit every week you're not doing too badly.

McKEAG: It's very interesting to see that such operating systems, which because of

limited hardware only provide certain limited facilities, are found to be quite
adequate by a great many users; this fact is often forgotten by designers of the
general purpose operating systems. Admittedly there are occasions when one does
require the more complicated and more expensive facilities. The Titan system
provides two modes, one of which is relatively cheap and relatively available for
simple interaction, simple editing and so on, and the other is the more complicated
and more expensive mode of full interaction. What extra facilities, which are not
present because of the limitations of the hardware, would NPL like and would be
prepared to pay for by less efficiency of utilization of resources; what extra
facilities do you think would justify the extra cost?

WICHMANN: The limitations are not just a matter of hardware; they're a matter
of firmware. The system is a modification of the standard ICL system and that is
where most of the limitations come from. If you started from the basic hardware
of the KDF9, you could write a substantially better multi-access system but we
weren't in that position, and within the framework with which the Leeds system
is devised it does fairly well.

What things could one do if one were starting from the hardware? One could
provide interactive processing with some fairly rigid rationing system. One could
provide a better disc access system; and tune one's compilers to the multi-access
system.

RANDELL: Lynch's paper is different from the normal description of yet another
operating system and is an attempt to distil a large number of years' experience on
a succession of operating systems developed for Univac 1107 and its successors.

The first of these, Exec II, was built in 1962 by Computer Sciences; this system
on the 1107, for the typical Fortran job shop, considerably outperformed the IBM
equivalent, to the considerable embarrassment of the IBM software people. The
Exec II had a very good drum and made brilliant use of it. The set of systems
analysed by Lynch describe the consequences of that original decision. From his
paper you get a very different definition of an operating system from that of
Hoare who implies that the idea of an operating system is to share resources; from
Lynch you have the feeling that the idea of an operating system is to avoid sharing
resources. A goal of Exec II and its successors was to minimize multiprogramming.
Multiprogramming, like sharing, is not a good thing, it's something you're forced
into. In order to get away with a very low level of multiprogramming it was
necessary to minimize input/output waiting; this necessitated a spooling system
(to a fast drum, not to a flailing arm disc) and an extremely fancy loader, moving
information between the drum and core store at very high speed.

The Exec III system, which was developed in 1965, was used at Case Western
Reserve University for a completely open job shop with multiple remote job
entry, with no operators, with students queueing up at terminals, and achieving
a five minute cycle time between successive inputs of the same job. That was on a
very heavily loaded system where the computer room tended to look rather like
Grand Central Station.

They wanted to minimize input/output waiting; they also wanted to minimize
input/output, and a very good way of doing that was to give a very good turn
around. If that turn around time went up then so did the amount of output the
people wanted. At 9 o'clock in the morning when the system was switched on there
was a great rush of users causing an initial transient that might take some hours

to work out. What they did was to schedule not only the system but also their users: they chopped any job that had been in the system for more than an hour waiting for execution; thereby 9 o'clock was no longer an especially good time to get on the system. From then on it was very unusual to see a job in the system for more than 5 minutes, and within a very short time not a single job was ever chopped. In scheduling, you have to realize that the users are taking countermeasures and you must have countermeasures to their countermeasures.[1]

The problems in Exec II which led to Exec III were the problems of deadlock and security. Exec III avoided all deadlocks but could get itself into the state of working at only 1/10,000th of its more normal operating speed. It wouldn't deadlock but it would make such slow progress that you couldn't even wait until the job had reached a restart point in order to, as Lynch so elegantly puts it, "re-boot" it. Lynch looked very askance at formal logical treatments of the problem of deadlock, which is much more of a statistical problem than a logical one. The same for security: they believed that Exec III was absolutely secure until a very good group of undergraduates, having been challenged to break the system, did so in ten weeks when armed with complete listings.

Exec IV followed three years later because of the transfer from the 1107 to the 1108. It was intended to provide for tape jobs and also to provide some on-line filing. They made a great step in this system: they grudgingly went up to a multi-programming level of 2. As a result the filing system was designed very differently from what you might otherwise expect: large chunks of file store are moved at vast speeds from the disc to the drum and are only then accessed.

The reasons for Chios are to deal with a far larger number of remote job terminals than the fifteen or so that Exec IV supports, and also to enable ordinary teletype terminals to be added on in fair numbers. Lynch makes the point that when you have fifty or sixty jobs active (in the sense of being attached to users who are sitting in front of terminals) then this isn't necessarily the same sort of multiprogramming as the multiprogramming that is used to cover up input/output waits.

There is a resemblance to the BCC1 system[2] which was designed by a group of refugees from the University of California at Berkeley. They wanted to investigate the problems of providing a time-sharing system to a very large number of terminals, but they didn't like the figures they got when they scaled up core store size from the fifty-terminal systems that they had designed beforehand to about five hundred terminals. Therefore they went back to a multiprogramming level of 1. In the BCC1 system the plan is to use almost the entire store for the one job currently being executed, together with the previous job, which is on its way out to the drum at a vast speed, and the next job, which is on its way in. The operating system is distributed amongst a set of special purpose high-speed mini-computers; in particular, one of these is looking after the problems of scheduling drum transfers and allocating drum space to ensure that in general a job can be swapped in and another one can be swapped out in just one revolution of the drum. So the BCC1 system and the Exec series of systems really have a surprising amount in common.

Lynch characterizes the Exec systems as evolving from performance specifications

---

[1] Coffman, E. V. and Kleinrock, L., "Computer scheduling methods and their countermeasures," AFIPS Spring Joint Conference, pp. 11–21, 1968.

[2] Greenberg, M. L., "An algorithm for drum storage management in time-sharing systems," *Third ACM Symposium on Operating Systems Principles,* Palo Alto (October, 1971).

rather than from functional specifications; right from the start they've aimed at getting excellent performance and in the succession of systems they have gradually added functional capability. This is very different from several large operating systems that have always had great functional capability and are gradually evolving into having good performance. Clearly one would hope that these two roads to heaven will meet rather than pass.

It's very important to realize how phenomenally successful this set of systems has been. The essence of the point that Lynch is trying to make is that serial allocation leads to a higher performance than parallel allocation; and that, although serial allocation algorithms are considerably more difficult to design, they can be, and they are, worth it.

FRASER: At Bell Labs I have been looking at the way they design communications gear: it's a system that is assembled from a lot of components, some of which are as difficult to analyse as are the components of a software system; but there is an extraordinary difference between the ways in which these two industries set about designing and manufacturing their products, and I think that what Lynch has shown is that it is definitely possible, even in the computer industry, to behave like an engineer and manufacture systems to a specification.

There are some difficulties: when you're trying to make something for an unknown market. If you engineer it too highly it's pretty difficult to change it. Almost the first program that I wrote after leaving university was to analyze Stock Exchange data; I wanted to get high performance out of Pegasus which was a drum machine with delay lines, so I was forced to write an algorithm that was very dependent upon the serial properties of the drums and delay lines. It ran like the wind and the customers were very satisfied. But they wanted a slight modification and that just about killed the whole project. The program had been engineered to slightly the wrong specification, and so highly engineered that it was well nigh impossible to change.

HOARE: May I endorse the approach of both speakers? My only regret is that Randell has produced an artificial conflict between my views and Lynch's. Whether you share by time-slicing or by space-slicing is to me a matter of efficiency and technique; I also prefer time division multiplexing for the same practical reasons that Lynch does.

LIPPS: On the problem of serial or parallel working I agree with what has been said, but it depends on what sort of hardware you have, what your balance is between CPU speed, I/O speed and memory size. I would question whether one can make a general statement that serial processing is generally more efficient than parallel processing, it's a matter of degree.

RANDELL: The point that is implicit here is not that serialism is always to be preferred to parallelism but rather that multiprogramming level is rather like the number of passes of a multipass compiler: never accept n unless you have convinced yourself that n−1 is not sufficient. You can be sloppy with the scheduling and convince yourself not that n but that n^2 is necessary; if you put more money into the scheduling you can bring n down; if you bring n down then you can do the same job with less resources.

WICHMANN: I have an example to illustrate the problem of "serial versus parallel". The Technical Support Unit of the Department of Trade and Industry decided to do a series of tests which were concerned with Fortran compilations and executions.

There were nine tests altogether and, almost as a joke, they decided "Oh, let's try this multiprogramming lark." Putting all the programs in at once, every multiprogramming system (and they tried quite a few) took longer than doing one after another and the time with one system was 54 minutes as against only 26 minutes when done serially.

BRINCH HANSEN: I have come to the conclusion that human beings can only think in terms of highly sequential processes and it now turns out that equipment evidently has the same limitation. My favourite example is that of teaching history; history is a highly concurrent process that can be taught in different ways. When I was at school we learned it country by country, Danish history, German history, English history, and so on, and at examination time I could faithfully reproduce Danish history, etc., but if my teacher asked me "Could you give me a cross-section of European history around 1830?" I started to do a lot of sequential searching in my mind. Nowadays you present history almost as one revolution or catastrophe after another, and you make time-slices across European or world history. But I strongly suspect that if you ask the student "Could you explain to me what happened in Denmark in the last century?" the student will do a lot of sequential searching again but in the orthogonal direction.

As human beings we can only understand concurrent processes by looking at sequential sub-sets of them, and people who say that some day we'll have equipment which permits parallel execution down to the instruction level and that we must start looking for the ideal language for expressing that degree of parallelism are living in a fool's paradise. Even if hardware development came to that stage we would still find ourselves partitioning our problem into fairly large sequential chunks which we could analyse step by step. It's certainly worth remembering that for reasons of understanding and efficiency we should try to design our operating systems as sequentially as possible.

HOARE: Dijkstra says that the task of the programmer is to produce reasonably deterministic results. Parallelism is a feature which, if it is essential at all, is always capable of producing indeterministic results; and therefore if for some reason — efficiency mainly — you feel that you have to go parallel this is always an unfortunate necessity. A final comment is that programmers who demand that their programming languages should be able to express parallelism, collaterality, tasking, or whatever it's now called, really do not understand their own best interests.

FRASER: The analysis of serial systems is easier than for parallel systems; however, mathematics isn't used very much in the design of computer systems. When I was talking to one of our engineers at Bell Labs. about designing a file system; he asked me why I hadn't done the traffic engineering on it. It was almost the first thing that he would have done, and if I did it at all it would have been almost the last thing I would have done.

VINCE: This system relies very much on the fact that you've got a fast drum available and you're spooling on to it from slower devices to cover up their input/output waits. What worries me from the point of view of a commercial manufacturer is the file integrity, because you're bringing files from the file store to what is essentially a more volatile medium, and doubling the number of transfers.

RANDELL: Let me correct one misconception: Exec II might have been built by Computer Sciences Corporation but it was under contract to Univac, and this was in fact a standard system on the 1107 machine. It was very much a commercial success so if there were problems they must have been surmounted.

HUXTABLE: The time during which a file is open in a multiprogramming system is longer than it need be in a single programming system, so Lynch's system seems to improve the problems of file integrity and not increase them.[1]

NEWELL: I must say I feel like someone who's had his religion kicked from under him. The last sentence that "Serial allocation algorithms have proven to be much more difficult to construct than the corresponding parallel allocation algorithms but their results have amply rewarded these efforts," may be fine in a batch environment but how on earth does it work in an on-line one with large random access files or even large serial ones? The amount of drum space you need if you have fifty users, each with a program and three files open, must be phenomenal.

BRINCH HANSEN: I think the sentence should actually read "Good serial allocation algorithms have proven to be much more difficult to construct than the corresponding bad parallel allocation algorithms."

RANDELL: They tried very hard, knowing the relative speeds of drum and disc, to do a good engineering job of calculating buffer sizes and number of buffers. Very often people have used multiprogramming as an excuse for avoiding taking on the very complex task of designing appropriate buffering. The other point is that the multiprogramming that you do for terminal interactions and terminal waits is something that's done on a device like a drum and not in core.

LIPPS: One point that somewhat reconciles these two aspects is that buffering is fine if you have sequential data sets, and in this case you can do a very good job provided you also have sufficiently fast access and sufficiently good discs, which is exactly the case in the Univac situation and is by no means the case in the typical IBM installation. Time-sharing brings with it many small programs which require random access to small amounts of data. That's the sort of situation that you cannot combat with a large amount of buffering and therefore the best you can do instead is to have a larger number of jobs in parallel.

[1] LYNCH: The fast file transfer was added at the Exec IV stage and is peculiar to the Chi (commercial computer utility) environment. File integrity is in fact maintained by a combination of the basic reliability of the I/O devices and the very low exposure times conjectured by Huxtable. Since the disc copy is not deleted until the updated file is copied back to the disc, the file is vulnerable only during the actual file transfer.

MISCELLANEOUS OPERATING SYSTEMS II

Speakers: D. J. Howarth, "A re-appraisal of certain design features of the Atlas I supervisory system."

G. Newell, "On unifying a batch system with a multiaccess system." (by H. P. Goodman)

Replier: C. A. R. Hoare

A RE-APPRAISAL OF CERTAIN DESIGN FEATURES OF THE ATLAS I SUPERVISORY SYSTEM

D. J. Howarth

Institute of Computer Science.
University of London,
London

1. INTRODUCTION

The Atlas I Supervisory system was designed, in parallel with hardware design, during the early 1960's. At that time the concepts of operating system design, and of the services required of operating systems, were quite undeveloped, and to that extent, the design was a pioneering effort. The present paper reviews some of the important design features in the light of improved understanding of the problem, and draws the conclusion that the principal weaknesses of the design lie in the different characteristics of the "virtual machines" seen by the supervisor and by the user programs operating under supervisor control.

The aims of the Atlas system are reviewed in Section 2. It is important in any critical discussion of a product to recognize the tasks that the product is designed to carry out; it is all to easy to confuse discussion of the design with discussion of the aims of the design. The aims resolve themselves in practice into an implementation of a "virtual machine" occupied by user programs, and the characteristics of this machine are reviewed briefly in Section 3. This virtual machine is that described in most of the published Atlas literature; it is the machine which the user "sees". It differs in many important respects from the "virtual machine" used by the supervisor itself. Section 4 outlines the significant characteristics of the supervisor virtual machine, emphasizing the design criteria which dictated the differences between supervisor and user virtual machines.

These differences affect markedly the effort required to design and maintain the supervisor, and the consequences of the differences are discussed in Section 5. We then investigate the extent to which the virtual machines could have borne a closer resemblance; it is concluded that, in order to achieve this whilst maintaining the characteristics which make the virtual machines suitable for their particular tasks, major architectural revision would be necessary. Not surprisingly, the result of a successful pioneering effort is an awareness of the architectural features which are desirable in future comparable systems.

2. AIMS OF THE ATLAS SUPERVISORY SYSTEM

The aim of the Atlas I supervisory system was to implement what is now known as a "remote-job-entry batch system". Users were expected to submit jobs, either via a human operator or remotely over a data link, which would be processed by

371

the system and the results returned to the user, again through the medium of an operator or over the data link used to submit the job.

The prime objective behind this system was the efficient exploitation of a hardware system capable of time-shared operation (in that processor and peripherals could function in parallel, time-sharing the central stores of the system), and involving in particular a fast processing unit. It was regarded as more efficient to implement a batch mode of operation than an interactive mode, both in terms of the exploitation of real resources and in terms of the activity of users. There can be no doubt that the design objective was achieved in terms of real resource utilization; in particular, the processing unit utilization achieved is higher than in any other comparable system.

In order to achieve this objective, the real resources of the system are mapped into a set of virtual machines, each of which comprises a subset of the overall real resources together with supervisory procedures which manage these resources and the mapping, and provide additional services. The virtual machines are protected from each other by the mapping mechanisms, so that multiprogramming may be exploited to enhance real resource utilization. We shall describe in following sections the salient characteristics of these virtual machines, and contrast these with the environment within which supervisor activities function. It is convenient to describe the virtual machine as a picture of a hypothetical real machine, comprising a processing unit, a store, and mechanisms with which it can communicate with its environment. In a real machine, the environment comprises peripheral equipments; in a virtual machine, the environment is supplied by the supervisor, and may comprise supervisor facilities, filed information, peripheral devices, and processes in other virtual machines.

3. THE USER VIRTUAL MACHINE

3.1 The processor

The processor is capable of obeying a sequence of instructions each of which couple a register with an operand by means of an elementary operation, leaving the result in the register or in store. The operand may be a literal, the contents of a store location, or the contents of a register, and in some cases the operand is not used (e.g. an instruction to standardize a floating point accumulator). Literals and store addresses may be modified by the addition of the contents of one or two registers.

The registers comprise an accumulator, which can be used for either fixed or floating point arithmetic, and 90 fixed point registers, or B-lines, which can be used for fixed point arithmetic and as modifiers. There is addressing capability for accessing 127 B-lines, but B lines 91–127 are used by the supervisor, and are in general not visible to the user virtual machine.

The instruction code of the user virtual machine comprises some five hundred instruction codes, of which about half are implemented by the hardware processor, and the remainder, known as Extracodes, are implemented by supervisor software. To this end, extracodes use fixed registers not visible to the user (nine B-lines together with a few words of a private working store).

The processor can be assigned to a user virtual machine, or recovered from a user virtual machine, at any time by restoring or preserving the registers and extracode work-space in the main store. Since, as we shall see later, all reference to other real resources is by a virtual name, the real environment can be altered at will without effect upon a user virtual machine, so that re-assignment of processor in no way affects the dynamic mapping of real resources. The appearance to the user virtual machine is of dedicated use of a processor, and the user is unaware of the re-allocation of the real processor.

The design of the processor is strongly influenced by the requirements of high-level languages. The single accumulator is suited for use in common assignment statements; the large number of index registers eases the task of dynamic mapping; ability to re-assign the real processor without implying the structuring of store or peripheral references allows a freedom to compiler writers which leads to compilation of efficient object code.

3.2 The store

The virtual store, which holds instructions and operands, comprises a number of blocks of information; each block is of size 512 words, and blocks are uniquely numbered in the range 0–1791 (decimal). These blocks are mapped by the supervisor onto the real storage devices, core store and drum, implementing what is known as a "one-level store" system. The processor can only access information resident in core, and blocks of information are transferred to core store when their need is signified by occurrence of a "non-equivalence" interrupt. The mapping mechanism is assisted by hardware associative address conversion if the block resides in core; the associative store, or "page address registers" contain the block label, which is compared with the requested block label, and contain a single digit which is not visible to the user virtual machine, but which allows the supervisor to share the page address registers.

Under supervisor control, any block label may be used, provided a pre-specified total number of blocks is not exceeded. Thus, users, and especially compiler writers, can use scattered virtual addressing to implement a simple form of segmentation. Note, however, that blocks of a virtual machine store are in no way protected within that virtual machine-presence of the block implies read and write access permission; they are, however, totally protected from access by any other user virtual machine. The absence of selective protection leads immediately to the total separation of virtual stores; there is no possibility of sharing information in a protected manner by sharing areas of virtual store.

3.3 Communication with the environment

3.3.1 *Communication with fast peripherals*

The virtual machine can control, by use of supervisory routines, fast peripheral devices including disc and magnetic tape. Blocks of information may be read from or written to these devices; assignment of the devices is by request for assignment of a titled device, the title being recorded in the form of an information block on the disc area or magnetic tape. The access method may be serial or, on blocked devices (such as disc or one-inch magnetic tape), may be random access to numbered blocks.

3.3.2 *Communication with serial peripheral files*

Character and line peripherals such as paper tape or card devices and printers, are not controlled on-line by user virtual machines. The user virtual machine "sees" one or more sequential files which can be accessed by extracode instructions to move characters or records between the files and virtual store. The information so transferred is essentially device independent; the files are assigned to the virtual machine again by assignment of titled objects. The files may be transient, forming a supervisor-controlled buffer between user and real peripherals, or may be permanent, recorded as a user file on disc or tape; files cannot be shared at any one time between different user virtual machines.

3.3.3 *Communication with the Supervisor*

This communication is achieved both by the use of extracode instructions, during execution of a program, or by statements in a job description or job control language. The extracode instructions can invoke supervisory routines to assign and control fast peripherals and serial files, and to call for other supervisory functions such as starting and ending processes, control of virtual store etc.

The above mechanisms of communication with the environment are well suited to the jobs which are principally concerned with data-processing, be they scientific or commercial. The device independence of serial files, the system buffering, are all features which can be exploited both by user and system. It is, however, in this area that the user virtual machine appears most restrictive, and it is in this area in particular that the supervisor virtual machine shows the most marked divergence.

4. THE SUPERVISOR VIRTUAL MACHINE

Because the nature of supervisor activities is such that they interact one with another, and because the batch system relies on time-sharing the supervisor (in control of peripherals) with user programs (using processor), the user virtual machine is not a suitable vehicle for use by the supervisor. Switching of activities would be slow, due to the number of central registers involved, and there is no mechanism at all for communication between virtual machines. The design therefore incorporated a distinct supervisor virtual machine (or SVM) and we describe below the chief differences between the SVM and the User Virtual Machine described above.

4.1 The SVM processor

In order to avoid costly switching of registers and extracode working space, the SVM processor comprises 11 B-lines (distinct from those of the user virtual machine) and the hardware implemented order code. Other registers can only be used by explicitly preserving and restoring their current values; extracode instructions cannot be used since, amongst other properties, they rely on return link set for user processes but not set for supervisor activities.

4.2 The SVM store

In common with user virtual machines, the supervisor itself uses a virtual store, comprising block labels 1792—2047 (decimal). It also uses two further "segments" of store — a read-only store, and a working store which is used in the same way as permanently locked-down core store. The conditions attached to the generation of non-equivalence interrupts are different from those relevant to user virtual machines, however; supervisor activities are obeyed one-at-a-time, and the processor cannot be reassigned without cognisance of the supervisor activities, since they make specific reference to the real environment, and this environment must be changed only when expected by supervisor activities. Since one-level store transfers themselves change the environment, it follows that supervisor activities must in some sense be aware of such transfers; the rule applied is that following any such transfer, a supervisor activity is resumed not at the instruction causing the transfer, but at a "re-entry address", preset by each activity, from which it can reconstruct any environmental features which may have changed. This consciousness of the mapping of virtual store is in direct contrast to the total unconsciousness displayed by a user virtual machine.

4.3 SVM communication with the environment

4.3.1 *Communication with peripherals*
In contrast to User Virtual Machines, the SVM communicates with peripherals by use of unprotected executive routines, suppling a device identifier as a parameter. Theoretically, any SVM can access any device, and special precautions are required in the executive in the event of changes in device identifiers. Such changes can occur by the physical redistribution of peripheral equipments (e.g. a switch of magnetic tape units on channels).

4.3.2 *Communication with other supervisor activities*
All SVM's share a common virtual store (comprising blocks of one-level store together with fixed (read-only) store and working store). They can thus communicate freely via shared store, and there is need for synchronization in access to common store areas. In some instances, private "semaphores" are used to guard access to common resources; in most cases, however, the fact that the processor is never re-assigned to another supervisor activity without cognisance by the current activity is used to ensure uninterrupted sequences of instructions where required. Although an efficient technique, this approach invites abuse in that the possible occurrence of non-equivalence interrupts must be carefully foreseen — these cause suspension of the current activity, and care must be taken to ensure consistency of all common data whenever such a suspension occurs.

5. CONSEQUENCES OF DIFFERENT VIRTUAL MACHINE CHARACTERISTICS

We have outlined the differing nature of the virtual machines created for the user and the supervisor, and have shown how these differences are a result of conscious design aims to achieve efficiency in the differing tasks these virtual machines are called upon to support. These differences have consequences which have serious repercussions on the construction and maintenance effort consumed by the supervisor. The salient consequences are as follows:

1. The tools and services made available to user virtual machines are not applicable to SVM's. For example, compilers designed to produce object code using the register and store structure of the user virtual machine are useless in the environment of an SVM, with its different register and store structure.

2. Although both virtual machines use a virtual store, the SVM must to some extent be conscious of the mapping onto real store. The particular rules applied, whilst logically sound and highly efficient, are a potential source of obscure errors, and are very difficult to implement in any language other than assembly code.

3. The ease with which the user virtual machine can handle peripheral devices of various types is not carried through to the SVM, which is aware of differing peripheral characteristics.

4. The resilience afforded to user virtual machines by their protected virtual store is not available to supervisor activities, with their common virtual store; for this reason, it was considered not worthwhile to protect the executive interface, and so one error in a supervisor activity is sufficient to invalidate the entire system.

5. The free, undisciplined communication between SVM's is to be contrasted with the absence of any communication between user virtual machines. These two extreme positions are a direct result of design aims, and contribute to the high performance observed, but emphasize again the fundamental difference in characteristics.

6. IN SEARCH OF COMMON VIRTUAL MACHINES

It is apparent that the differences in virtual machines are to be deplored even though they result in high performance. On the one hand, supervisor construction is rendered non-standard and complex, and SVM's are unprotected one from another. On the other hand, although user virtual machines reflect the independent nature of batch jobs, the lack of communication facilities and facility to share store areas makes them totally unsuitable vehicles for other applications such as dedicated time-sharing or transaction processing.

It is clear from the above analysis that an attempt to preserve efficiency whilst using common virtual machines would involve fundamental architectural changes, of which the following are examples:

1. Controlled communication between protected virtual machines demands a *segmented* virtual store, with segments individually protected (e.g. read only, read-write, execute only) and individually shareable between virtual machines.

2. Protected SVM's demand a protected executive interface, at which all reference to real resources are logical references, invariant to changes in the real environment.

3. Software extensions to the instruction code must be "invisible" to SVM as well as user virtual machine, and should be capable of recursive use. The obvious implication is hardware implementation of a stack to record procedural history and provide local work space.

4. If SVM's and user virtual machines are to have a common register and store structure, processor switching time demands a redesign of the associative store

mapping, to include process number as well as block number in the mapping. Demands of processor switching efficiency also require a redesign of the register structure to avoid the penalty of swopping large banks of registers, whilst preserving the advantage of compilers of a flexible register structure.

CONCLUSIONS

We conclude that the performance of the Atlas I supervisor system has justified the use of different virtual machines to implement the tasks of the user and supervisor; we further conclude that these differences impose penalties in terms of flexibility, design effort and resilience, but that to overcome these differences requires fundamental architectural redesign not only of software but of many major aspects of hardware.

ON UNIFYING A BATCH SYSTEM WITH A MULTI-ACCESS SYSTEM

H. P. Goodman

ICL,
Putney,
London

INTRODUCTION

George 3 is the major operating system for the larger members of the ICL 1900 Series of Computers. The decision to produce a large batch operating system for the 1906 and 1907 (the top end of the range as first announced) was taken in late 1964. In early 1965 a clear marketing requirement appeared for a multi-access system for the 1907 — this was christened MOP (multiple on-line processing). After some preliminary design work on both George 3 and MOP it rapidly became apparent that the two systems had much in common and a decision was taken to implement one operating system for both batch and multi-access work. The consequences of that decision form the subject of this paper.

Since a multi-access capability was one of the early design aims of George 3, these facilities are built into the heart of the system rather than being added on afterwards. In some cases, of course, compromises had to be made between multi-access and batch requirements but such cases turned out to be few—in nearly all parts of the system it was found possible to design facilities that would suit both batch and multi-access users. Detailed discussion of three areas — the filestore, the command language and swapping — now follows.

FILESTORE

The heart of the George 3 system, as it now exists, is the file store. This contains many different sorts of file both for use by the system itself and by user programs. The George 3 file store is basically a tree structure with all but the terminal nodes occupied by directories. Each directory corresponds to a user of the system and the tree structure mirrors a hierarchical structure among users — users may have other users below (i.e. inferior) to them in the tree structure as well as terminal files. The depth of the tree may vary widely from one installation to another (subject to a maximum depth of 64) depending on the requirements of the installation.

The diagram below represents a simple example of a filestore. Square boxes represent directories, round boxes represent terminal files. Some of the names on the right-hand side of the diagram will be explained later in this paper.

Terminal files, i.e. all the files except directories, each have an owner (i.e. the immediately superior user) who has the power to permit or deny access in various ways to the file both to himself and to other users. Files can only be created and erased by their owners. There is also an elaborate system of incremental dumping on magnetic tape which serves two purposes — it preserves the filestore against the possibility of corruption due to a system error and it allows little used files to be kept off-line until required on-line thus allowing the total filestore to be larger than the on-line filestore.

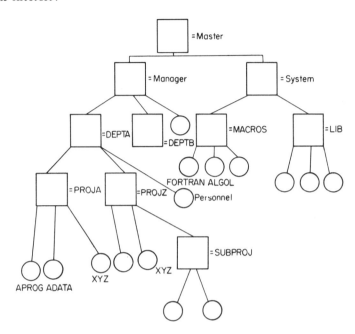

All these aspects of the George 3 filestore are the sort of thing one would expect from any self respecting general purpose multi-access operating system. Since these facilities are available, it was found that they could also be of great use to batch jobs. Batch users can profit equally with multi-access users from the facility of keeping programs and data in files which the system looks after. They do not have to concern themselves with such mundane matters as where exactly their files are and what to do with files which they must keep in case they are needed — they all go into the filestore and have only to be referred to by name to be recalled and opened by the system. The security system which protects against unauthorized access is also valuable for the patch user.

Since the filestore is designed as an integral part of the George 3 operating system, it can be used by the system for its own purposes. For example, standard items of software, such as compilers, are kept in the filestore where they can be made generally available. They are kept under a special user called SYSTEM and all users are given EXECUTE access to such files. These items of software are, however, perfectly normal files and all the usual filestore mechanisms can be used to operate them. It is, for example, a routine matter to replace a compiler by a later version and any installation can easily replace compilers or other software issued by ICL. The filestore is also used to hold job descriptions and macro commands for running user and systems programs — this will be discussed more fully later in the paper.

There are a number of files in the filestore which are used for internal purposes by the operating system. For example, George 3 includes a tape librarian. This keeps records of all magnetic tapes known to the system against owners. Each user directory contains, besides the names of files belonging to the user, information about tapes the user owns. There is also an overall file containing details of all tapes. Then if a tape is requested by the name in the header label, for example, the system can look up the serial number and ask the operators to load the tape. The system will not allow one user to access another user's tapes, except with his permission. This tape librarian system is clearly a facility for batch users but it was made possible by the provision of the George 3 filestore which was initially aimed at the requirements of multi-access users.

A standard feature of batch processing operating systems is off-lining of input and output — sometimes called spooling. Input data from cards or paper tape is read onto backing store before it is to be read by the object program and similarly output from object programs goes to backing store for later output, at the system's convenience, to printers and punches. In the case of George 3, this concept has been combined with the filestore. Programs and data can be read into the filestore at any time from cards or paper tape. Each program or piece of data becomes a file which can then be read by a subsequent job. The user can choose whether to leave the file in the filestore for subsequent use (e.g. a source program which he may wish to edit and recompile) or whether to erase the file once read. Output also goes to the filestore and the user explicitly lists all or part of it as required. Again, he may retain it for re-input to a subsequent program or not as he wishes. All these things can be done equally well for multi-access and batch jobs. In particular, the multi-access user, after off-lining (that is, filing) the output from his program, can then choose whether to list it on his console, on a printer (to be sent to him by post) or both. Often he will wish to see a few lines on his console before deciding to print it on a line printer. Similarly input from a console can go into the filestore and even later be used with a batch program if required.

THE COMMAND LANGUAGE

Any batch operating system requires a job description to be submitted with each job. This job description has been written in what may be called a language, though in many contemporary operating systems this language bears little relation to a programming language — consisting mainly of lists of parameters. Multi-access jobs also require operating instruction — in this case these instructions are typed by the programmer on his console. The language used for multi-access commands is usually much more like a programming language — usually consisting of a series of statements or commands, each of which consists of a verb and a number of parameters.

It was an early, and fundamental, decision in the design of Geroge 3 that the same language would be used for both batch and multi-access type jobs. The George 3 command language is very like a programming language with short individual commands. Each command consists of an optional label, a verb and a variable number of parameters. There are a great many elementary, or built-in, commands; some users say there are too many but casual users only need to remember a subset of the available commands. Nearly all the commands can be used by both batch and multi-access users, though there are a few exceptions.

Some examples of commands:

```
2LAB    LOAD    FRED
        ASSIGN *CRO, DATA
        ENTER
        IF NOT HALTED LD, GOTO 2LAB
23X     GOTO 2LAB
```

In the case of multi-access users the commands are, of course, typed one at a time and executed as they are typed. In the case of batch jobs the whole job description is read in first into a file and the commands executed from there. No attempt is, however, made to compile or pre-scan the job description — commands are read from the file and interpreted in exactly the same manner as if they were being read from a multi-access user's terminal. The multi-access user will often wish to see the result of one command, or job step, before inputting the rest; the corresponding facility for batch users is the IF command, which allows a great many conditions to be tested and alternative actions specified. The batch user also has a facility of declaring action to be taken on any command error — usually a jump to an error routine. This facility is not needed for multi-access users who can take direct action in such an eventually.

A multi-access user frequently needs replies to various commands output on his terminal. To give the batch user a corresponding facility we invented the "monitoring file". This is a file produced for every job run under George 3 which records the complete history of the job. It usually contains copies of all commands obeyed by the job, various messages and replies, time used etc. This information is recorded both for batch and multi-access jobs but in the case of multi-access jobs some or all of this information (at the user's option) is also output to the terminal. For example, the LISTDIR command requests a list of the names and properties of all files belonging to the user issuing the command. The MOP user gets the information on his terminal, the batch user will find it in his monitoring file when he gets his job back. The monitoring file is normally printed automatically for batch users, but not for multi-access users, at the end of the job. This facility was originally designed purely for compatibility but it turned out that the complete job history thus provided was a very valuable facility for the batch user. Besides using his terminal for the input of commands and the output of replies to such commands, the multi-access user may wish to use his terminal to interact directly with his program — i.e. for input and output of data. Instead of his program's input channels being connected to a file in the filestore or to on-line peripherals, he may request input for one or more channels direct from the terminal. The system then interprets read instructions on the specified channel (usually the program thinks of it as a card or paper tape reader), as a request for input from the terminal. Similarly, one or more output channels can be specified as the terminal and the system will direct (and label) the output accordingly. We wished to provide analogous facilities for batch users. On the input side this was done by introducing the concept of the "job source". A command was provided to connect an input channel of the program to the job source. For multi-access users this was interpreted as the terminal and for batch users it was the job description. Thus the batch user who has a small amount of data for one channel can embed this data in his job description instead of making it a separate file. Thus a program can be written to expect data from an on-line terminal and can subsequently be run in a batch mode with its data in its job description. It is also possible to embed a whole program in the job description—useful for small, frequently run jobs. On the output side the corresponding destination to the terminal is the monitoring file; this is again a convenient place for the batch user to send small quantities of output.

One of the most important facilities of the George 3 command language is that of macros. A macro-command, like a built in command, takes the format of a verb followed by a number of parameters. Macro definitions are held in the file-store and are of two types — system macros and user macros depending on whether they can be used by all users or only by individual users. A macro definition consists of a series of commands containing dummy parameters — the latter either refer to the nth parameter or to a parameter beginning with a keyword. Macros may be nested and may be recursive. System macros are used, for example, to interface standard software. All the complicated operations needed to run a compiler can be described inside the macro and the user only has to type, say, FORTRAN followed by parameters identifying, say, the source program and what he wants to do with the compiled program. A user macro is more likely to be used as a short way of describing a series of basic commands which the user wishes to obey frequently. Macros can, of course, be called equally well from a batch job description or from a multi-access terminal. While obeying the macro the multi-access job is more likely a batch job in that it takes its command from the macro definition file, not from the terminal. Thus batch type concepts like labelled commands and conditional jumps are often used inside macros and so these facilities have their use for the multi-access user. The same macro may well be used for both batch and multi-access work — this is often done with standard software. The writer of the macro does not need to know whether it will be used in a batch or multi-access environment — he can, possibly as an option, take input from the "job source" and send output to "the monitoring file system" and know that this will allow the multi-access user to run the program interactively while still making sense for the batch user.

Since the same language is used for both types of working it is possible for jobs to pass from one mode to the other. When a multi-access job is obeying commands from a macro the terminal user may break in, if he wishes, obey a few commands and then continue (or abandon) the macro. One of the commands he can type after breaking in is a DISCONNECT command which will then cause the job to continue obeying the macro as though it was a batch job description. The user can then use the terminal for another job or go home etc. as he wishes. He may, for instance, wish to initiate the job from a terminal and monitor its beginning. When he finds it is going smoothly he may happily leave it to be completed in a batch mode. Similarly there is a CONNECT facility to allow a user (who has identified himself by a password) to connect a batch job running under his user name to a terminal.

He can "break-in" and thus inquire about the progress of the job or change its course from that prescribed by the stored job description. Thus he can change jobs from multi-access control to batch type control at will.

It can be seen from the description above of various aspects of the command language that there are considerable benefits to the user from using the same language for controlling both batch and multi-access jobs. The unified system gives him considerable flexibility for such operations as testing programs in a multi-access environment and subsequently running them in a batch mode.

4. SCHEDULING AND CORE STORE MANAGEMENT

The decision to combine a multi-access with a batch system had less happy results in the areas of scheduling and core store management. The effect was to complicate the problem to an extent not foreseen in the early stages of the project. This was one of the main reasons for the inefficiency of early versions of George 3. Most of these problems are now solved, though in some cases the release of versions of George with problems solved is still in the future. The inefficiencies were not, however, of a theoretically unavoidable nature; they were due to an under-estimation of the problems by the system designers. In principle, it should certainly be possible to produce better schedulers and core store managers in a unified system than if an attempt is made to share the resources between two different systems — particularly if the multi-access workload is fluctuating.

As part of the system of time-slicing to spread CPU time among the various multi-access jobs, mechanisms had to be provided to roll multi-access programs out of core store when their time-slices were completed and roll them in again when their turns came round again. Since this mechanism was available, we used it as a major tool of core store management and there were many circumstances in which batch jobs could be rolled out. For example, if a job was held up for some reason — such as waiting for the operator to load a magnetic tape — it was rolled out and the store thus freed used either for starting another batch job or for multi-access work. This is clearly advantageous and could only be done because the mechanism was available for multi-access work — in a batch only system the job would probably have remained in core store during the hold-up.

We did, however, take this policy too far in some cases. For example, if a job wished to change its core store occupancy, either upwards or downwards, it was always rolled out and then a search made for a piece of store of the new size required by the program. This sort of thing is obviously much more elegant to program than sometimes relocating programs in core store (though this is allowed by 1900 architecture) but it is liable to lead to large overheads in some circumstances. In particular, a swapping philosophy for multi-access requires the availability of a fast drum for efficient operation. Many batch users of George 3, however, did not have such a drum and the resultant roll out to disc — with many head movements — proved inefficient. During the subsequent evolution of George 3, therefore, a number of changes have been made which discriminate between batch and multi-access jobs and avoid rolling out the former if at all possible. The core store management situation is still not entirely satisfactory but it is very much better than it was. My personal belief is that store fragmentation cannot be solved really efficiently on a datum/limit machine — some sort of paging is required. Paging is now available as an option on the four largest 1900 processors (the 1906S, 1906A, 1904S and 1904A) and George 4 — the paged version of George 3 is scheduled to be released later this year.

A somewhat similar problem was caused by excessive roll out of batch jobs due to time-slicing. It is normal practice for multi-access jobs to share time by time-slicing. Since George 3 multiprograms as well as time-slices, a program is not automatically rolled out when its time-slice is completed but it is likely to get rolled out if core store space is short. Thus several programs can be in core store at any one time — one because it is enjoying its time-slice and others because there is room for them. In early versions of George 3 the same low-level scheduler algorithms were used for both batch and multi-access jobs. This resulted in batch jobs frequently ending their time-slices and being rolled out in order to roll in other batch jobs. This continual interchange between batch jobs at intervals of a few seconds was clearly too inefficient to tolerate and the algorithms were modified so as not to roll out a batch job to let another batch job in. We now have a reasonably efficient system in this area although there are still some problems which we hope will be resolved by a new improved low-level scheduler to be released next year. One point we discovered was that sometimes it is necessary to treat multi-access jobs as if they were batch jobs. A terminal user may initiate a computation lasting an appreciable time — e.g. compilation of a large program. If several multi-access jobs are in this state it is clearly inefficient to keep rolling them in and out at short intervals — it is better to run each to completion. We altered the system to recognize this situation and to increase the time-slices for such jobs in such circumstances. This could easily be fitted into the system as we were already coping with batch work and normal multi-access work so this intermediate case did not present any special problems.

One major advantage, in the province of scheduling, for a combined system is that the system can be run efficiently in the not uncommon case of a sharply fluctuating multi-access workload in the presence of the continuous availability of batch work. The algorithms used by George 3 are such as to aim to provide a good response to multi-access users and to run batch work in the remaining CPU time and core store space. There is no difficulty in bringing batch work into core store when there is no multi-access work available and thus using the store efficiently. If there were two separate systems, then it would almost certainly be necessary to partition the store between batch and multi-access work and this leads to part of the store being left idle during short term drops in the multi-access workload.

CONCLUSIONS

There is no doubt that the advantages in terms of user facilities in integrating batch and multi-access modes are considerable in George 3. The user is presented with a unified coherent structure rather than two different and inevitably not entirely compatible systems. He can move jobs and files freely from one mode to the other and essentially has the combined power of both. He has the flexibility associated with a continuous graduation from all multi-access work to all batch work.

There were also some advantages to the writers of the system in that they only had one system to write, develop and maintain; furthermore the multi-access facilities were of considerable use while writing and testing the system. On the other hand, there are disadvantages due to greater complexity — the example of scheduling is described above. These disadvantages are largely in the greater difficulty of designing a more complex product and in the management involved in its implementation. The greater complexity has increased the time taken to produce the system and it is more difficult to maintain.

The overheads, measured as, for example, the proportion of CPU time or core store occupied by the system, are greater than they would be in a similar system; for installations which only require a small subset of the facilities provided this may be a real extra overhead. For other users, however, the extra flexibility and range of facilities outweighs these considerations and they are able to get more useful work done than in two separate systems.

Two separate systems could never have been enhanced to provide anything like the same range of facilities that are available with George 3; the system also has enormous potential for further enhancement.

It is, therefore, difficult to dispute that the decision to produce a unified batch and multi-access system has been entirely justified.

DISCUSSION

HOWARTH: I want to discuss not only the Atlas supervisory system, but also the system design of Atlas as a combined piece of software and hardware. Although the hardware was built before the software was completely developed, both were planned in parallel and their designs interacted with one another quite strongly.

If you read Atlas literature you find a rather curious confusion between the real hardware of the machine and what the user can do, e.g. the ABL manual (Atlas Basic Language Manual) is a description of a particular assembly language, but since that assembly language is really rather low-level, it turns out to be a description of the user version of the machine, i.e. the user virtual machine. There is another manual which is a description of the actual hardware, i.e. the supervisor's virtual machine which, being more primitive is nearer to the real machine. Behind the scenes, yet again, there are the engineer's logic drawings, etc., which really do describe the real hardware.

There are quite significant differences in the design of the user and supervisor virtual machines, since Atlas wasn't designed with these two concepts in mind. The user virtual machine was created for the batch running of isolated independent jobs. This is a very limited aim, although in the late '50's, and early '60's, when the machine was designed, it was an obvious objective. The user virtual machine has a single floating point accumulator, together with 90 fixed point accumulators which can also be used as modifiers, with a limited use of another 10 equivalent registers. It has a range of basic instructions composed of hardware instructions and software-implemented instructions, known in the Atlas terminology as extracodes. They look exactly the same to the user virtual machine except that one is slower than the other. The result is that when you wish to assign a processor to a user virtual machine you have to switch the 90 or 100 index registers, and also reload the fixed working space used by the extracode instructions. Process switching is therefore, by modern standards, a very time consuming affair, but when considered in conjunction with the aim of the Atlas designers it could afford to be.

If you read the hardware description of the store you find that the virtual store consists of 2000 blocks of virtual storage pages, a block being 512 words. In fact this is an incorrect description. In more modern terminology the store of the user virtual machine consists of (1) two read only segments; (a) the fixed store (16 blocks) which is "read only" from a hardware point of view, and (b) the working or subsidiary store (2 blocks) designed as workspace for the supervisor, to which read accesses are permitted by extracode. (2) About 1800 blocks of read/write memory, because some of the addressing capability of the hardware is locked off for supervisor use. So the user virtual machine has its one level store in which the block labels can range up to 1800.

Another difference between the real and user virtual machines is the way in which they communicate with their environment. The user has access to a large number of I/O channels, and these resemble the real peripherals of the machine. In particular the fast I/O channels were coupled directly to the fast I/O equipment, the magnetic tapes, discs, etc. Also the slow channels which, although they were made to look like actual slow devices, were attached to temporary files held in the input and output well. The user was under the impression he was reading from an idealized peripheral, and we used a common internal code so that the peculiarities of particular equipment were masked, but you could do on the virtual channels substantially what you could do on a real peripheral. The only other means of communication with the virtual machine environment was a set of supervisor commands allowing the user to call for supervisory activities.

The system was designed with the needs of high-level languages in mind, but not any one language in particular. In those days if you introduced a new machine you introduced a new language, e.g. Fortran was the language of the IBM 7094, Mercury Autocode was the language of Mercury, and naturally a new language appeared known as Atlas Autocode. There was not much attempt to standardize high-level languages. So some of the good features of Atlas were (1) a large number of index registers which eases the job of assignment of variables to registers; (2) a one-level store which considerably eases overlay problems associated with the compilation of object code via high-level languages; (3) a large instruction repertoire and (4) substantial device independence over the I/O channels. All these points facilitate writing moderately good compilers on Atlas.

There are limitations of course. It is a very bad Cobol machine because of the poor character handling facilities. Also the idea of communication with other processes in other virtual machines is absent. We limited channel properties to make them look rather like I/O devices. At the same time we refused to couple the slow I/O devices directly to these channels because we wished to avoid the inefficiency of matching up the speeds of I/O devices with the speeds of processing.

In contrast, the supervisor virtual machine uses 12 index registers and only the basic instruction set. The reason for this is to enable rapid switching between supervisor virtual machines, since they use the processor in very short bursts. Since we do not use extracode instructions there would be no dumping or restoring of the attached working space. Because there were no software instructions, the supervisor virtual machine was poorly equipped to do such things as shifting, for example, which in the user virtual machine is partially implemented by extracode.

All the supervisor virtual machines share the same virtual store, which comprises a read-only segment of 16 blocks which is the fixed store, a read/write segment of 2 blocks which is the working store, and 250 blocks which can be treated either as a set of segments or as one segment. The supervisor uses a common virtual machine for all its activities, since communication between the supervisor virtual machines is essential in that they are co-operating to do the same job. This is achieved through commonality of store; additionally we need some sort of synchronization mechanism. Synchronization was achieved by a semaphore operation obeyed at the start of the supervisor activity and it applied to the entire supervisor virtual machine; the net effect is that supervisor activities are done one at a time. This is a very crude mechanism, but it works quite well because no supervisor activity lasts very long. However, a nasty complication occurs when the supervisor requires information which is not resident in core. What we could have done was to arrange that the lock on the supervisor virtual machine could be maintained over the one level store transfer. The reason we didn't do this was in case the required part of the supervisor was not resident on drum, but on the library tape, which is effectively a third level of backing store. So not only would the entire drum system be called into play but also the entire tape system and that involves human interaction and therefore operator communication. We therefore arranged that the supervisor virtual machine was able to specify an exception condition address (generally known as the re-entry address), which is the address at which you resume the process should you have to take the lock off and put it back on again. If you want to ensure that the lock is never taken off, that you are essentially uninterrupted you can access every block in your subsequent sequence, one after another. When you have a page fault you return to the re-entry address again and access the whole lot again. By the time you have gone through a sequence of accesses you can guarantee that all those blocks accessed must be in core, otherwise you would never have arrived at that point. Hence you have essentially got a very controlled method of synchronization whereby you can hold that lock irrespective of other supervisory activities. Depending on the particular core store occupancy at any time, you will take different routes through the supervisor virtual machine, and so any idea of exhaustive checking is very difficult to achieve. Because of this the maintenance time on the Atlas supervisor was exceedingly lengthy, due especially to this re-entry technique. So the supervisor virtual machine was good from the point of view of efficiency, but bad from the point of view of lack of protection (because they all use a common virtual store and there is no lock-out on the stores), and also from the point of view of repeatability because of the one level store. It is furthermore very difficult to exploit high level languages to write code for execution in supervisor state.

Because of these two different machines the User and Supervisor virtual machines, you have a supervisor team and the rest of the users talking about different machines and there is no interaction between them. You get a lack of understanding; you find users asking for facilities which are difficult to implement because of the supervisor structure. If we had the same machine for both purposes it would have been apparent to the users what was easy and what was difficult. Hence we would have had a much more sensible set of demands from the users for facilities. Also although we built in services to make life easier for the user, it is more difficult to do this on the supervisor virtual machine, and you end up detracting from supervisor efforts in order to provide these services; you don't pick up any commonality.

Commonality of structure fulfils two purposes: it makes the supervisor's life easier, and secondly gets round the limits of the user virtual machine, because by the time you put facilities in which make the supervisor work well, you have removed some of the unpleasant restrictions which were attached to the particular user virtual machine on Atlas.

HOARE: If you are implementing an operating system function, there is one virtual machine on which it's logically impossible to implement that function, and that is the virtual machine in which that function already exists. Thus it is logically impossible to use identical virtual machines at all levels of the supervisor. Dijkstra's approach in the design of the T.H.E. system is the one needed to solve this sort of problem. But I can see how serious additional problems can emerge if the philosophy propounded by Howarth and Dijkstra is ill-advisedly applied. It's not obvious that the writing of the supervisor using other supervisor facilities is automatically going to be successful particularly on a modern operating system the size of OS 360. Even with maximum hardware assistance, the implementation of a single common virtual machine for supervisor and user processes can require as much or more supervisor code than the entire supervisor of the Atlas. Even worse, the code required to implement the same functions within this virtual machine could be more voluminous than it is at present, since interfacing to a virtual machine can be more tedious than interfacing to hardware. This is often due to the protection mechanism, which is unproductive, and unnecessary when programming the actual hardware. The net result could be that a well-structured well-protected operating system may be an order of magnitude more inefficient and voluminous than the present Atlas system, and provide no improvement in user service.

HOWARTH: Although it may be difficult to achieve total commonality, there is much to be gained from so doing one of the major criticisms from the user has been that when the system crashes, because the supervisor is using a common virtual machine, you can't guarantee the contents of any other supervisor virtual machine. We devised a monitor to give some indication of the area of the fault and isolate it, but because of the restrictive nature of the Atlas set-up it was almost impossible to do this satisfactorily. I agree with Hoare; you might get the problem of structuring of the common virtual machine, which is bigger than the entire supervisor. Unless the structure can be fairly simply constructed the exercise is of doubtful value.

NEEDHAM: Surely it's a mistaken view to say one wants a common virtual machine which all these processes run. What one really means is that the virtual machines in which these processes run differ in function but have a common structure — and this is much less of a requirement.

RANDELL: If you want the structure to be common you must be careful that what you need is matched at the hardware level.

HOARE: A practical point is that if you have structures, you should try to ensure that each level you implement works in a time scale which is an order of magnitude smaller than the time scale in which the next higher level works. Otherwise you take disproportionately complicated steps at your higher levels to avoid invoking your lower level, and this will lead to the complexity that I've been warning against.

NEWELL: One of the problems faced by the manufacturer is to cater for a variety of environments, and to do this he can take one of two approaches. He can write functional operating systems and try to get these to co-exist in some comfortable fashion; or he can write an "all singing all dancing" operating system in an integrated fashion. There are three main areas where the advantages of using the latter approach are to be seen; in the command language, in the file store and in scheduling. Firstly, certain features of the command language can be successfully used for both on-line and background work. A main principle of our job command language (JCL) is that since the operating system is to run a series of jobs, this can be described by means of a high-level language. Hence we use a programming language including basic facilities like conditional statements, counts and subroutines. Our JCL started off as a very powerful macro language, and eventually these macros have become procedures. Another reason for having the same JCL is that once you have developed your job sitting at a terminal you can then submit it as a background job: perhaps start something else and later interrupt that job to see for example if it were converging fast enough.

Our file store caters for all categories of file, all the compilers and the macros to run jobs, and all the spooling requirements. It is very advantageous to have the same file store for both on-line and background jobs and thus avoid the use of different file formats.

Scheduling is the area where we failed in trying to be all things to all men, since we were too on-line orientated. It took us a long time to realize, as Howarth says in his paper, that although maximizing throughput is not necessarily synonymous with optimizing response it's near enough to be true. At the moment we're at the intermediate stage, trying to recognize the current environment which changes very fast. If there are active on-line jobs then you time slice and try to guarantee response, and if they're all scratching their heads or it's all background work you run to completion of the time-slot. We need a way of enabling the customer to adjust the scheduler to his workload rather than giving preference to the on-line jobs.

Another scheduling difficulty is recognizing the difference between the truly interactive jobs and ordinary programs run from a terminal. Otherwise there's no point in time-slicing as everyone will suffer in response time and it would have been much better to wait your turn in the queue.

Finally we have to a certain extent adopted the other approach too, with George 2 and Minimop co-existing under operator's executive. Here we have all the disadvantages of different JCL's, different file formats, etc. If you partition your system into these different functional areas with different operating systems for each, you can't optimize your resources as you should and it's much more difficult to enhance your system.

HOARE: I agree that a single design team should take full responsibility for all users of the system, and design the system to share the machine between all classes of user. The pursuit of modularity leads to rather extreme classification of users of a computer. This has some practical advantages in simplifying the system and in some ways making it easier to control and adapt. Also it is easier to write subsystems that will be satisfactory to limited classes of users in a particular range. But if you decide to modularize as George 2 and Minimop have done, the overall design responsibility should remain with one conceptual person.

What is happening with George 3 is that the two approaches are moving closer together. The areas in which different treatment needs to be given to different classes of user, and in which economic advantage can be taken of certain polarization of demands, are coming to be recognized by system designers. The system designer can then achieve a certain degree of efficiency combined with modularity, based on limitations which the user himself is well advised to accept. Approaching from these two directions, I hope we will meet somewhere in the middle with good systems covering a wide range of users.

NEWELL: Another point about George 3 is, because of its huge size (300K instructions) it has got to be modular because it has to be produced by separate teams of people. The file store is about 75K instructions, and anyone not working on it sees it as a macro interface of some dozen macros. However the filestore routines do use all the common services, like the core allocation system, and have to be changed in the light of experience, and if you over-modularize them it's very difficult to do so.

RANDELL: As far as the OS 360 was concerned there was an original small design team that laid out basic ideas and looked for unified principles. Then the designs were divided up and done in parallel with the result that the conceptual uniformity did not become apparent in the actual system. One or two problems emerged and various halfway stages were produced. Another point which has emerged is the extent to which a difference in size of configuration would change the system similarity. IBM had originally thought that with the spectrum of uniformity given by a common processor architecture, a common I/O interface, they would be able to achieve greater commonality for compilers; but in fact they had to now design different compilers for different sizes of core store. Often these would be done by different teams in different locations. These are the sort of things that can go wrong with an attempt to get communality.

HOWARTH: Our problem is that we never do the same thing again. We get a lot of experience on our first simple system, and then when it comes to doing the same thing again with a better designed hardware, with all the tools we know we need, we try and produce something which is ten times more complicated and fall into exactly the same trap. We do not stabilize on something nice and simple and say "let's do it again, but do it very well this time".